Author's Message:

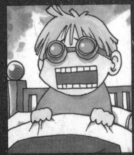

Art GB Yamamoto

NOBUYUKI ANZAI
安西信行
PRESENTS

I'm working hard...
But not too hard.

MÄR
Vol. 4
Story and Art by Nobuyuki Anzai

English Adaptation/Gerard Jones
Translation/Kaori Inoue
Touch-up Art & Lettering/James Gaubatz
Design/Izumi Evers
Editor/Pancha Diaz

Editor in Chief, Books/Alvin Lu
Editor in Chief, Magazines/Marc Weidenbaum
VP of Publishing Licensing/Rika Inouye
VP of Sales/Gonzalo Ferreyra
Sr. VP of Marketing/Liza Coppola
Publisher/Hyoe Narita

© 2004 Nobuyuki ANZAI/Shogakukan Inc. First published by
Shogakukan Inc. in Japan as "MÄR." All rights reserved.
Some art has been modified from the original Japanese edition.
The stories, characters and incidents mentioned in this
publication are entirely fictional.

No portion of this book may be reproduced or transmitted in any
form or by any means without written permission from the
copyright holders.

The rights of the author(s) of the work(s) in this publication to
be so identified have been asserted in accordance with the
Copyright, Designs and Patents Act 1988. A CIP catalogue
record for this book is available from the British Library.

Printed in Canada

Published by VIZ Media, LLC
P.O. Box 77010
San Francisco, CA 94107

10 9 8 7 6 5 4 3
First printing, October 2005
Third printing, May 2008

www.viz.com
store.viz.com

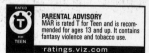

PARENTAL ADVISORY
MAR is rated T for Teen and is recom-
mended for ages 13 and up. It contains
fantasy violence and tobacco use.
ratings.viz.com

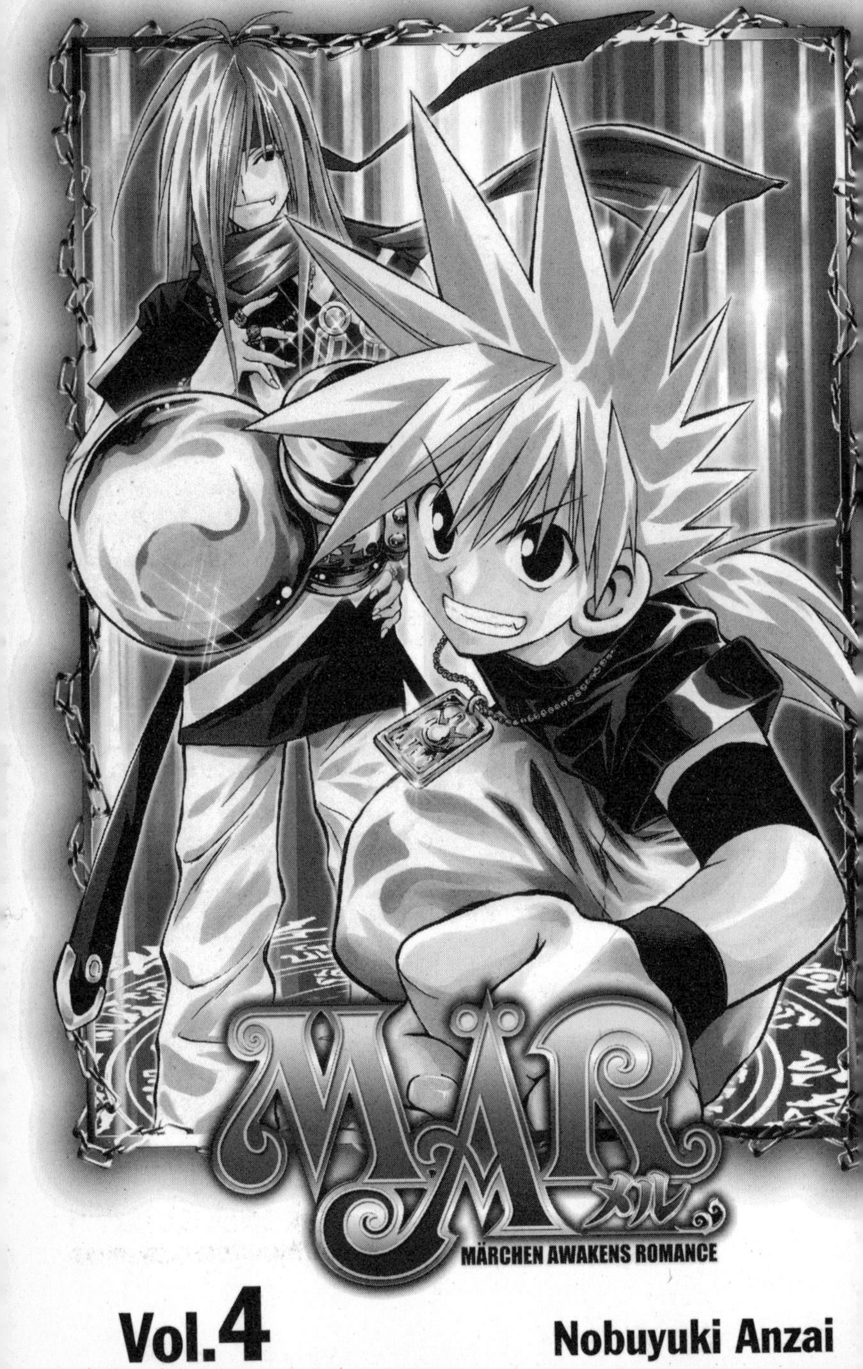

MÄR

MÄRCHEN AWAKENS ROMANCE

Vol.4

Nobuyuki Anzai

Characters

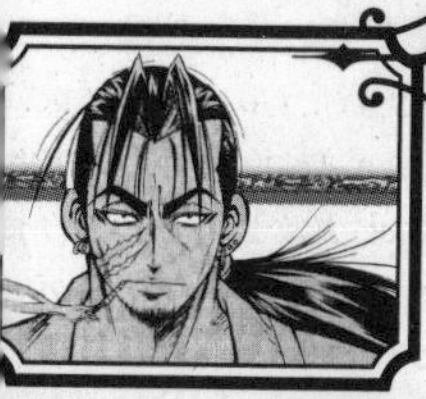

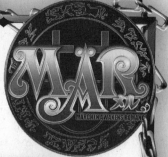

Edward (Human)

A warrior who played a major role in the war six years ago. Back then, his name was Alan, but due to a curse he now takes on the appearance of a dog.

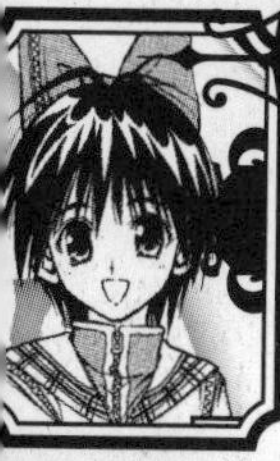

Snow

The Princess of the Great Kingdom of Lestava. Rescued from a frozen state by Ginta.

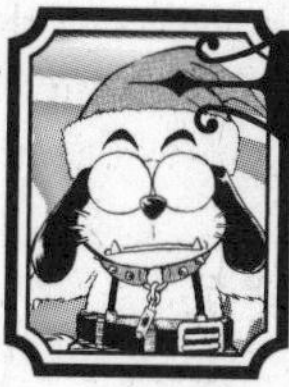

Edward (Canine)

Devotedly serves Princess Snow. Appears as a human after falling asleep three times.

Dorothy

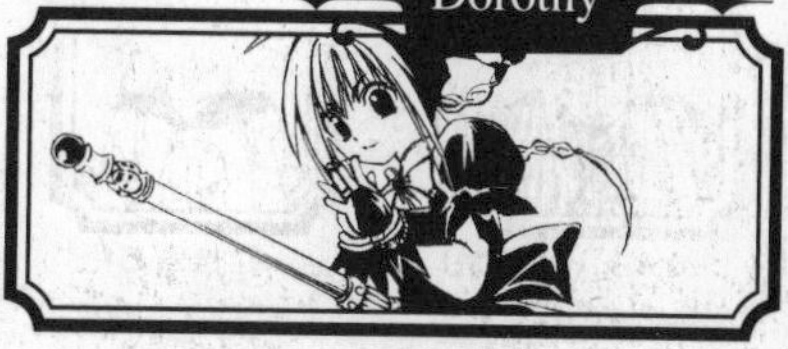

A witch. She got close to Ginta in order to find Babbo, but could her feelings for Ginta have turned amorous…?!

Alviss

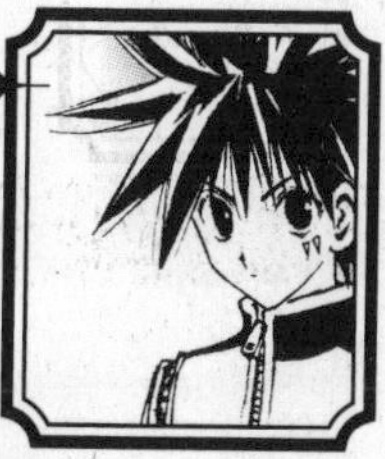

e called Ginta to
är Heaven
ing the
imension ÄRM
Gate Keeper
own."

Babbo

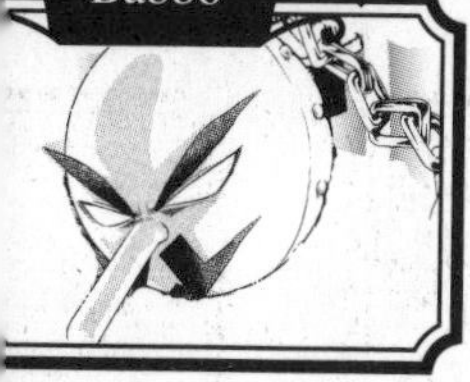

alking ÄRM, rare through-
t the world. He has a dark
st, having once been
antom's possession…

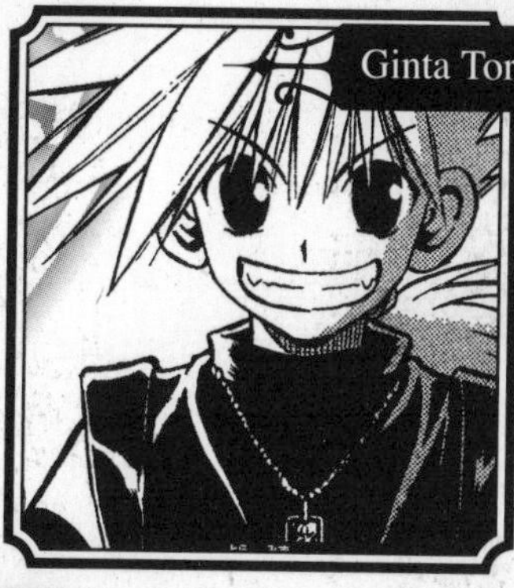

Ginta Toramizu

A normal second-year middle school student who loves to dream about the world of fairy tales (Märchen). He is enjoying his adventures in the other world.

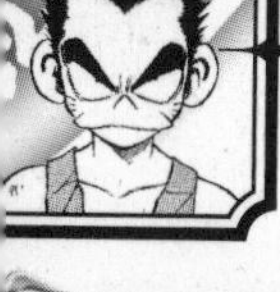

Jack

He was living with his mother and growing crops, and ends up going on a journey through Mär Heaven with Ginta.

Previous Volume

Ginta Toramizu, a middle school student who dreams of Märchen and land of fairy tales, finds himself jumping into another world through a "door" that one day suddenly appeared in his classroom. Ginta accidentally gains possession of the ÄRM Babbo, and becomes embroiled in a plot. As Ginta's adventure continues, Babbo's dark past, the existence of the Chess Pieces, and countless other things become clear. Furthermore, Ginta and his friends have completed the grueling 180 training with flying colors in order to prepare for the battle against the Chess Pieces…

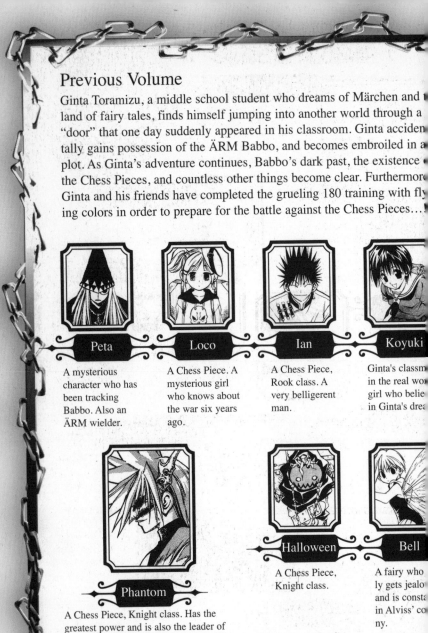

Peta

A mysterious character who has been tracking Babbo. Also an ÄRM wielder.

Loco

A Chess Piece. A mysterious girl who knows about the war six years ago.

Ian

A Chess Piece, Rook class. A very belligerent man.

Koyuki

Ginta's classm in the real wo girl who belie in Ginta's dre

Phantom

A Chess Piece, Knight class. Has the greatest power and is also the leader of the combat force.

Halloween

A Chess Piece, Knight class.

Bell

A fairy who ly gets jealo and is consta in Alviss' co ny.

CONTENTS

AKT.31/ MÄR

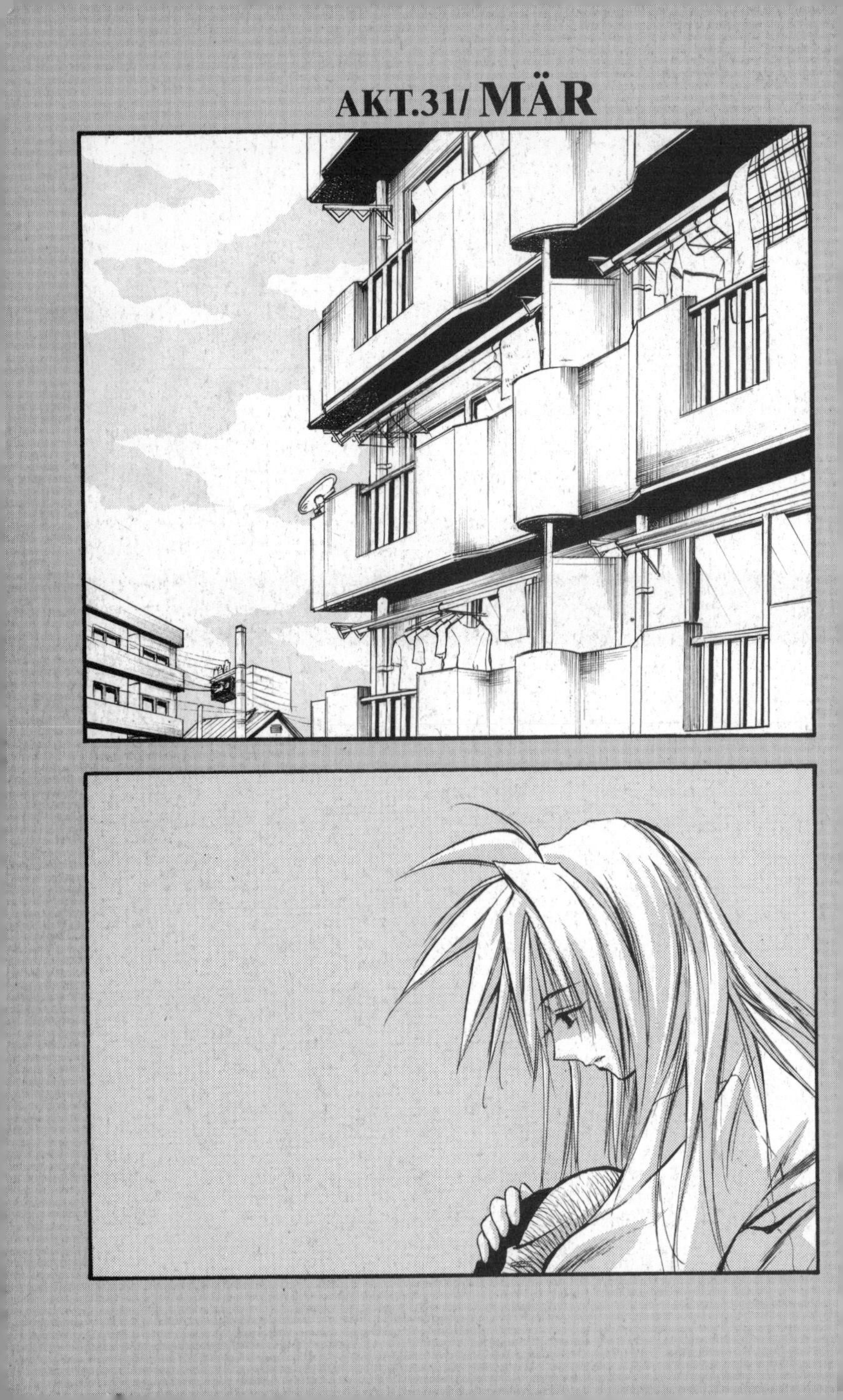

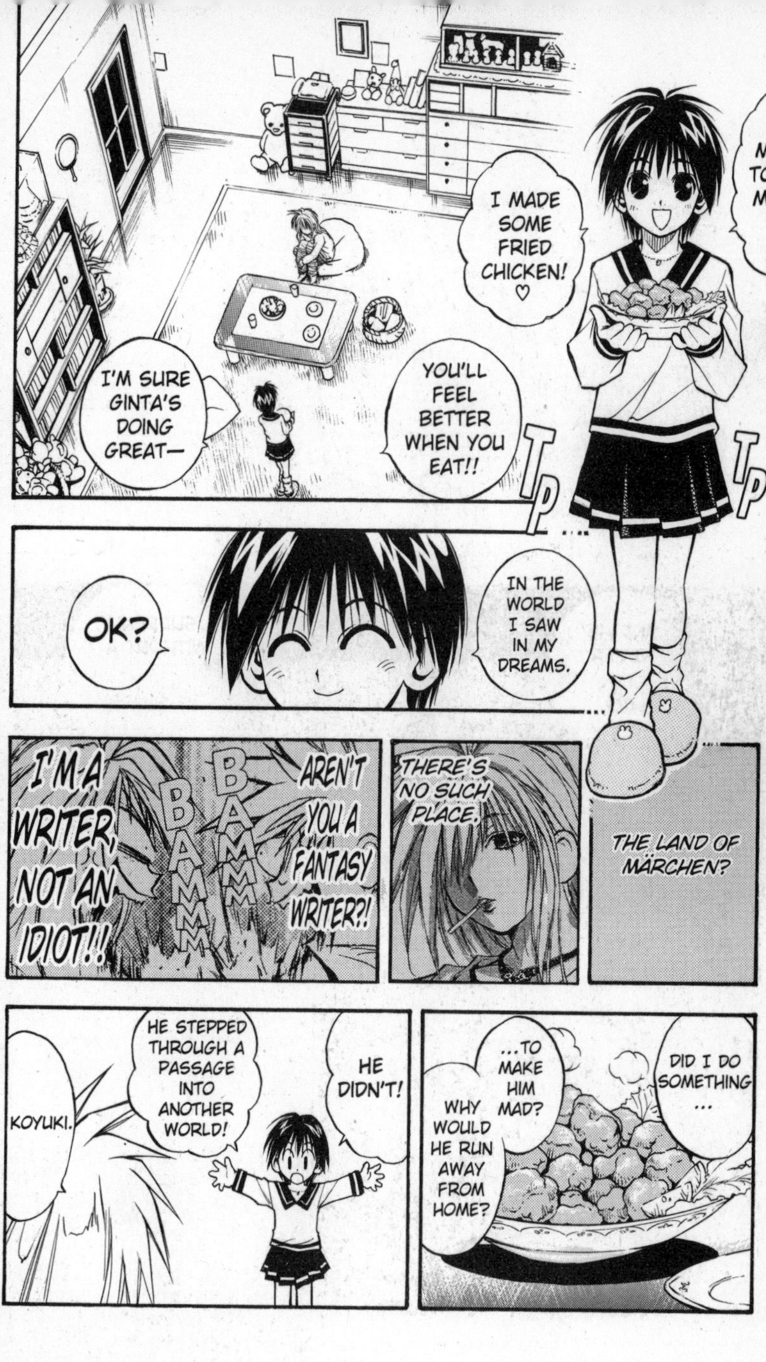
MRS. TORA-MIZU!
I MADE SOME FRIED CHICKEN! ♡
TP
TP
YOU'LL FEEL BETTER WHEN YOU EAT!!
I'M SURE GINTA'S DOING GREAT—
IN THE WORLD I SAW IN MY DREAMS.
OK?
THE LAND OF MÄRCHEN?
THERE'S NO SUCH PLACE.
AREN'T YOU A FANTASY WRITER?!
BAMMM
BAMMM
I'M A WRITER, NOT AN IDIOT!!
DID I DO SOMETHING ...
...TO MAKE HIM MAD?
WHY WOULD HE RUN AWAY FROM HOME?
HE DIDN'T!
HE STEPPED THROUGH A PASSAGE INTO ANOTHER WORLD!
KOYUKI.

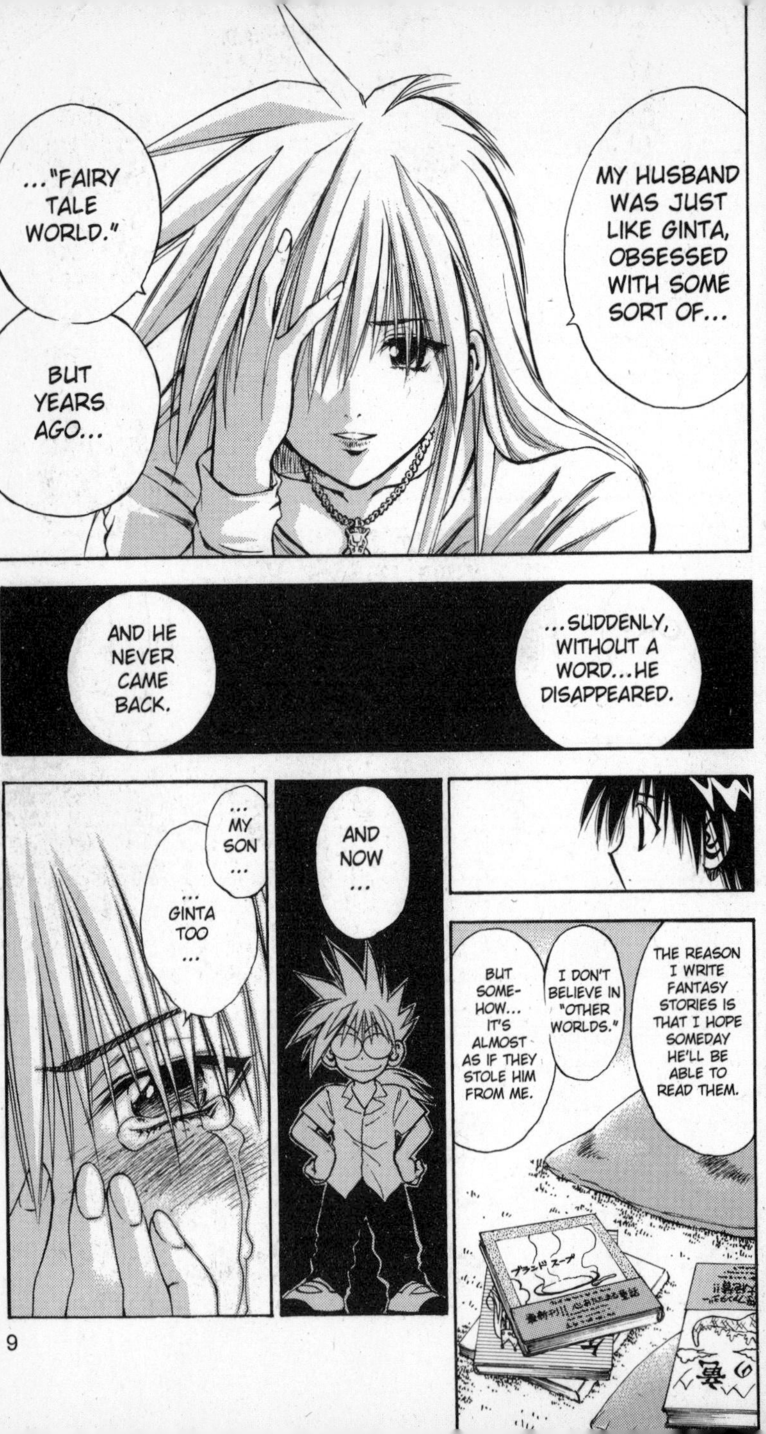
MY HUSBAND WAS JUST LIKE GINTA, OBSESSED WITH SOME SORT OF...
..."FAIRY TALE WORLD."
BUT YEARS AGO...
...SUDDENLY, WITHOUT A WORD...HE DISAPPEARED.
AND HE NEVER CAME BACK.
THE REASON I WRITE FANTASY STORIES IS THAT I HOPE SOMEDAY HE'LL BE ABLE TO READ THEM.
I DON'T BELIEVE IN "OTHER WORLDS."
BUT SOME-HOW... IT'S ALMOST AS IF THEY STOLE HIM FROM ME.
AND NOW ...
... MY SON ...
... GINTA TOO ...

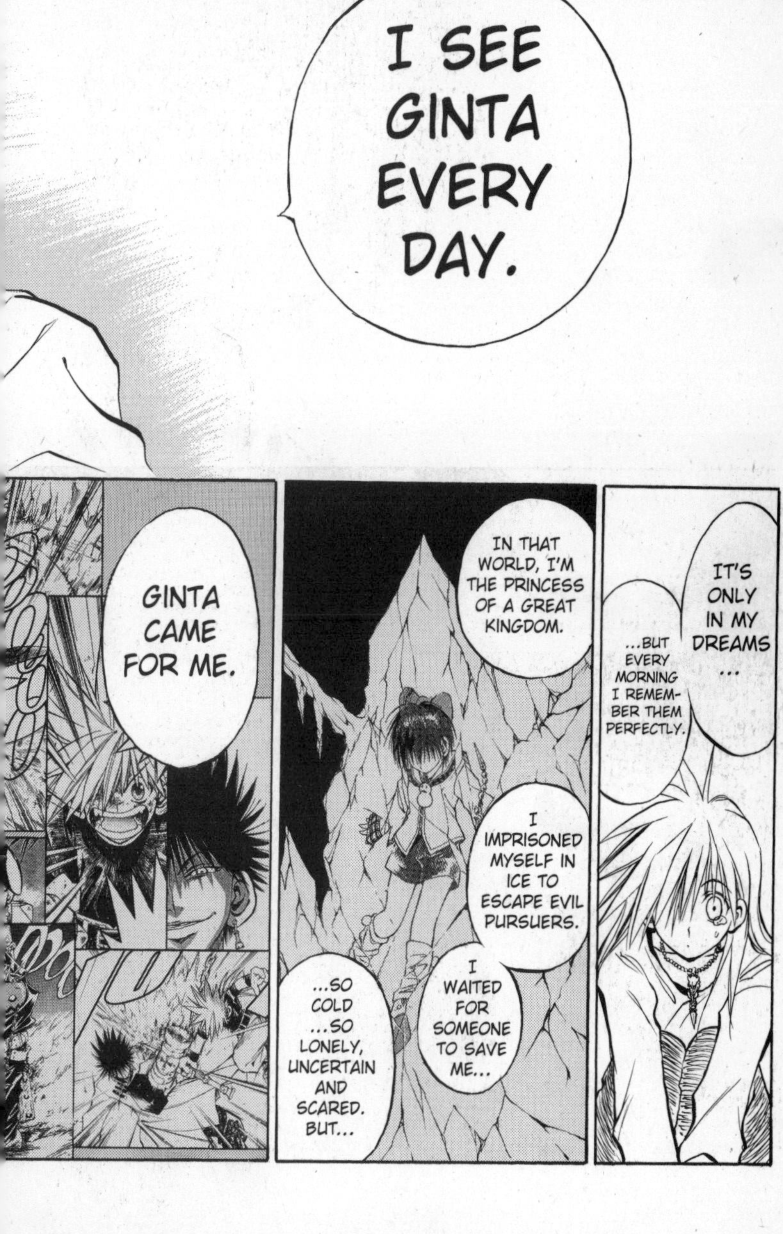
I SEE GINTA EVERY DAY.
IT'S ONLY IN MY DREAMS...
...BUT EVERY MORNING I REMEMBER THEM PERFECTLY.
IN THAT WORLD, I'M THE PRINCESS OF A GREAT KINGDOM.
I IMPRISONED MYSELF IN ICE TO ESCAPE EVIL PURSUERS.
I WAITED FOR SOMEONE TO SAVE ME...
...SO COLD ...SO LONELY, UNCERTAIN AND SCARED. BUT...
GINTA CAME FOR ME.

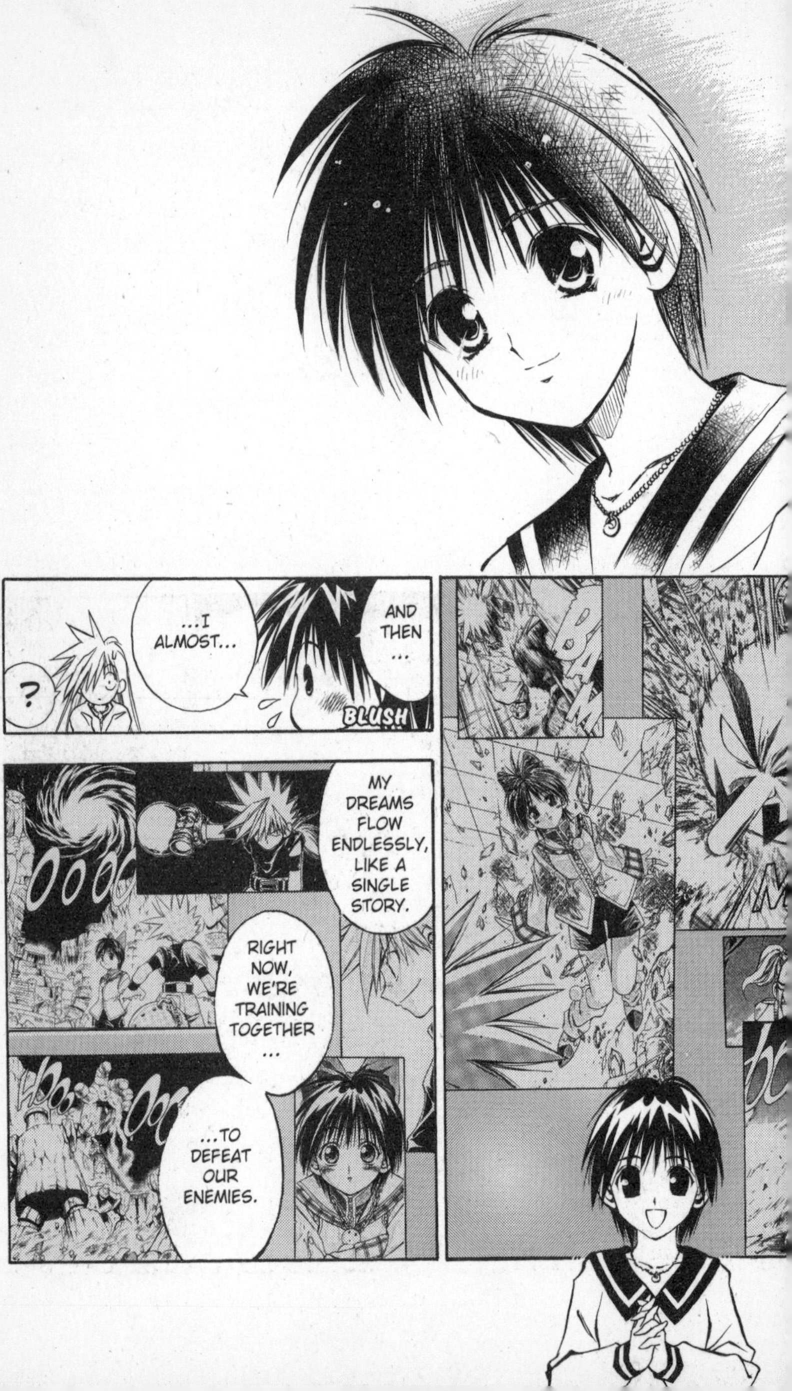
AND THEN ...
...I ALMOST...
BLUSH
?
MY DREAMS FLOW ENDLESSLY, LIKE A SINGLE STORY.
RIGHT NOW, WE'RE TRAINING TOGETHER ...
...TO DEFEAT OUR ENEMIES.

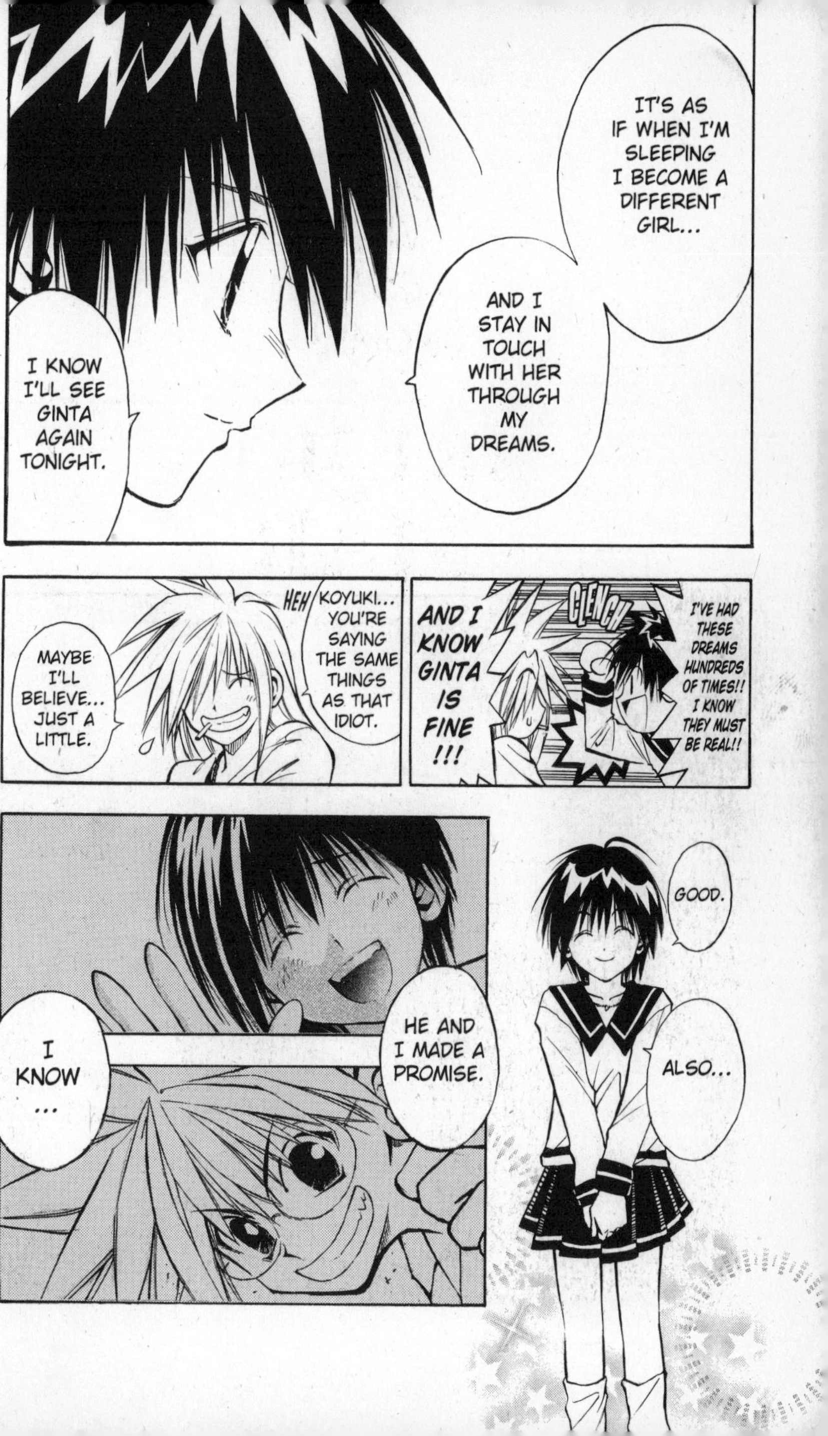

IT'S AS IF WHEN I'M SLEEPING I BECOME A DIFFERENT GIRL...
AND I STAY IN TOUCH WITH HER THROUGH MY DREAMS.
I KNOW I'LL SEE GINTA AGAIN TONIGHT.
I'VE HAD THESE DREAMS HUNDREDS OF TIMES!! I KNOW THEY MUST BE REAL!!
CLENCH
AND I KNOW GINTA IS FINE!!!
HEH
KOYUKI... YOU'RE SAYING THE SAME THINGS AS THAT IDIOT.
MAYBE I'LL BELIEVE... JUST A LITTLE.
GOOD.
ALSO...
HE AND I MADE A PROMISE.
I KNOW ...

... THAT GINTA WILL COME HOME!

AKT.31/ MÄR

HEY!
GINTA!!

WHAT'S THAT?
A NEW ÄRM?

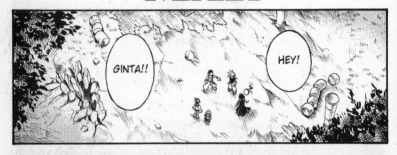

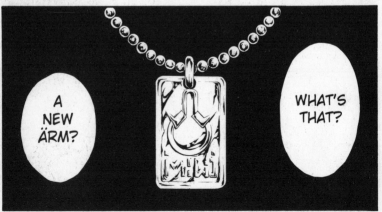

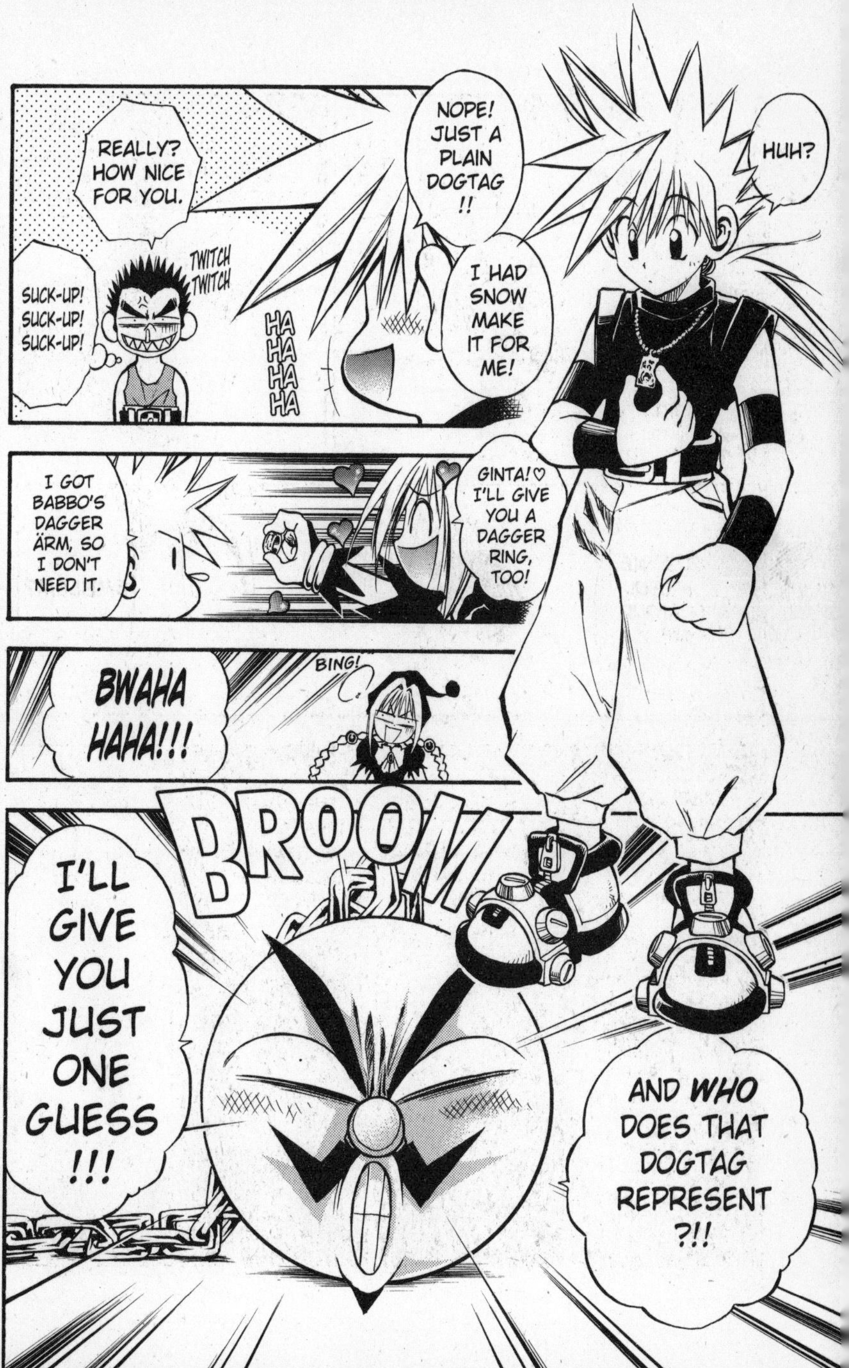
HUH?
NOPE! JUST A PLAIN DOGTAG!!
I HAD SNOW MAKE IT FOR ME!
HA HA HA HA HA
REALLY? HOW NICE FOR YOU.
TWITCH TWITCH
SUCK-UP! SUCK-UP! SUCK-UP!
GINTA!♡ I'LL GIVE YOU A DAGGER RING, TOO!
I GOT BABBO'S DAGGER ÄRM, SO I DON'T NEED IT.
BING!
BWAHA HAHA!!!
AND WHO DOES THAT DOGTAG REPRESENT?!!
BROOM
I'LL GIVE YOU JUST ONE GUESS!!!

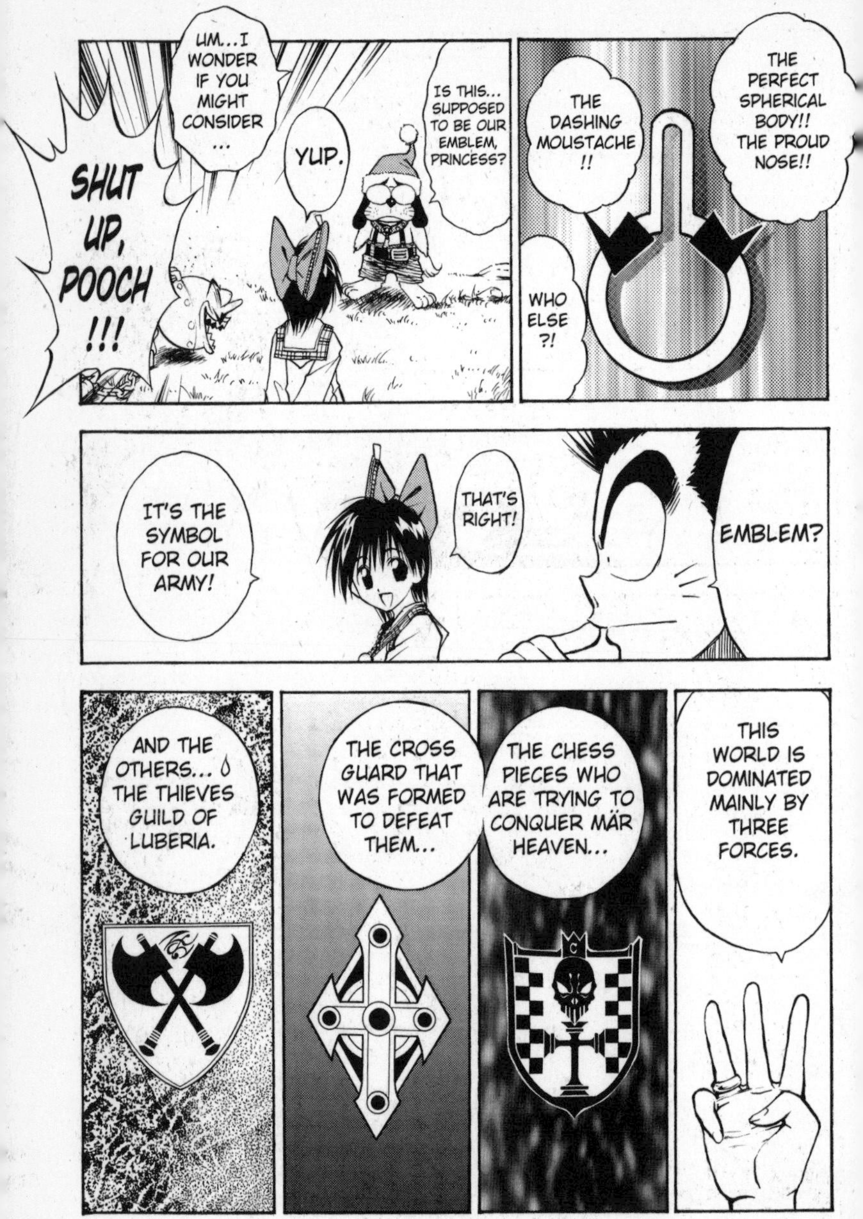
THE PERFECT SPHERICAL BODY!! THE PROUD NOSE!!
THE DASHING MOUSTACHE !!
WHO ELSE ?!
IS THIS... SUPPOSED TO BE OUR EMBLEM, PRINCESS?
YUP.
UM...I WONDER IF YOU MIGHT CONSIDER ...
SHUT UP, POOCH !!!
EMBLEM?
THAT'S RIGHT!
IT'S THE SYMBOL FOR OUR ARMY!
THIS WORLD IS DOMINATED MAINLY BY THREE FORCES.
THE CHESS PIECES WHO ARE TRYING TO CONQUER MÄR HEAVEN...
THE CROSS GUARD THAT WAS FORMED TO DEFEAT THEM...
AND THE OTHERS... THE THIEVES GUILD OF LUBERIA.

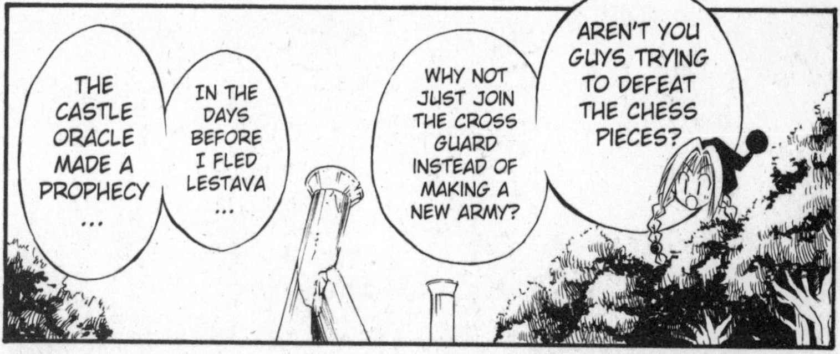
AREN'T YOU GUYS TRYING TO DEFEAT THE CHESS PIECES?
WHY NOT JUST JOIN THE CROSS GUARD INSTEAD OF MAKING A NEW ARMY?
IN THE DAYS BEFORE I FLED LESTAVA ...
THE CASTLE ORACLE MADE A PROPHECY ...

THEN...

FLEE THE CASTLE, PRINCESS.

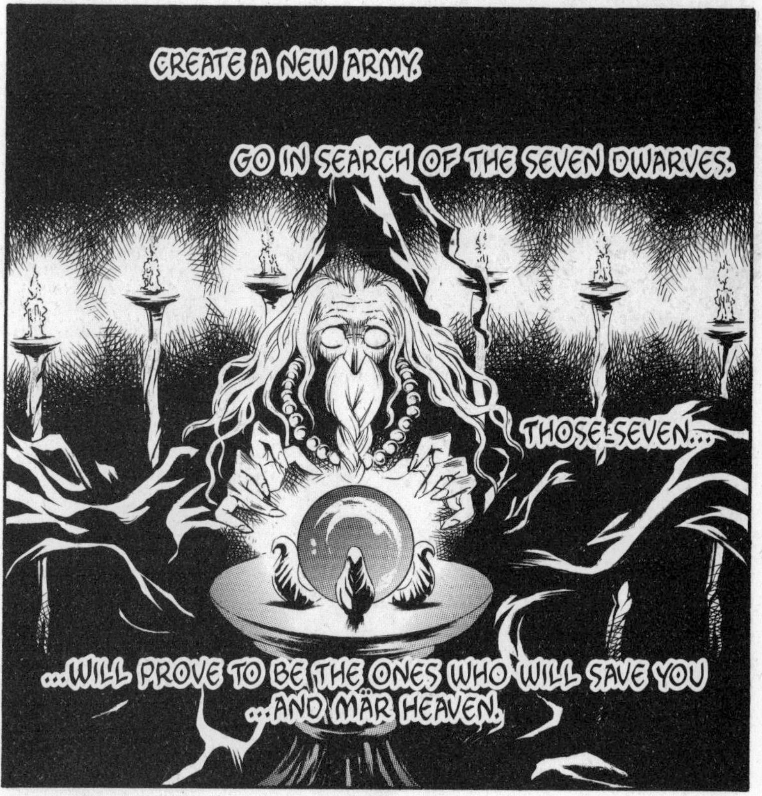
CREATE A NEW ARMY.
GO IN SEARCH OF THE SEVEN DWARVES.
THOSE SEVEN...
...WILL PROVE TO BE THE ONES WHO WILL SAVE YOU ...AND MÄR HEAVEN.

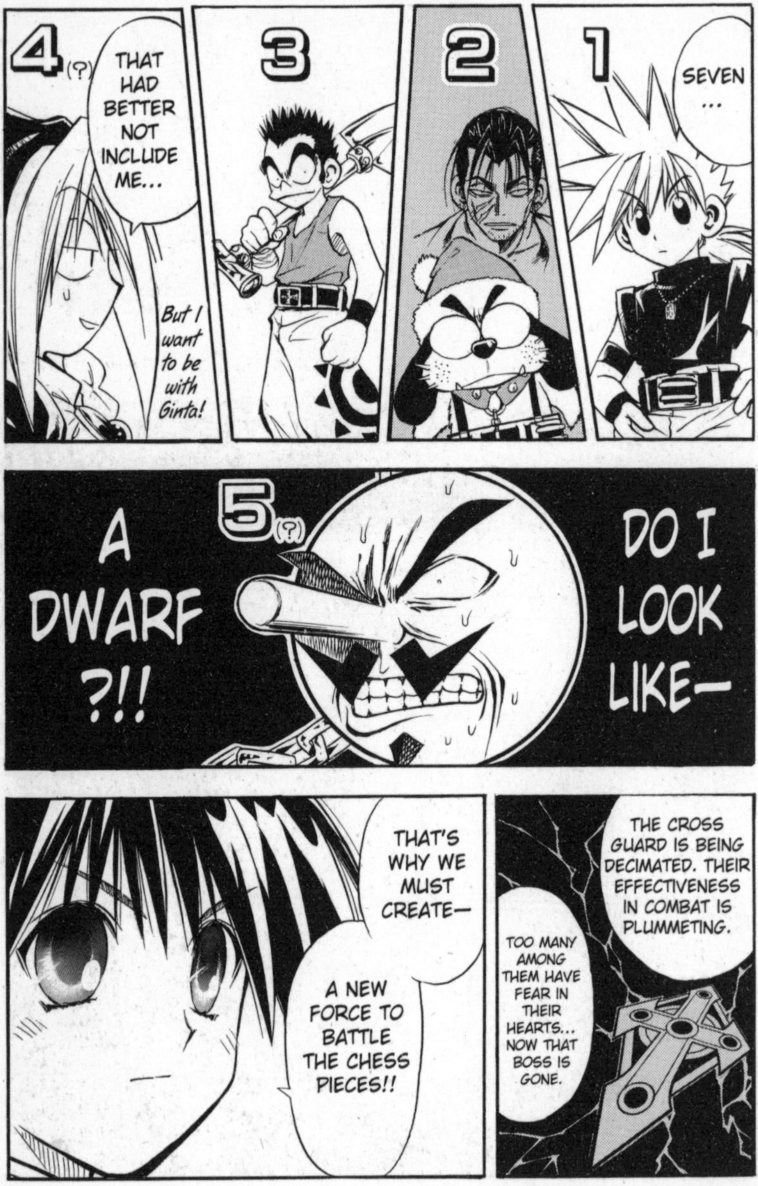
1
SEVEN ...
2
3
4(?)
THAT HAD BETTER NOT INCLUDE ME...
But I want to be with Ginta!
DO I LOOK LIKE—
5(?)
A DWARF ?!!
THE CROSS GUARD IS BEING DECIMATED. THEIR EFFECTIVENESS IN COMBAT IS PLUMMETING.
TOO MANY AMONG THEM HAVE FEAR IN THEIR HEARTS... NOW THAT BOSS IS GONE.
THAT'S WHY WE MUST CREATE—
A NEW FORCE TO BATTLE THE CHESS PIECES!!

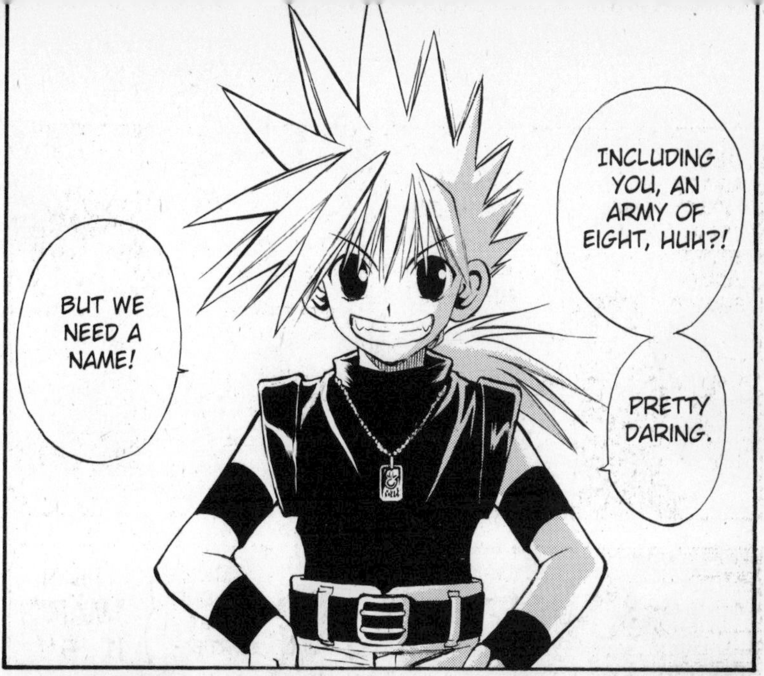
INCLUDING YOU, AN ARMY OF EIGHT, HUH?!
PRETTY DARING.
BUT WE NEED A NAME!

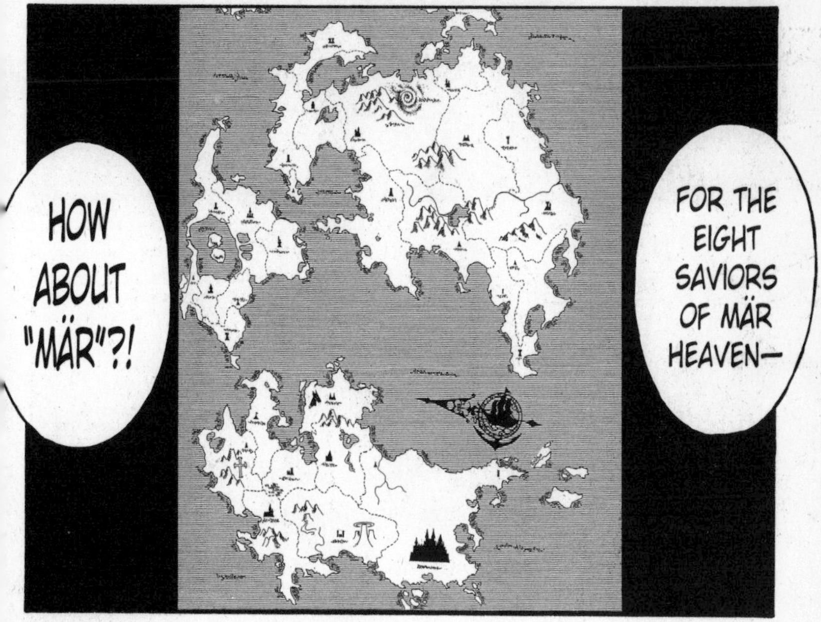
FOR THE EIGHT SAVIORS OF MÄR HEAVEN—
HOW ABOUT "MÄR"?!

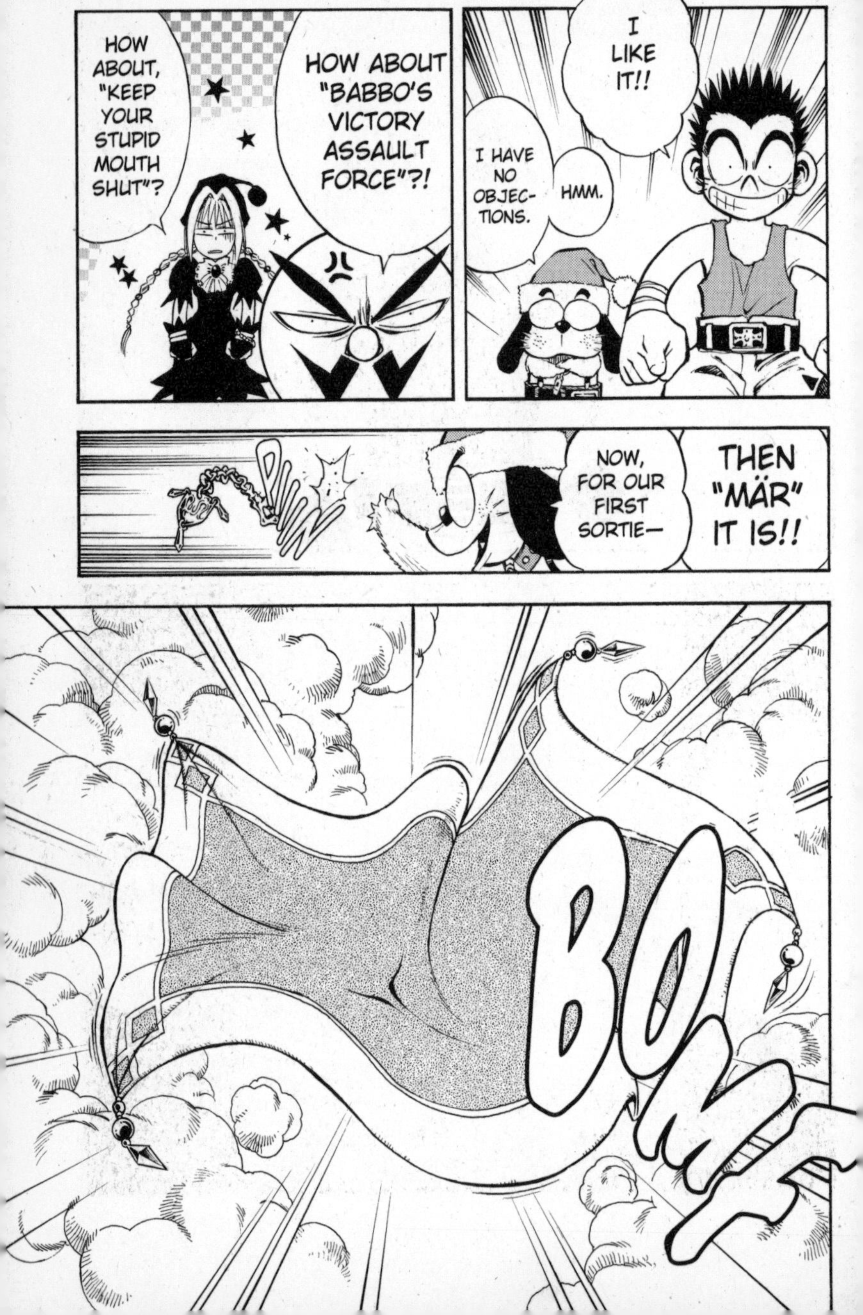
I LIKE IT!!
HMM.
I HAVE NO OBJECTIONS.
HOW ABOUT "BABBO'S VICTORY ASSAULT FORCE"?!
HOW ABOUT, "KEEP YOUR STUPID MOUTH SHUT"?
THEN "MÄR" IT IS!!
NOW, FOR OUR FIRST SORTIE—
BOM

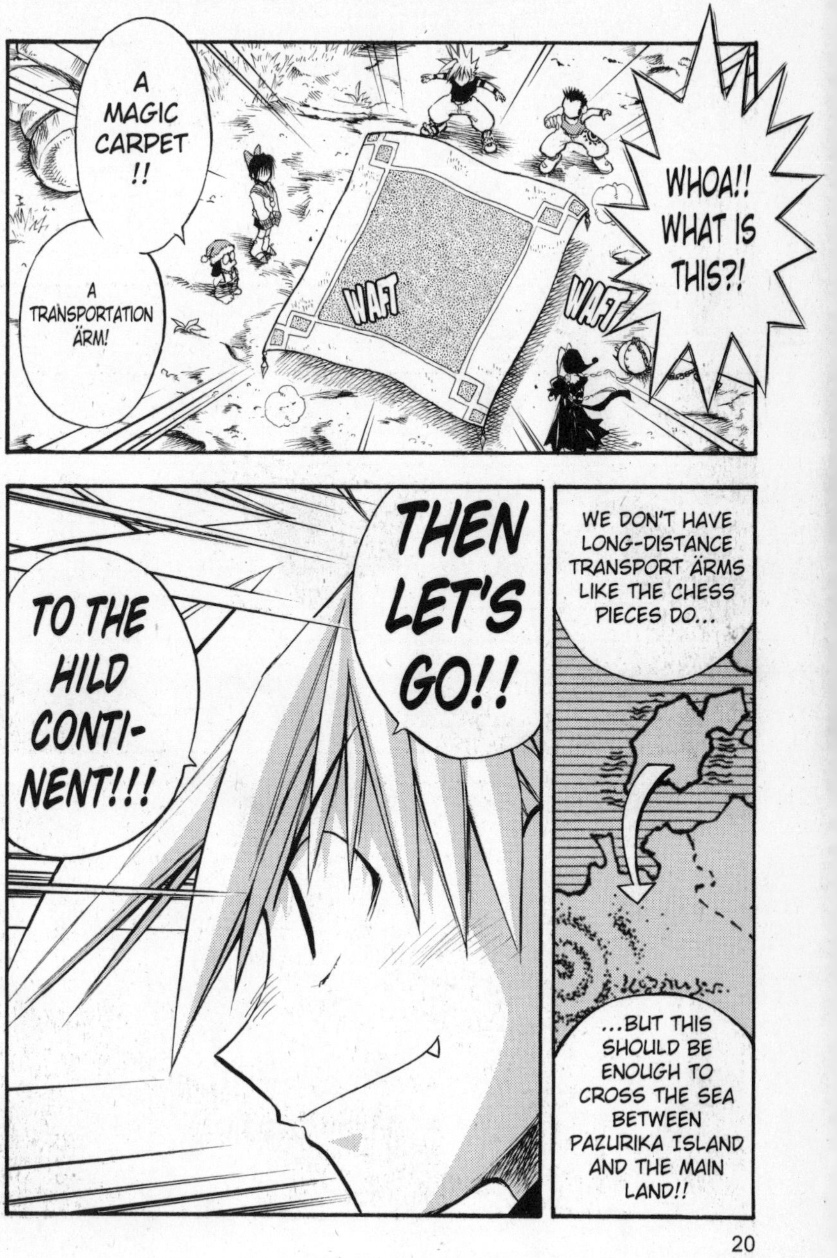
WHOA!! WHAT IS THIS?!
WAFT
WAFT
A MAGIC CARPET !!
A TRANSPORTATION ÄRM!
WE DON'T HAVE LONG-DISTANCE TRANSPORT ÄRMS LIKE THE CHESS PIECES DO...
...BUT THIS SHOULD BE ENOUGH TO CROSS THE SEA BETWEEN PAZURIKA ISLAND AND THE MAIN LAND!!
THEN LET'S GO!!
TO THE HILD CONTI-NENT!!!

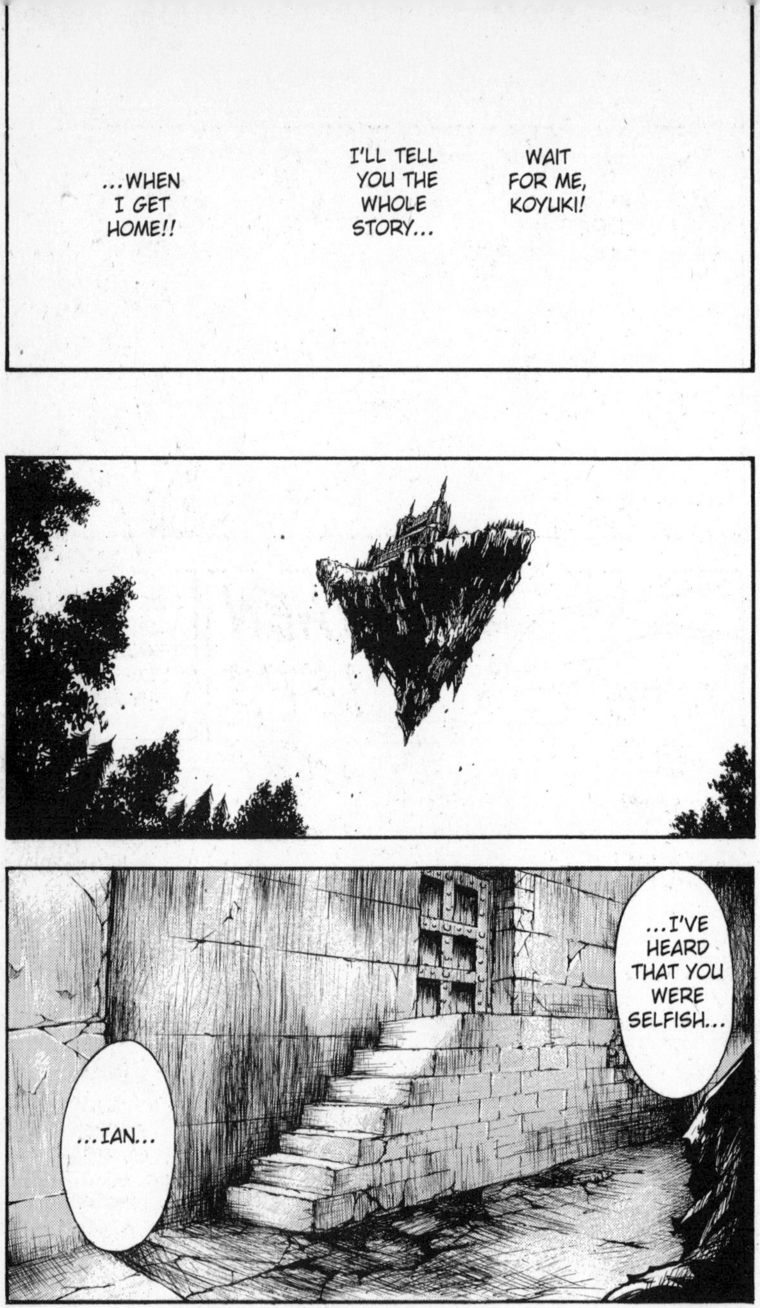
WAIT FOR ME, KOYUKI!
I'LL TELL YOU THE WHOLE STORY...
...WHEN I GET HOME!!
...I'VE HEARD THAT YOU WERE SELFISH...
...IAN...

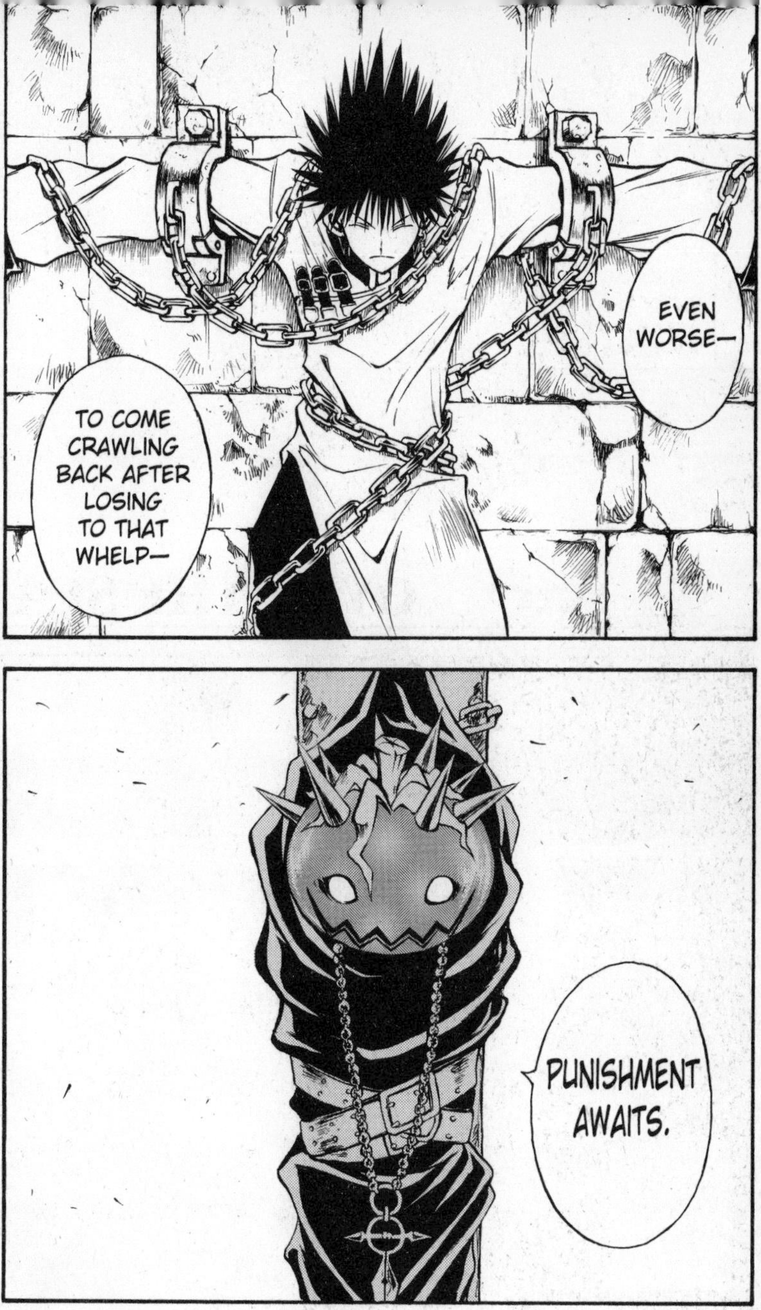
EVEN WORSE—
TO COME CRAWLING BACK AFTER LOSING TO THAT WHELP—
PUNISHMENT AWAITS.

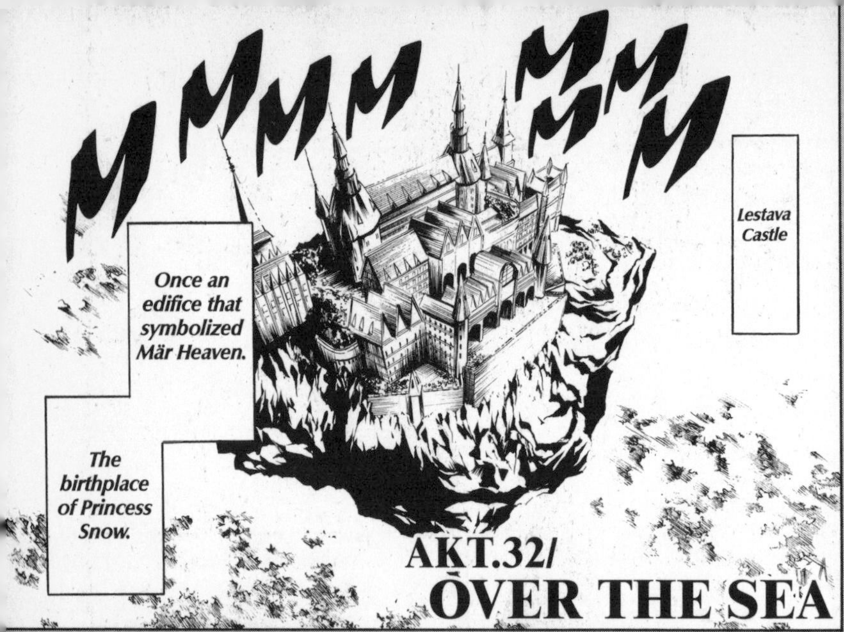
MMMM MMMM
Lestava Castle
Once an edifice that symbolized Mär Heaven.
The birthplace of Princess Snow.
AKT.32/
ÖVER THE SEA
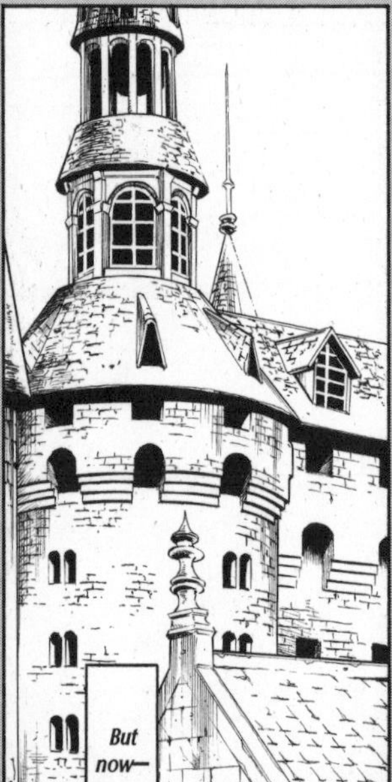
But now—
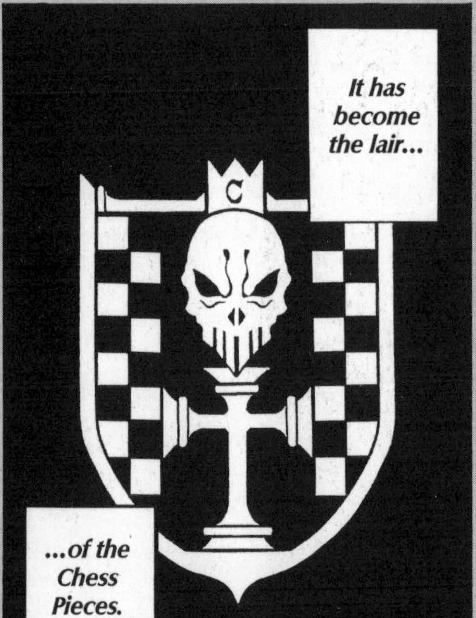
It has become the lair...
...of the Chess Pieces.

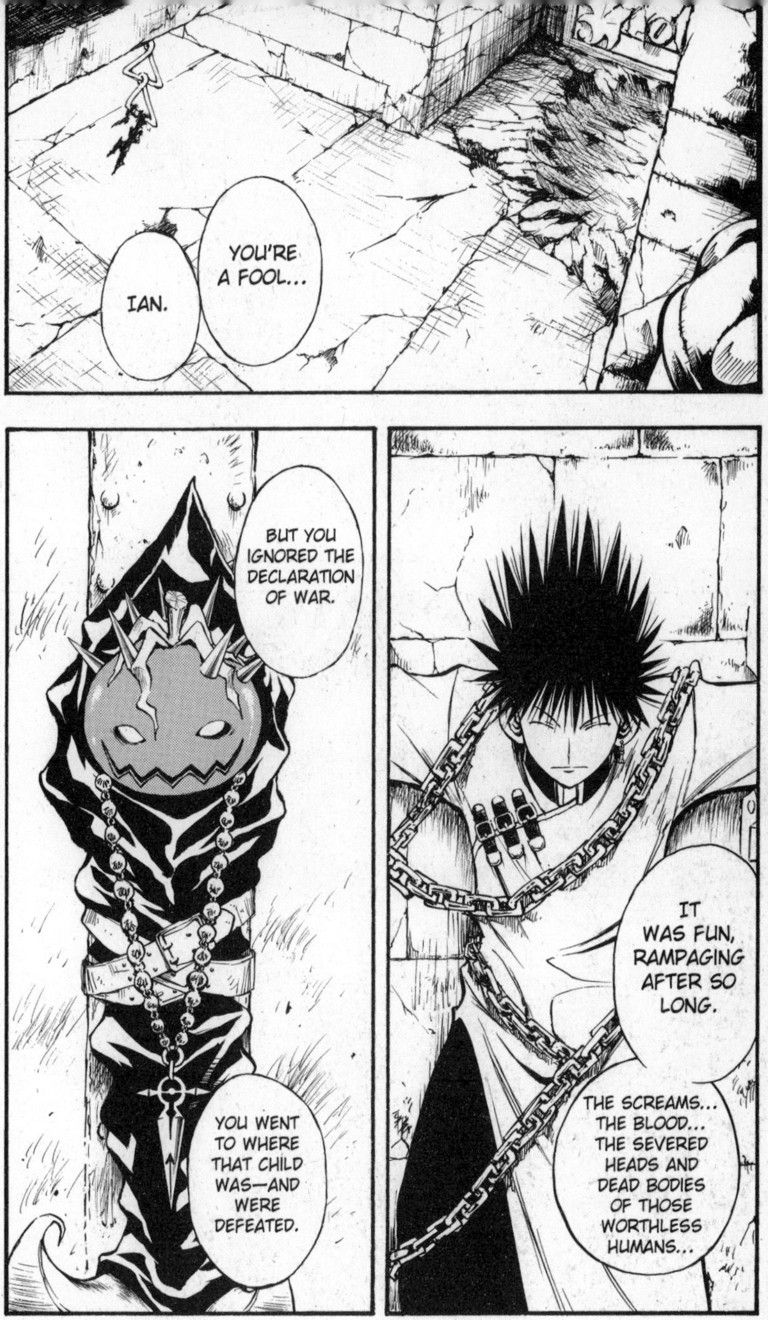
YOU'RE A FOOL...
IAN.
IT WAS FUN, RAMPAGING AFTER SO LONG.
THE SCREAMS... THE BLOOD... THE SEVERED HEADS AND DEAD BODIES OF THOSE WORTHLESS HUMANS...
BUT YOU IGNORED THE DECLARATION OF WAR.
YOU WENT TO WHERE THAT CHILD WAS—AND WERE DEFEATED.

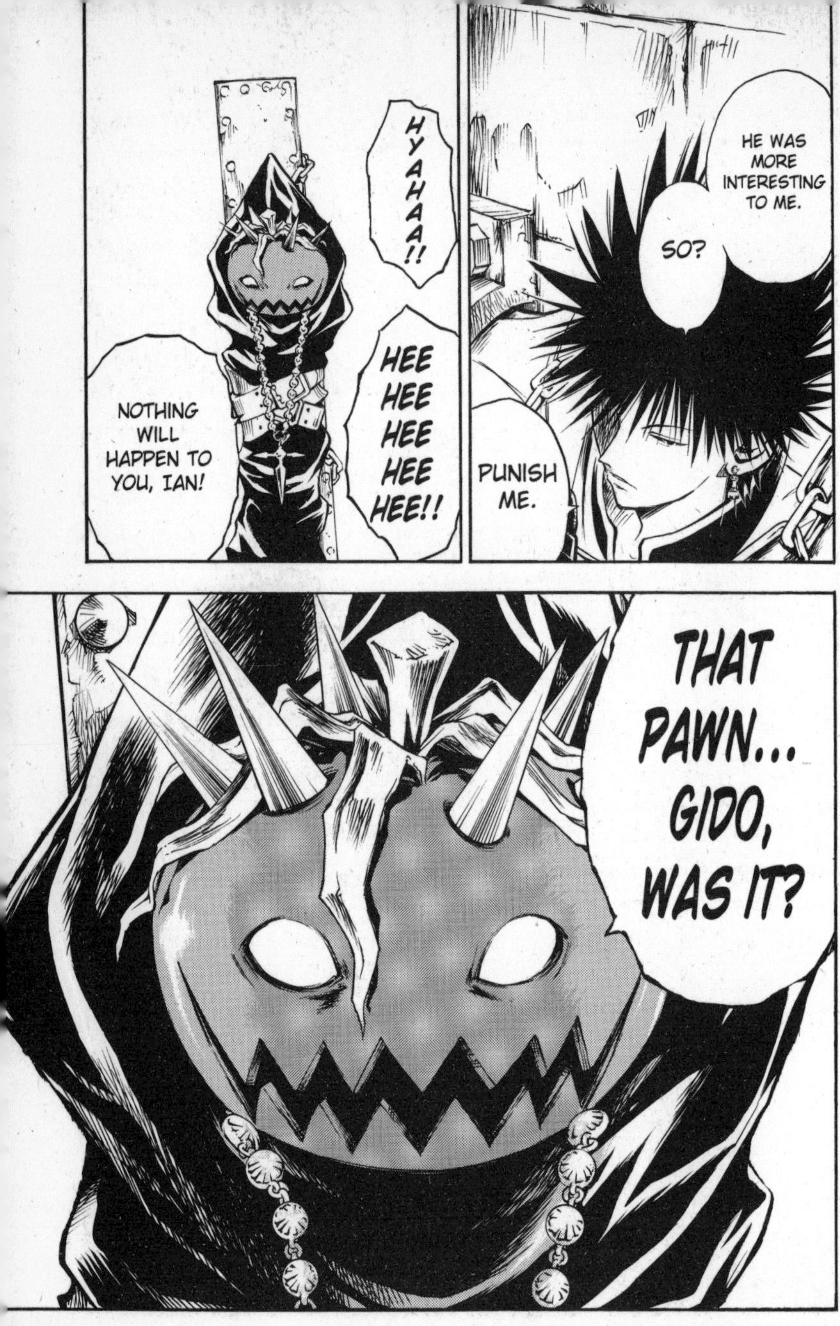
HE WAS MORE INTERESTING TO ME.
SO?
PUNISH ME.
HYAHAAA!!
HEE HEE HEE HEE HEE!!
NOTHING WILL HAPPEN TO YOU, IAN!
THAT PAWN... GIDO, WAS IT?

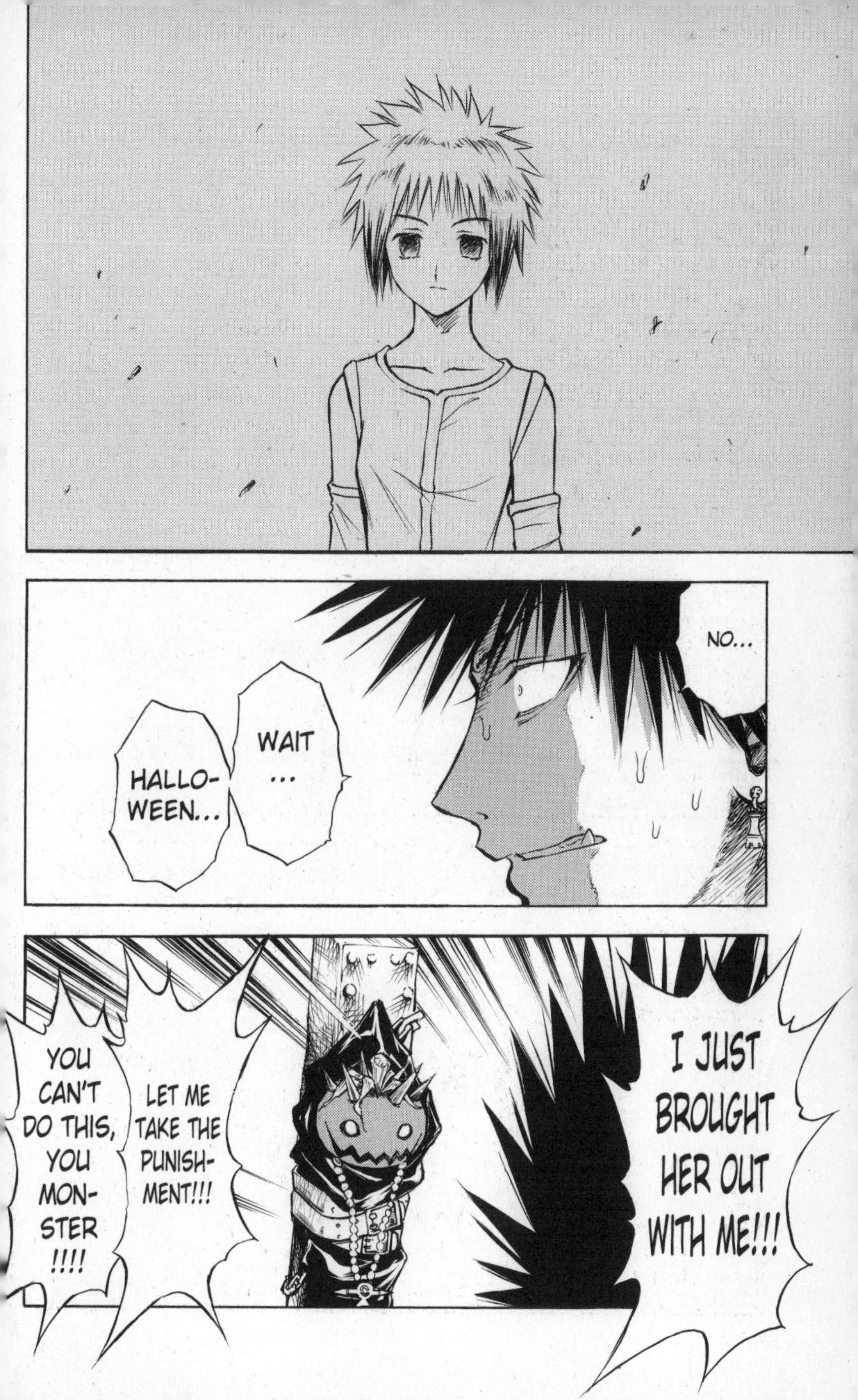
NO...
WAIT ...
HALLO-WEEN...
I JUST BROUGHT HER OUT WITH ME!!!
LET ME TAKE THE PUNISH-MENT!!!
YOU CAN'T DO THIS, YOU MON-STER !!!!

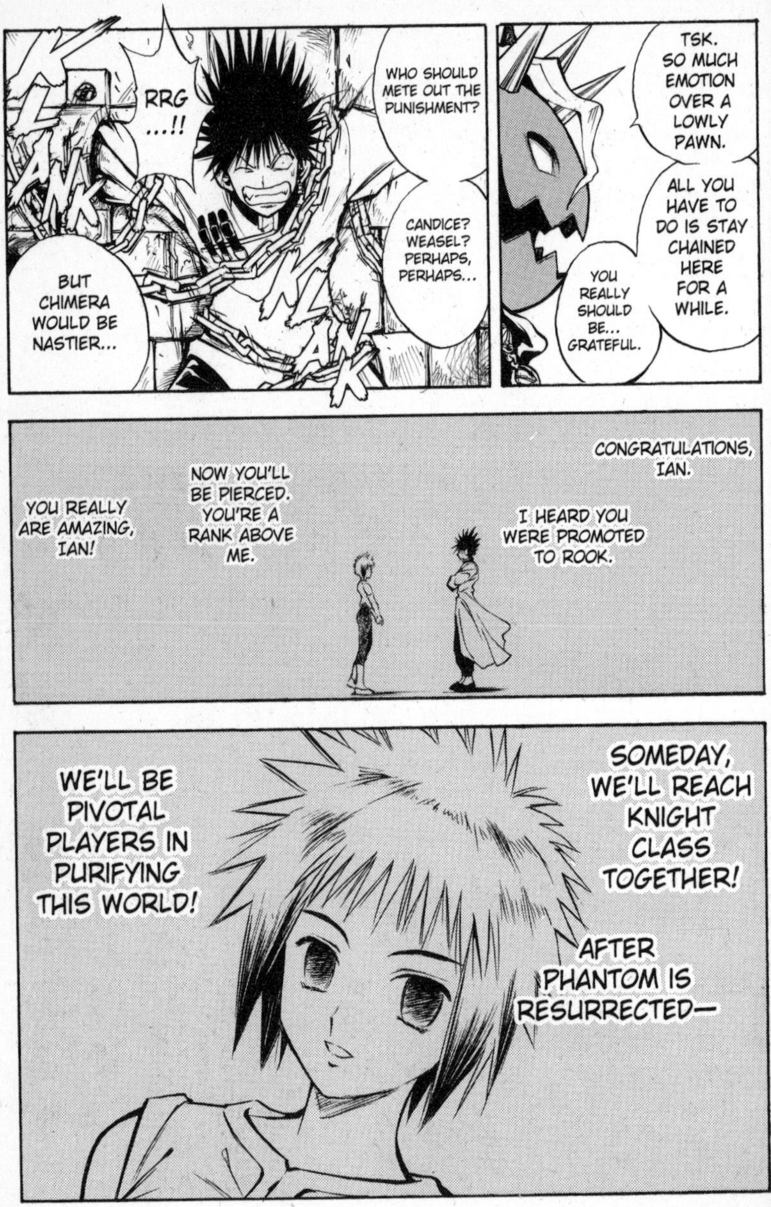
TSK. SO MUCH EMOTION OVER A LOWLY PAWN.
ALL YOU HAVE TO DO IS STAY CHAINED HERE FOR A WHILE.
YOU REALLY SHOULD BE... GRATEFUL.
WHO SHOULD METE OUT THE PUNISHMENT?
CANDICE? WEASEL? PERHAPS, PERHAPS...
RRG ...!!
KLANK
KLANK
BUT CHIMERA WOULD BE NASTIER...
CONGRATULATIONS, IAN.
I HEARD YOU WERE PROMOTED TO ROOK.
NOW YOU'LL BE PIERCED. YOU'RE A RANK ABOVE ME.
YOU REALLY ARE AMAZING, IAN!
SOMEDAY, WE'LL REACH KNIGHT CLASS TOGETHER!
AFTER PHANTOM IS RESURRECTED—
WE'LL BE PIVOTAL PLAYERS IN PURIFYING THIS WORLD!

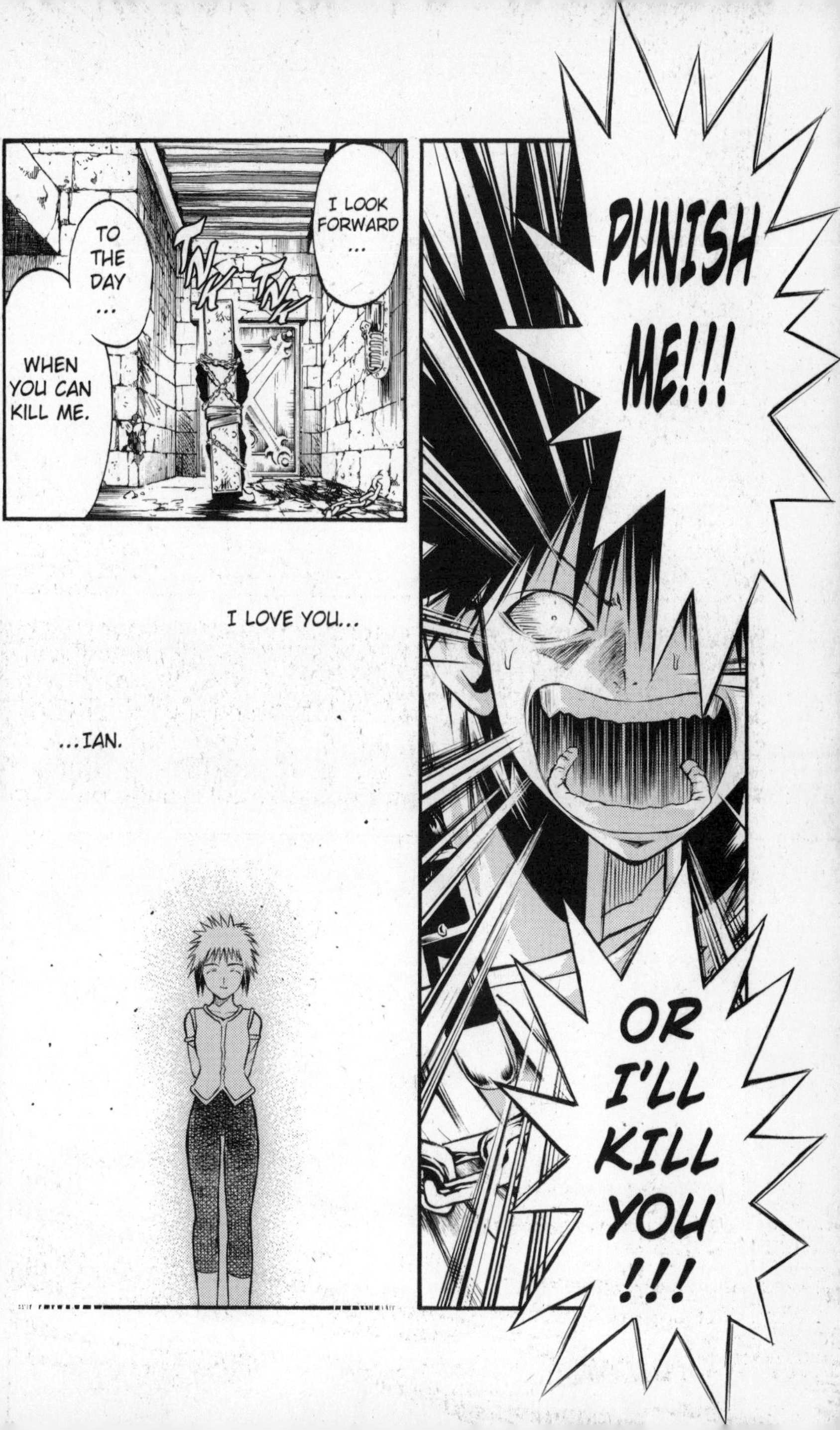
PUNISH ME!!!
OR I'LL KILL YOU!!!
I LOOK FORWARD ...
TO THE DAY ...
WHEN YOU CAN KILL ME.
TNK TNK
I LOVE YOU...
...IAN.

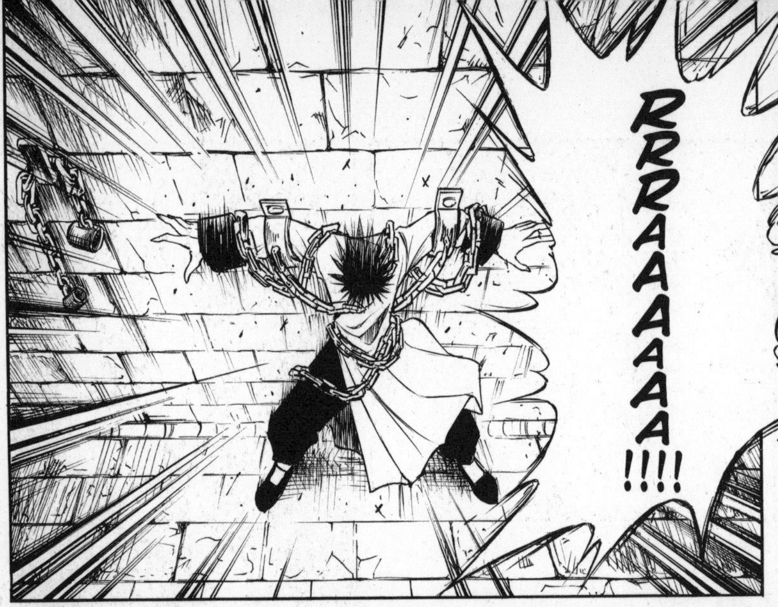
RRRAAAAAA!!!!

AKT.32/ OVER THE SEA

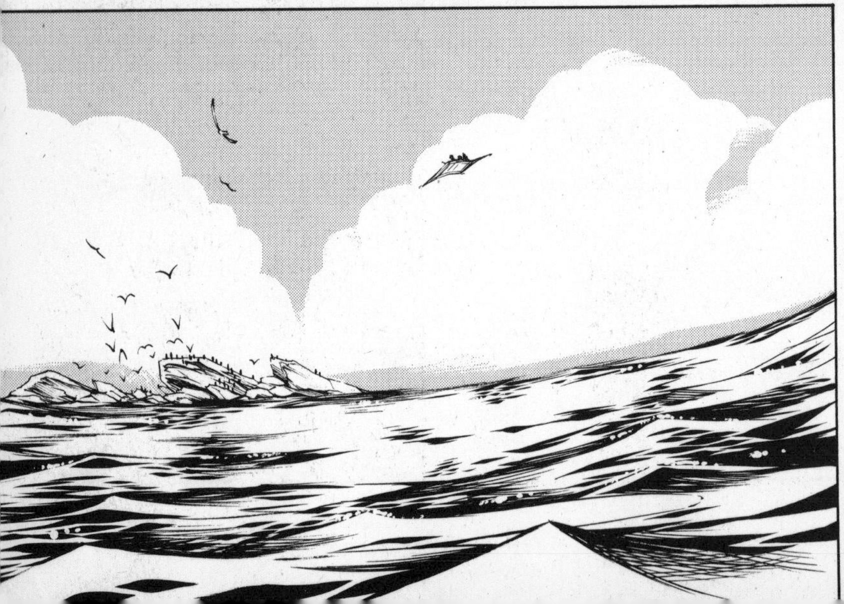

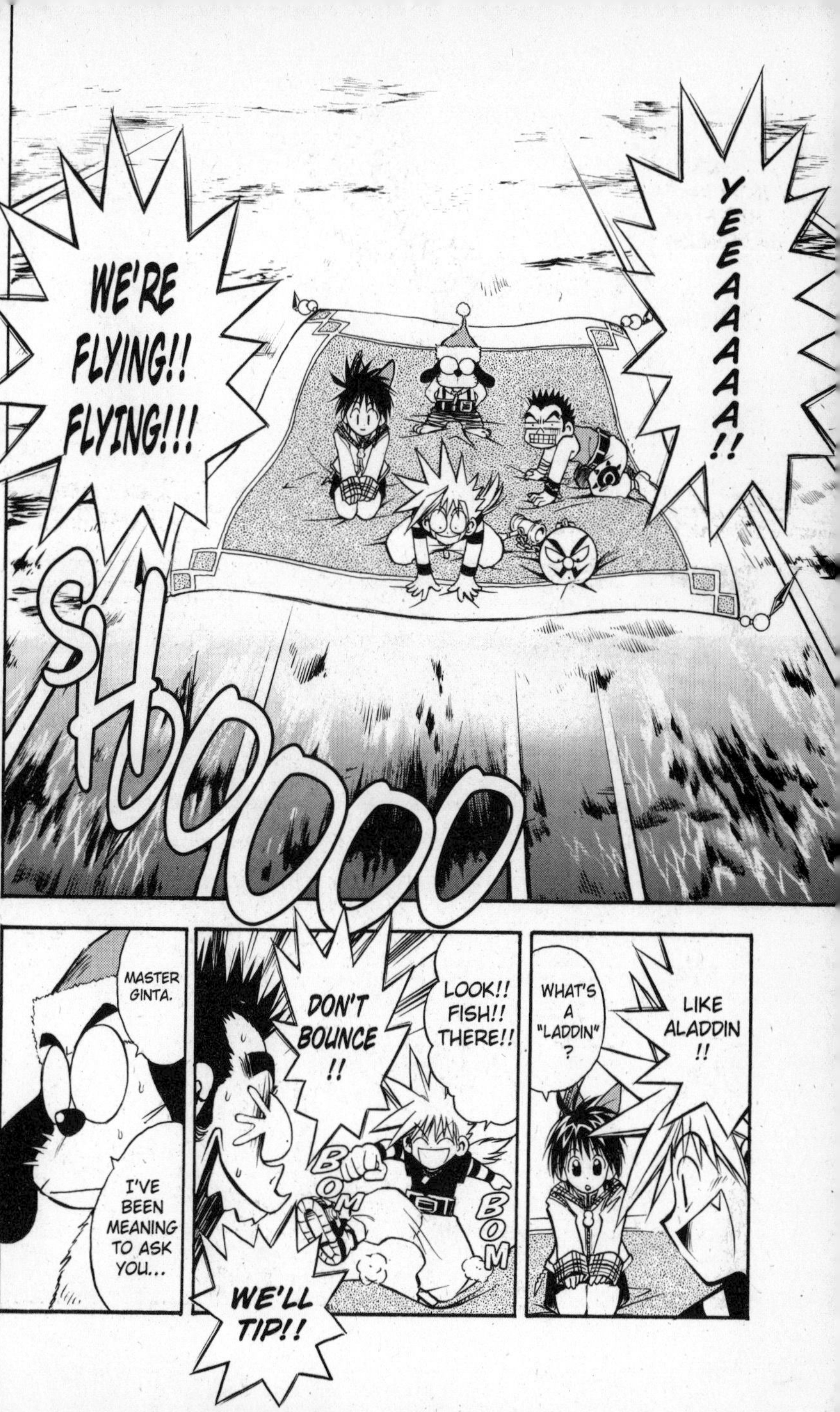
YEEAAAAAA!!
WE'RE FLYING!! FLYING!!!
SHOOOOO
LIKE ALADDIN!!
WHAT'S A "LADDIN"?
LOOK!! FISH!! THERE!!
DON'T BOUNCE!!
BOM
BOM
BOM
WE'LL TIP!!
MASTER GINTA.
I'VE BEEN MEANING TO ASK YOU...

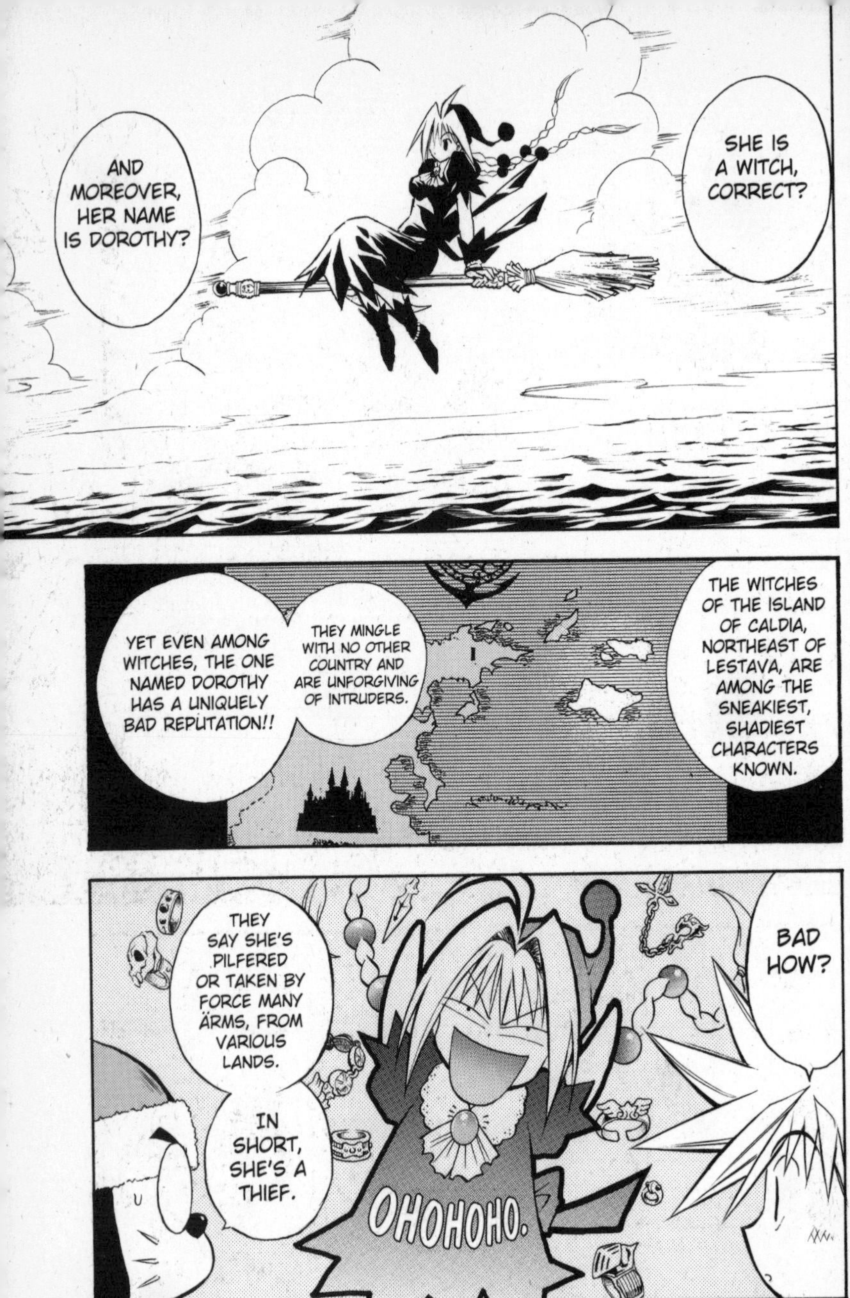
SHE IS A WITCH, CORRECT?
AND MOREOVER, HER NAME IS DOROTHY?
THE WITCHES OF THE ISLAND OF CALDIA, NORTHEAST OF LESTAVA, ARE AMONG THE SNEAKIEST, SHADIEST CHARACTERS KNOWN.
THEY MINGLE WITH NO OTHER COUNTRY AND ARE UNFORGIVING OF INTRUDERS.
YET EVEN AMONG WITCHES, THE ONE NAMED DOROTHY HAS A UNIQUELY BAD REPUTATION!!
BAD HOW?
THEY SAY SHE'S PILFERED OR TAKEN BY FORCE MANY ÄRMS, FROM VARIOUS LANDS.
IN SHORT, SHE'S A THIEF.
OHOHOHO.

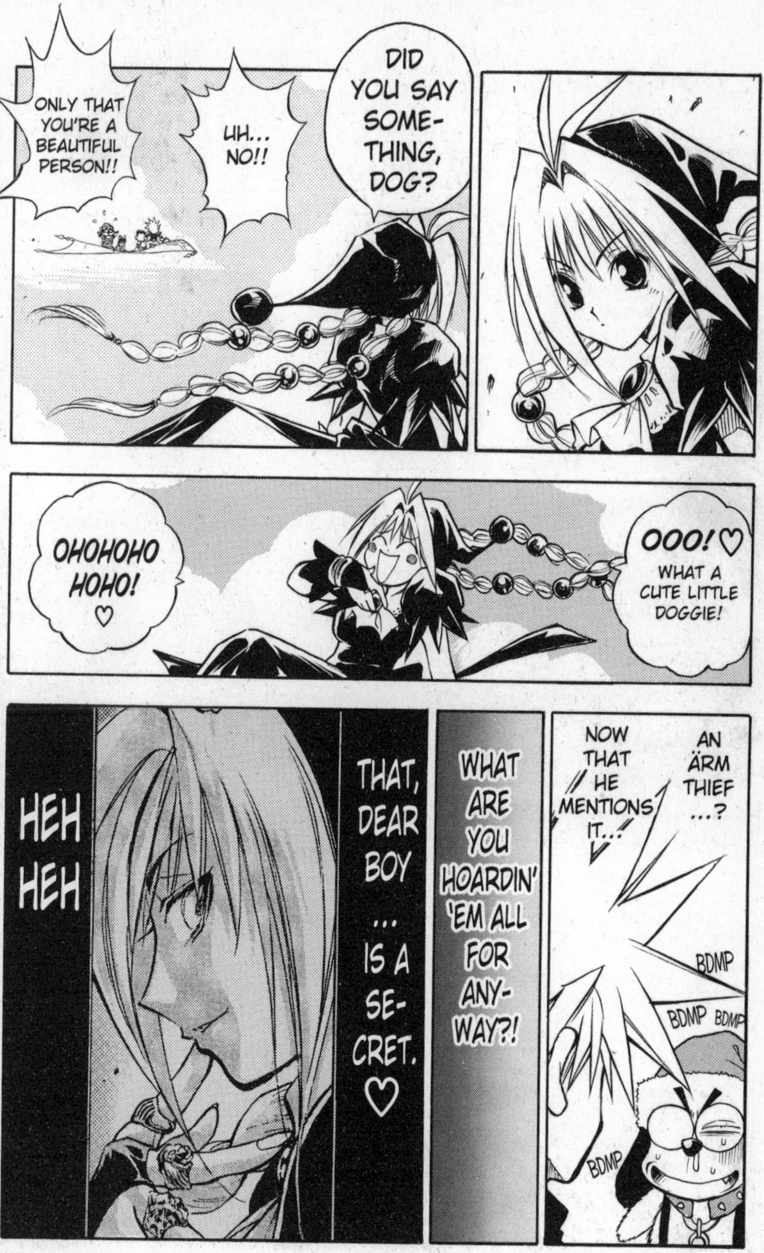
DID YOU SAY SOME-THING, DOG?
UH... NO!!
ONLY THAT YOU'RE A BEAUTIFUL PERSON!!
OOO! ♡ WHAT A CUTE LITTLE DOGGIE!
OHOHOHO HOHO! ♡
AN ÄRM THIEF ...?
NOW THAT HE MENTIONS IT...
BDMP
BDMP BDMP
BDMP
WHAT ARE YOU HOARDIN' 'EM ALL FOR ANY-WAY?!
THAT, DEAR BOY ... IS A SE-CRET. ♡
HEH HEH

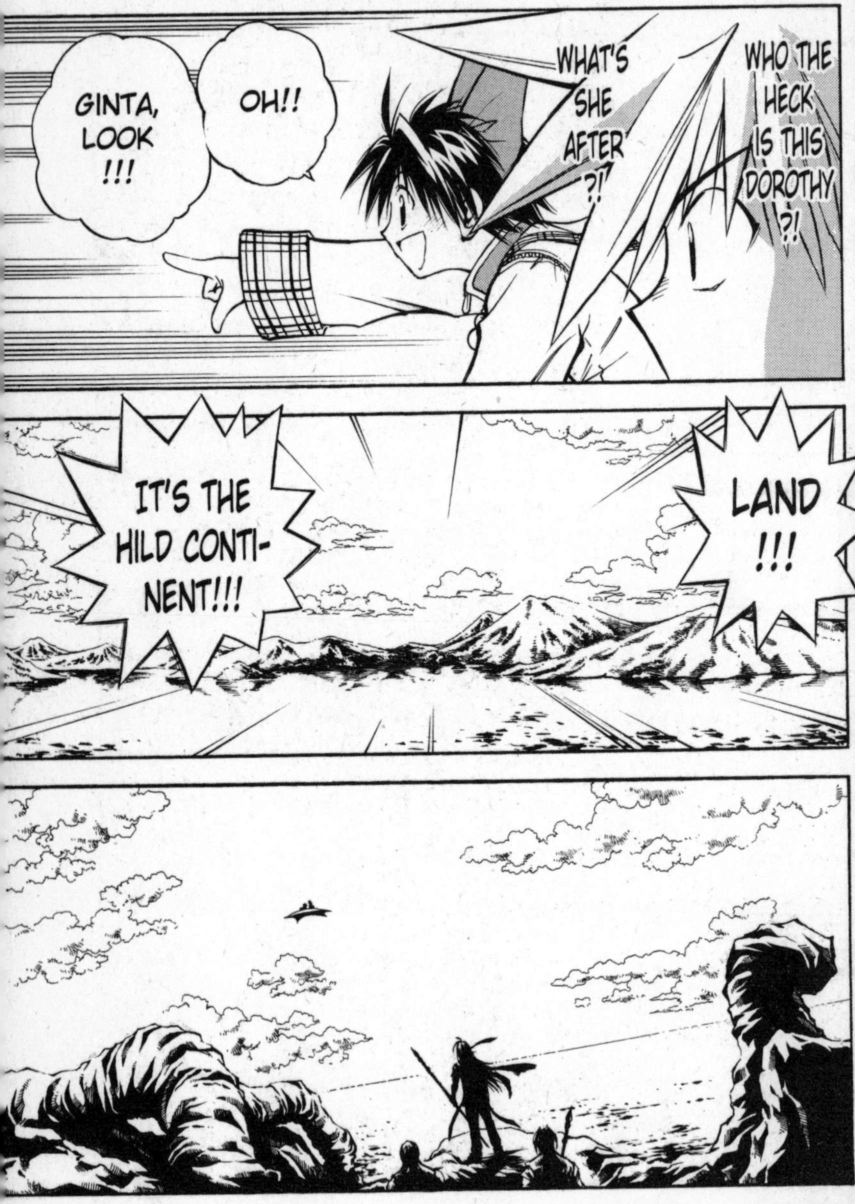
WHO THE HECK IS THIS DOROTHY ?!
WHAT'S SHE AFTER ?!
OH!!
GINTA, LOOK !!!
LAND !!!
IT'S THE HILD CONTI-NENT!!!

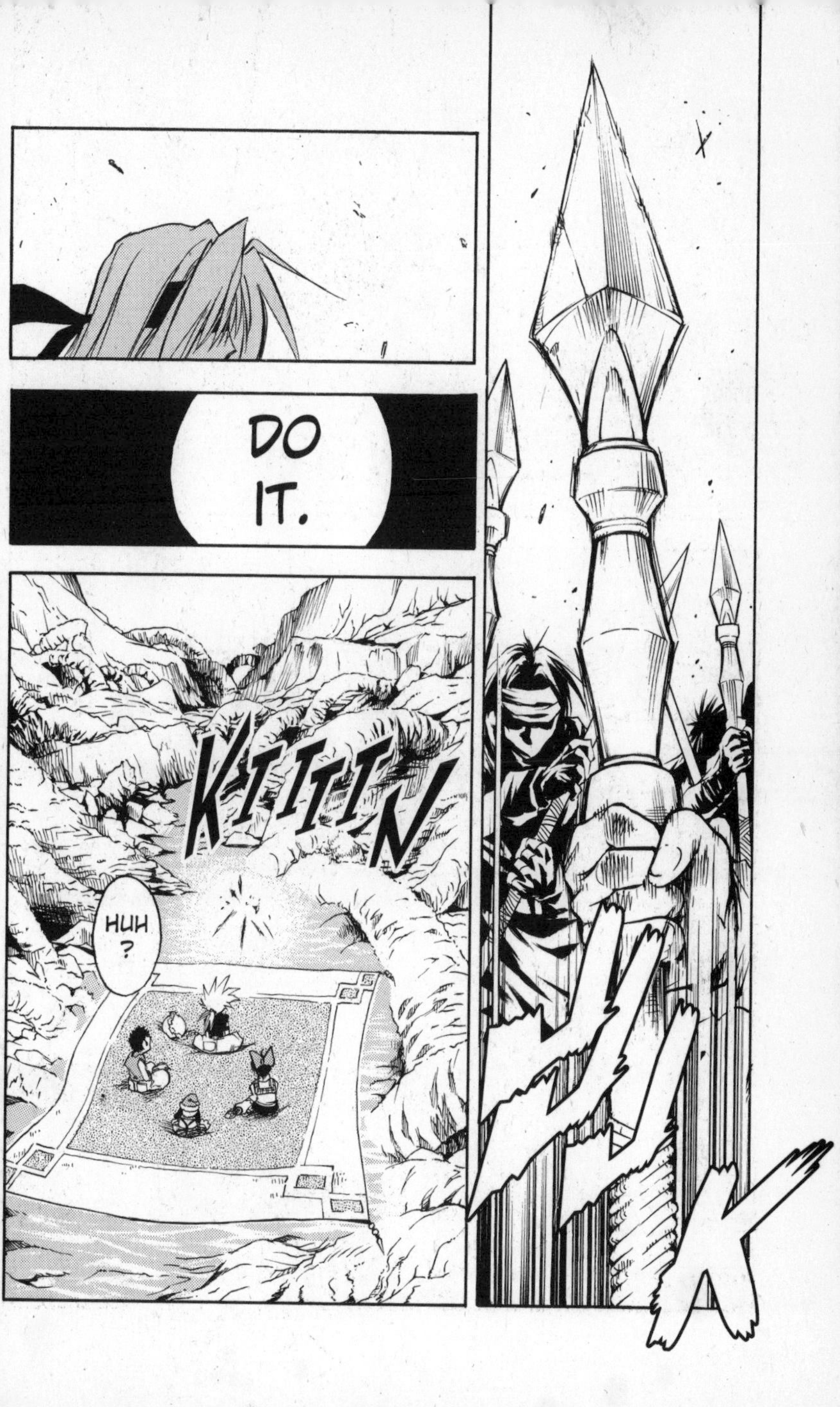
DO IT.
KIIIIN
HUH ?

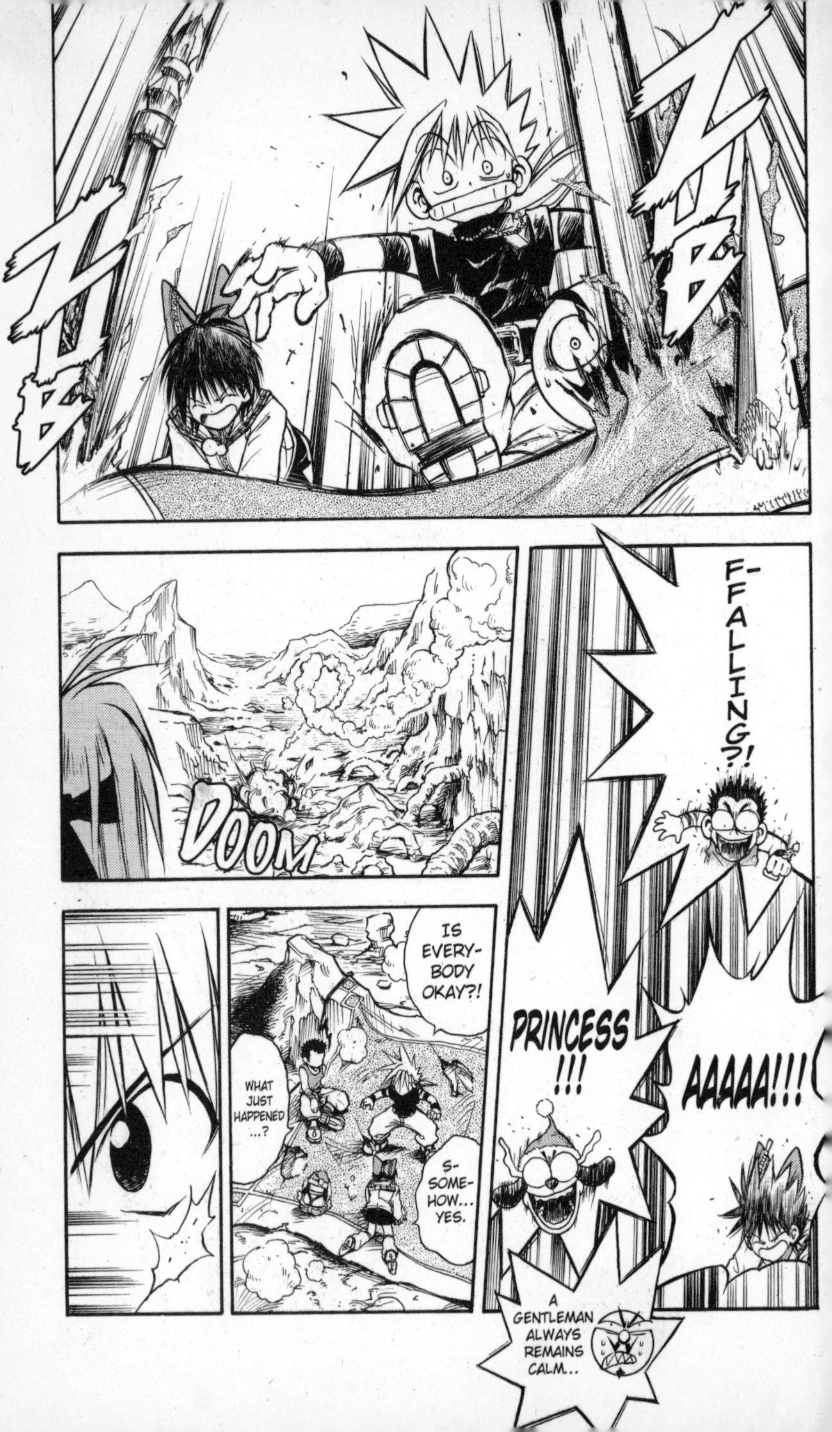
F-FFALLING?!
AAAAA!!!
PRINCESS!!!
A GENTLEMAN ALWAYS REMAINS CALM...
DOOM
IS EVERY-BODY OKAY?!
WHAT JUST HAPPENED...?
S-SOMEHOW... YES.

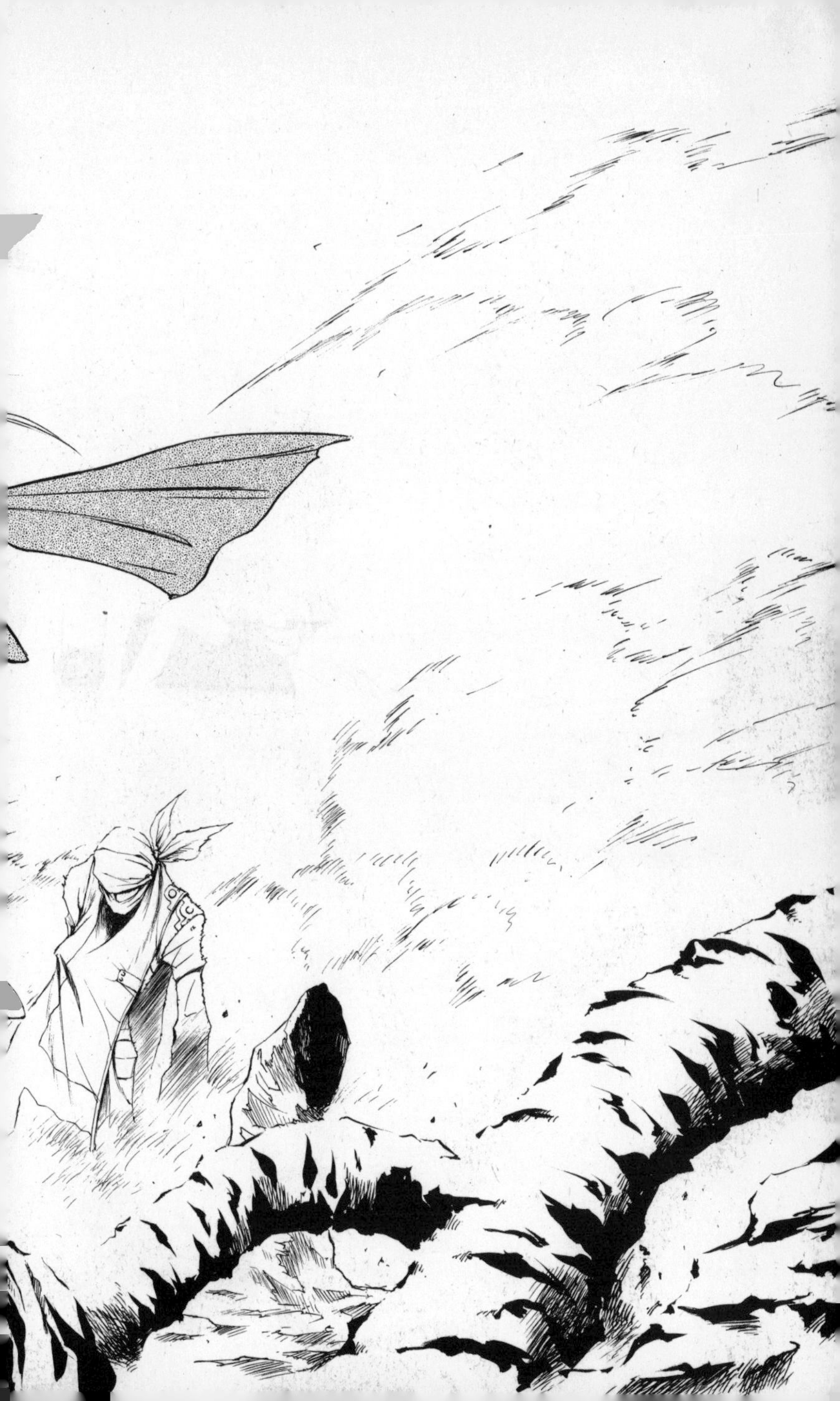

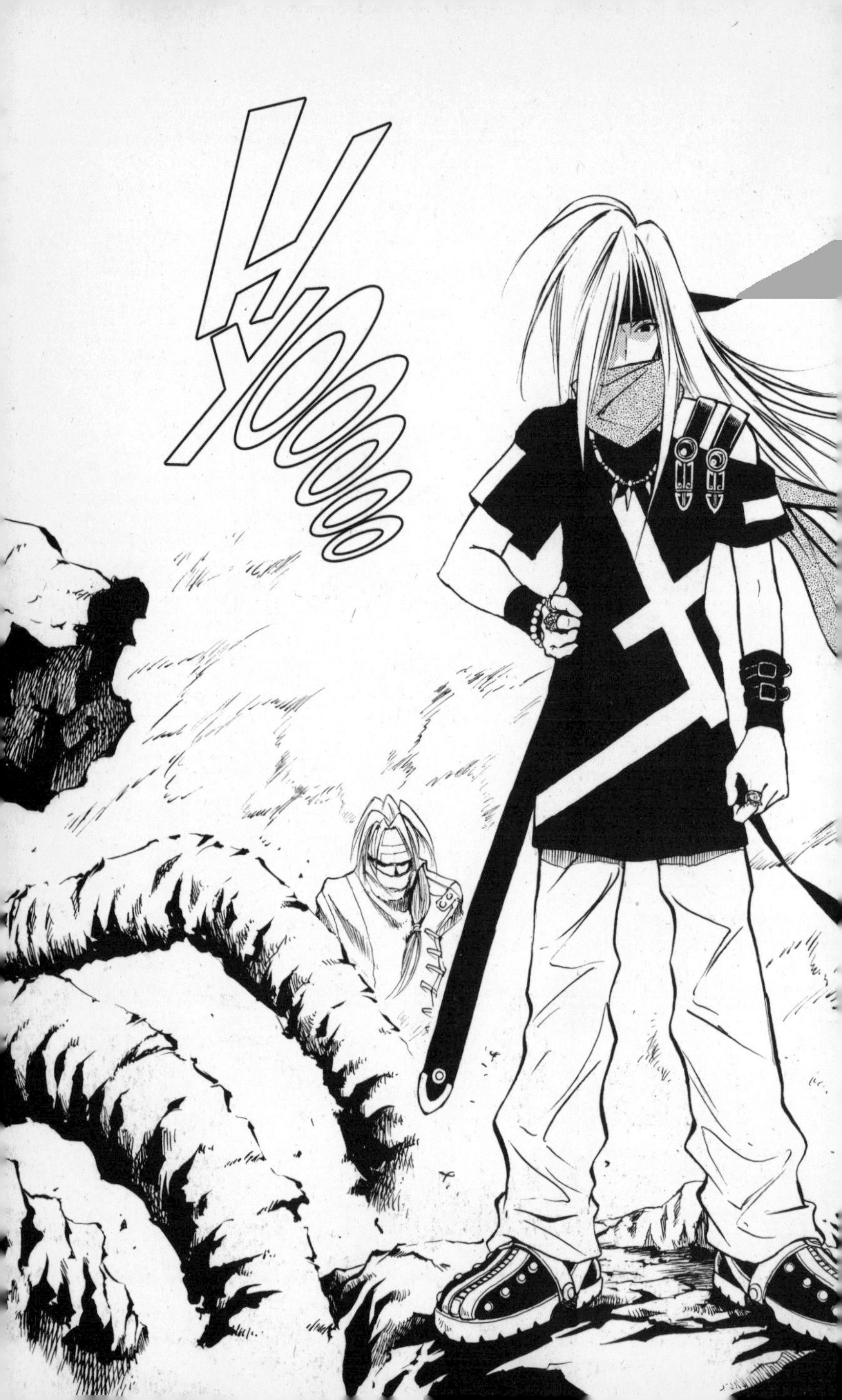
VWOOOOOO

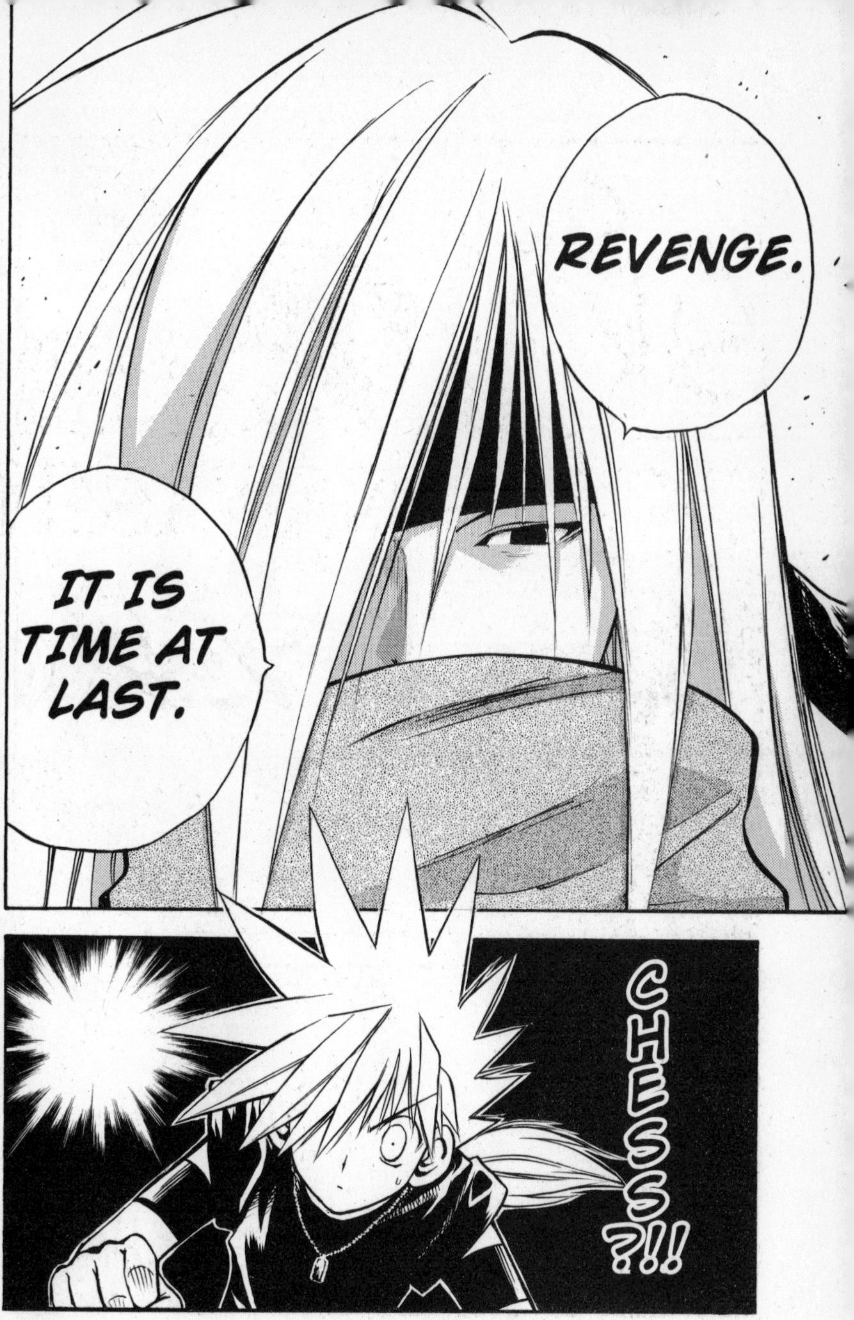
REVENGE.
IT IS TIME AT LAST.
CHESS?!!

AKT.33/ NANASHI

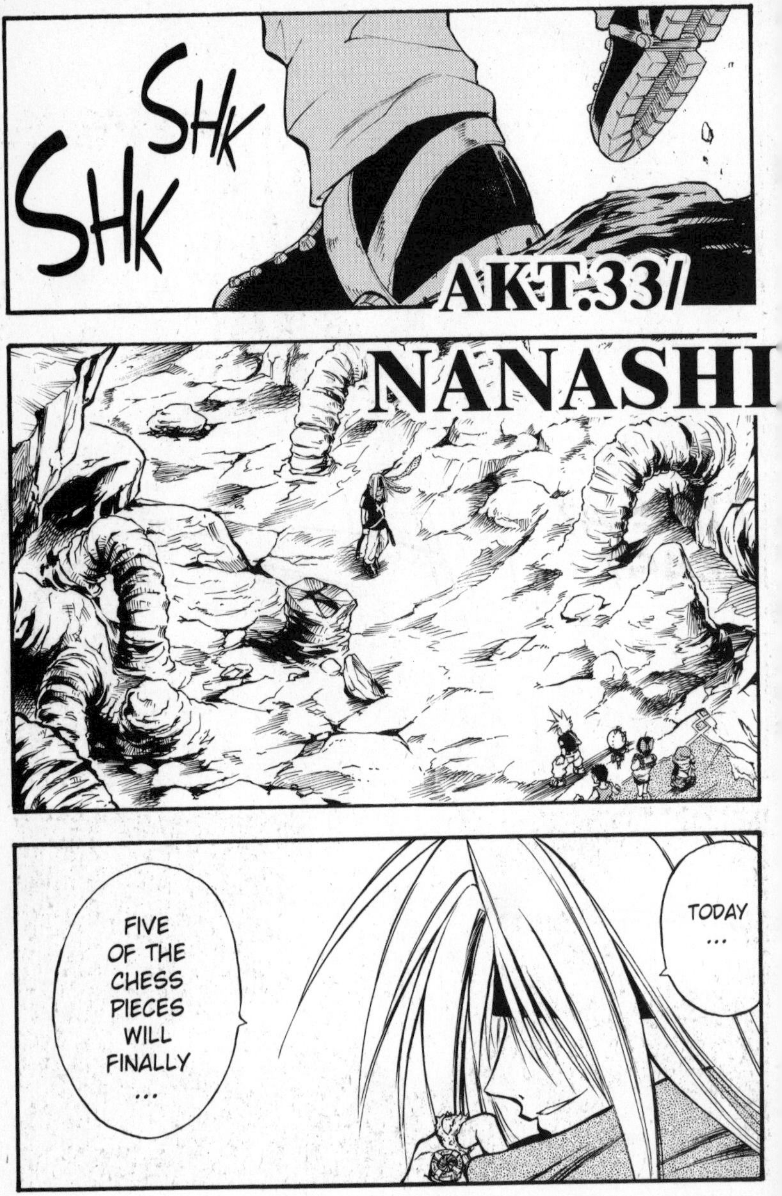
SHK SHK
TODAY ...
FIVE OF THE CHESS PIECES WILL FINALLY ...

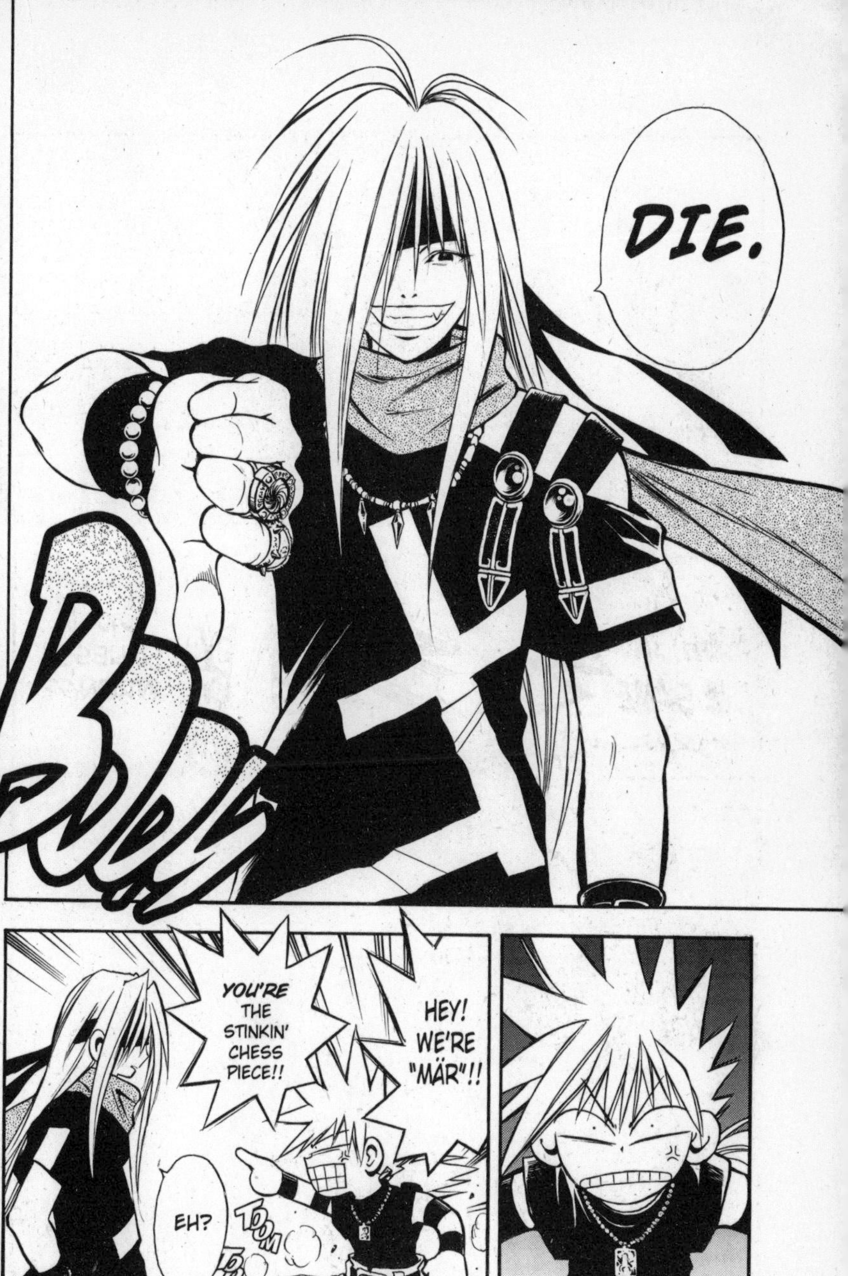
DIE.
HEY! WE'RE "MÄR"!!
YOU'RE THE STINKIN' CHESS PIECE!!
TOOM TOOM
EH?

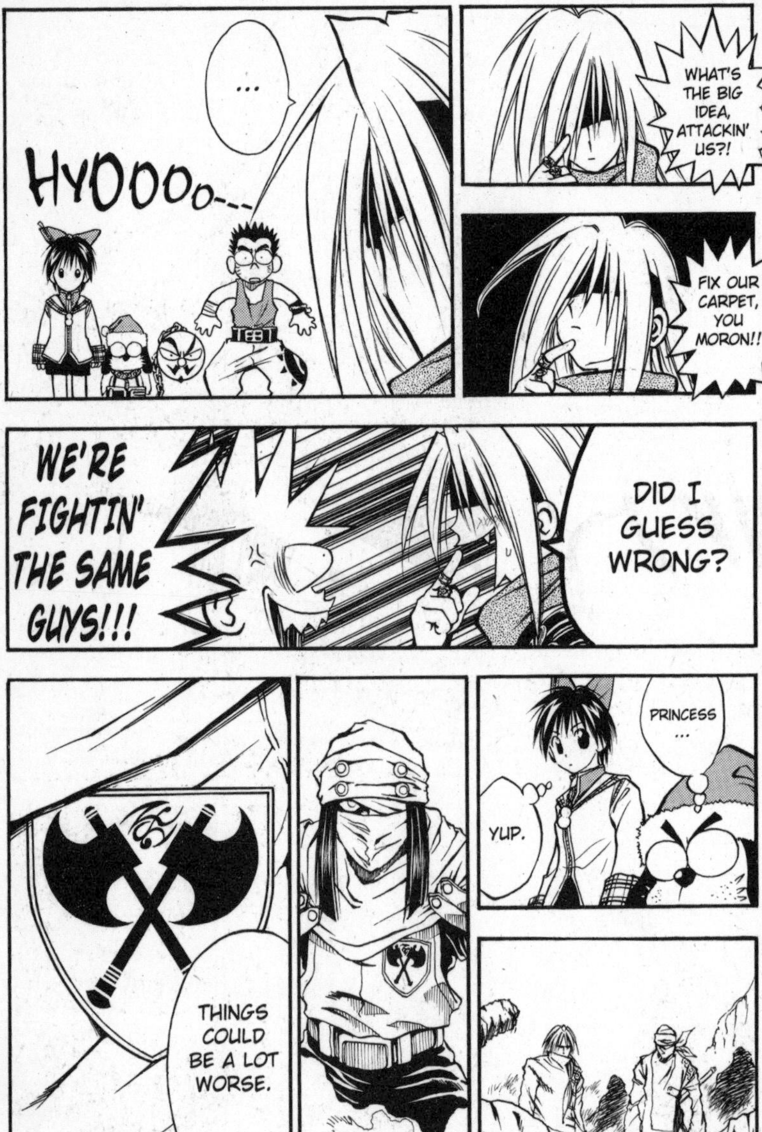
WHAT'S THE BIG IDEA, ATTACKIN' US?!
FIX OUR CARPET, YOU MORON!!
...
HYOOOo---
DID I GUESS WRONG?
WE'RE FIGHTIN' THE SAME GUYS!!!
PRINCESS ...
YUP.
THINGS COULD BE A LOT WORSE.

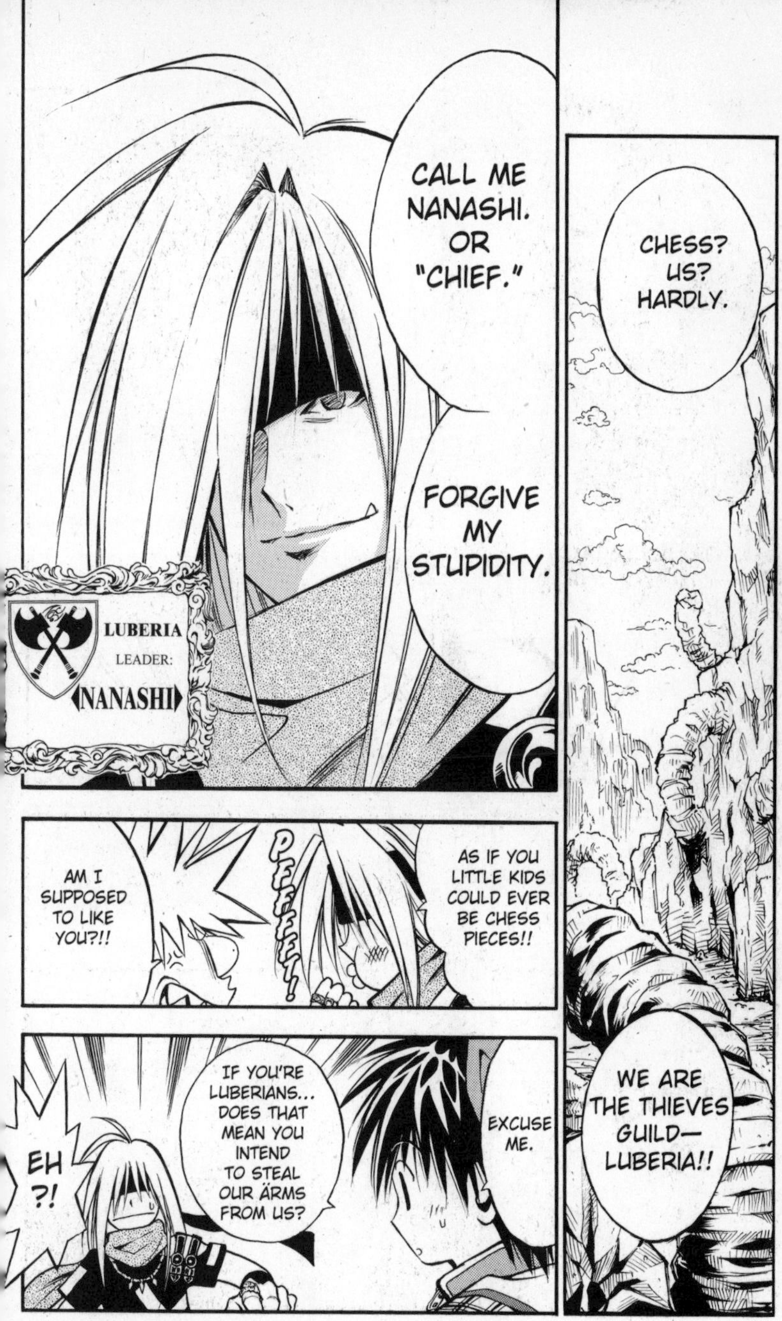
CHESS? US? HARDLY.
WE ARE THE THIEVES GUILD— LUBERIA!!
CALL ME NANASHI. OR "CHIEF."
FORGIVE MY STUPIDITY.
LUBERIA
LEADER:
NANASHI
AS IF YOU LITTLE KIDS COULD EVER BE CHESS PIECES!!
PFFFFT!
AM I SUPPOSED TO LIKE YOU?!!
EXCUSE ME.
IF YOU'RE LUBERIANS... DOES THAT MEAN YOU INTEND TO STEAL OUR ÄRMS FROM US?
EH ?!

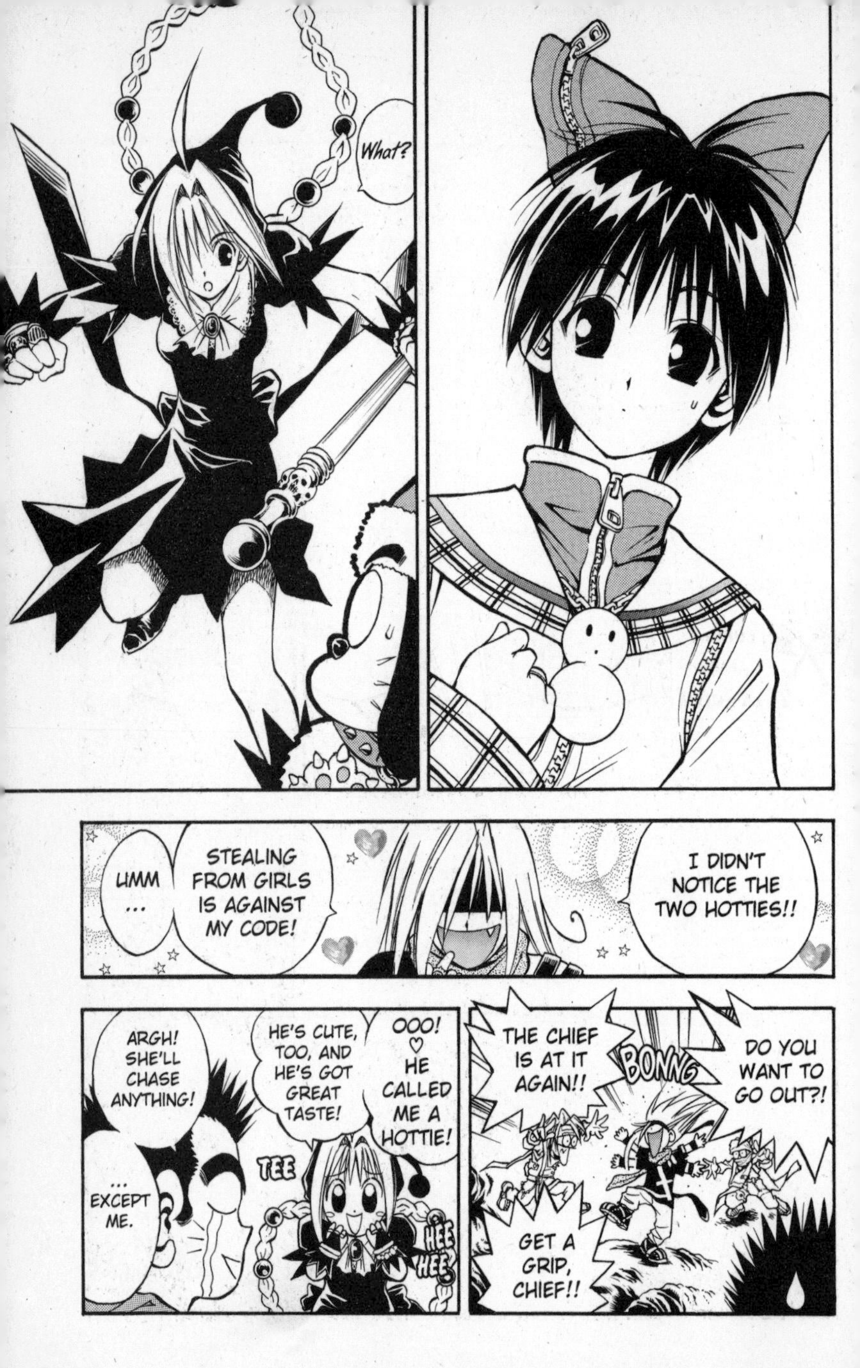
What?
I DIDN'T NOTICE THE TWO HOTTIES!!
STEALING FROM GIRLS IS AGAINST MY CODE!
UMM ...
DO YOU WANT TO GO OUT?!
BONNG
THE CHIEF IS AT IT AGAIN!!
GET A GRIP, CHIEF!!
OOO! ♡ HE CALLED ME A HOTTIE!
HE'S CUTE, TOO, AND HE'S GOT GREAT TASTE!
TEE
HEE HEE
ARGH! SHE'LL CHASE ANYTHING!
... EXCEPT ME.

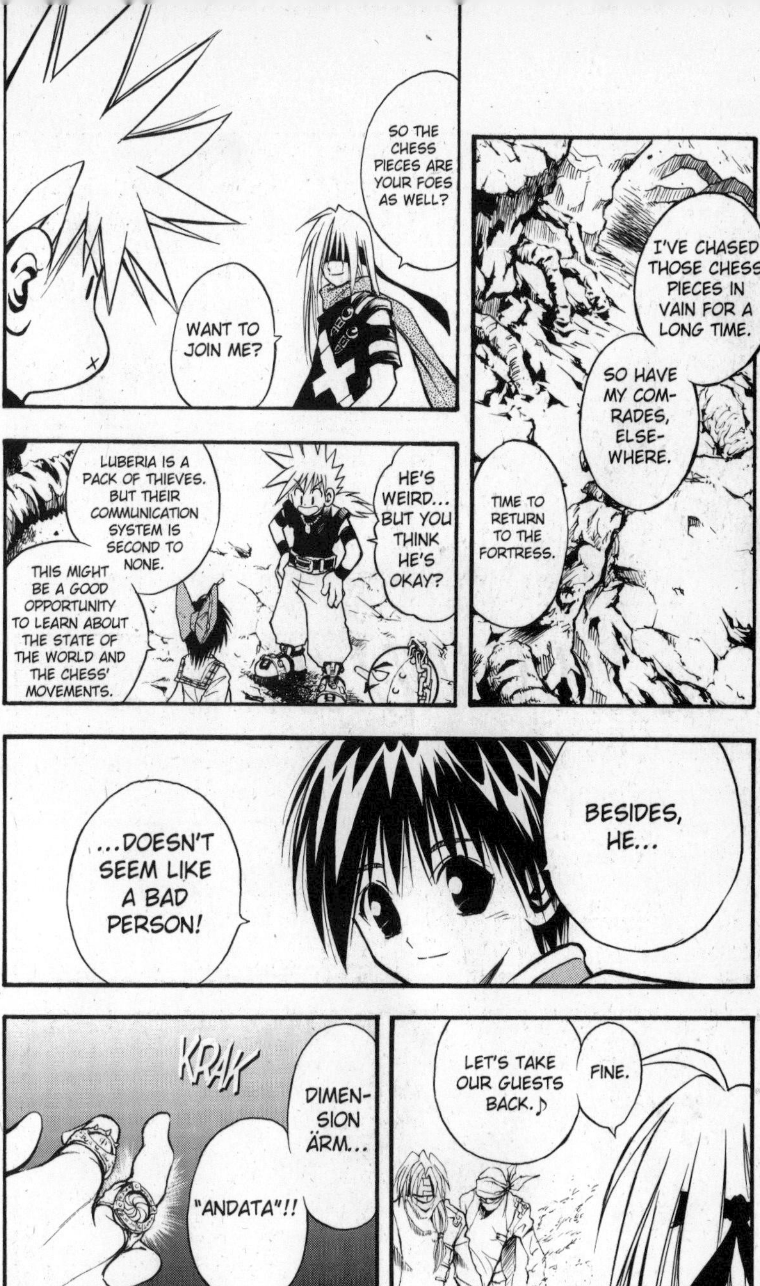

I'VE CHASED THOSE CHESS PIECES IN VAIN FOR A LONG TIME.
SO HAVE MY COM-RADES, ELSE-WHERE.
TIME TO RETURN TO THE FORTRESS.
SO THE CHESS PIECES ARE YOUR FOES AS WELL?
WANT TO JOIN ME?
HE'S WEIRD... BUT YOU THINK HE'S OKAY?
LUBERIA IS A PACK OF THIEVES. BUT THEIR COMMUNICATION SYSTEM IS SECOND TO NONE.
THIS MIGHT BE A GOOD OPPORTUNITY TO LEARN ABOUT THE STATE OF THE WORLD AND THE CHESS' MOVEMENTS.
BESIDES, HE...
...DOESN'T SEEM LIKE A BAD PERSON!
FINE.
LET'S TAKE OUR GUESTS BACK.♪
DIMEN-SION ÄRM...
KRAK
"ANDATA"!!

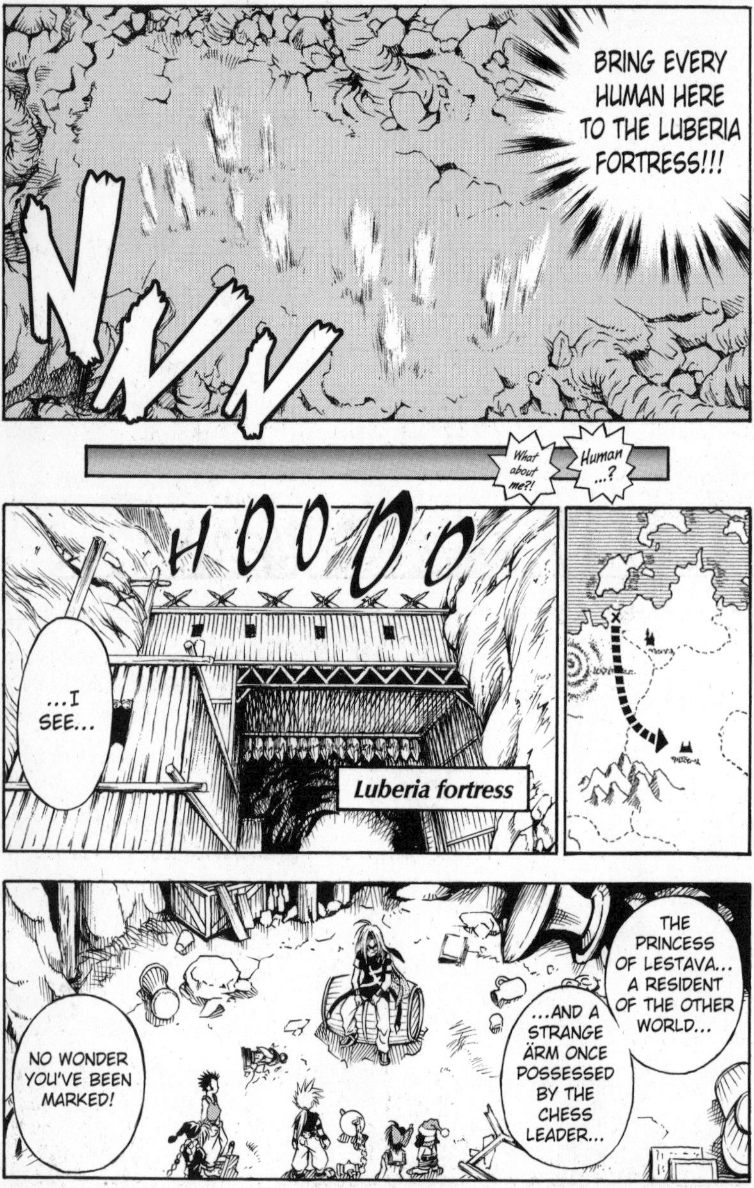
BRING EVERY HUMAN HERE TO THE LUBERIA FORTRESS!!!
NNN
Human ...?
What about me?!
HOOOOO
Luberia fortress
...I SEE...
THE PRINCESS OF LESTAVA... A RESIDENT OF THE OTHER WORLD...
...AND A STRANGE ÄRM ONCE POSSESSED BY THE CHESS LEADER...
NO WONDER YOU'VE BEEN MARKED!

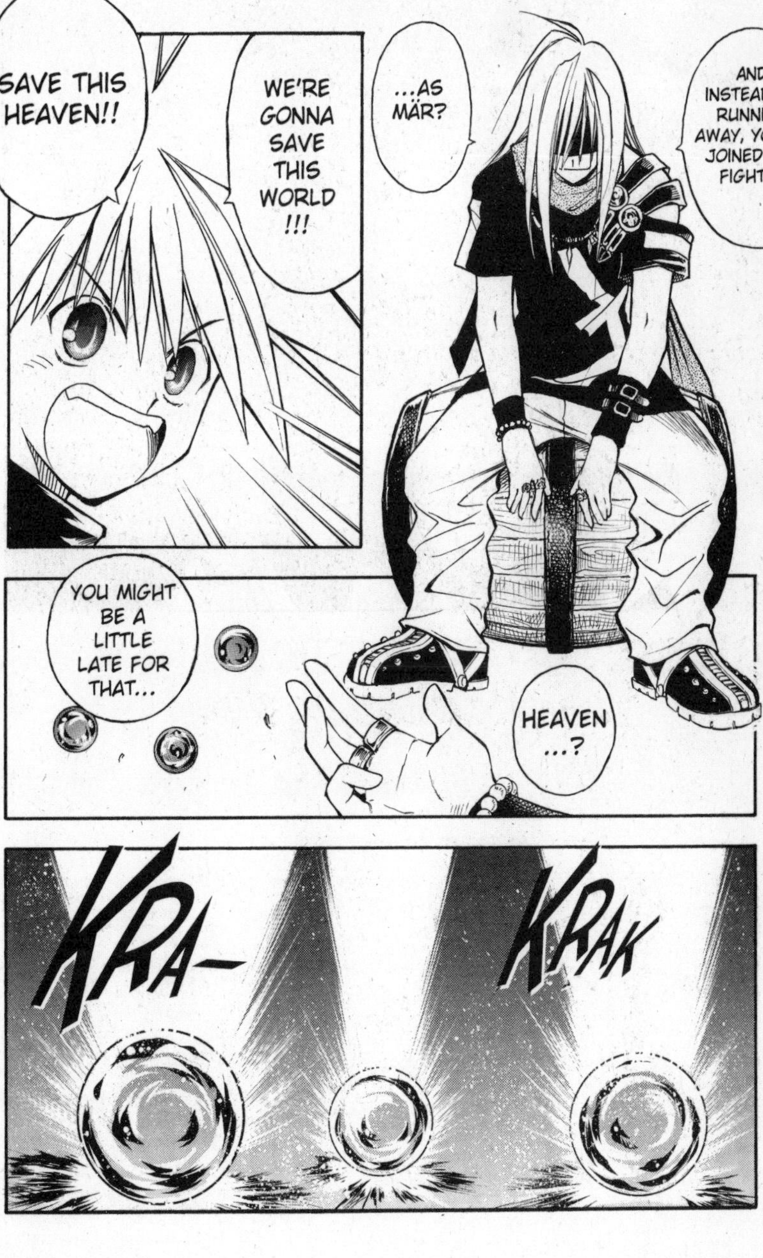
AND INSTEAD OF RUNNING AWAY, YOU'VE JOINED THE FIGHT...
...AS MÄR?
WE'RE GONNA SAVE THIS WORLD!!!
SAVE THIS HEAVEN!!
HEAVEN...?
YOU MIGHT BE A LITTLE LATE FOR THAT...
KRA-
KRAK

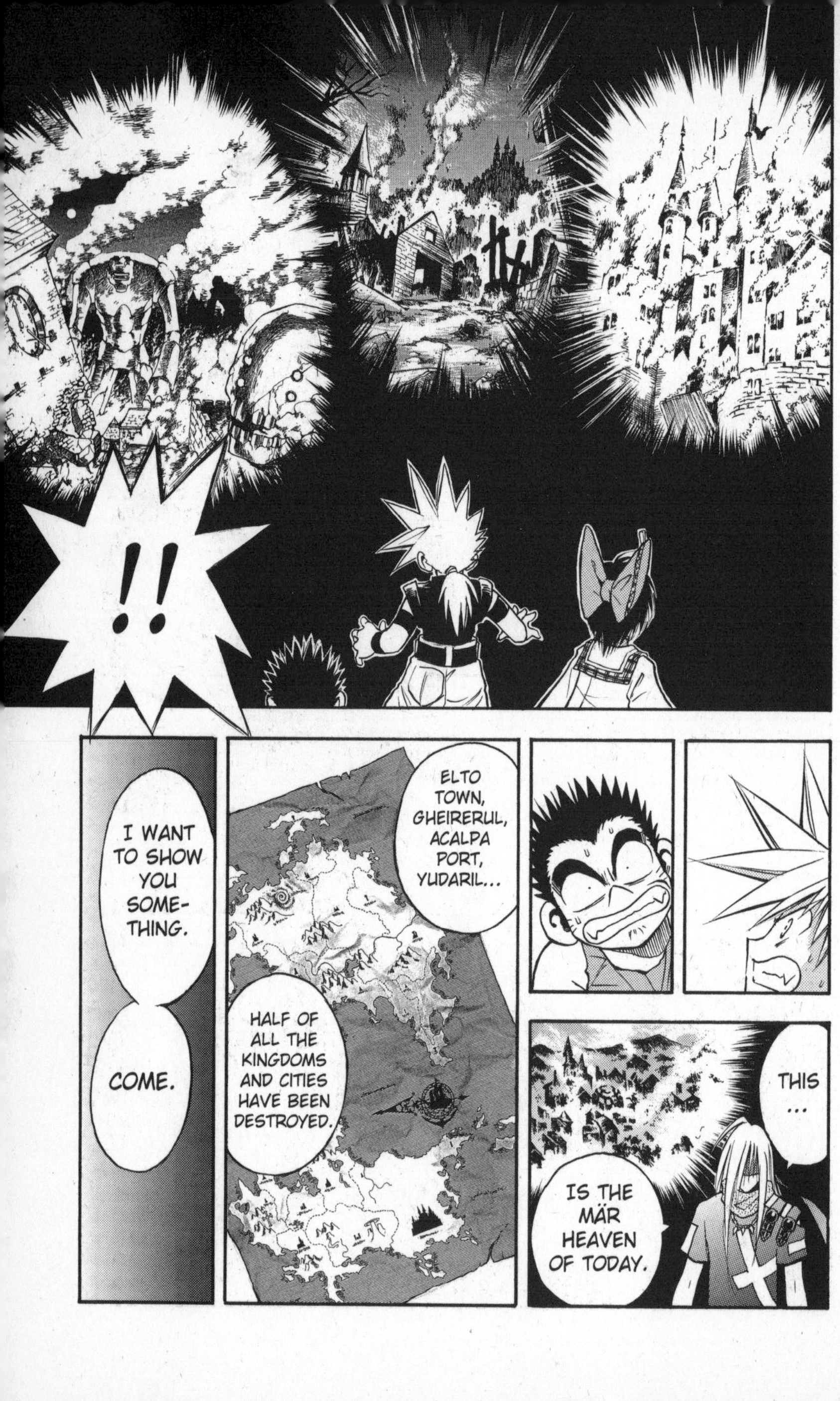
!!
THIS...
IS THE MÄR HEAVEN OF TODAY.
ELTO TOWN, GHEIRERUL, ACALPA PORT, YUDARIL...
HALF OF ALL THE KINGDOMS AND CITIES HAVE BEEN DESTROYED.
I WANT TO SHOW YOU SOMETHING.
COME.

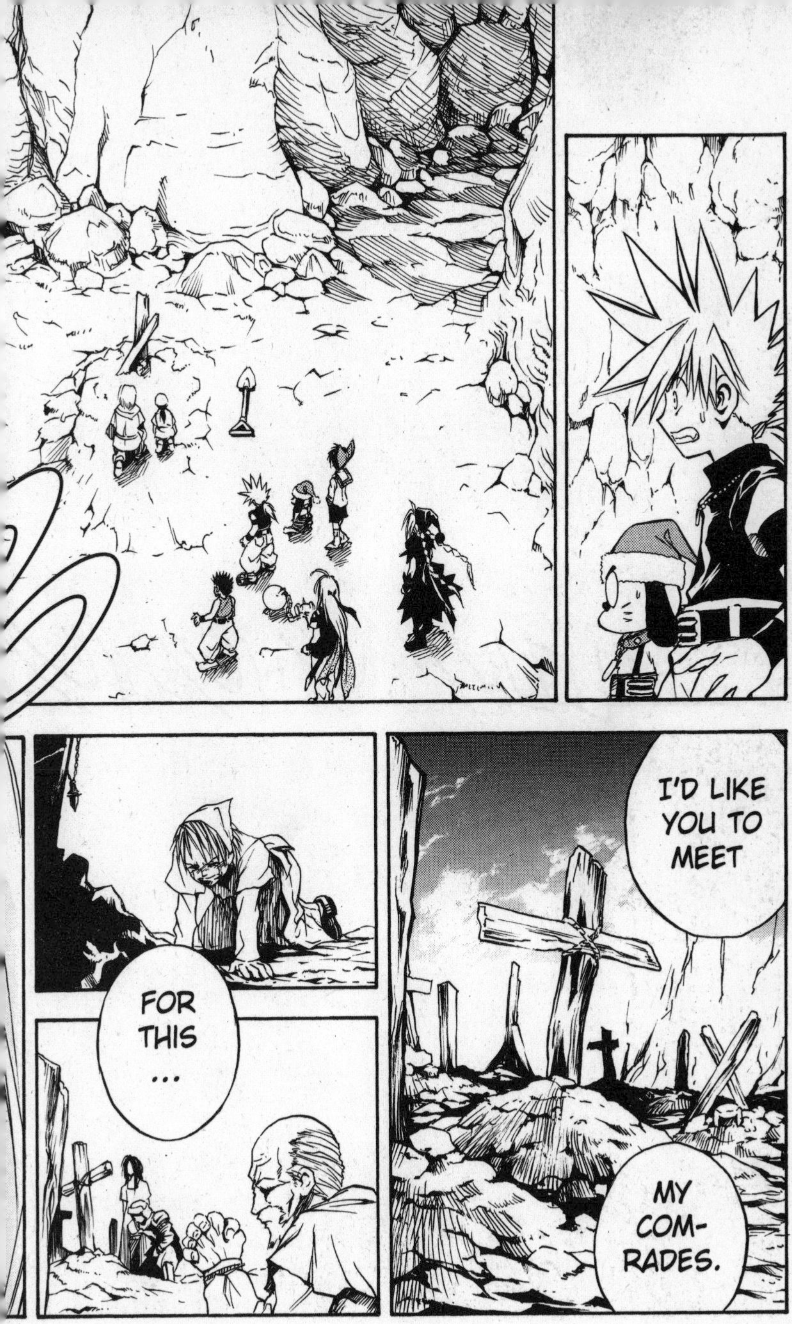
I'D LIKE YOU TO MEET
MY COM-RADES.
FOR THIS ...

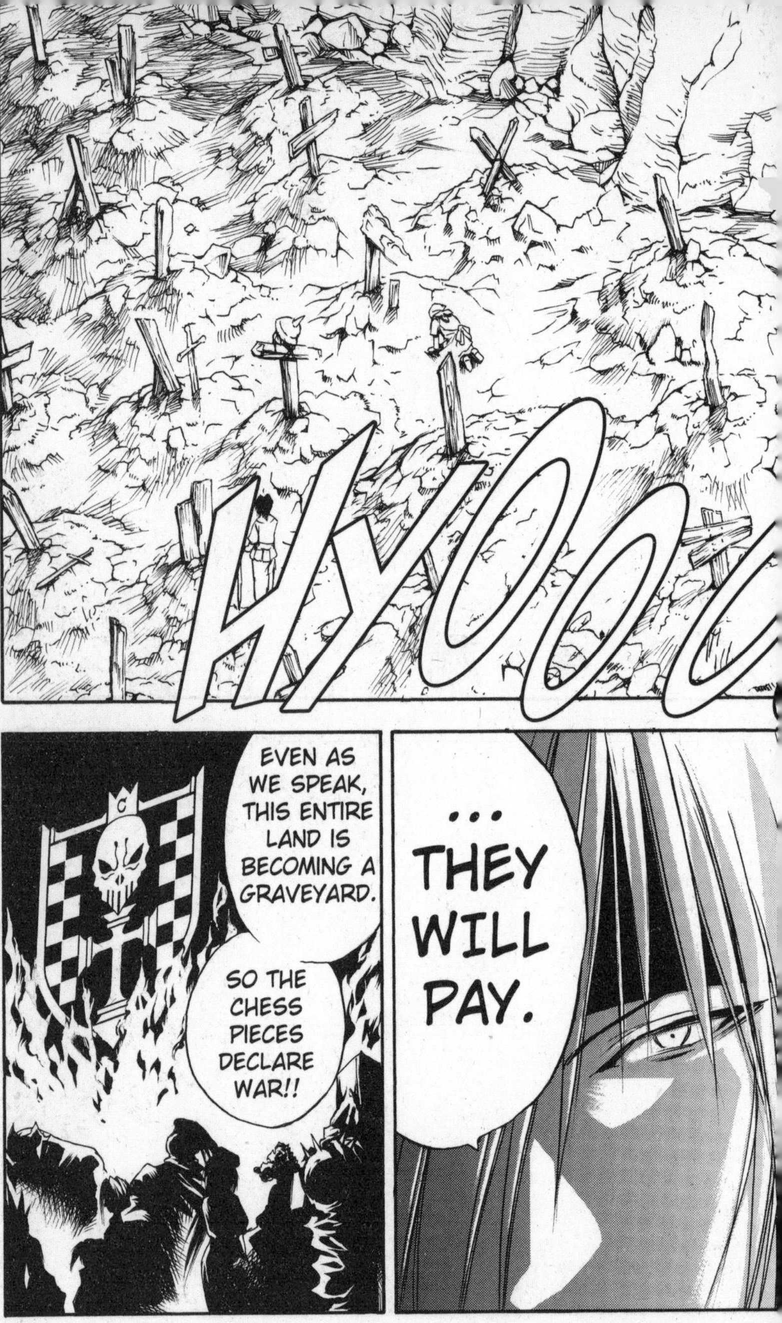
HYOOO
... THEY WILL PAY.
EVEN AS WE SPEAK, THIS ENTIRE LAND IS BECOMING A GRAVEYARD.
SO THE CHESS PIECES DECLARE WAR!!

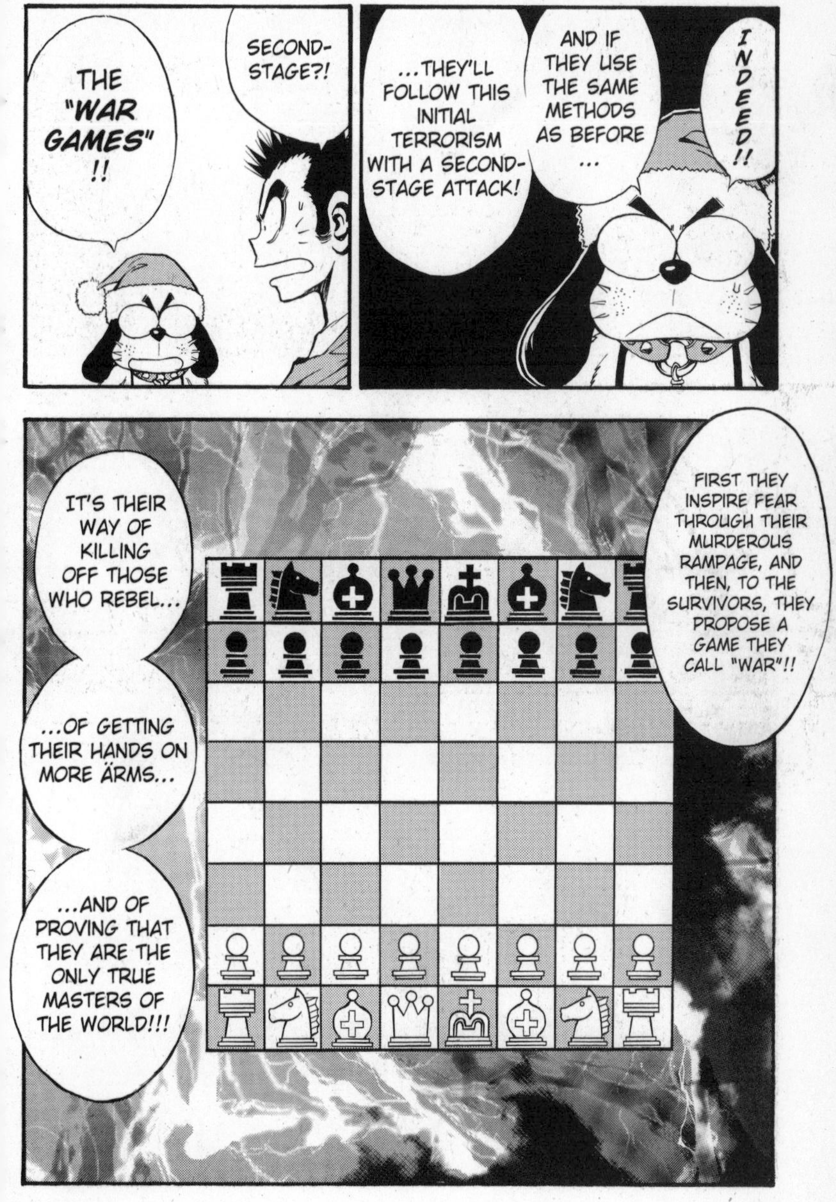
INDEED!!
AND IF THEY USE THE SAME METHODS AS BEFORE ...
...THEY'LL FOLLOW THIS INITIAL TERRORISM WITH A SECOND-STAGE ATTACK!
SECOND-STAGE?!
THE "WAR GAMES" !!
FIRST THEY INSPIRE FEAR THROUGH THEIR MURDEROUS RAMPAGE, AND THEN, TO THE SURVIVORS, THEY PROPOSE A GAME THEY CALL "WAR"!!
IT'S THEIR WAY OF KILLING OFF THOSE WHO REBEL...
...OF GETTING THEIR HANDS ON MORE ÄRMS...
...AND OF PROVING THAT THEY ARE THE ONLY TRUE MASTERS OF THE WORLD!!!

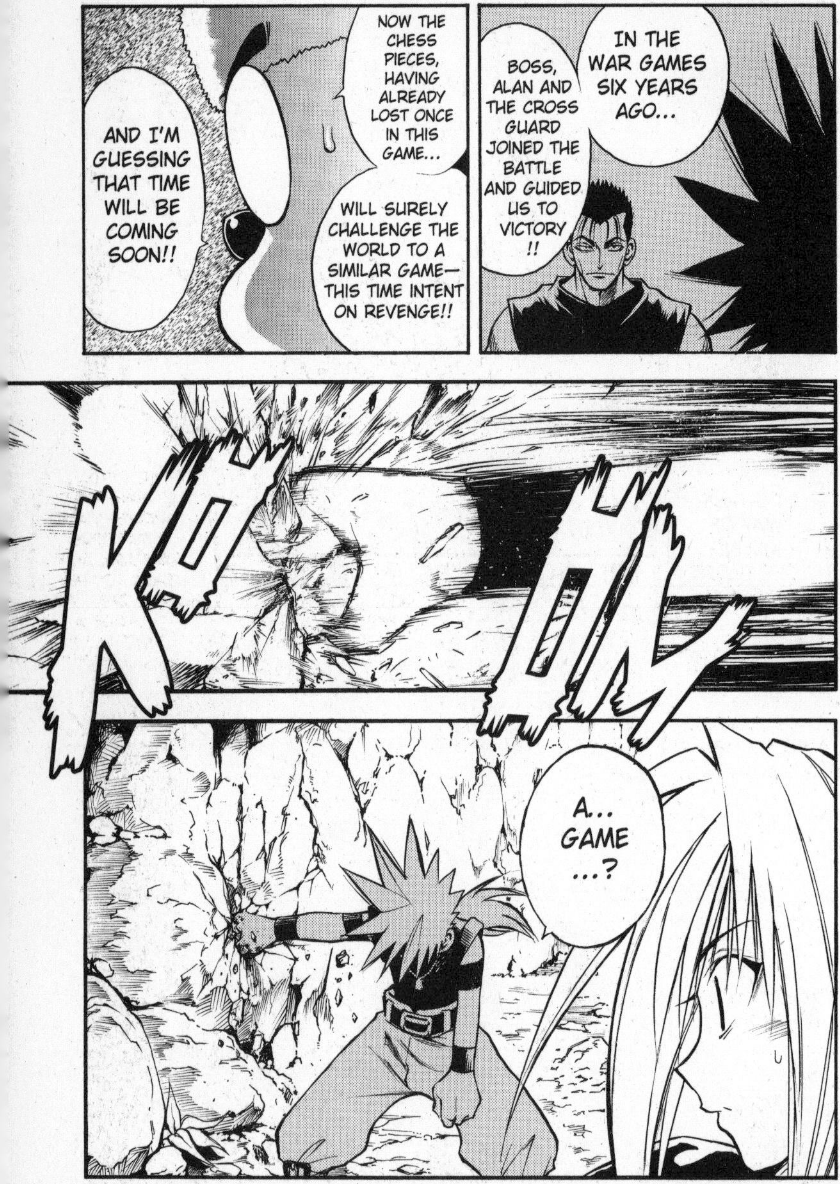
IN THE WAR GAMES SIX YEARS AGO...
BOSS, ALAN AND THE CROSS GUARD JOINED THE BATTLE AND GUIDED US TO VICTORY!!
NOW THE CHESS PIECES, HAVING ALREADY LOST ONCE IN THIS GAME...
WILL SURELY CHALLENGE THE WORLD TO A SIMILAR GAME— THIS TIME INTENT ON REVENGE!!
AND I'M GUESSING THAT TIME WILL BE COMING SOON!!
A... GAME ...?

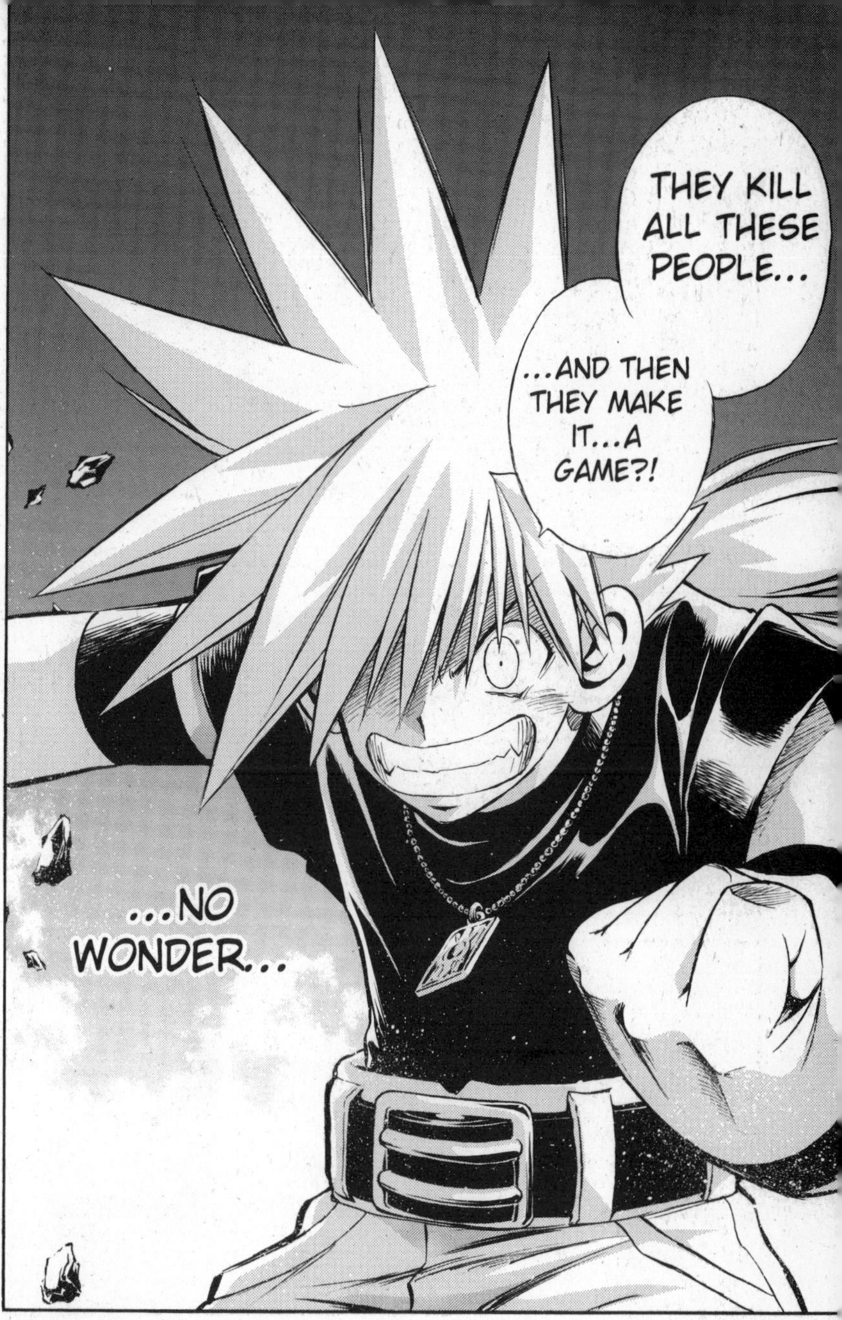
THEY KILL ALL THESE PEOPLE...
...AND THEN THEY MAKE IT...A GAME?!
...NO WONDER...

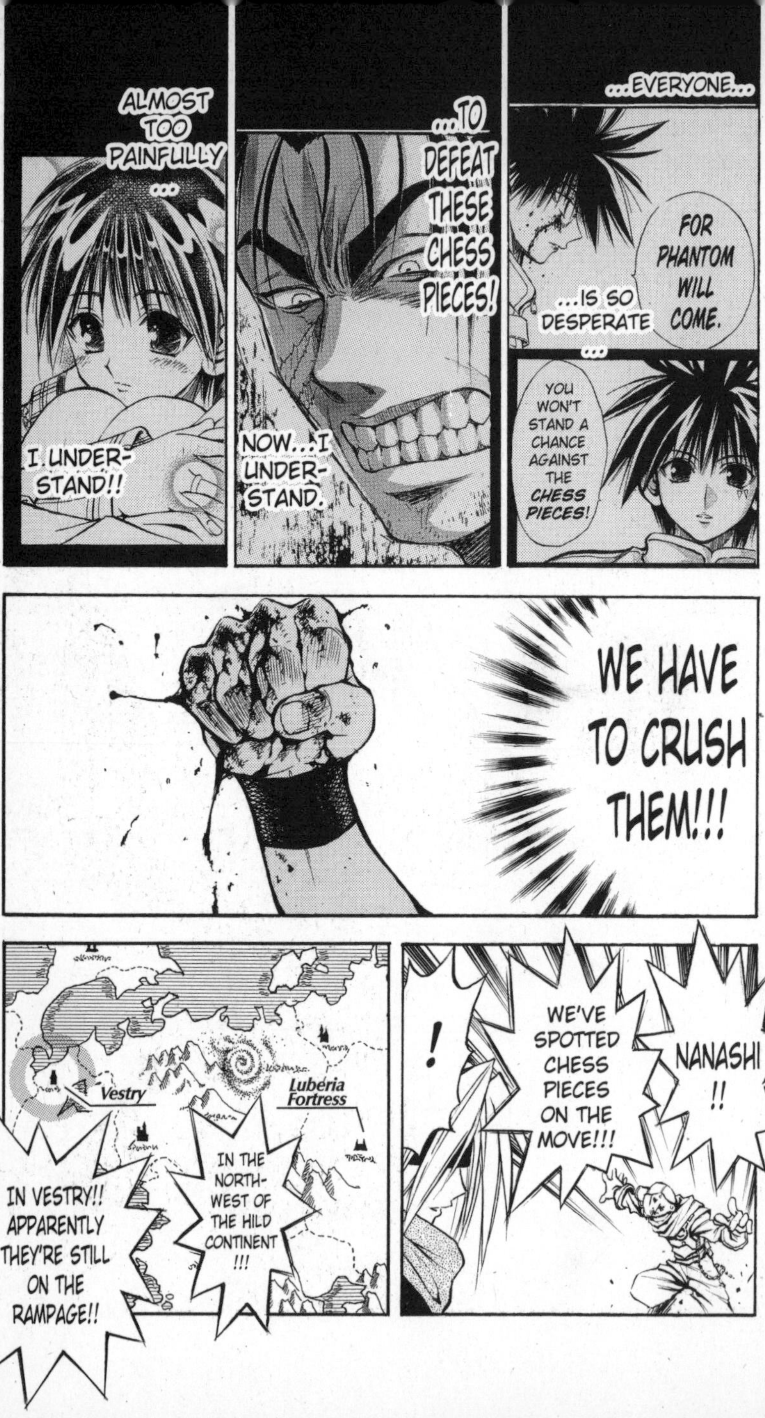
...EVERYONE...
FOR PHANTOM WILL COME.
...IS SO DESPERATE...
YOU WON'T STAND A CHANCE AGAINST THE CHESS PIECES!
...TO DEFEAT THESE CHESS PIECES!
NOW...I UNDERSTAND.
ALMOST TOO PAINFULLY...
I UNDERSTAND!!
WE HAVE TO CRUSH THEM!!!
NANASHI!!
WE'VE SPOTTED CHESS PIECES ON THE MOVE!!!
!
Luberia Fortress
Vestry
IN THE NORTHWEST OF THE HILD CONTINENT!!!
IN VESTRY!! APPARENTLY THEY'RE STILL ON THE RAMPAGE!!

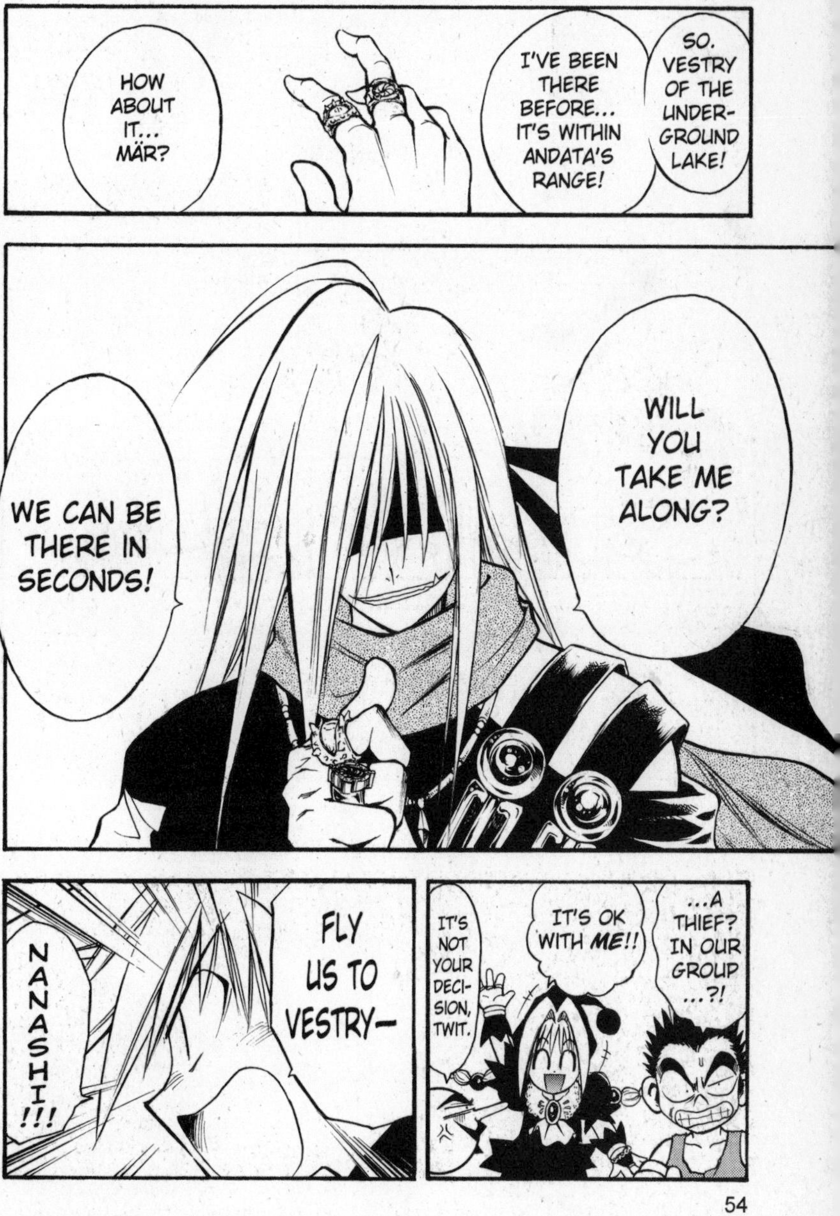
SO. VESTRY OF THE UNDER-GROUND LAKE!
I'VE BEEN THERE BEFORE... IT'S WITHIN ANDATA'S RANGE!
HOW ABOUT IT... MÄR?
WILL YOU TAKE ME ALONG?
WE CAN BE THERE IN SECONDS!
...A THIEF? IN OUR GROUP ...?!
IT'S OK WITH *ME*!!
IT'S NOT YOUR DECI-SION, TWIT.
FLY US TO VESTRY—
NANASHI!!!

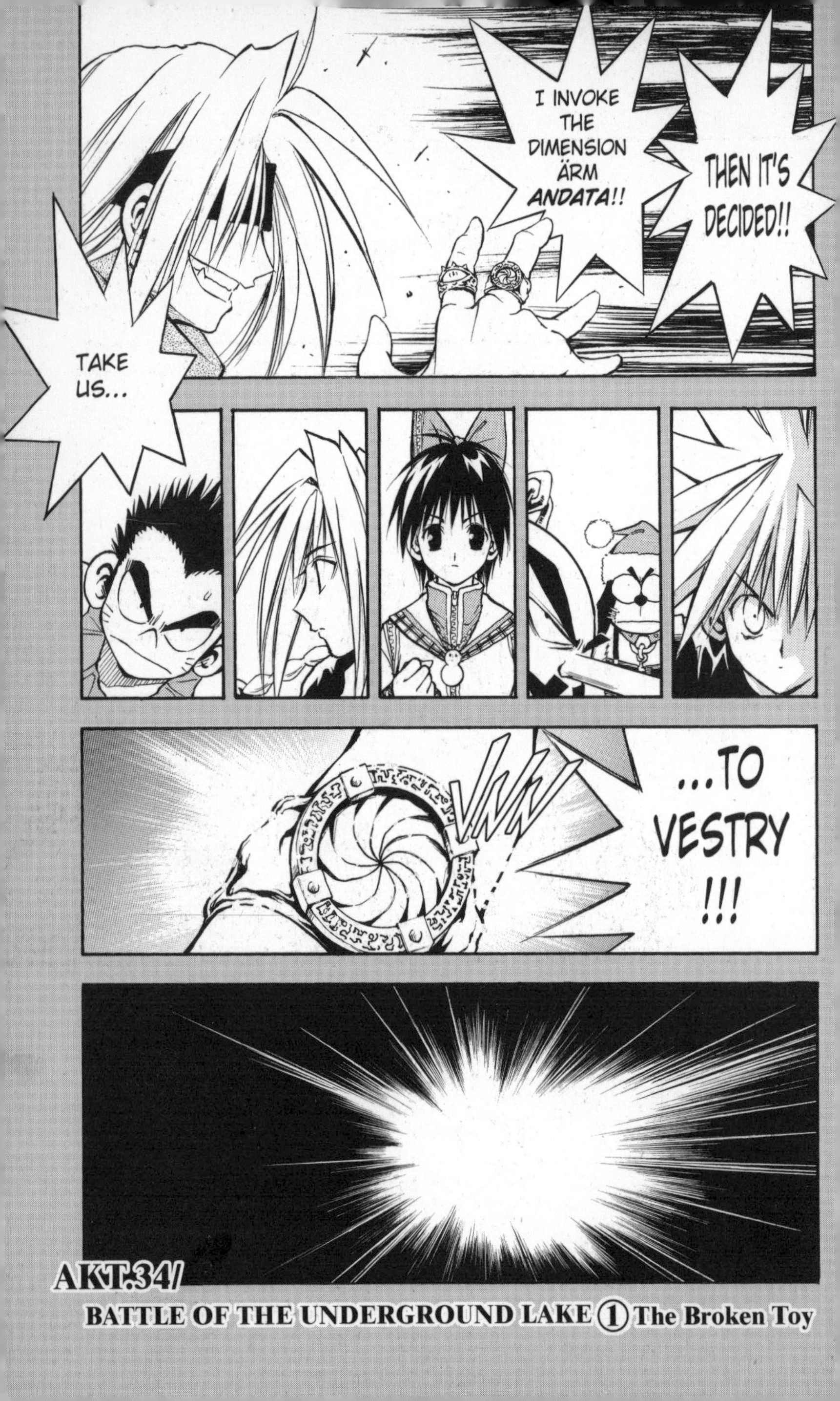
THEN IT'S DECIDED!!
I INVOKE THE DIMENSION ÄRM ANDATA!!
TAKE US...
...TO VESTRY !!!

AKT.34/

BATTLE OF THE UNDERGROUND LAKE ① The Broken Toy

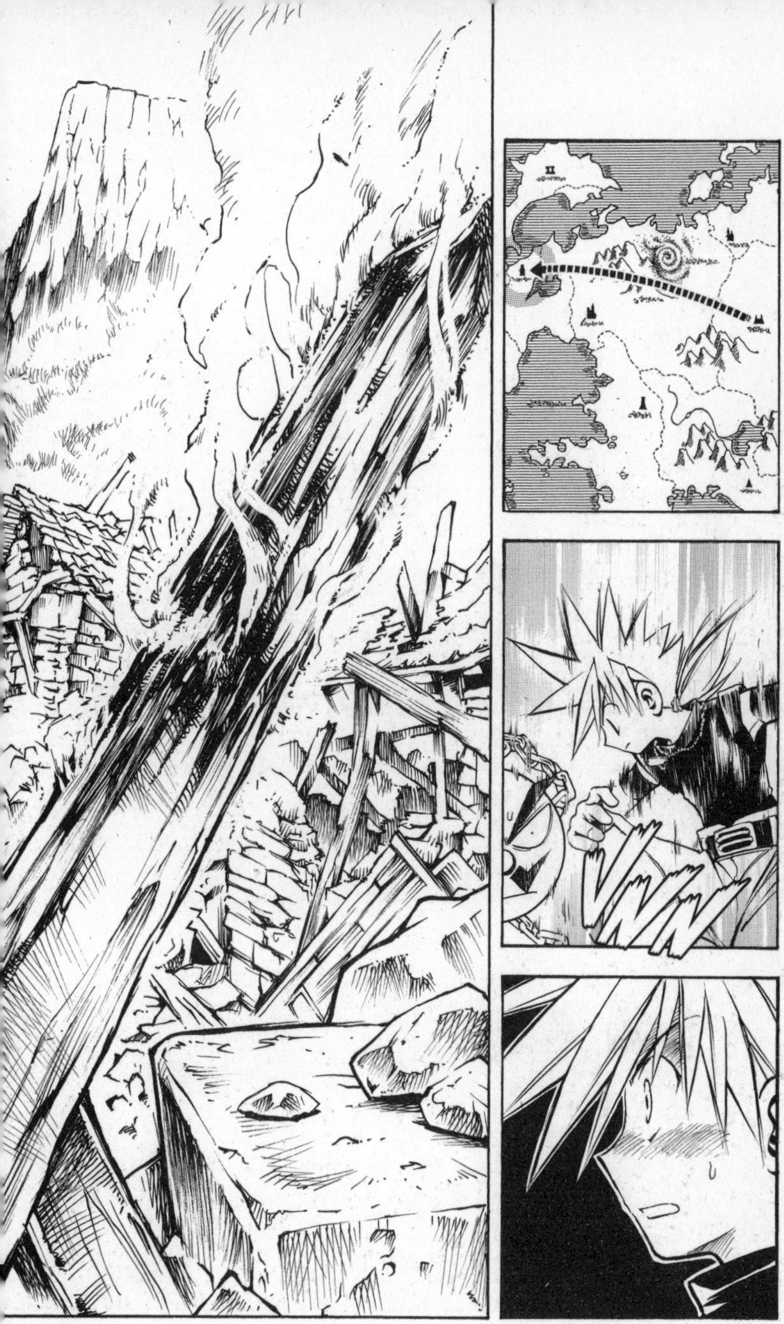
VNN

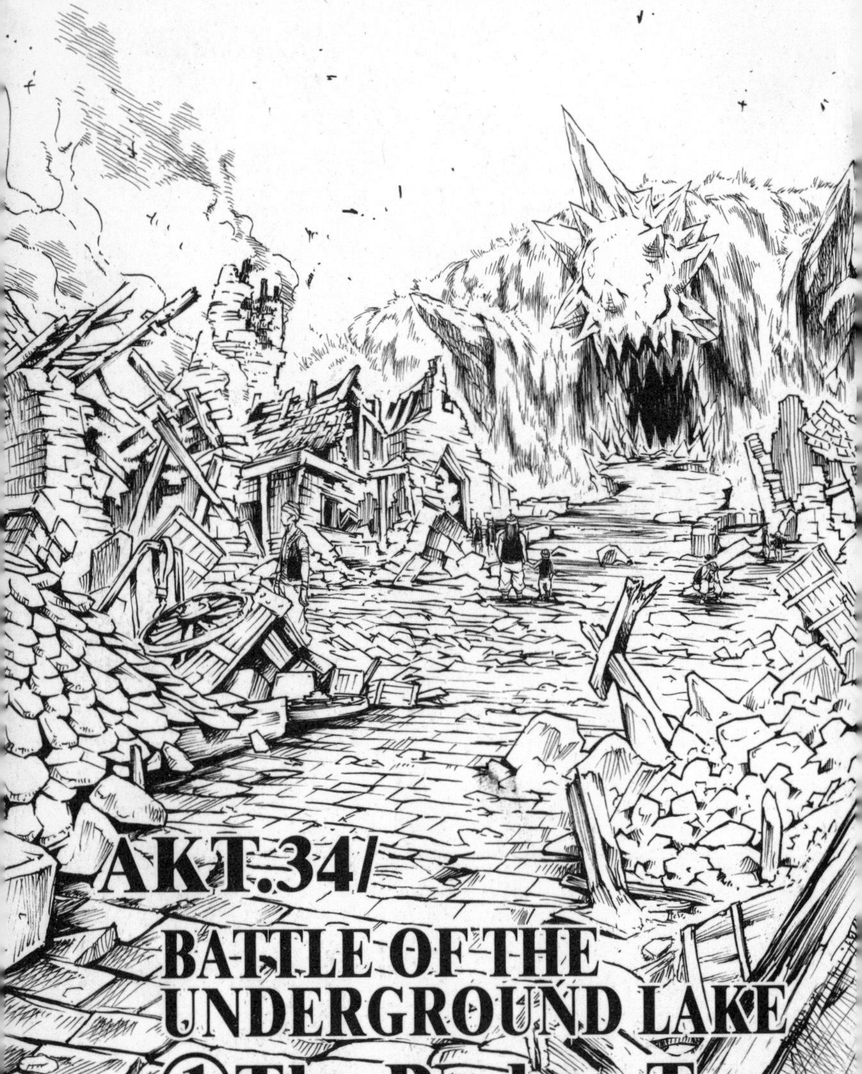
AKT.34/
BATTLE OF THE UNDERGROUND LAKE
① The Broken Toy

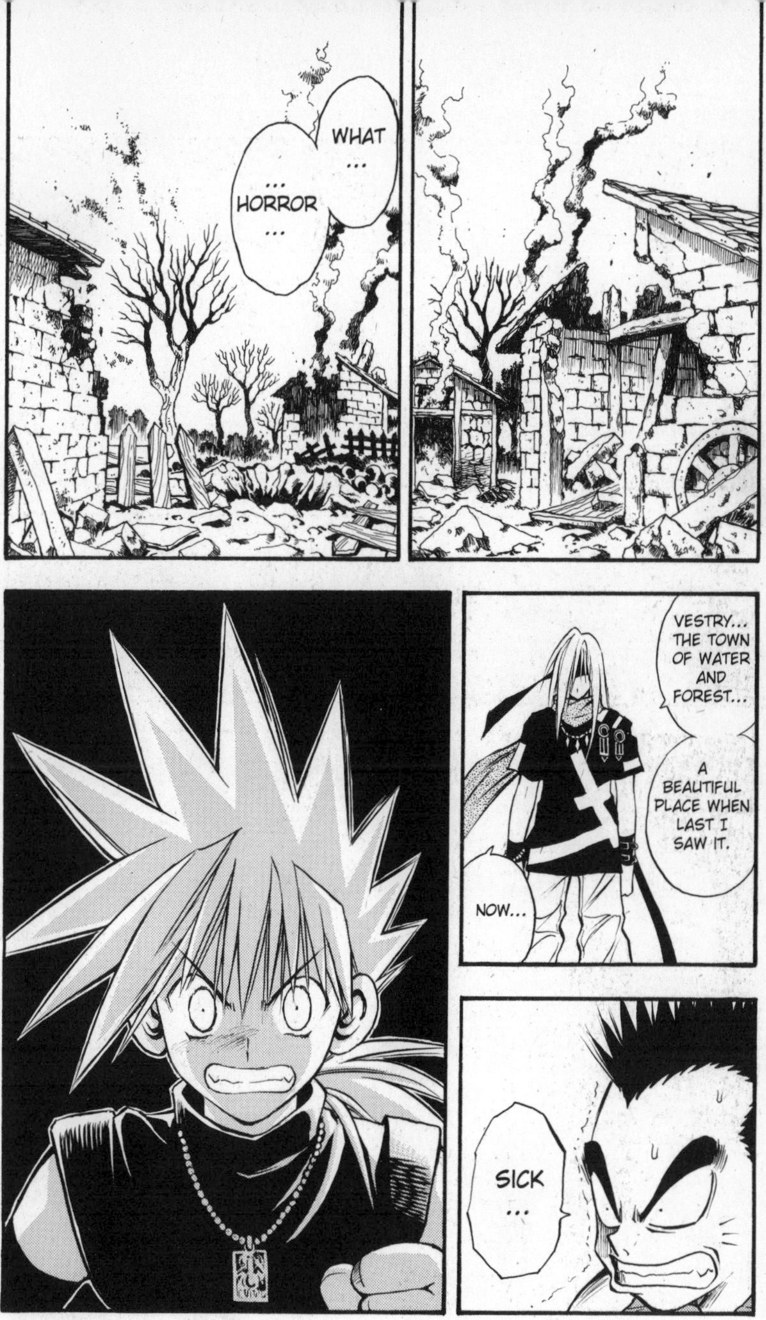
WHAT ...
... HORROR ...
VESTRY... THE TOWN OF WATER AND FOREST...
A BEAUTIFUL PLACE WHEN LAST I SAW IT.
NOW...
SICK ...

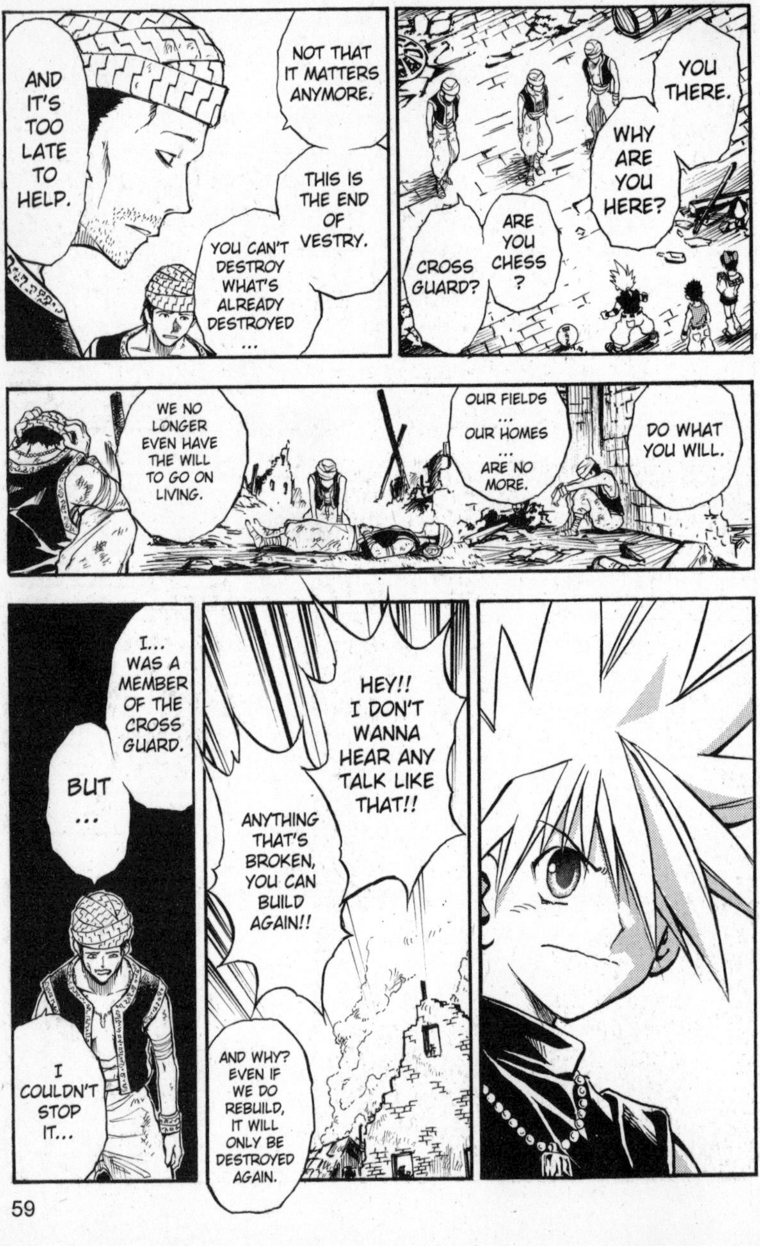
YOU THERE.
WHY ARE YOU HERE?
ARE YOU CHESS?
CROSS GUARD?
NOT THAT IT MATTERS ANYMORE.
AND IT'S TOO LATE TO HELP.
THIS IS THE END OF VESTRY.
YOU CAN'T DESTROY WHAT'S ALREADY DESTROYED...
DO WHAT YOU WILL.
OUR FIELDS... OUR HOMES... ARE NO MORE.
WE NO LONGER EVEN HAVE THE WILL TO GO ON LIVING.
HEY!! I DON'T WANNA HEAR ANY TALK LIKE THAT!!
ANYTHING THAT'S BROKEN, YOU CAN BUILD AGAIN!!
AND WHY? EVEN IF WE DO REBUILD, IT WILL ONLY BE DESTROYED AGAIN.
I... WAS A MEMBER OF THE CROSS GUARD.
BUT...
I COULDN'T STOP IT...

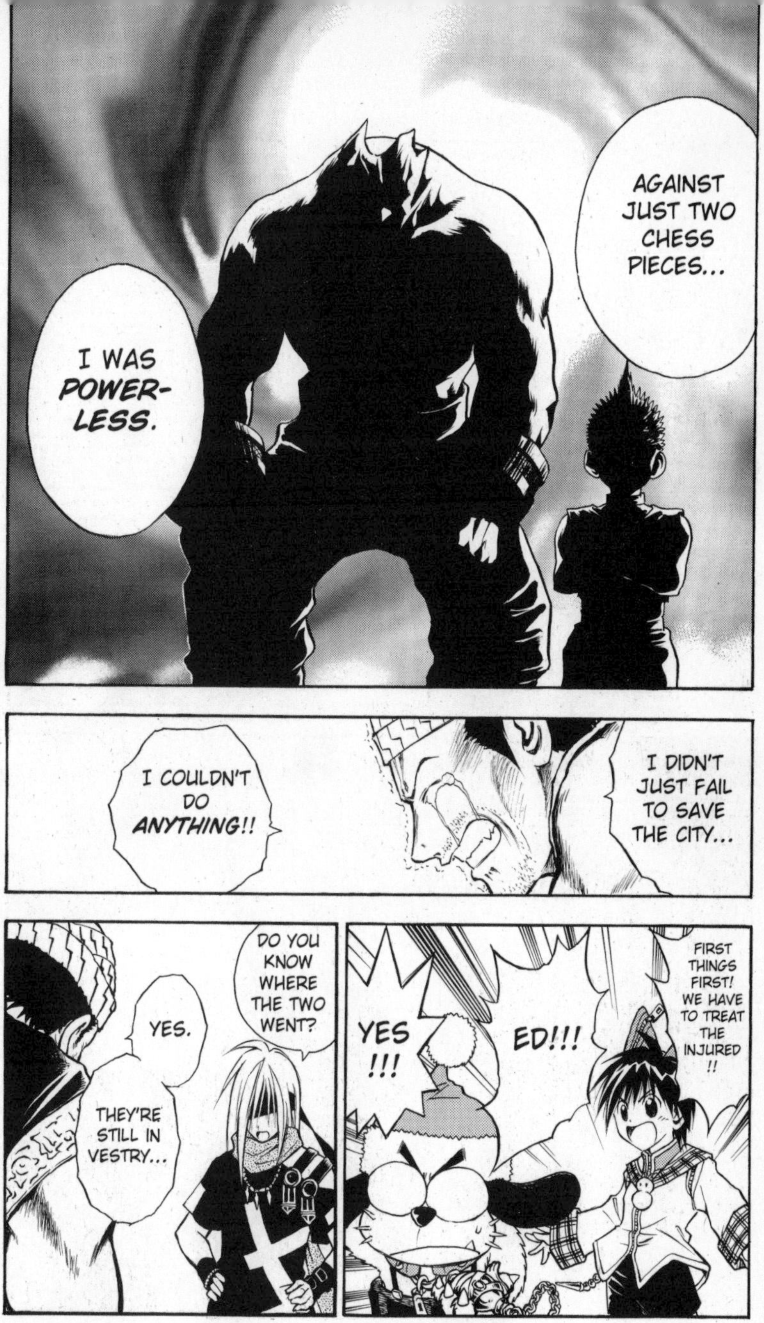

AGAINST JUST TWO CHESS PIECES...
I WAS *POWER-LESS.*
I DIDN'T JUST FAIL TO SAVE THE CITY...
I COULDN'T DO *ANYTHING!!*
FIRST THINGS FIRST! WE HAVE TO TREAT THE INJURED!!
ED!!!
YES!!!
DO YOU KNOW WHERE THE TWO WENT?
YES.
THEY'RE STILL IN VESTRY...

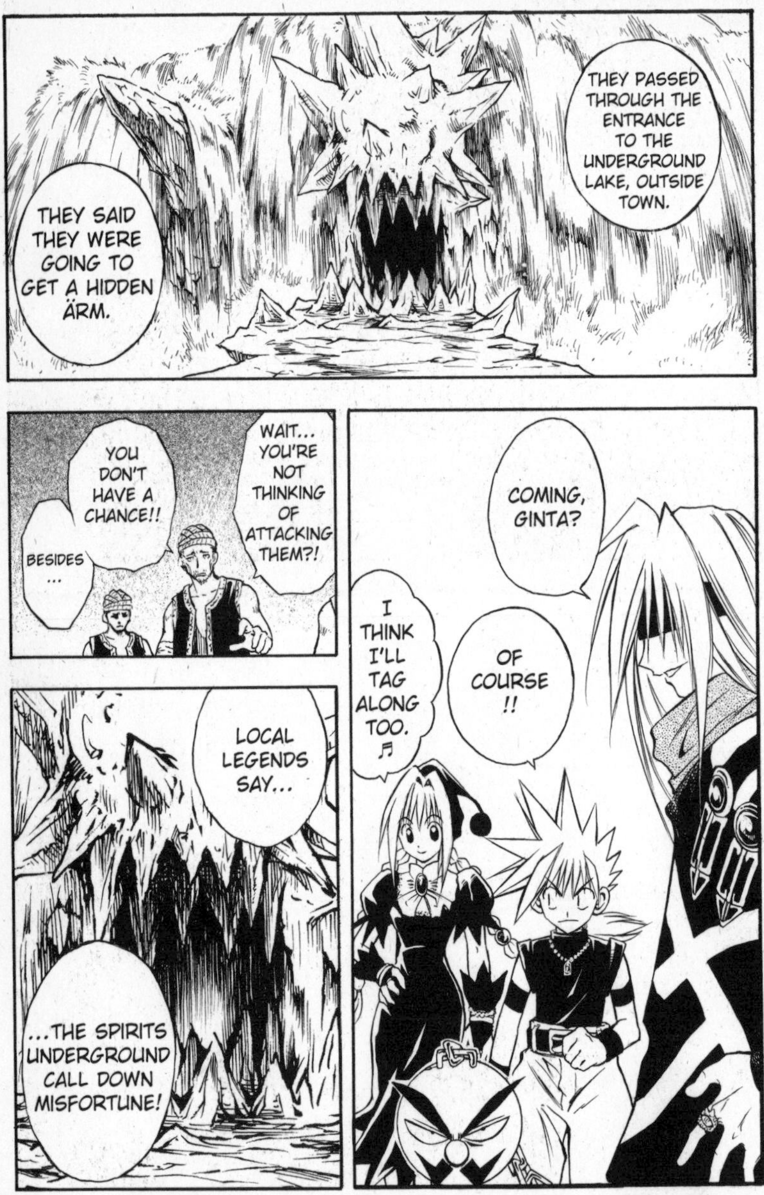
THEY PASSED THROUGH THE ENTRANCE TO THE UNDERGROUND LAKE, OUTSIDE TOWN.
THEY SAID THEY WERE GOING TO GET A HIDDEN ÄRM.
COMING, GINTA?
OF COURSE !!
I THINK I'LL TAG ALONG TOO. ♬
WAIT... YOU'RE NOT THINKING OF ATTACKING THEM?!
YOU DON'T HAVE A CHANCE!!
BESIDES ...
LOCAL LEGENDS SAY...
...THE SPIRITS UNDERGROUND CALL DOWN MISFORTUNE!

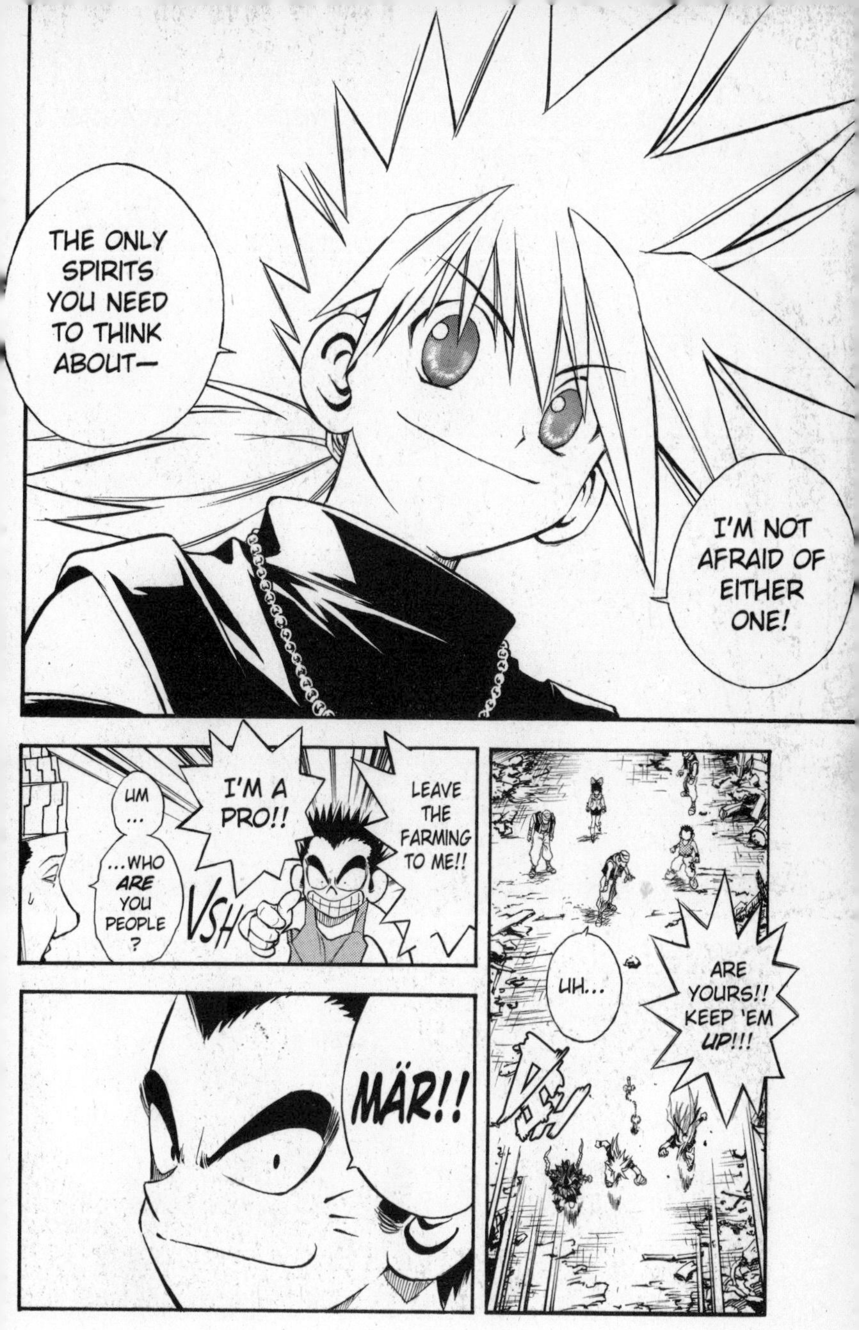
I'M NOT AFRAID OF EITHER ONE!
THE ONLY SPIRITS YOU NEED TO THINK ABOUT—
ARE YOURS!! KEEP 'EM UP!!!
UH...
LEAVE THE FARMING TO ME!!
I'M A PRO!!
VSH
UM ...
...WHO ARE YOU PEOPLE?
MÄR!!

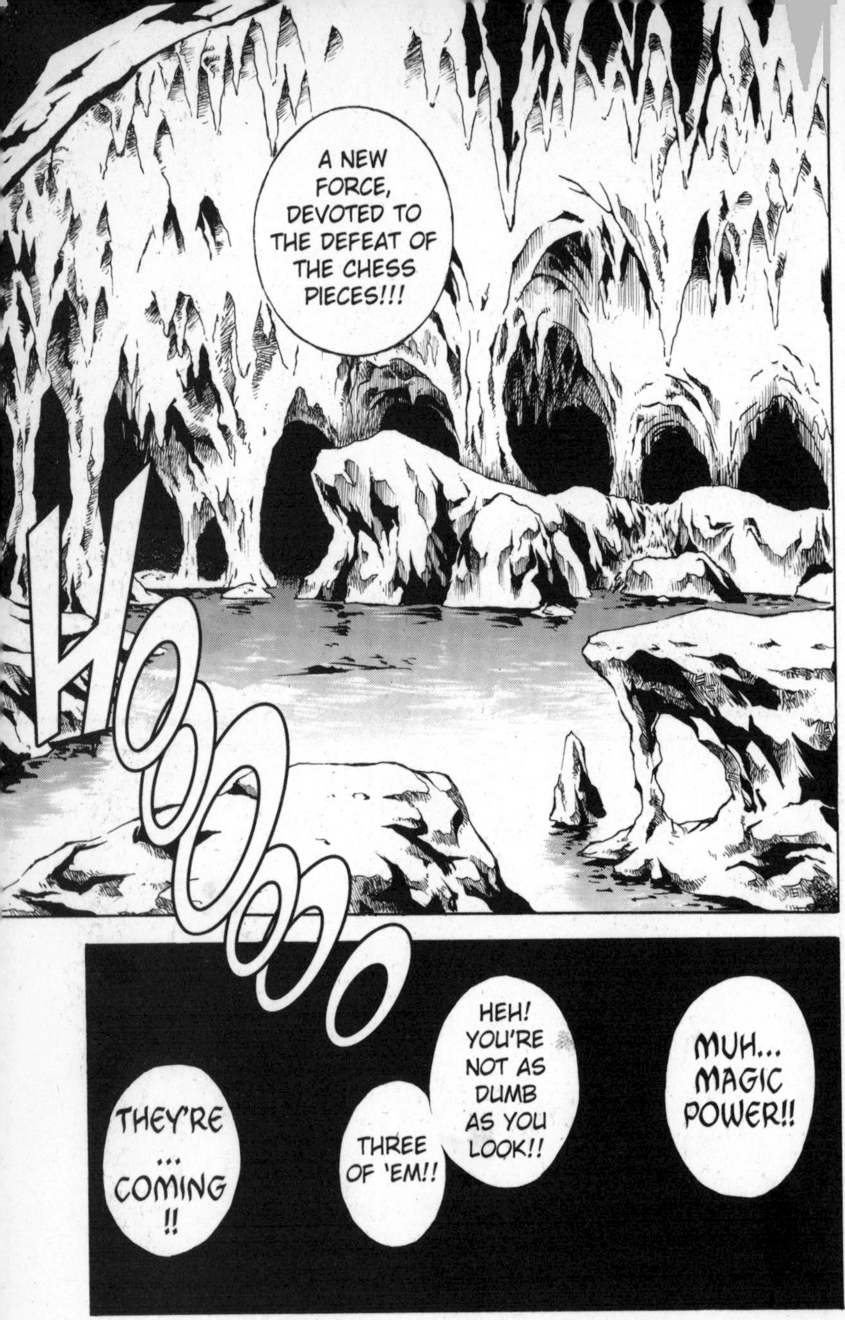
A NEW FORCE, DEVOTED TO THE DEFEAT OF THE CHESS PIECES!!!
HOOOOOO
MUH... MAGIC POWER!!
HEH! YOU'RE NOT AS DUMB AS YOU LOOK!!
THREE OF 'EM!!
THEY'RE ... COMING !!

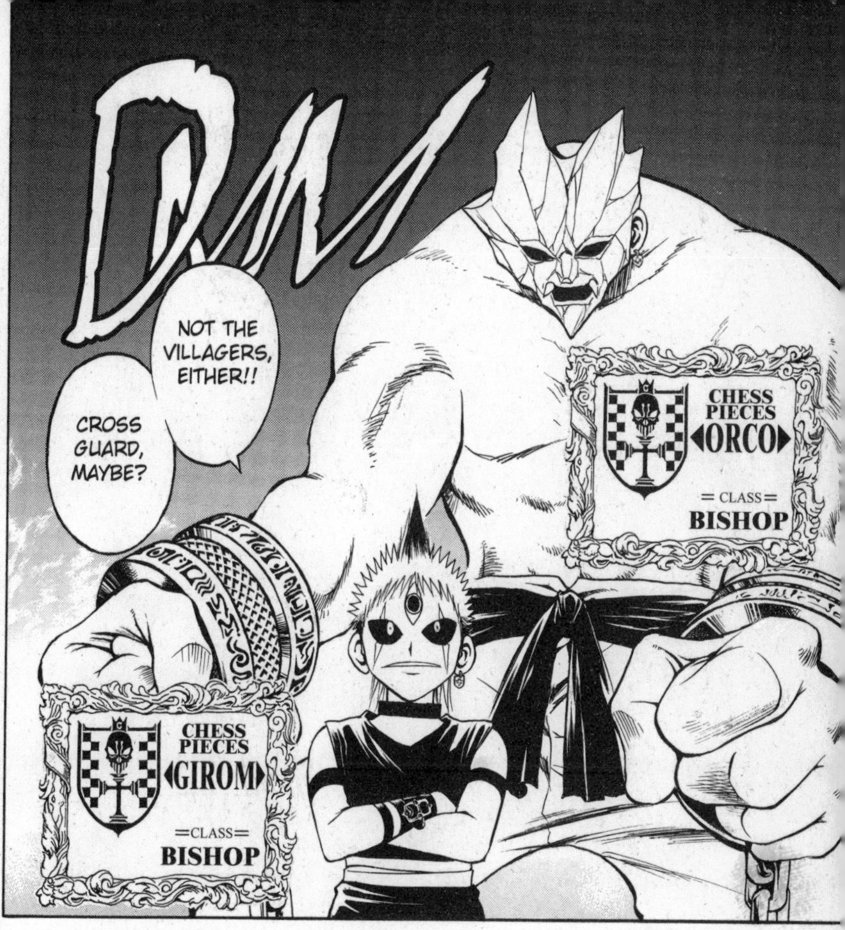
DM
NOT THE VILLAGERS, EITHER!!
CROSS GUARD, MAYBE?
CHESS PIECES ◀ORCO▶ =CLASS= BISHOP
CHESS PIECES ◀GIROM▶ =CLASS= BISHOP

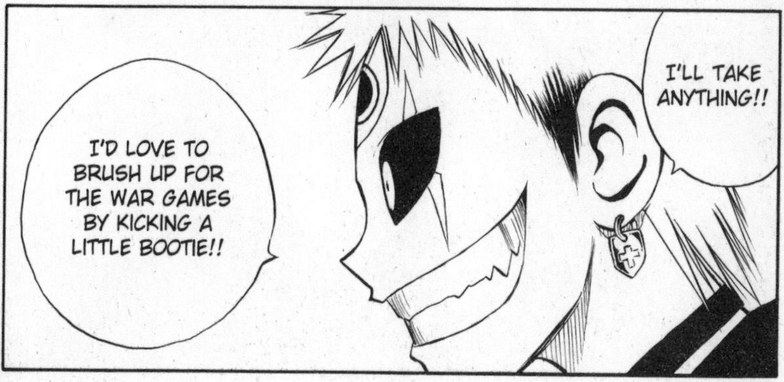
I'LL TAKE ANYTHING!!
I'D LOVE TO BRUSH UP FOR THE WAR GAMES BY KICKING A LITTLE BOOTIE!!

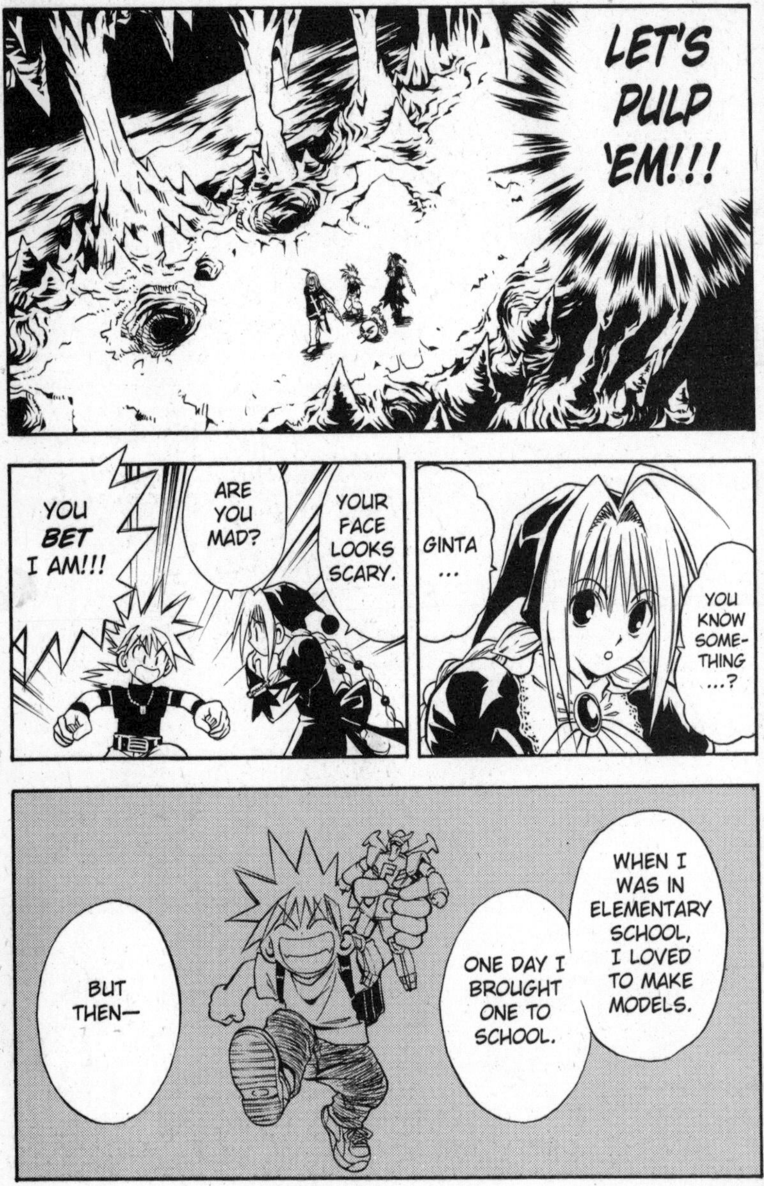
LET'S PULP 'EM!!!
GINTA ...
YOU KNOW SOME-THING ...?
YOUR FACE LOOKS SCARY.
ARE YOU MAD?
YOU BET I AM!!!
WHEN I WAS IN ELEMENTARY SCHOOL, I LOVED TO MAKE MODELS.
ONE DAY I BROUGHT ONE TO SCHOOL.
BUT THEN—

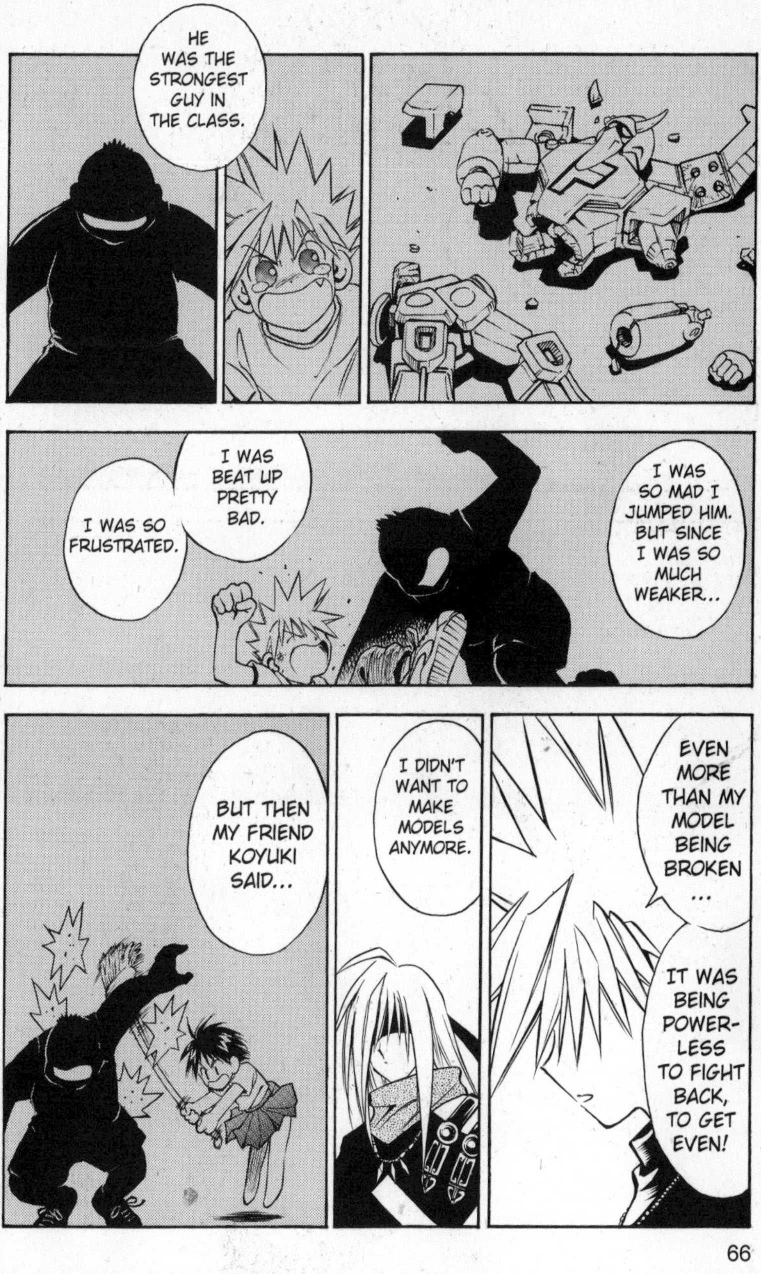
HE WAS THE STRONGEST GUY IN THE CLASS.
I WAS SO MAD I JUMPED HIM. BUT SINCE I WAS SO MUCH WEAKER...
I WAS BEAT UP PRETTY BAD.
I WAS SO FRUSTRATED.
EVEN MORE THAN MY MODEL BEING BROKEN...
IT WAS BEING POWER-LESS TO FIGHT BACK, TO GET EVEN!
I DIDN'T WANT TO MAKE MODELS ANYMORE.
BUT THEN MY FRIEND KOYUKI SAID...

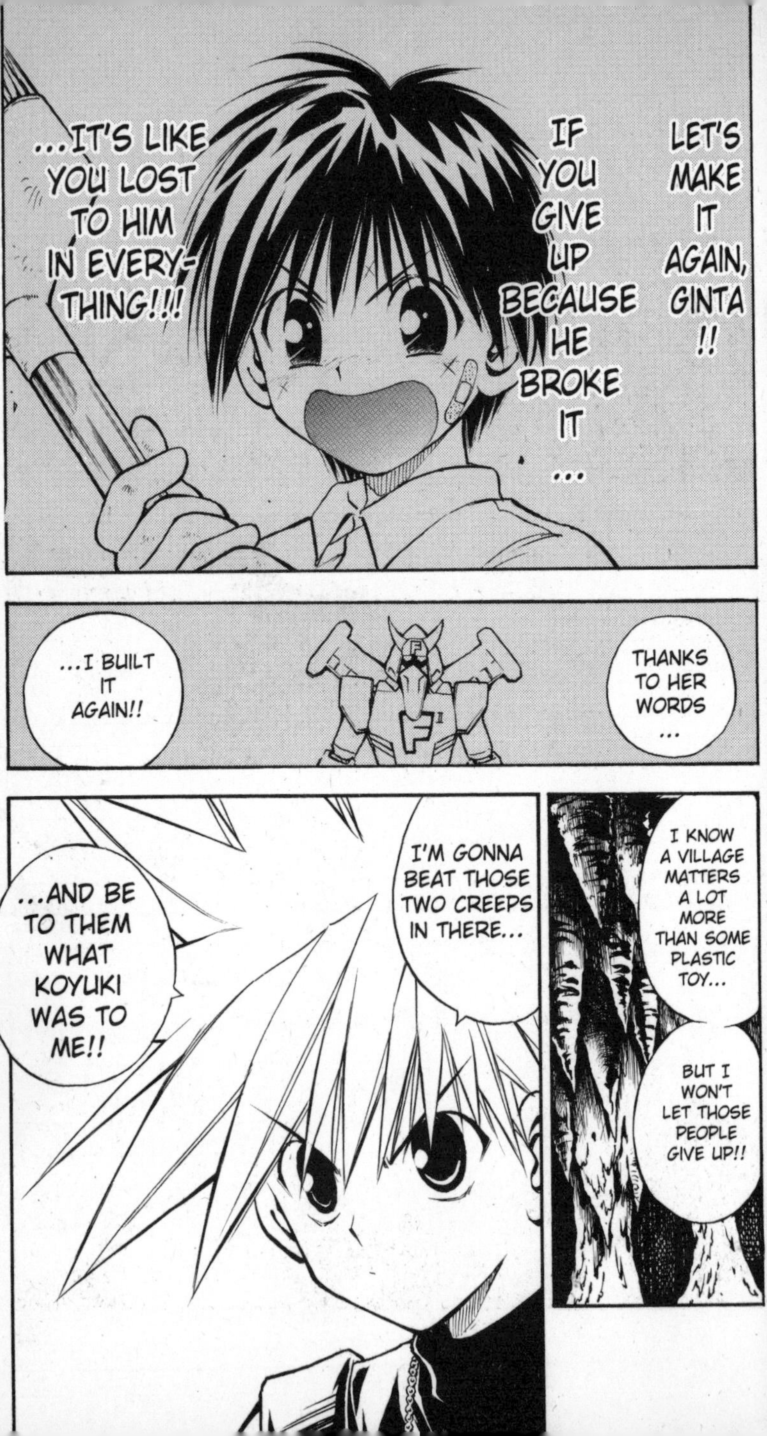
LET'S MAKE IT AGAIN, GINTA!!
IF YOU GIVE UP BECAUSE HE BROKE IT...
...IT'S LIKE YOU LOST TO HIM IN EVERY-THING!!!
THANKS TO HER WORDS...
...I BUILT IT AGAIN!!
I KNOW A VILLAGE MATTERS A LOT MORE THAN SOME PLASTIC TOY...
BUT I WON'T LET THOSE PEOPLE GIVE UP!!
I'M GONNA BEAT THOSE TWO CREEPS IN THERE...
...AND BE TO THEM WHAT KOYUKI WAS TO ME!!

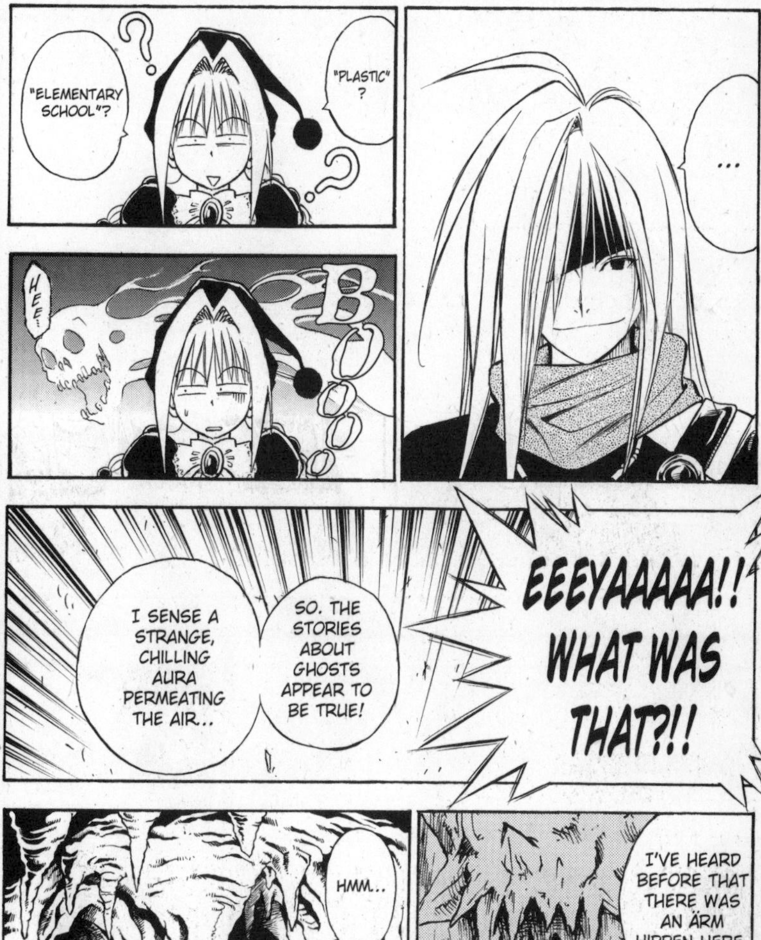
...
"PLASTIC"?
"ELEMENTARY SCHOOL"?
BOOOOOO
HEE!!
EEEYAAAAA!! WHAT WAS THAT?!!
SO. THE STORIES ABOUT GHOSTS APPEAR TO BE TRUE!
I SENSE A STRANGE, CHILLING AURA PERMEATING THE AIR...
I'VE HEARD BEFORE THAT THERE WAS AN ÄRM HIDDEN HERE.
I TRIED TO STEAL IT A LONG TIME AGO, BUT THE PEOPLE OF VESTRY HAD SEALED THE ENTRANCE.
MOST LIKELY THAT'S WHY THEY WERE ATTACKED NOW.
HMM...
THERE ARE TWO PATHS.
WE'VE GOT TO SPLIT UP!!

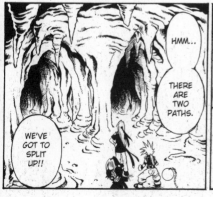

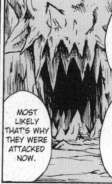

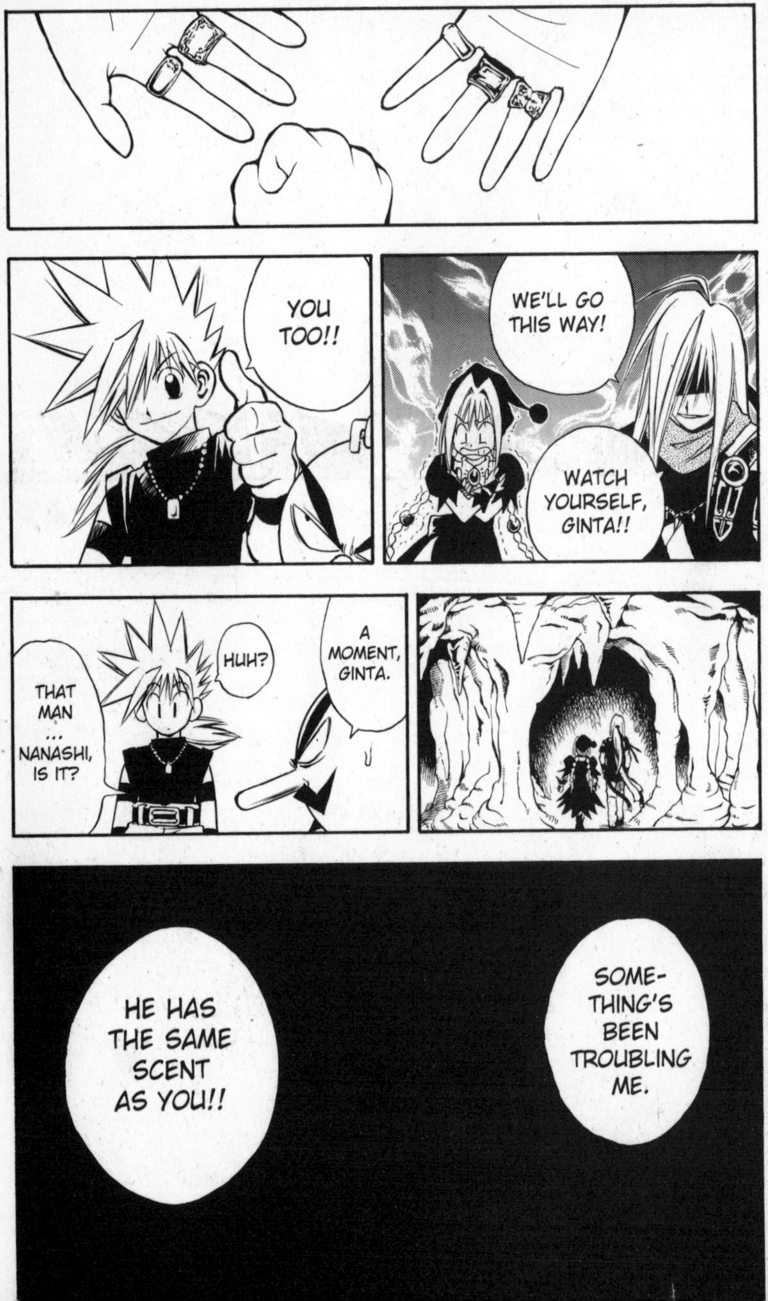
WE'LL GO THIS WAY!
WATCH YOURSELF, GINTA!!
YOU TOO!!
A MOMENT, GINTA.
HUH?
THAT MAN ... NANASHI, IS IT?
SOME-THING'S BEEN TROUBLING ME.
HE HAS THE SAME SCENT AS YOU!!

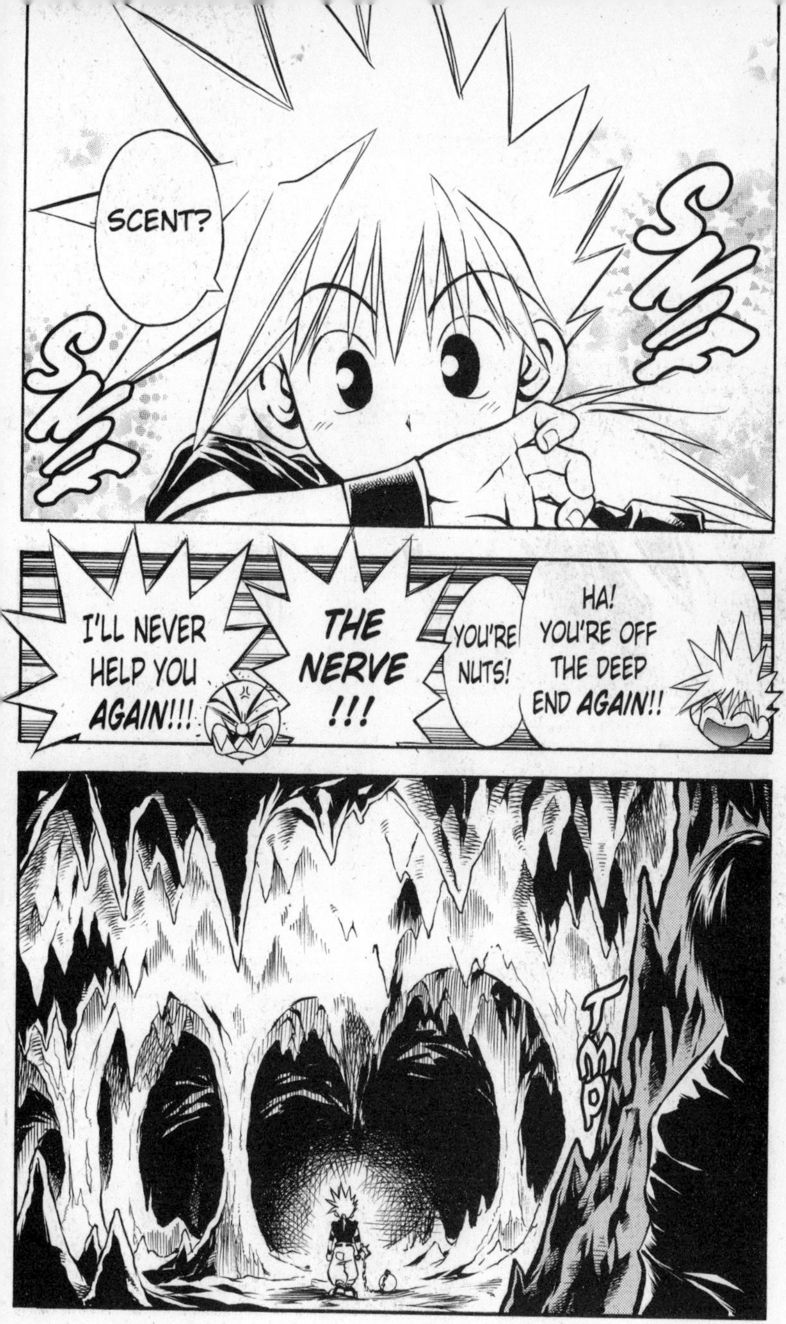
SNIFF
SCENT?
SNIFF
HA! YOU'RE OFF THE DEEP END AGAIN!!
YOU'RE NUTS!
THE NERVE!!!
I'LL NEVER HELP YOU AGAIN!!!
TMP

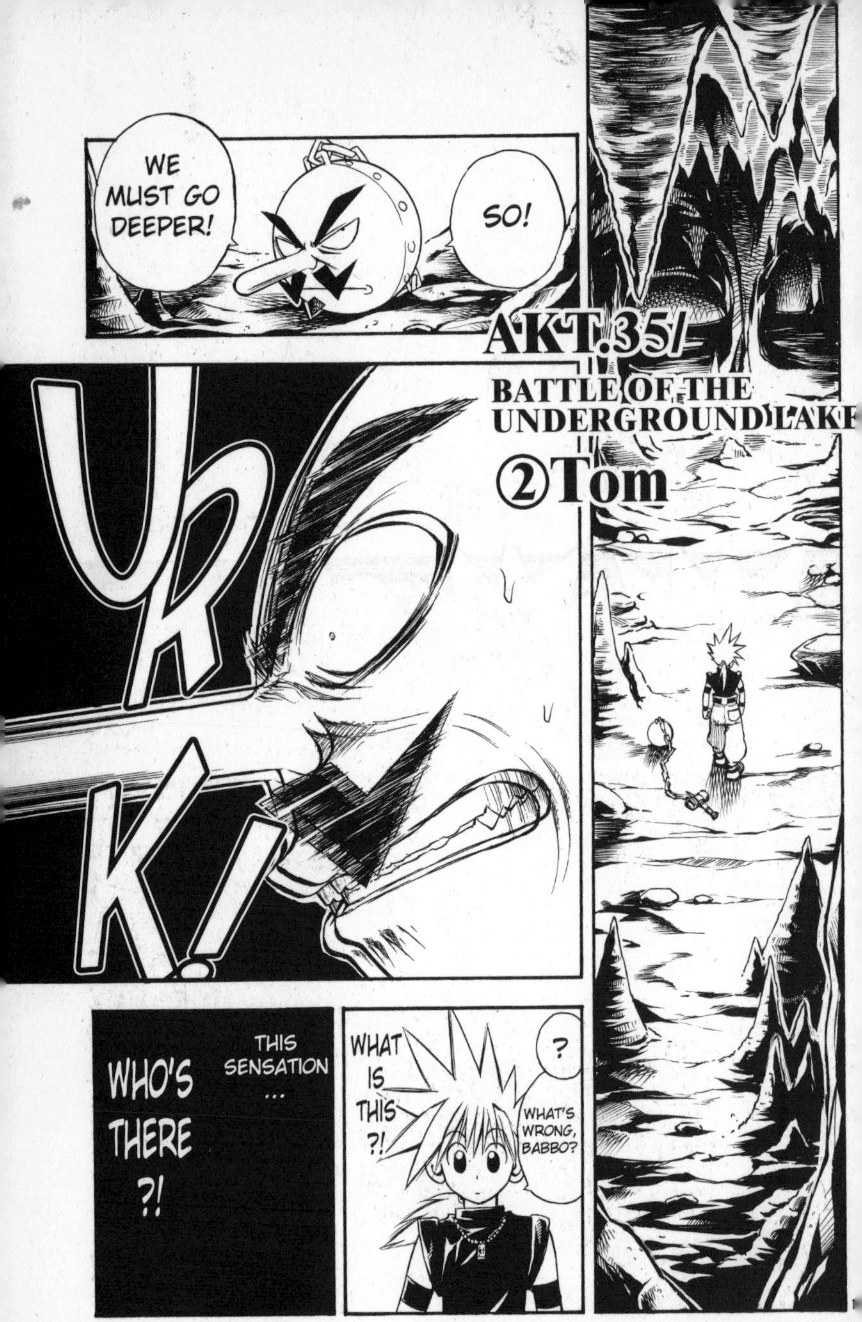
AKT.35/
BATTLE OF THE UNDERGROUND LAKE
②Tom
SO!
WE MUST GO DEEPER!
UK!
?
WHAT'S WRONG, BABBO?
WHAT IS THIS ?!
THIS SENSATION ...
WHO'S THERE ?!

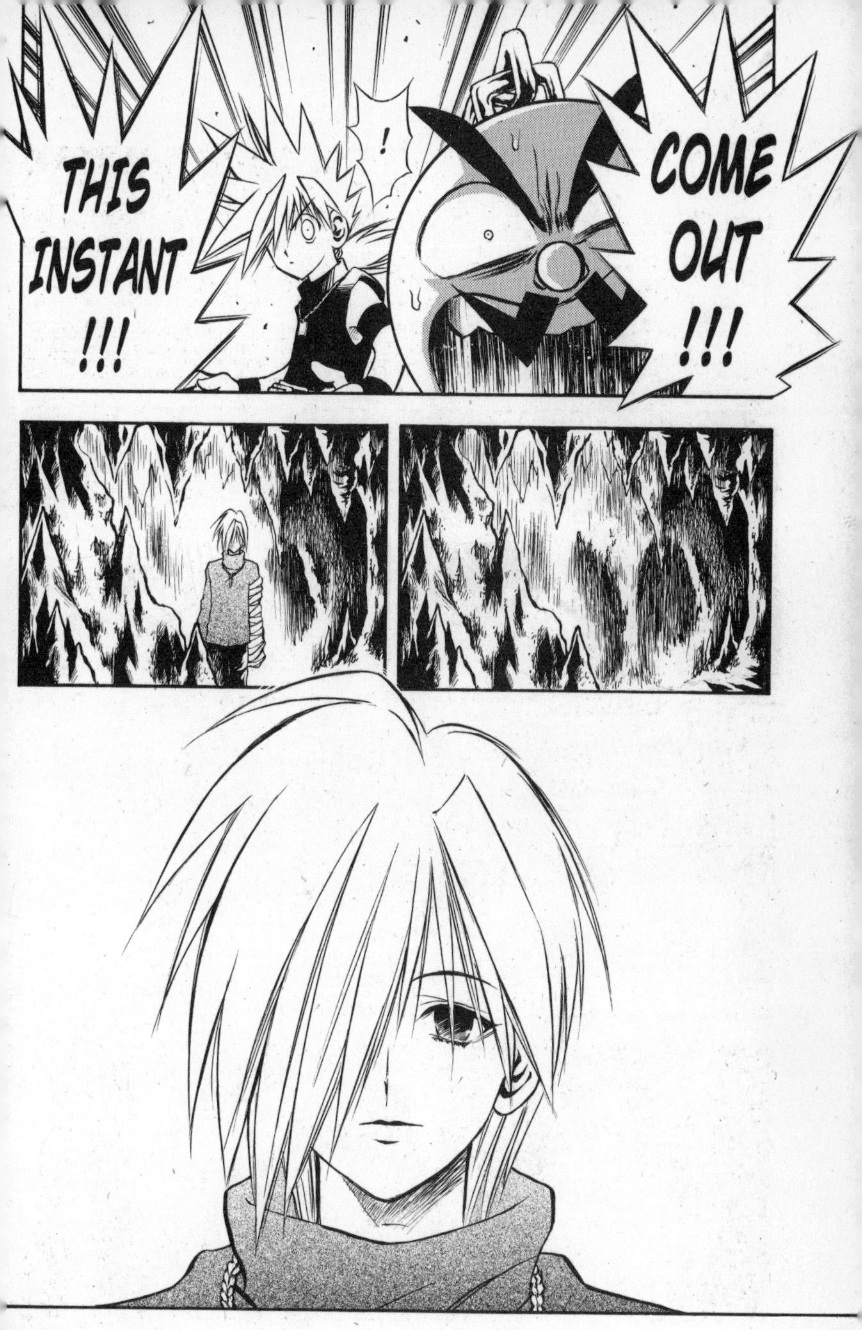
COME OUT !!!
!
THIS INSTANT !!!

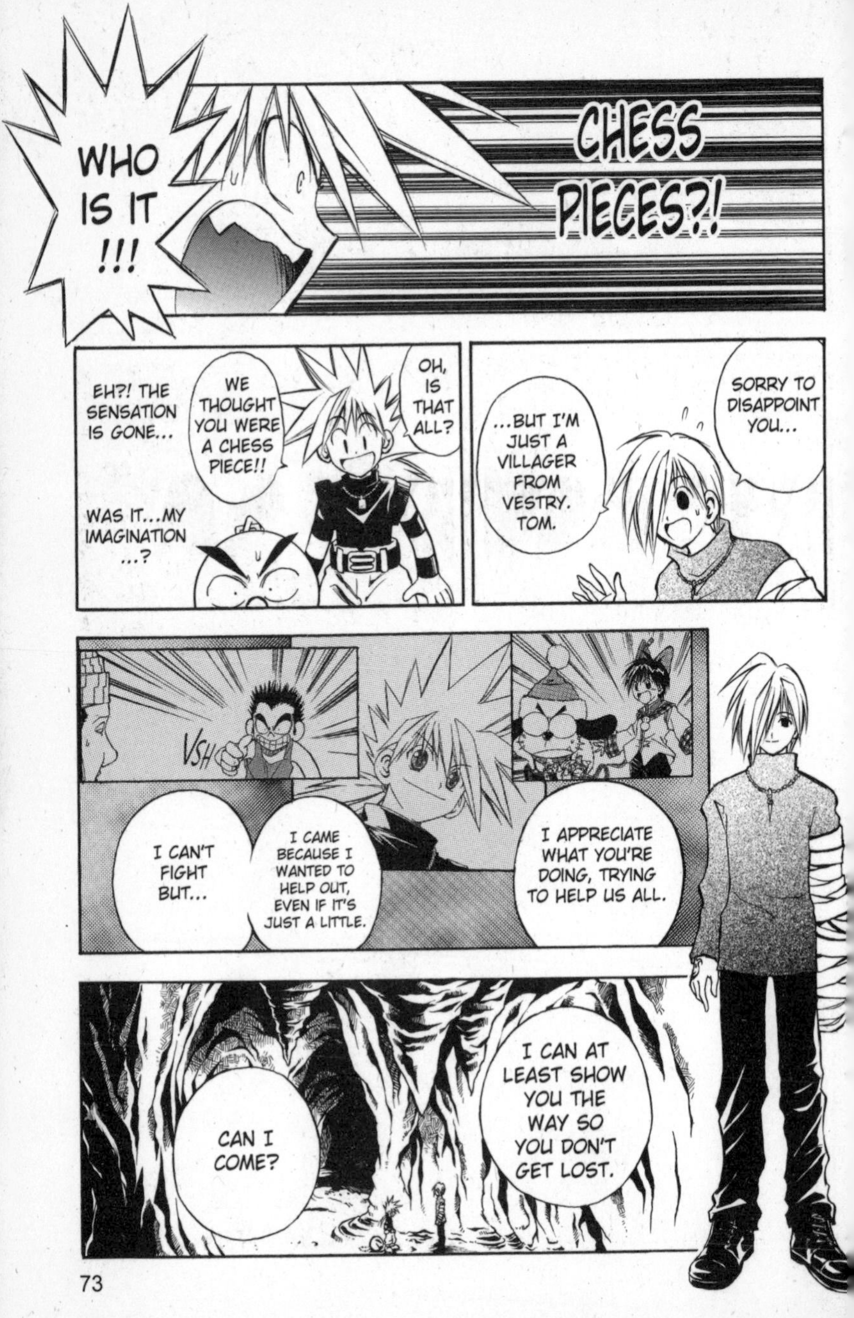
CHESS PIECES?!
WHO IS IT !!!
SORRY TO DISAPPOINT YOU...
...BUT I'M JUST A VILLAGER FROM VESTRY. TOM.
OH, IS THAT ALL?
WE THOUGHT YOU WERE A CHESS PIECE!!
EH?! THE SENSATION IS GONE...
WAS IT...MY IMAGINATION ...?
I APPRECIATE WHAT YOU'RE DOING, TRYING TO HELP US ALL.
I CAME BECAUSE I WANTED TO HELP OUT, EVEN IF IT'S JUST A LITTLE.
I CAN'T FIGHT BUT...
VSH
I CAN AT LEAST SHOW YOU THE WAY SO YOU DON'T GET LOST.
CAN I COME?

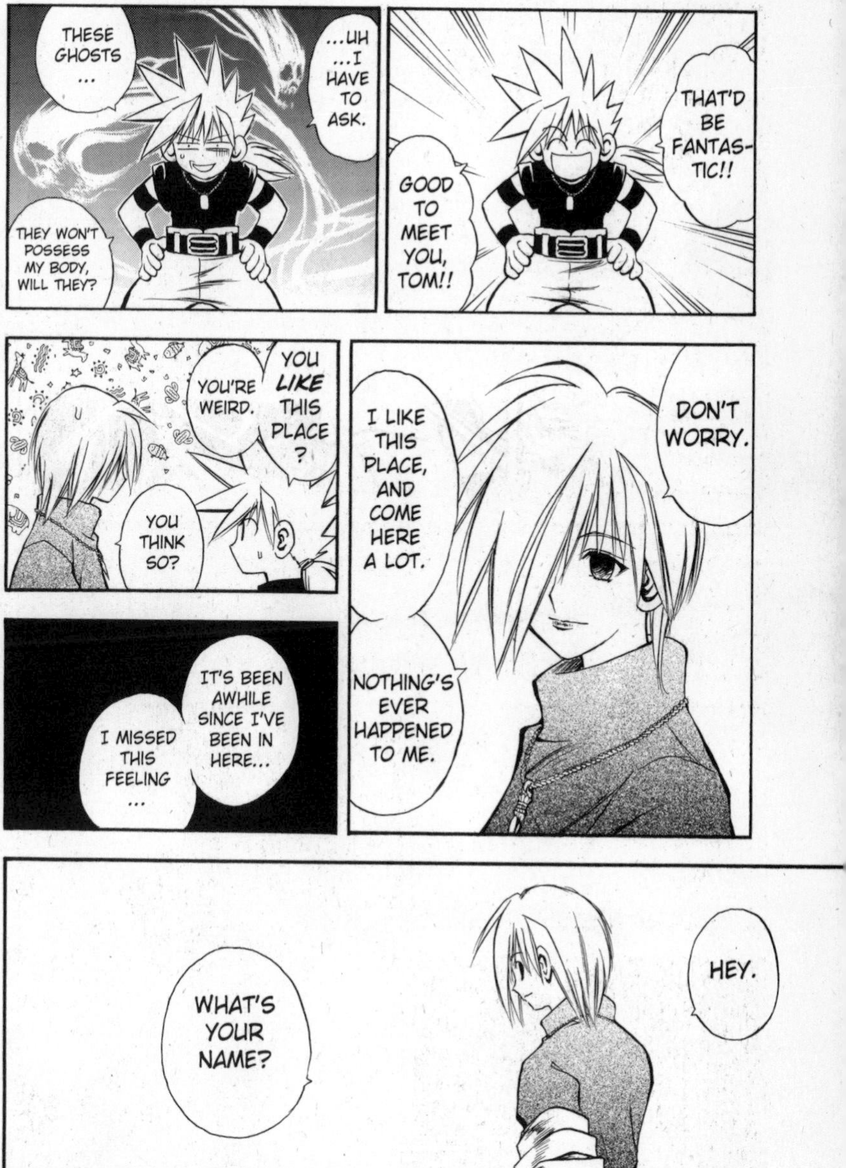
THAT'D BE FANTAS-TIC!!
GOOD TO MEET YOU, TOM!!
...UH ...I HAVE TO ASK.
THESE GHOSTS ...
THEY WON'T POSSESS MY BODY, WILL THEY?
DON'T WORRY.
I LIKE THIS PLACE, AND COME HERE A LOT.
NOTHING'S EVER HAPPENED TO ME.
YOU *LIKE* THIS PLACE?
YOU'RE WEIRD.
YOU THINK SO?
IT'S BEEN AWHILE SINCE I'VE BEEN IN HERE...
I MISSED THIS FEELING ...
HEY.
WHAT'S YOUR NAME?

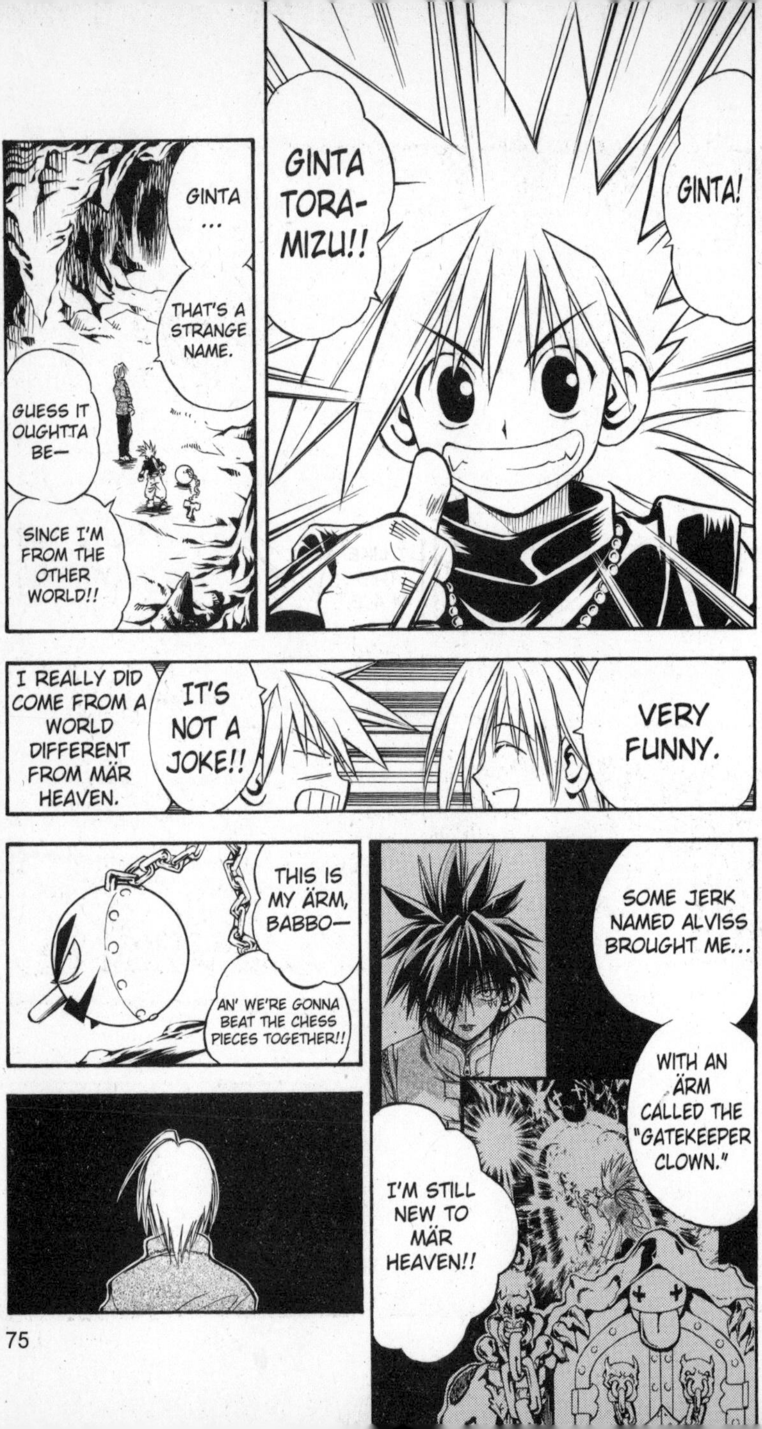
GINTA!
GINTA TORA-MIZU!!
GINTA ...
THAT'S A STRANGE NAME.
GUESS IT OUGHTTA BE—
SINCE I'M FROM THE OTHER WORLD!!
VERY FUNNY.
IT'S NOT A JOKE!!
I REALLY DID COME FROM A WORLD DIFFERENT FROM MÄR HEAVEN.
SOME JERK NAMED ALVISS BROUGHT ME...
WITH AN ÄRM CALLED THE "GATEKEEPER CLOWN."
I'M STILL NEW TO MÄR HEAVEN!!
THIS IS MY ÄRM, BABBO—
AN' WE'RE GONNA BEAT THE CHESS PIECES TOGETHER!!

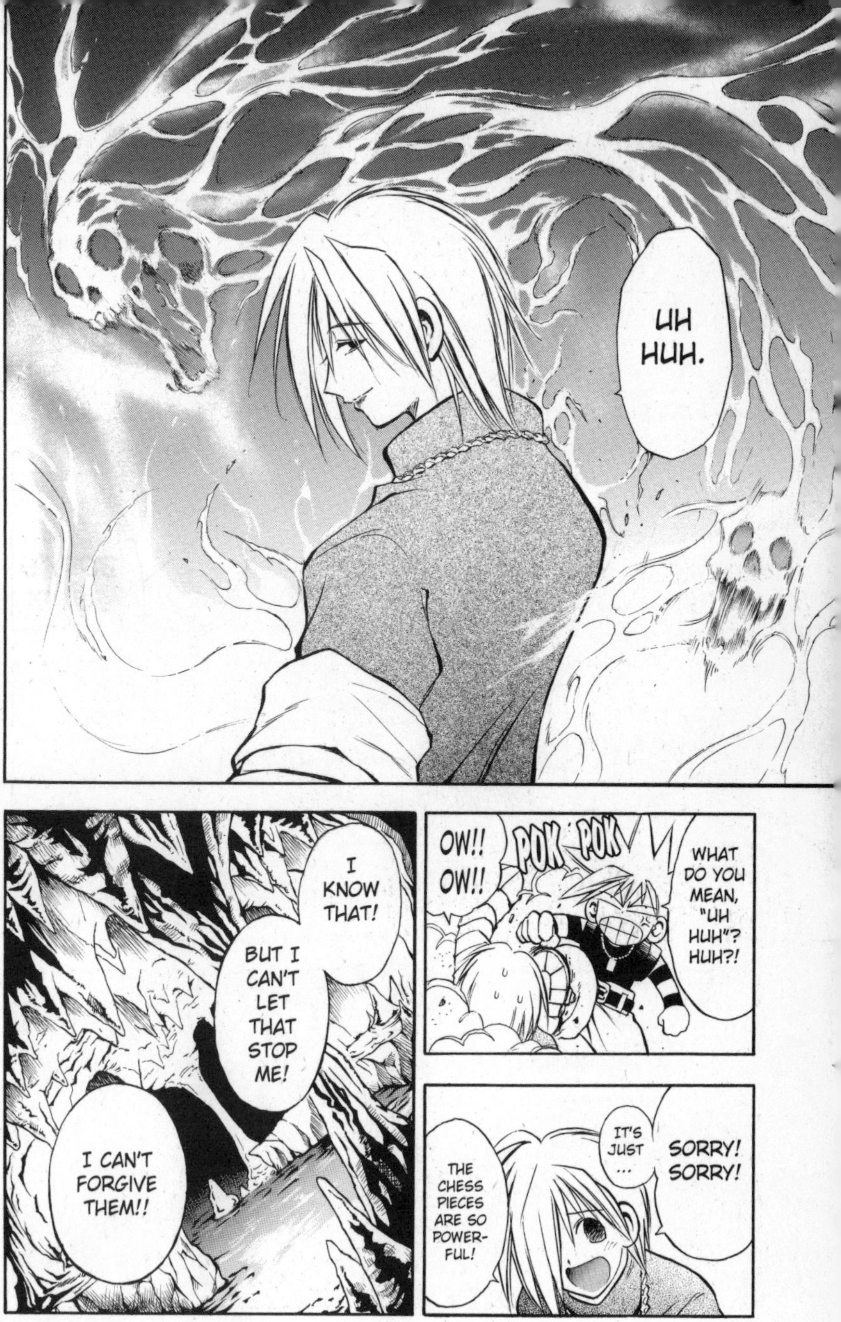
UH HUH.
WHAT DO YOU MEAN, "UH HUH"? HUH?!
POK POK
OW!! OW!!
SORRY! SORRY!
IT'S JUST ...
THE CHESS PIECES ARE SO POWER-FUL!
I KNOW THAT!
BUT I CAN'T LET THAT STOP ME!
I CAN'T FORGIVE THEM!!

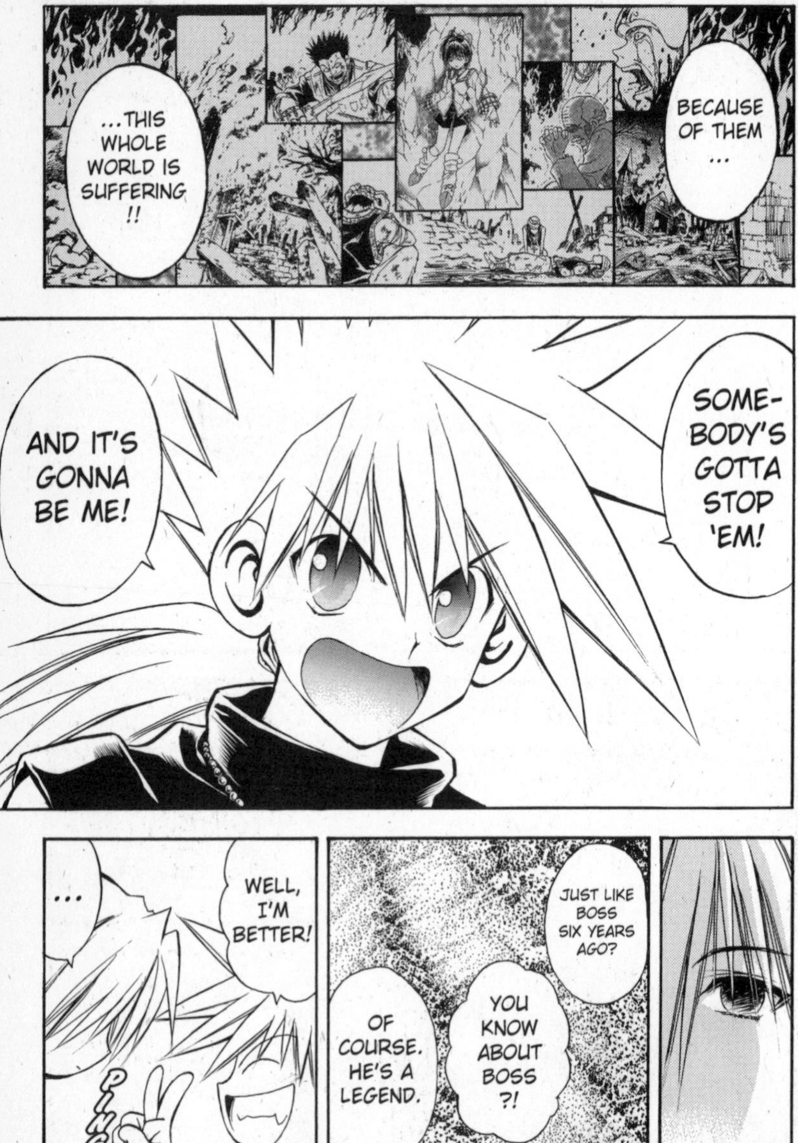
BECAUSE OF THEM ...
...THIS WHOLE WORLD IS SUFFERING !!
SOME-BODY'S GOTTA STOP 'EM!
AND IT'S GONNA BE ME!
JUST LIKE BOSS SIX YEARS AGO?
YOU KNOW ABOUT BOSS ?!
OF COURSE. HE'S A LEGEND.
WELL, I'M BETTER!
...
PING!

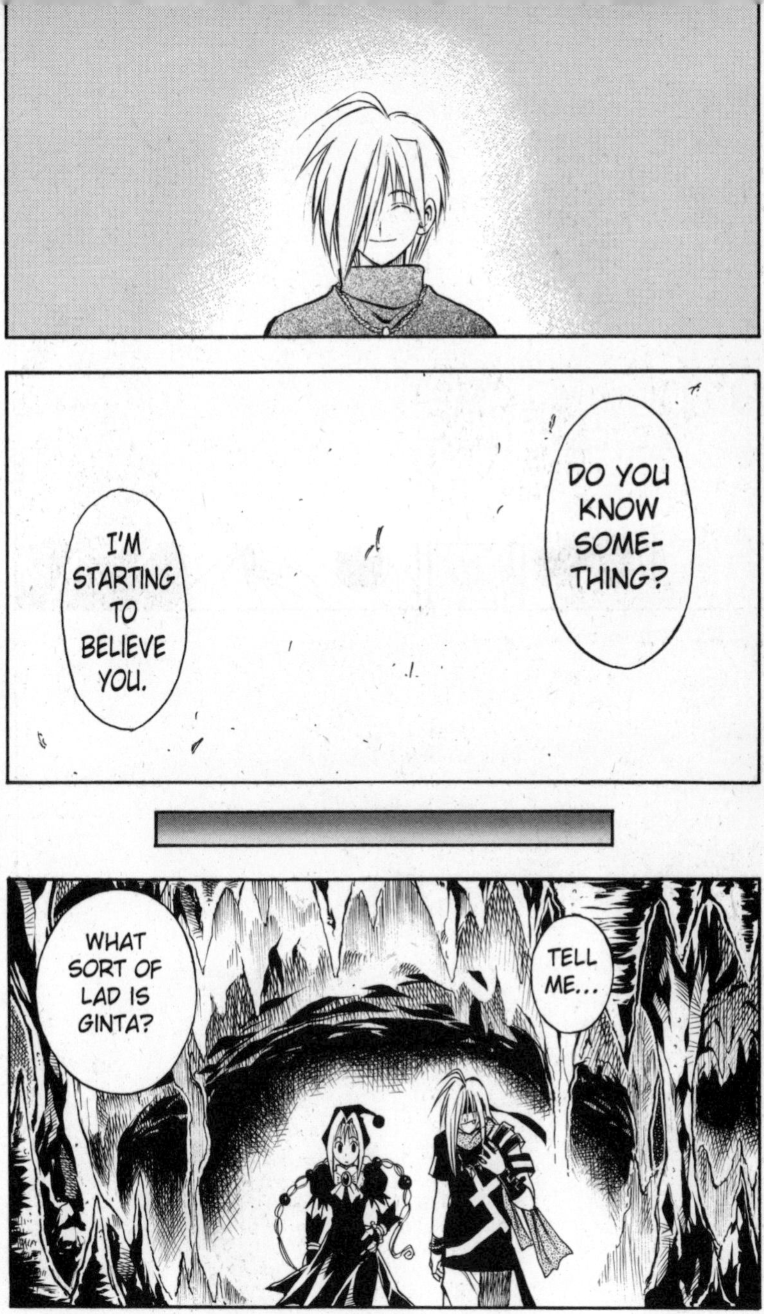
DO YOU KNOW SOME-THING?
I'M STARTING TO BELIEVE YOU.
TELL ME...
WHAT SORT OF LAD IS GINTA?

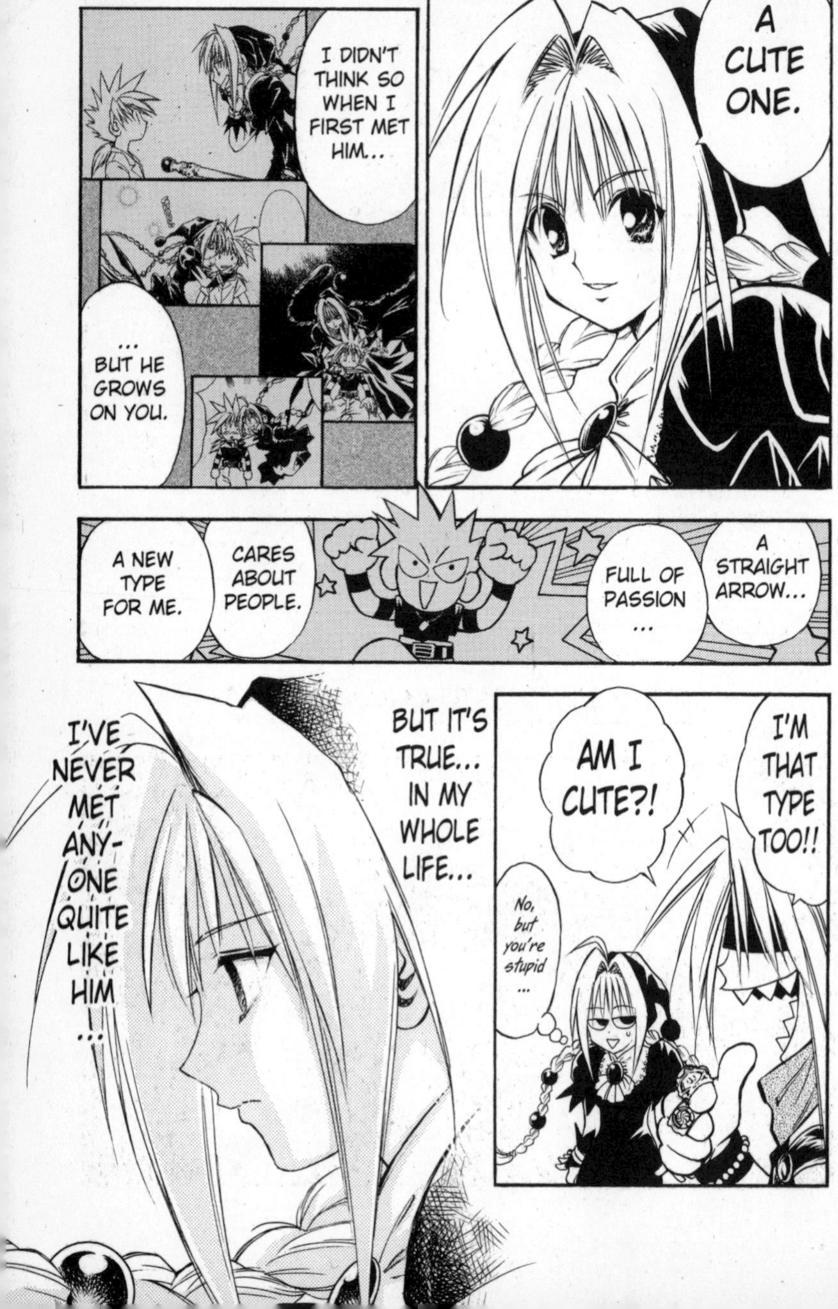
A CUTE ONE.
I DIDN'T THINK SO WHEN I FIRST MET HIM...
...BUT HE GROWS ON YOU.
A STRAIGHT ARROW...
FULL OF PASSION ...
CARES ABOUT PEOPLE.
A NEW TYPE FOR ME.
I'M THAT TYPE TOO!!
AM I CUTE?!
No, but you're stupid ...
BUT IT'S TRUE... IN MY WHOLE LIFE...
I'VE NEVER MET ANY-ONE QUITE LIKE HIM...

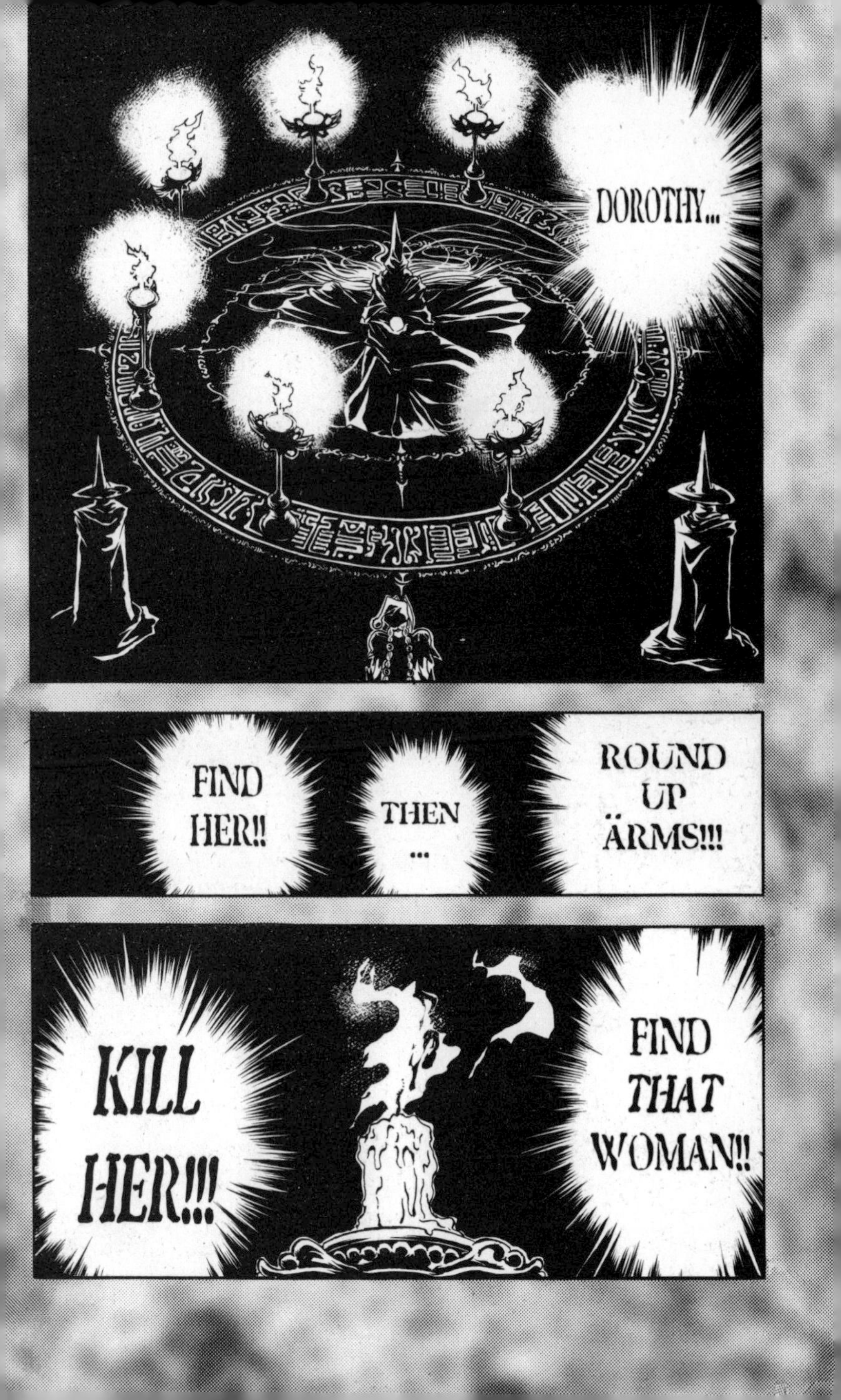
DOROTHY...
ROUND UP ÄRMS!!!
THEN ...
FIND HER!!
FIND THAT WOMAN!!
KILL HER!!!

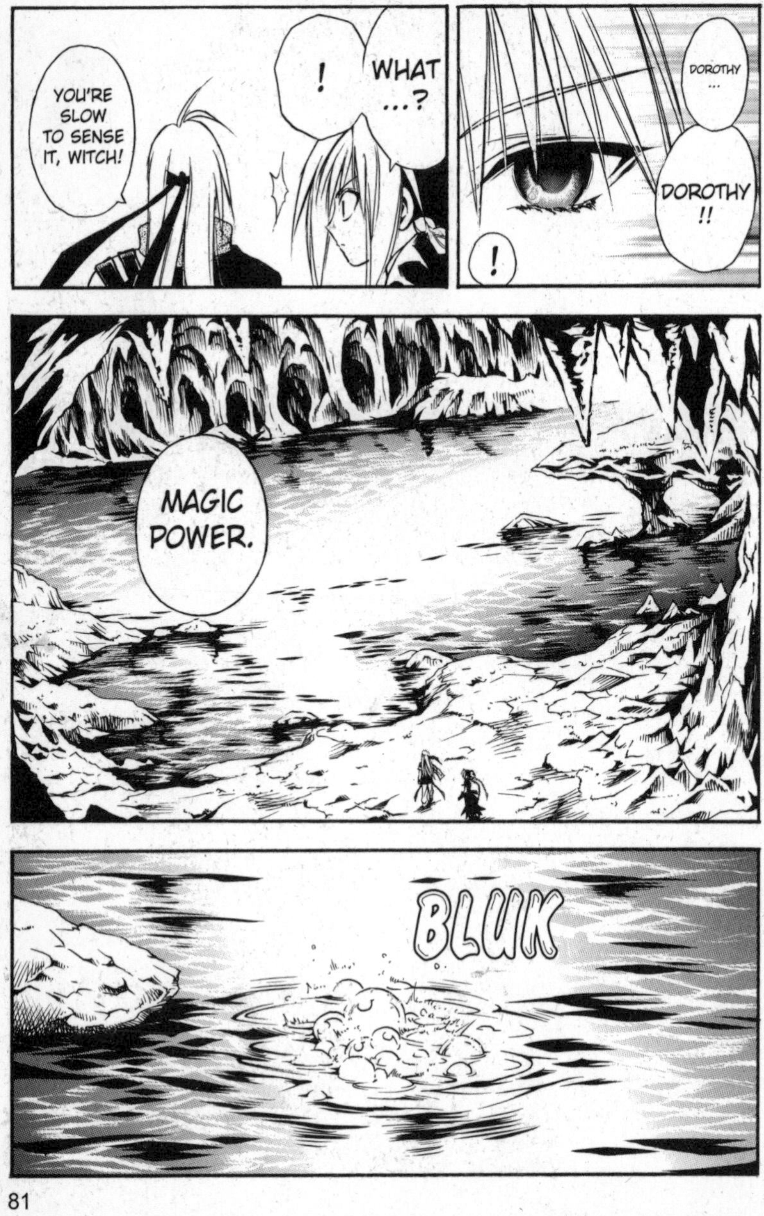
DOROTHY ...
DOROTHY !!
!
WHAT ...?
!
YOU'RE SLOW TO SENSE IT, WITCH!
MAGIC POWER.
BLUK

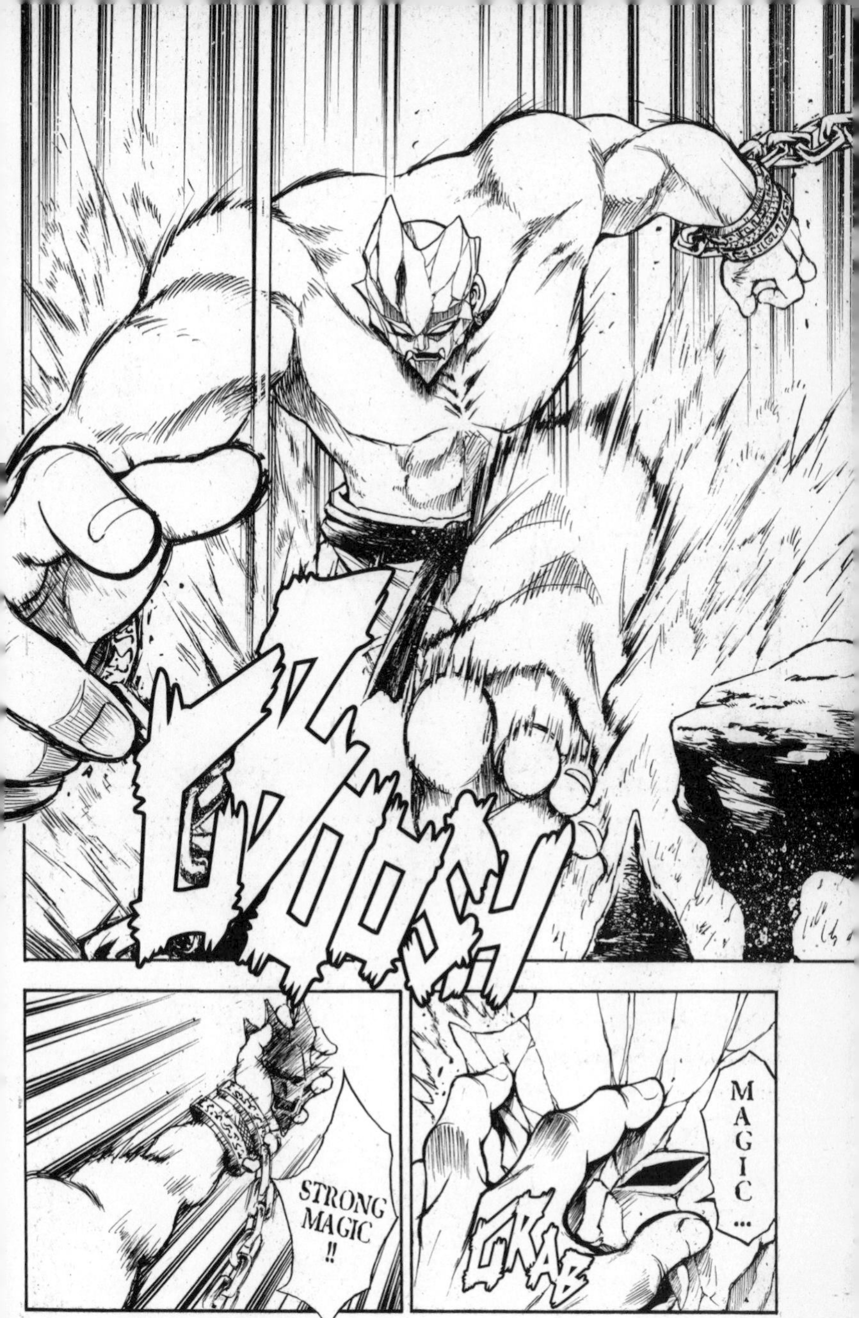
MAGIC…
GRAB
STRONG MAGIC !!

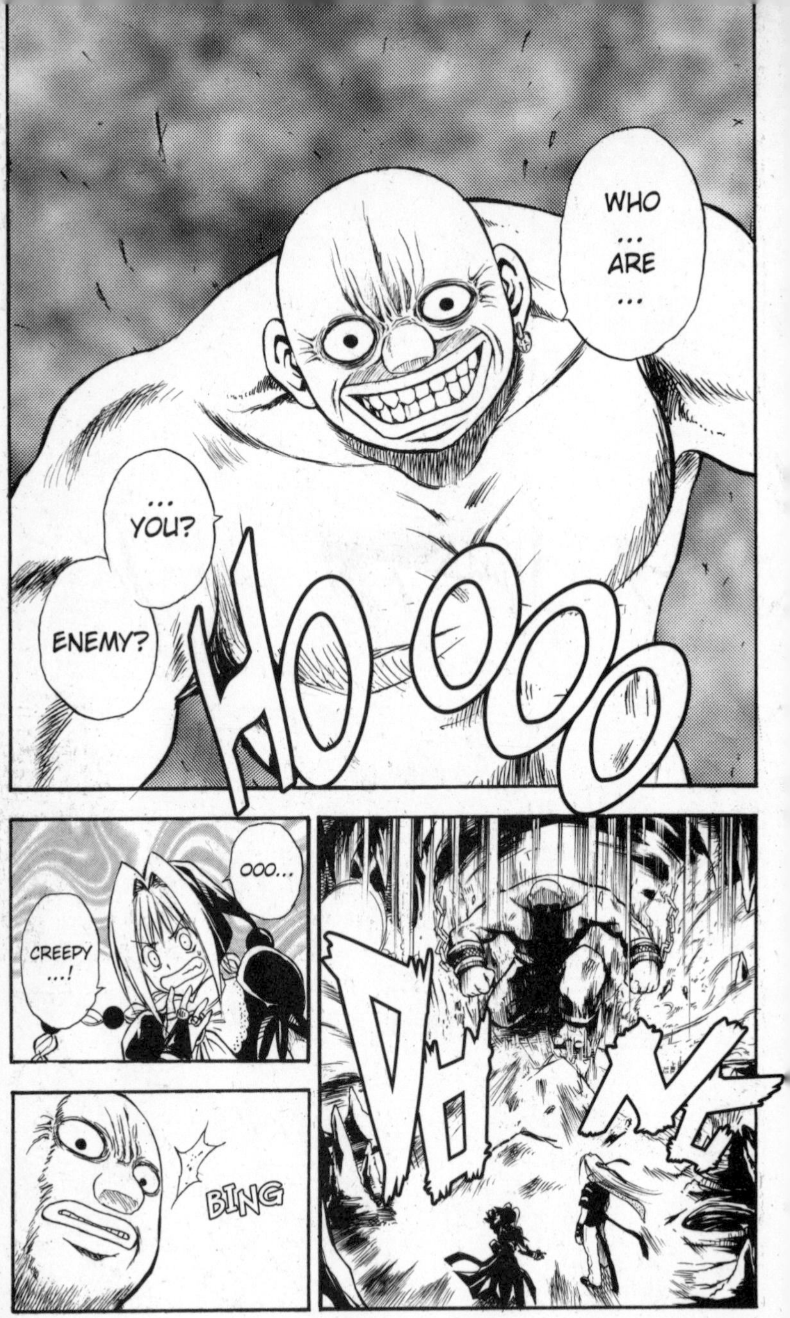
WHO ... ARE ...
... YOU?
ENEMY?
HO-OOO
OOO...
CREEPY ...!
BING

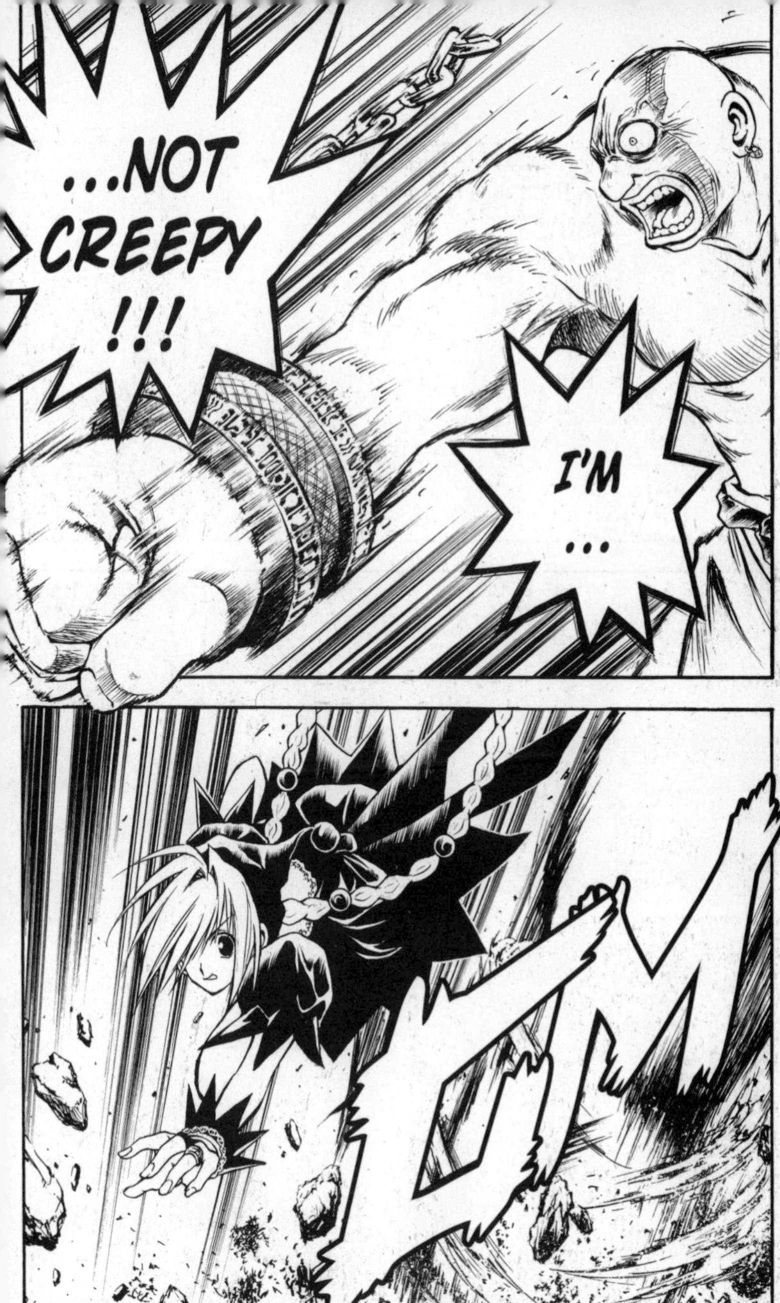
I'M ...
...NOT CREEPY !!!

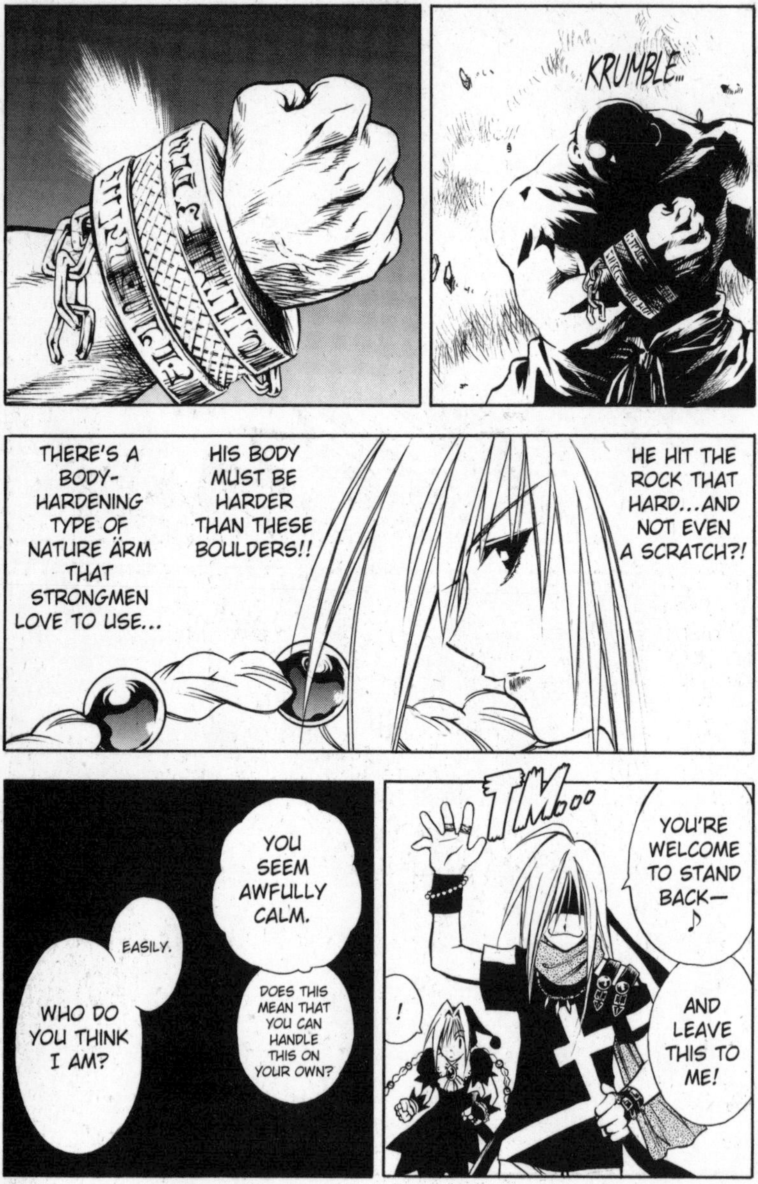
KRUMBLE...
HE HIT THE ROCK THAT HARD...AND NOT EVEN A SCRATCH?!
HIS BODY MUST BE HARDER THAN THESE BOULDERS!!
THERE'S A BODY-HARDENING TYPE OF NATURE ÄRM THAT STRONGMEN LOVE TO USE...
TM
YOU'RE WELCOME TO STAND BACK—♪
AND LEAVE THIS TO ME!
!
YOU SEEM AWFULLY CALM.
DOES THIS MEAN THAT YOU CAN HANDLE THIS ON YOUR OWN?
EASILY.
WHO DO YOU THINK I AM?

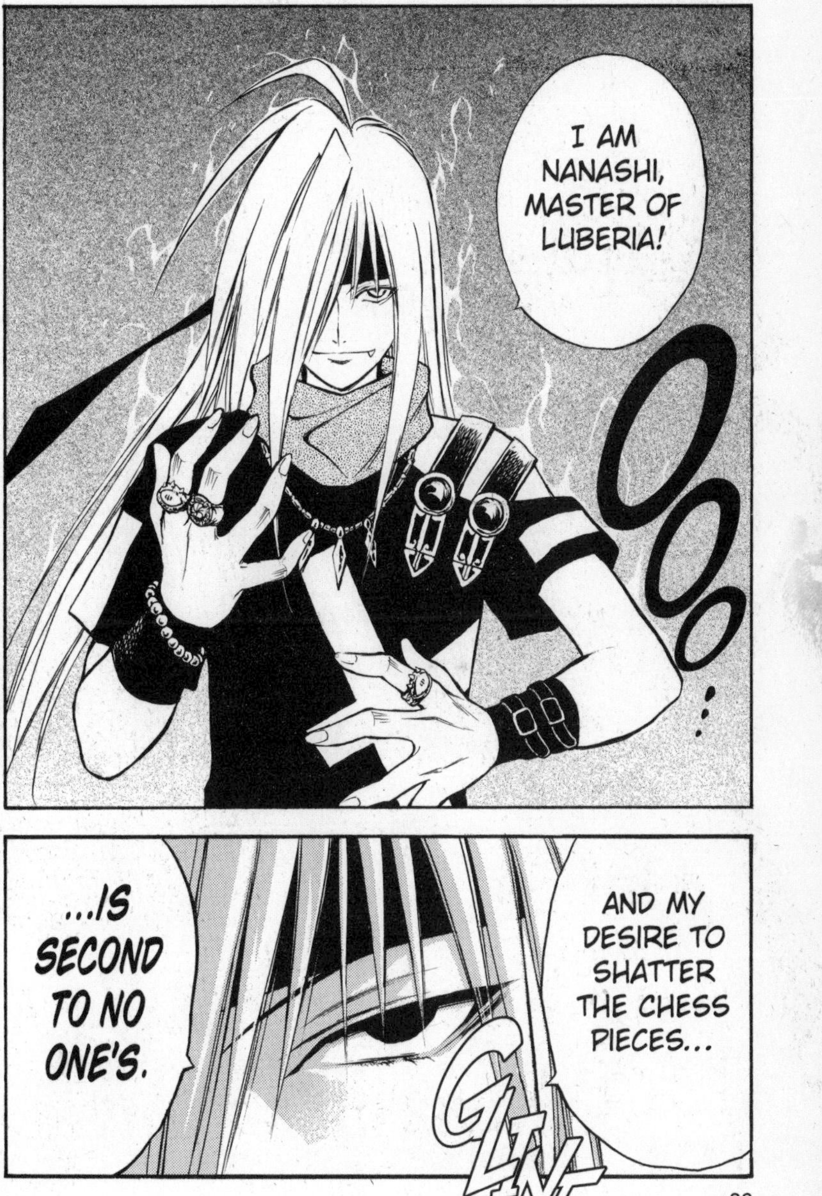
I AM NANASHI, MASTER OF LUBERIA!
OOOO...
AND MY DESIRE TO SHATTER THE CHESS PIECES...
...IS SECOND TO NO ONE'S.
GLINT

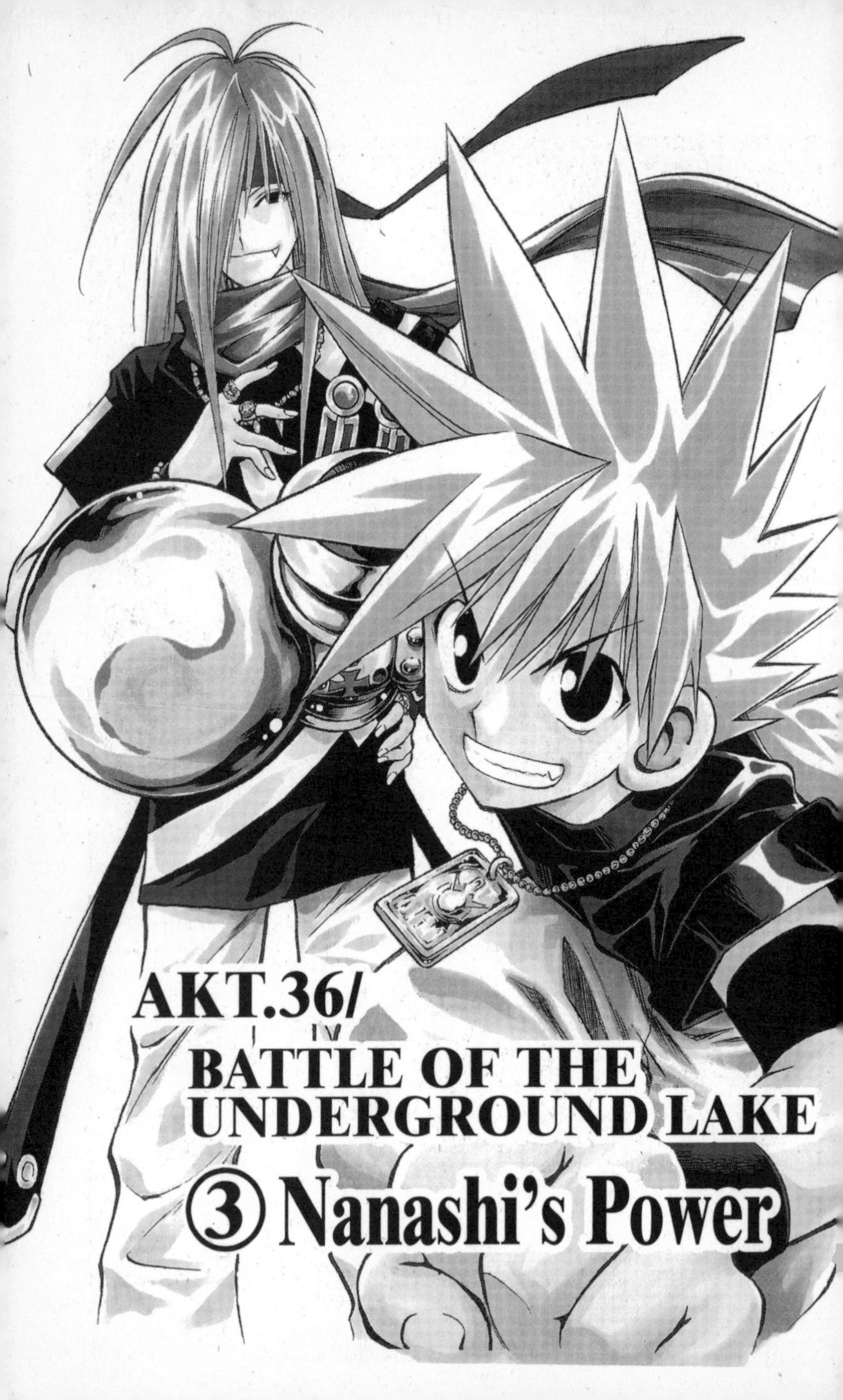
AKT.36/
BATTLE OF THE UNDERGROUND LAKE
③ Nanashi's Power

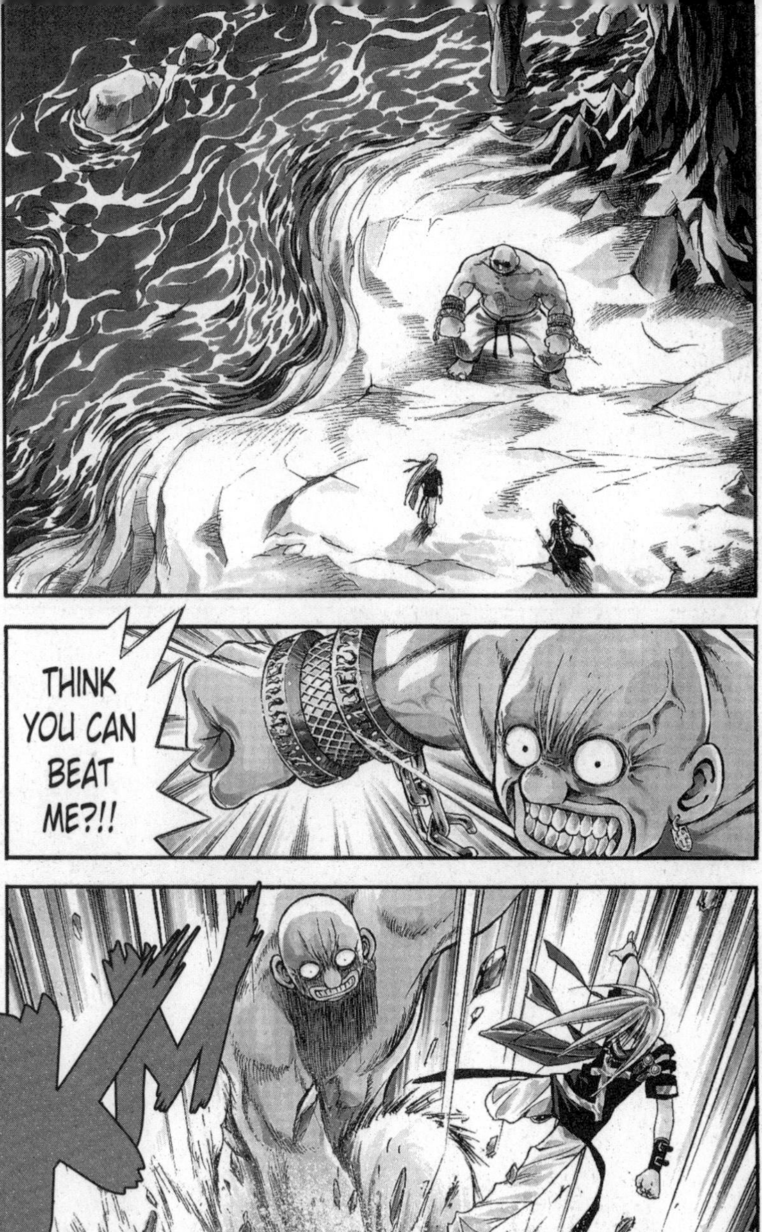
THINK YOU CAN BEAT ME?!!

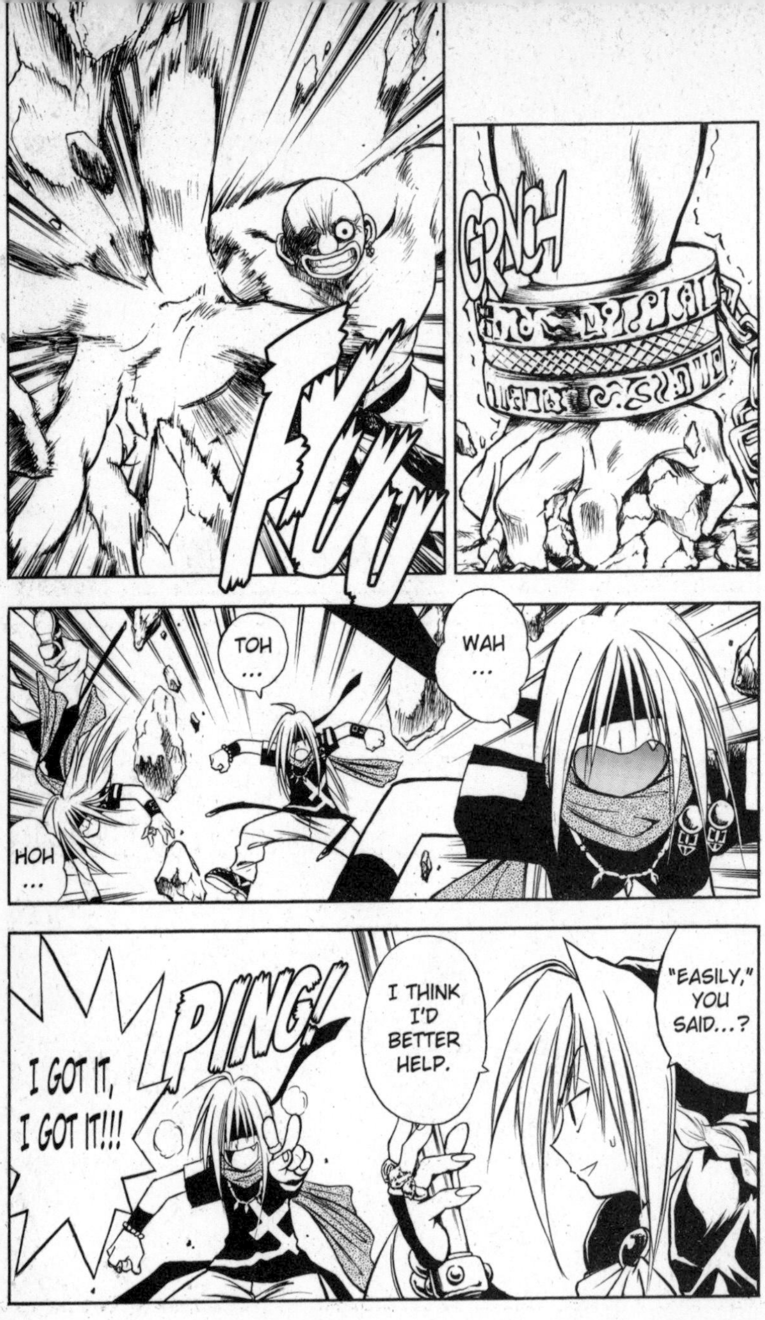
GRNCH
WAH ...
TOH ...
HOH ...
"EASILY," YOU SAID...?
I THINK I'D BETTER HELP.
PING!
I GOT IT, I GOT IT!!!

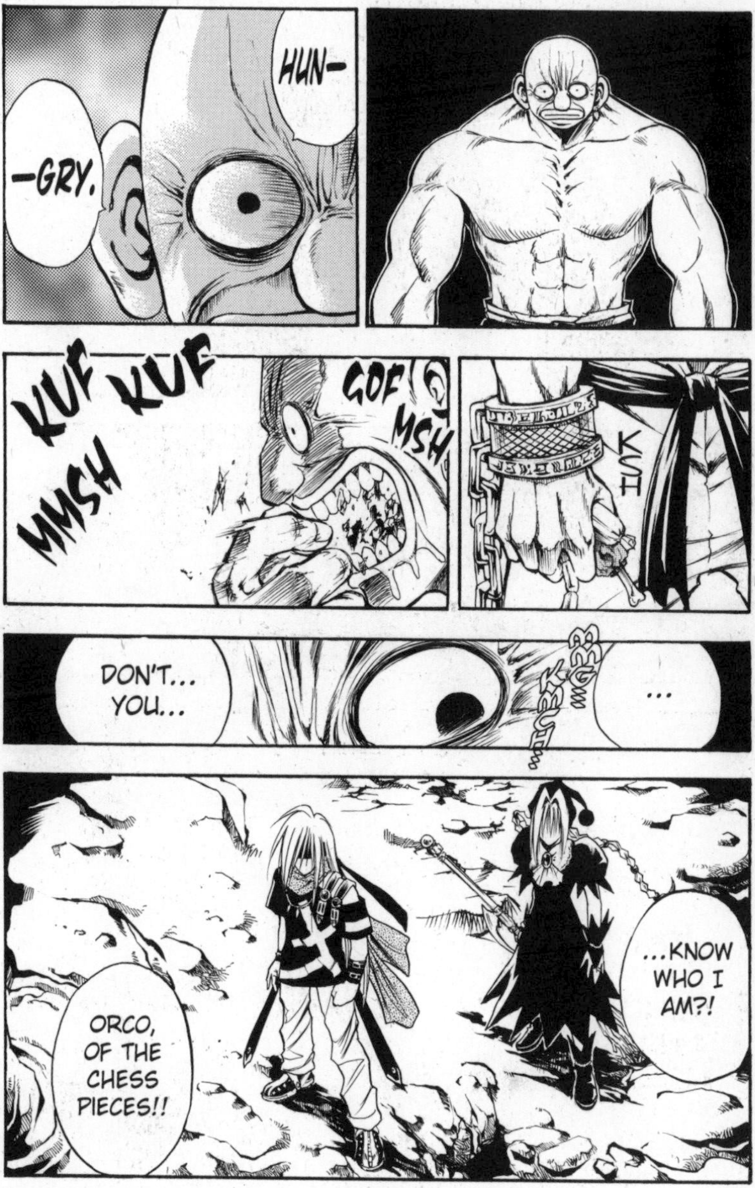
HUN-
-GRY.
KSH
GOF
MSH
KUF KUF
MMSH
...
DON'T... YOU...
...KNOW WHO I AM?!
ORCO, OF THE CHESS PIECES!!

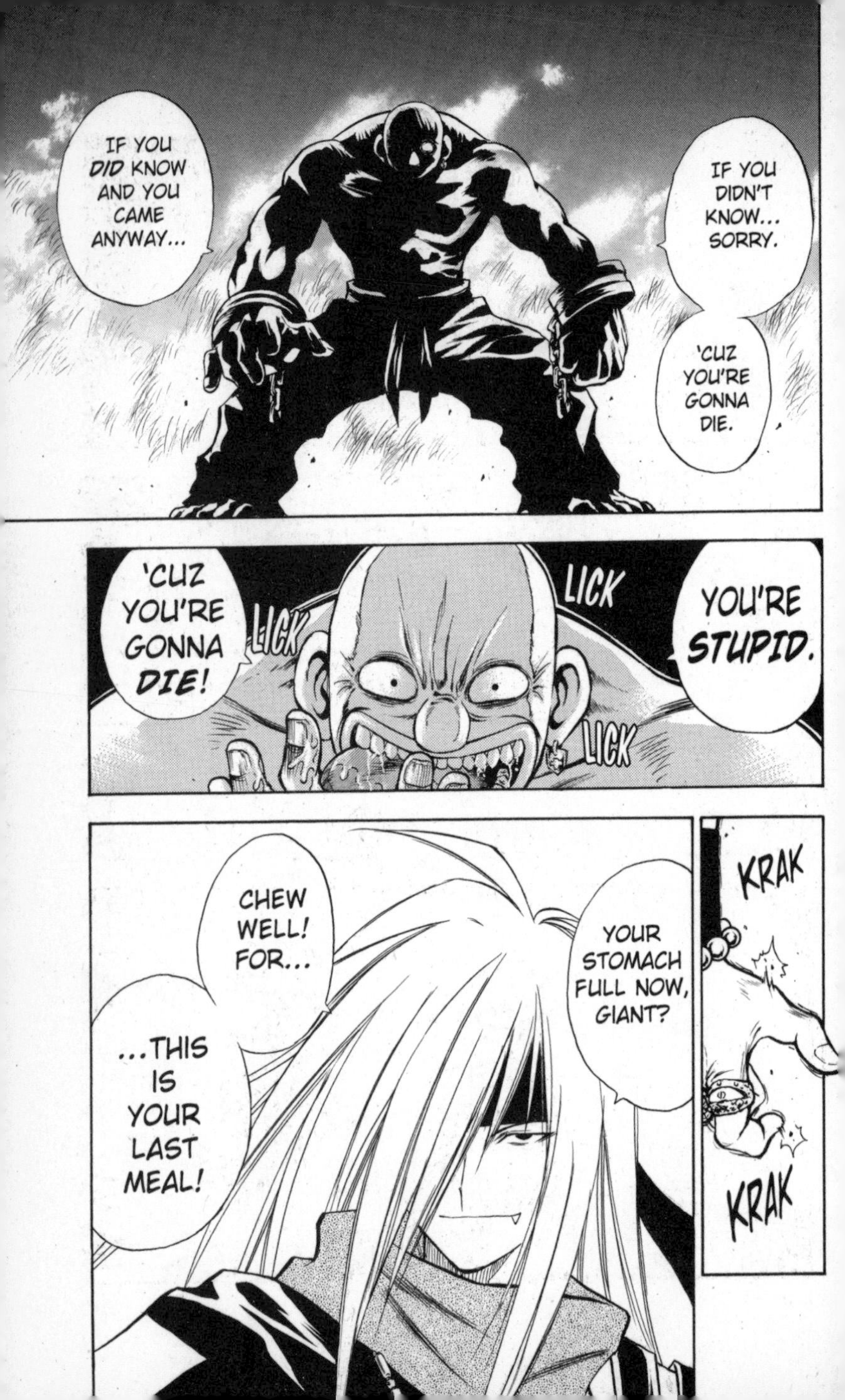
IF YOU DIDN'T KNOW... SORRY.
'CUZ YOU'RE GONNA DIE.
IF YOU DID KNOW AND YOU CAME ANYWAY...
YOU'RE STUPID.
LICK
LICK
LICK
'CUZ YOU'RE GONNA DIE!
KRAK
KRAK
YOUR STOMACH FULL NOW, GIANT?
CHEW WELL! FOR...
...THIS IS YOUR LAST MEAL!

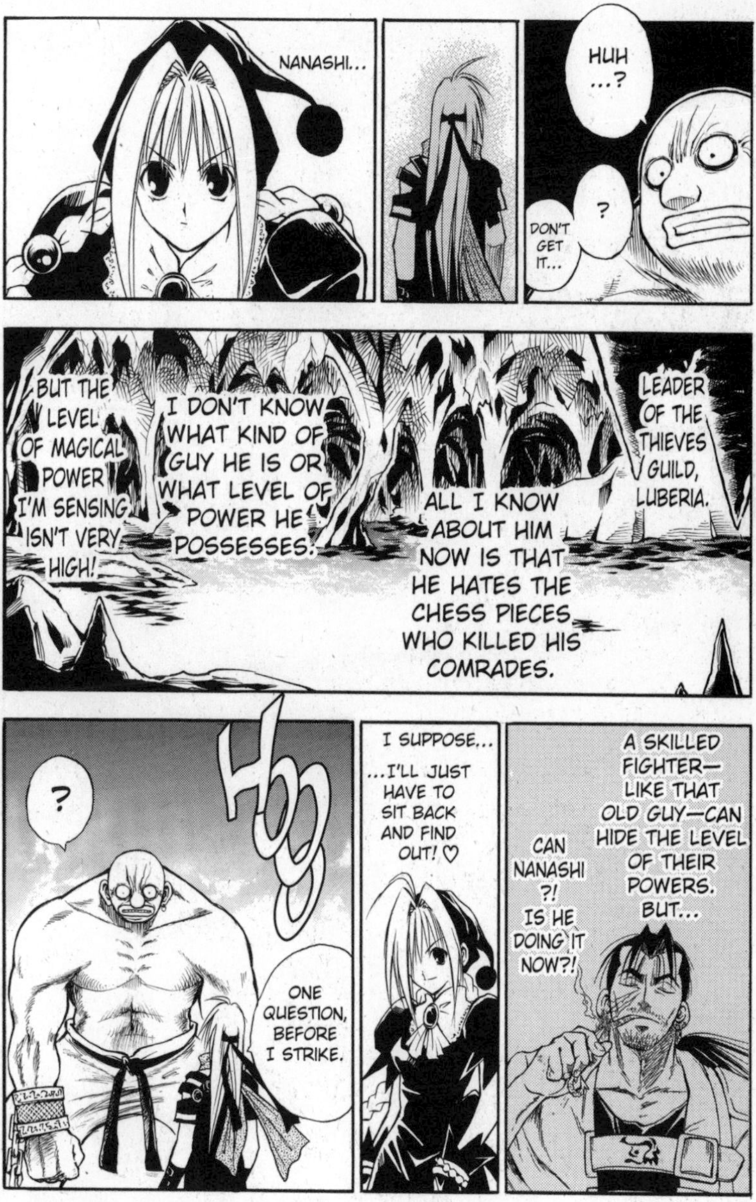
HUH ...?
?
DON'T GET IT...
NANASHI...
LEADER OF THE THIEVES GUILD, LUBERIA.
ALL I KNOW ABOUT HIM NOW IS THAT HE HATES THE CHESS PIECES WHO KILLED HIS COMRADES.
I DON'T KNOW WHAT KIND OF GUY HE IS OR WHAT LEVEL OF POWER HE POSSESSES.
BUT THE LEVEL OF MAGICAL POWER I'M SENSING ISN'T VERY HIGH!
A SKILLED FIGHTER—LIKE THAT OLD GUY—CAN HIDE THE LEVEL OF THEIR POWERS. BUT...
CAN NANASHI ?! IS HE DOING IT NOW?!
I SUPPOSE...
...I'LL JUST HAVE TO SIT BACK AND FIND OUT! ♡
HOO
?
ONE QUESTION, BEFORE I STRIKE.

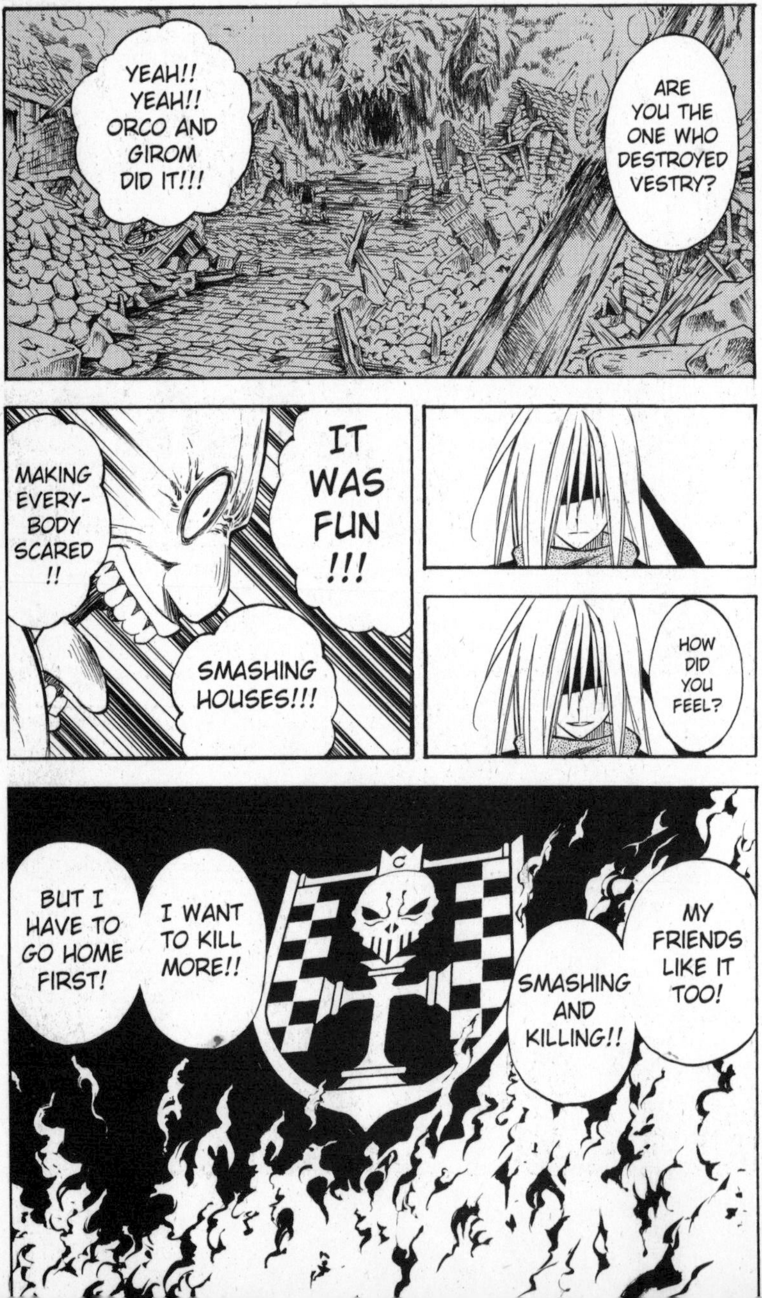
ARE YOU THE ONE WHO DESTROYED VESTRY?
YEAH!! YEAH!! ORCO AND GIROM DID IT!!!
HOW DID YOU FEEL?
IT WAS FUN!!!
MAKING EVERY-BODY SCARED!!
SMASHING HOUSES!!!
MY FRIENDS LIKE IT TOO!
SMASHING AND KILLING!!
I WANT TO KILL MORE!!
BUT I HAVE TO GO HOME FIRST!

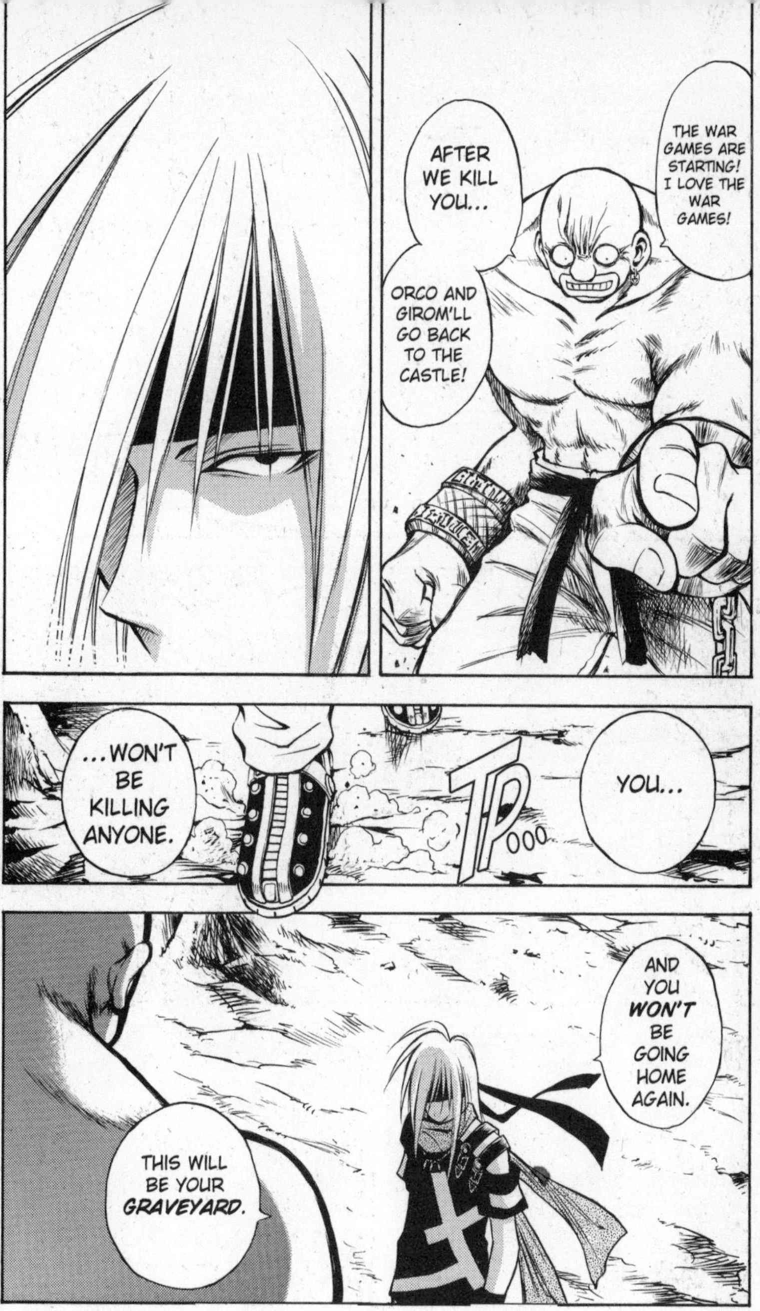
THE WAR GAMES ARE STARTING! I LOVE THE WAR GAMES!
AFTER WE KILL YOU...
ORCO AND GIROM'LL GO BACK TO THE CASTLE!
YOU...
TPOOO
...WON'T BE KILLING ANYONE.
AND YOU *WON'T* BE GOING HOME AGAIN.
THIS WILL BE YOUR *GRAVEYARD*.

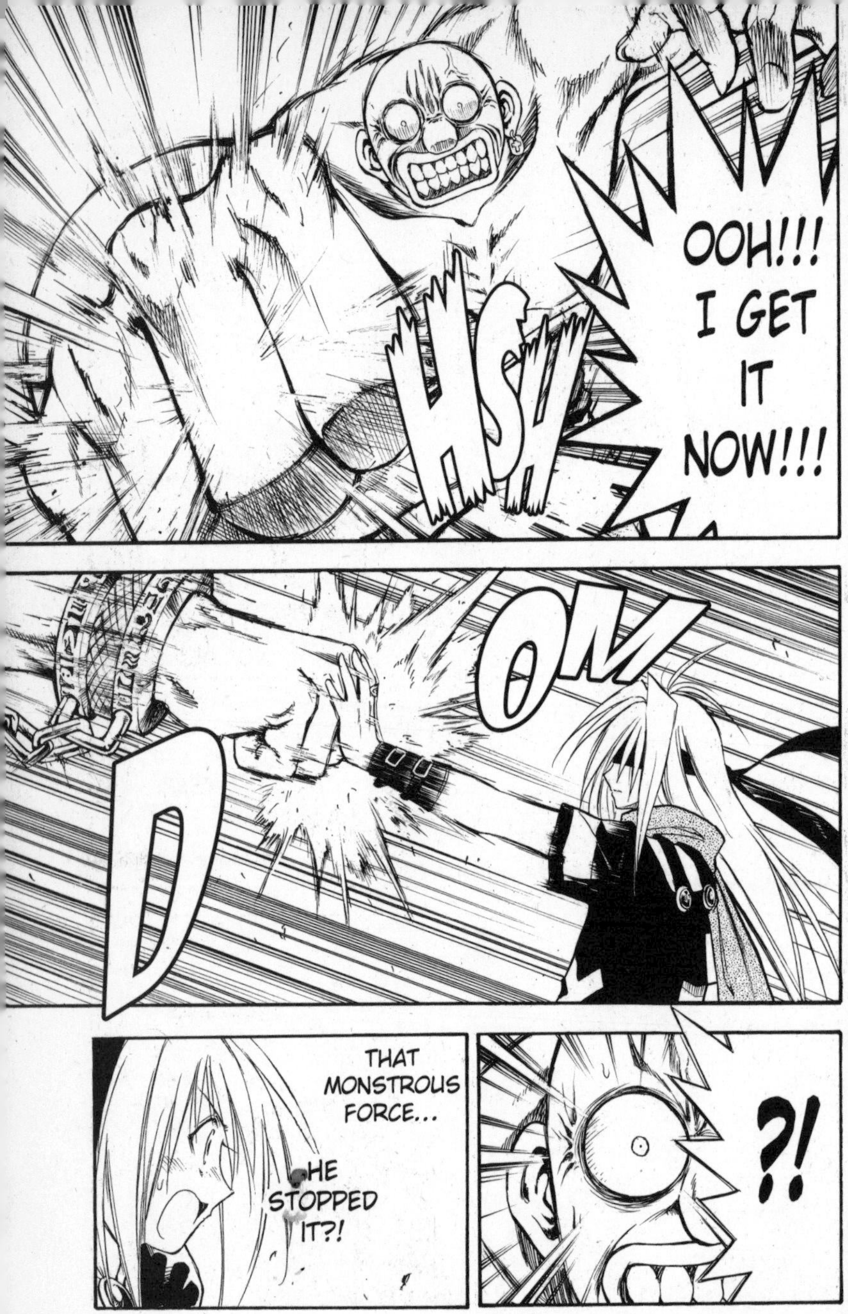

OOH!!! I GET IT NOW!!!
HSH
OM
D
?!
THAT MONSTROUS FORCE...
HE STOPPED IT?!

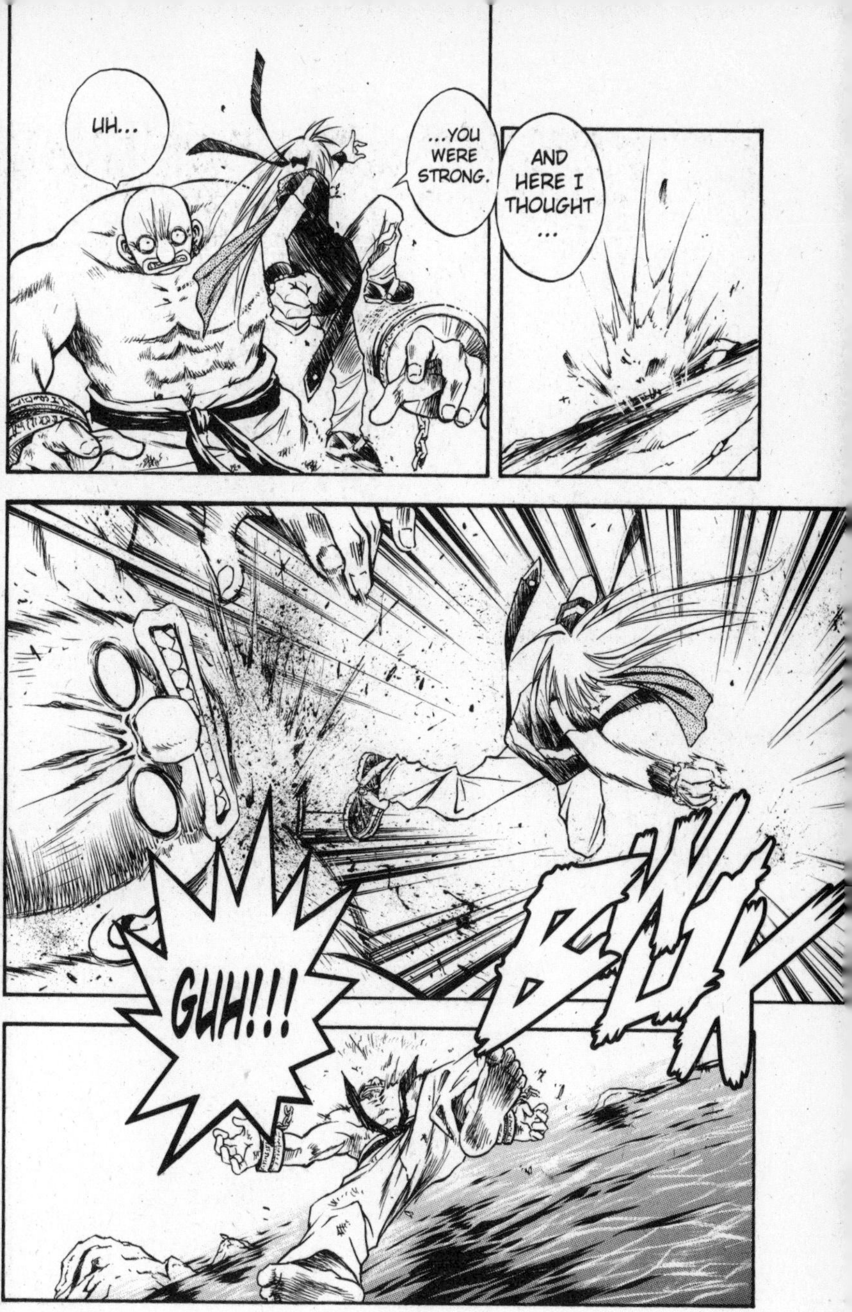
AND HERE I THOUGHT ...
...YOU WERE STRONG.
UH...
BLK
GUH!!!

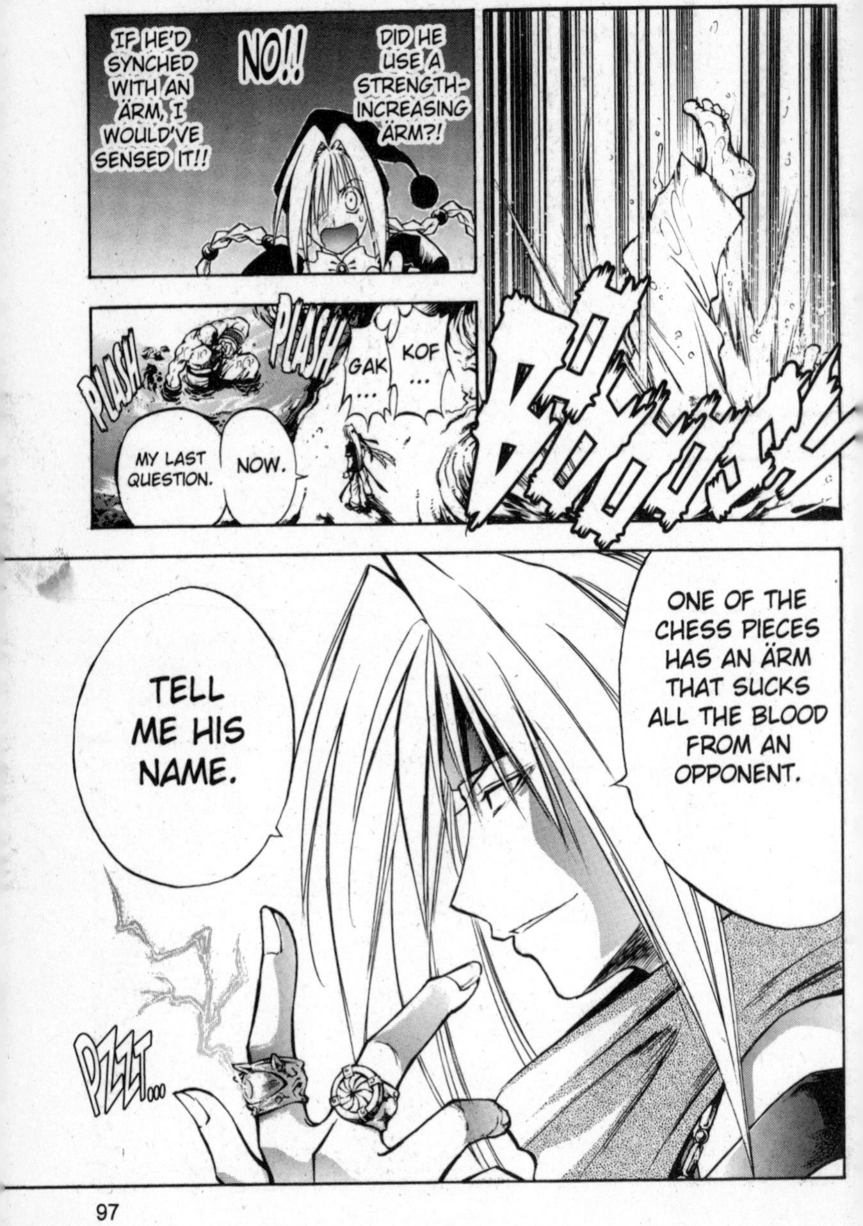
DID HE USE A STRENGTH-INCREASING ÄRM?!
NO!!
IF HE'D SYNCHED WITH AN ÄRM, I WOULD'VE SENSED IT!!
PLASH
KOF...
GAK...
PLASH
NOW.
MY LAST QUESTION.
ONE OF THE CHESS PIECES HAS AN ÄRM THAT SUCKS ALL THE BLOOD FROM AN OPPONENT.
TELL ME HIS NAME.
PZZZT...

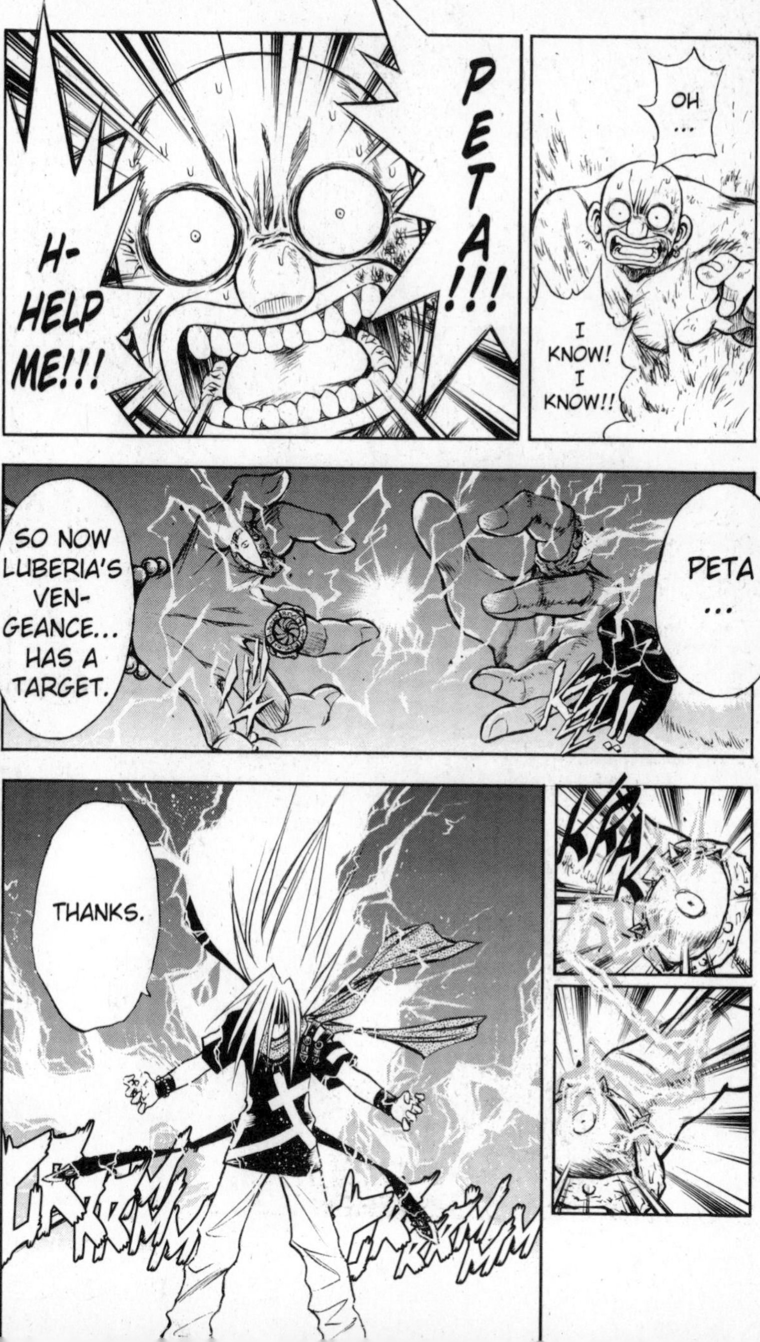
OH ...
I KNOW! I KNOW!!
PETA!!!
H-HELP ME!!!
PETA ...
SO NOW LUBERIA'S VEN-GEANCE... HAS A TARGET.
KRAK
THANKS.

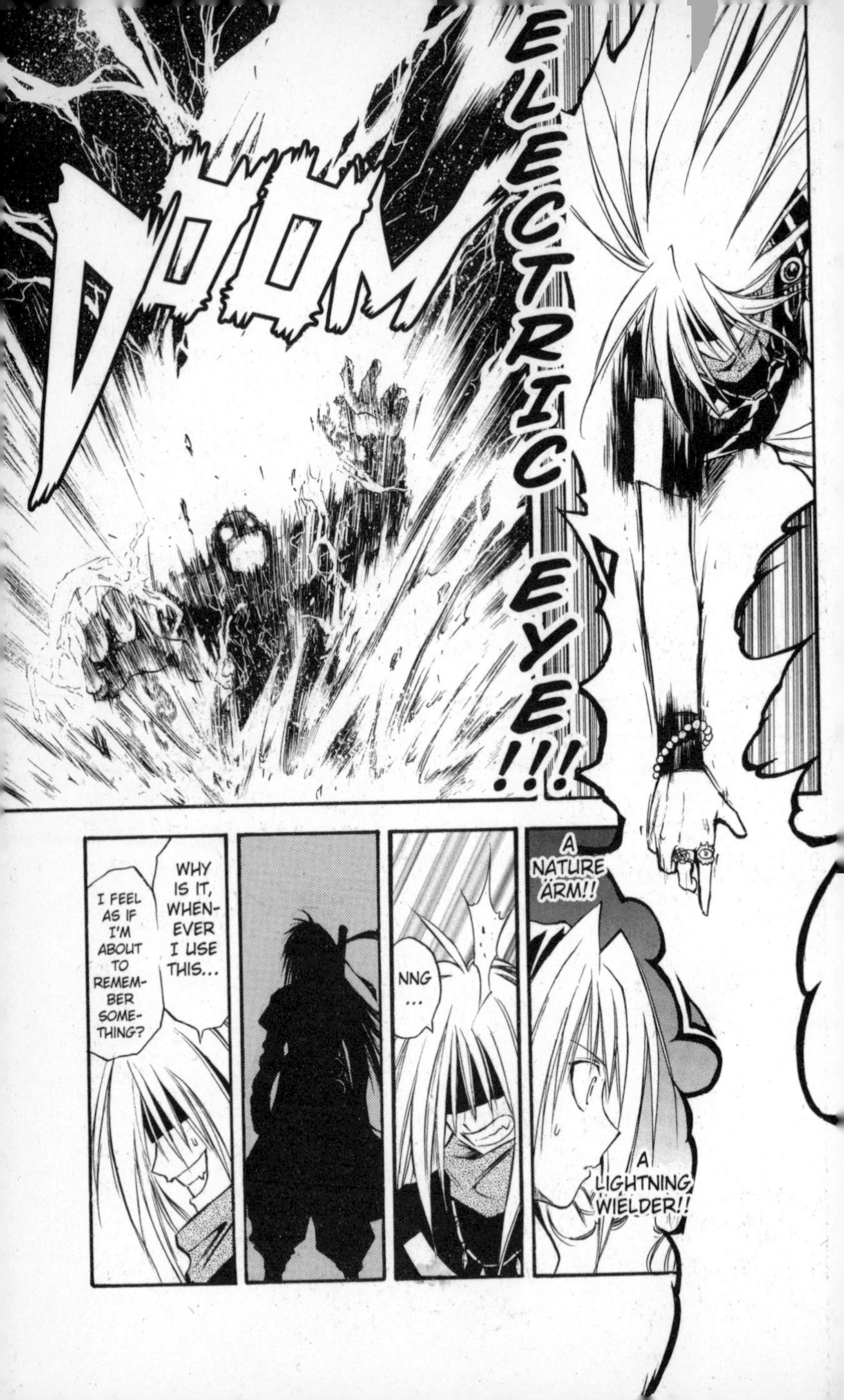
ELECTRIC EYE!!!
DOOM
A NATURE ARM!!
A LIGHTNING WIELDER!!
NNG...
WHY IS IT, WHENEVER I USE THIS...
I FEEL AS IF I'M ABOUT TO REMEMBER SOMETHING?

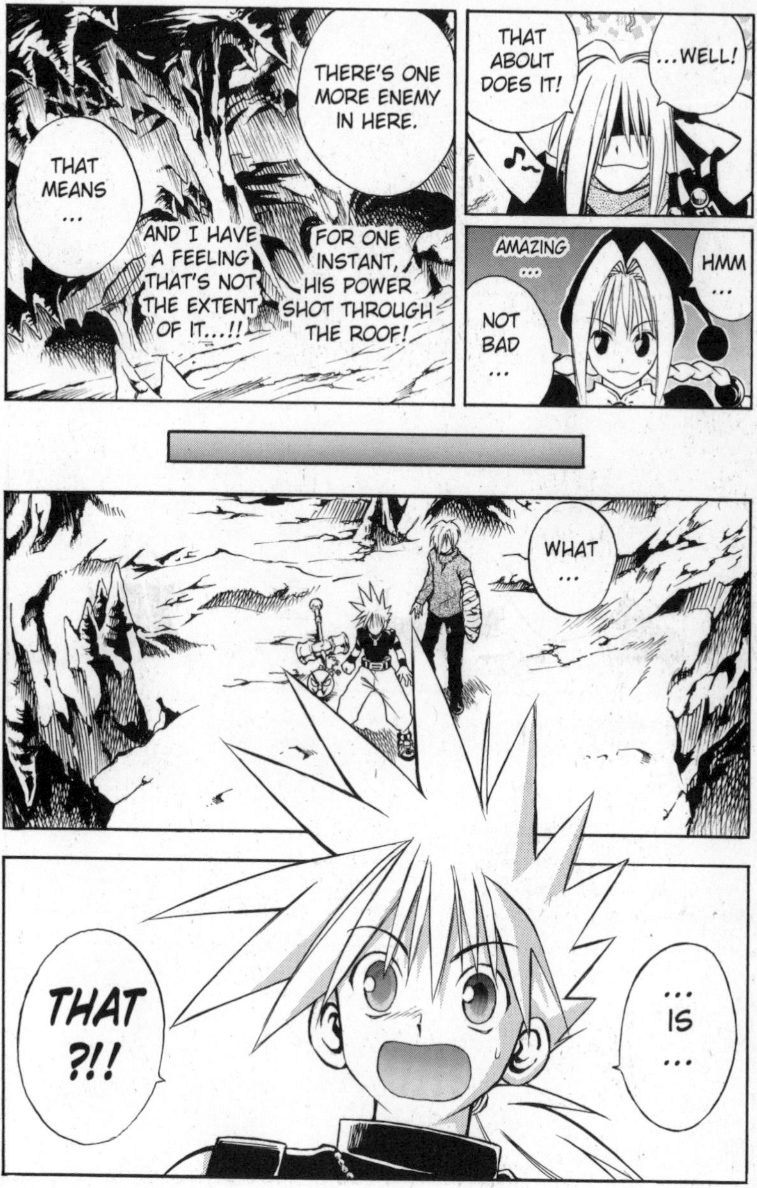
...WELL!
THAT ABOUT DOES IT!
HMM...
AMAZING...
NOT BAD...
THERE'S ONE MORE ENEMY IN HERE.
THAT MEANS...
FOR ONE INSTANT, HIS POWER SHOT THROUGH THE ROOF!
AND I HAVE A FEELING THAT'S NOT THE EXTENT OF IT...!!
WHAT...
...IS...
THAT ?!!

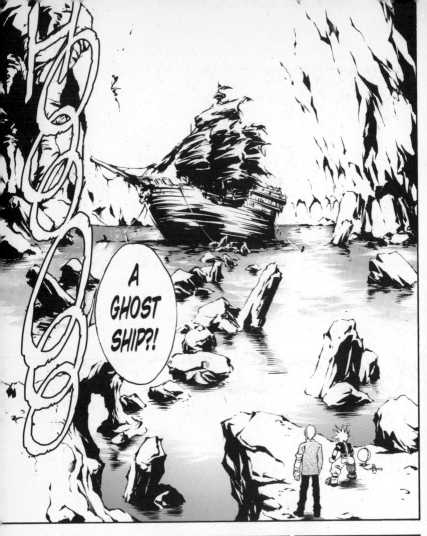

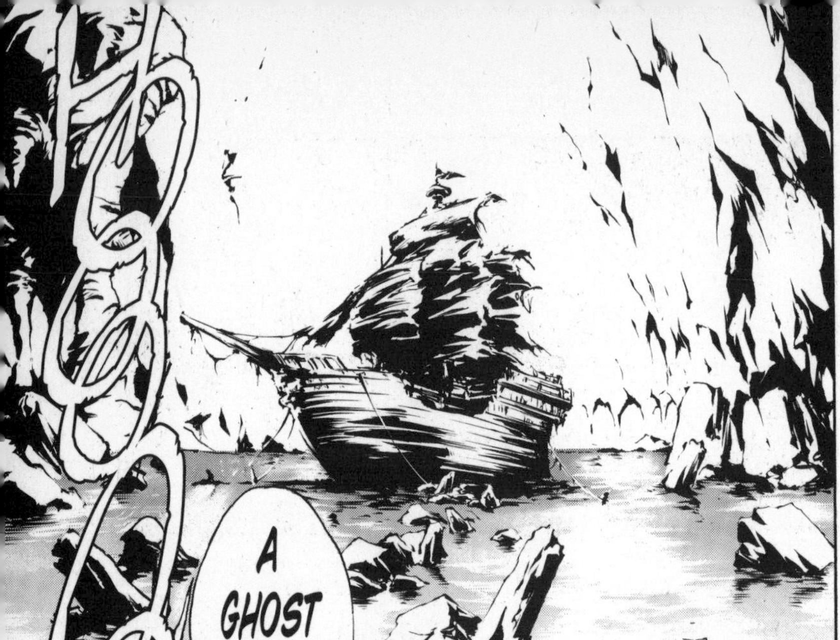
A GHOST SHIP?!

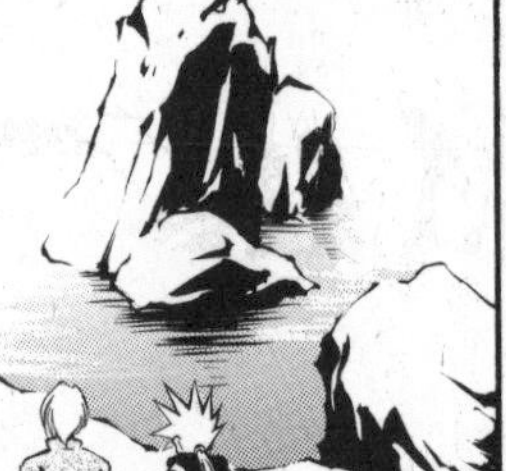

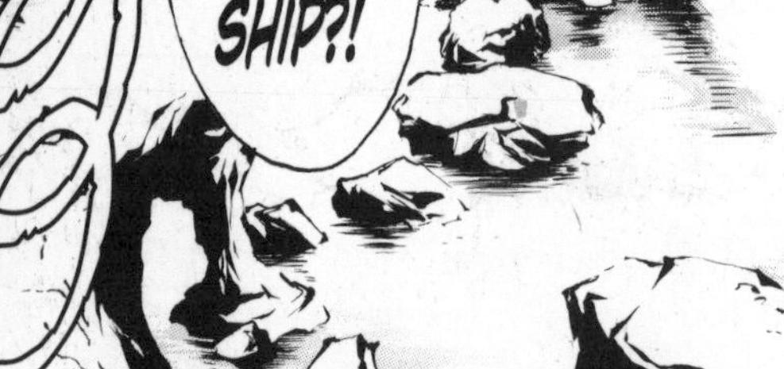
STAND BACK, TOM!
WHAT ?
MAGIC POWERS.
WHICH MEANS ...

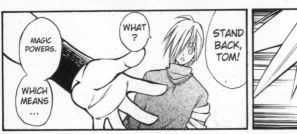

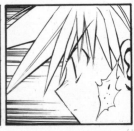

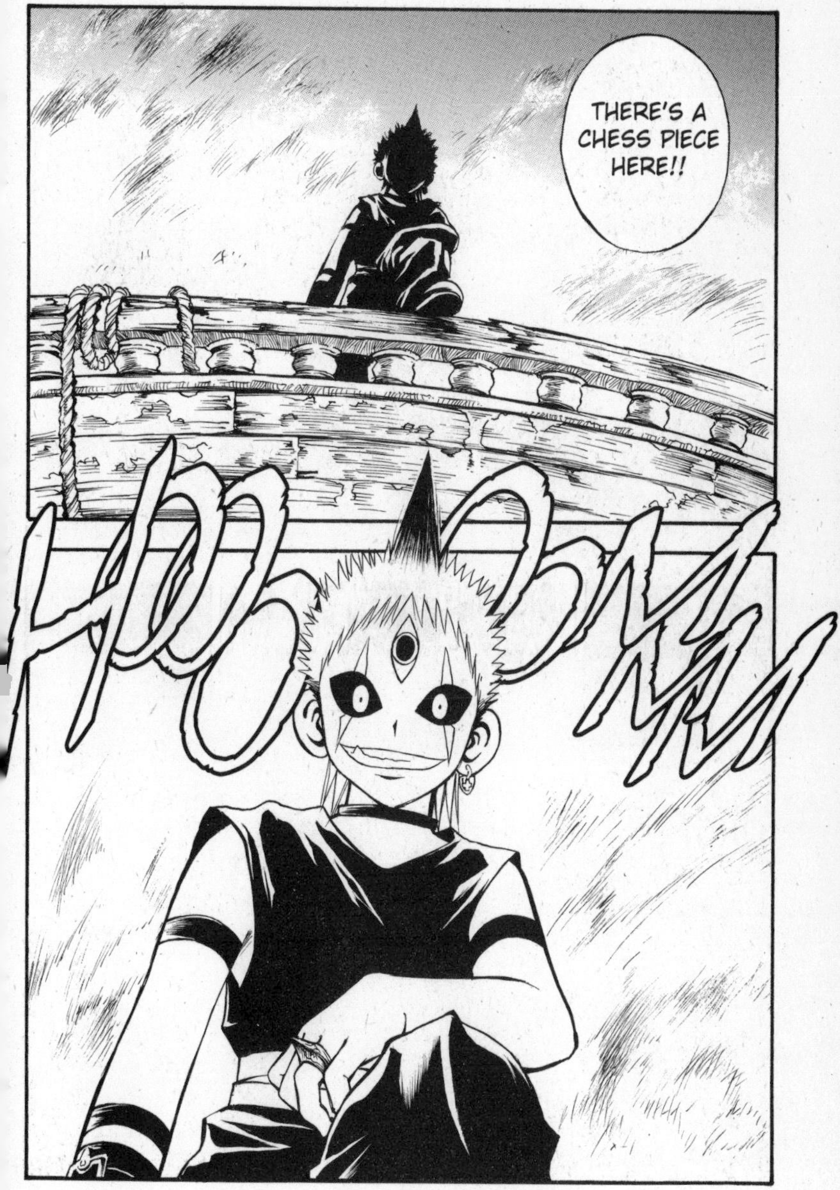
THERE'S A CHESS PIECE HERE!!
HOOOMM

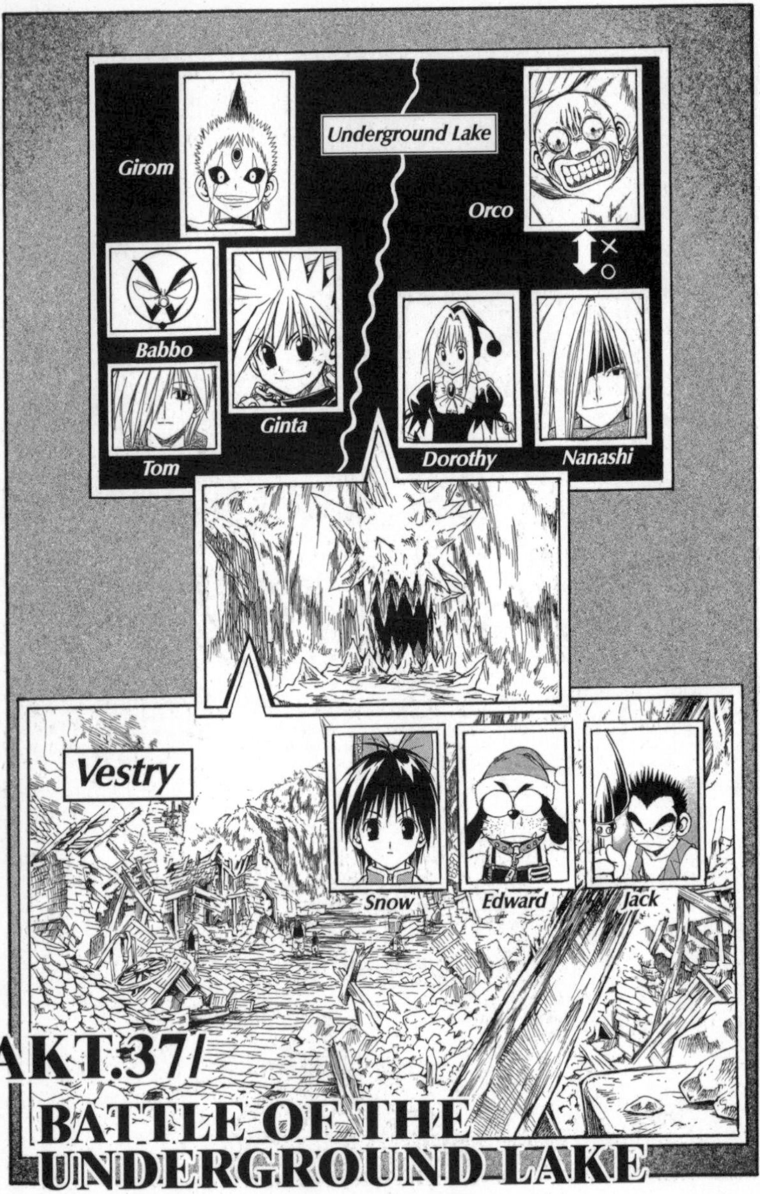
Underground Lake
Orco
Nanashi
Dorothy
Girom
Ginta
Babbo
Tom
Vestry
Jack
Edward
Snow

AKT.37/ BATTLE OF THE UNDERGROUND LAKE ④ Version ③

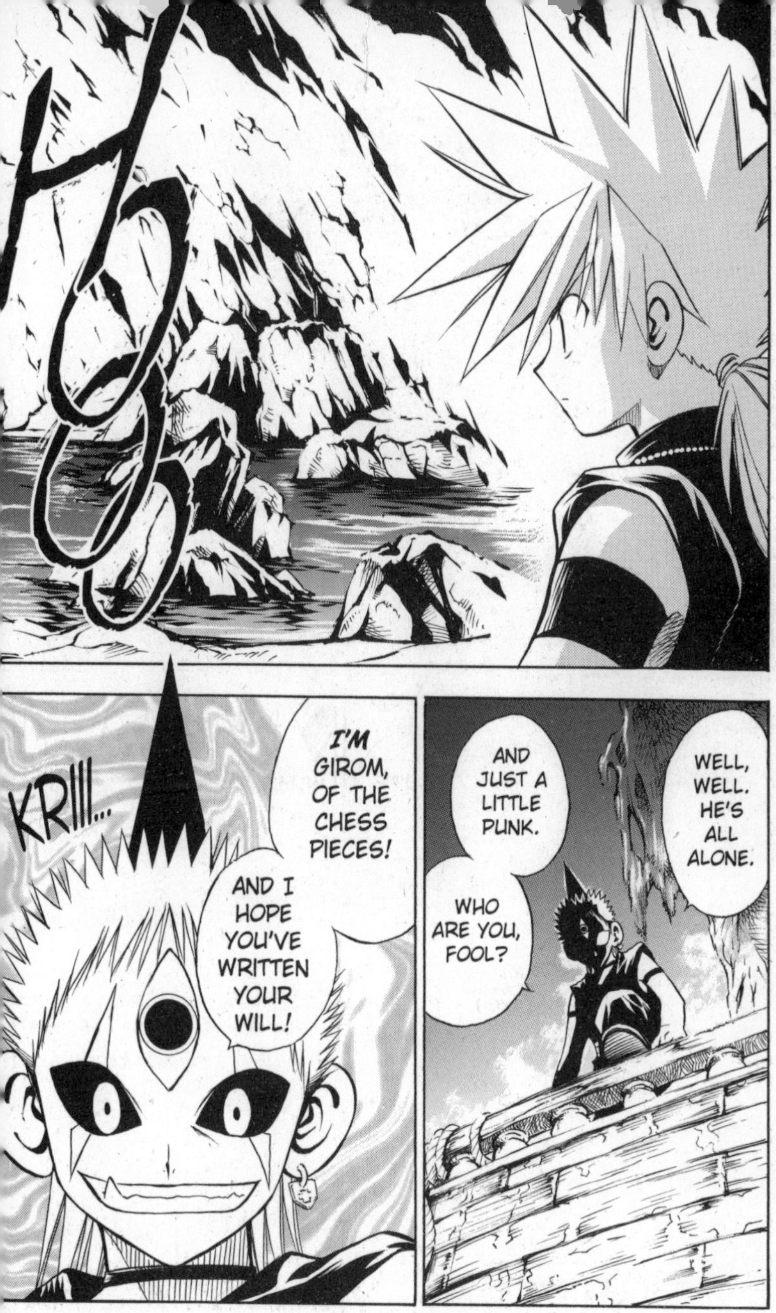
WELL, WELL. HE'S ALL ALONE.
AND JUST A LITTLE PUNK.
WHO ARE YOU, FOOL?
I'M GIROM, OF THE CHESS PIECES!
KRIII...
AND I HOPE YOU'VE WRITTEN YOUR WILL!

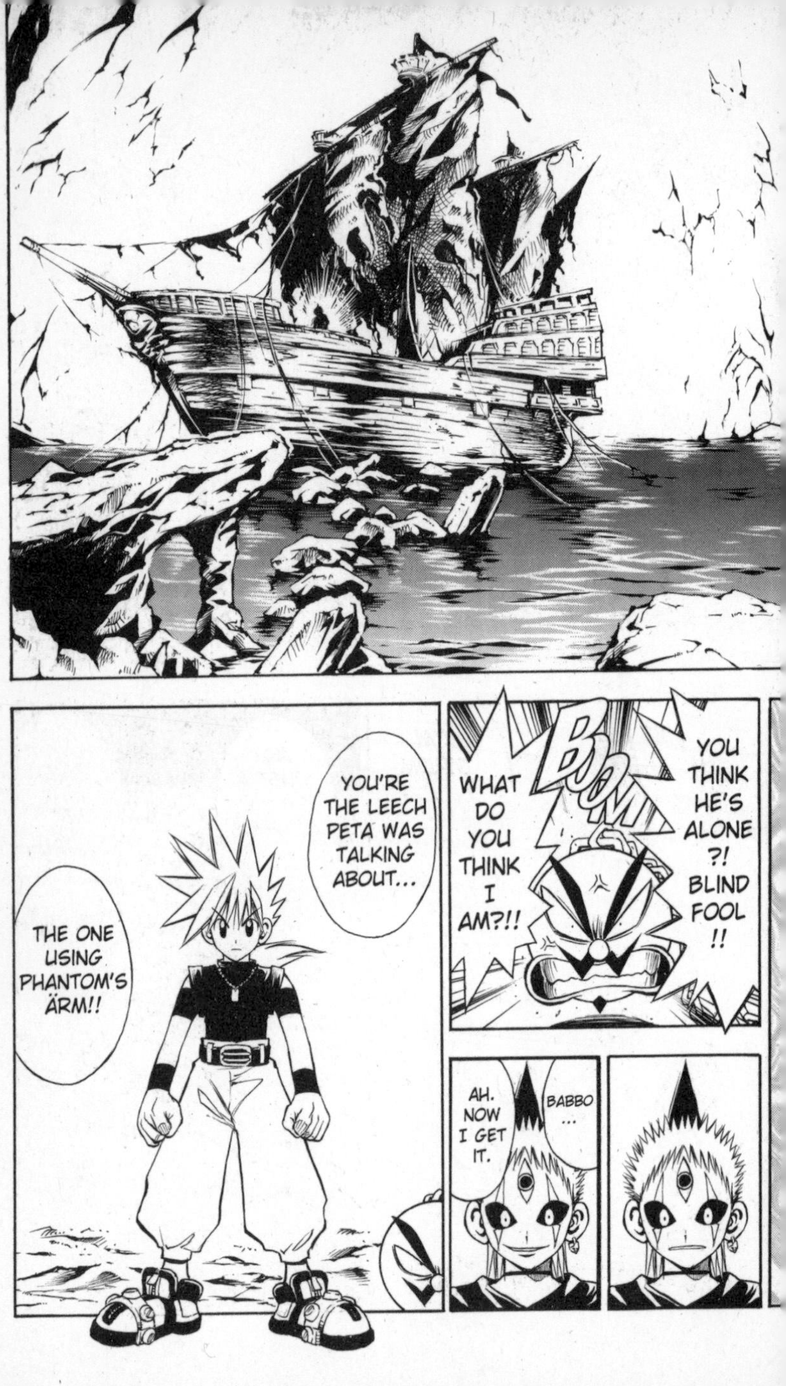
YOU THINK HE'S ALONE ?! BLIND FOOL !!
BOOM
WHAT DO YOU THINK I AM?!!
BABBO ...
AH. NOW I GET IT.
YOU'RE THE LEECH PETA WAS TALKING ABOUT...
THE ONE USING PHANTOM'S ÄRM!!

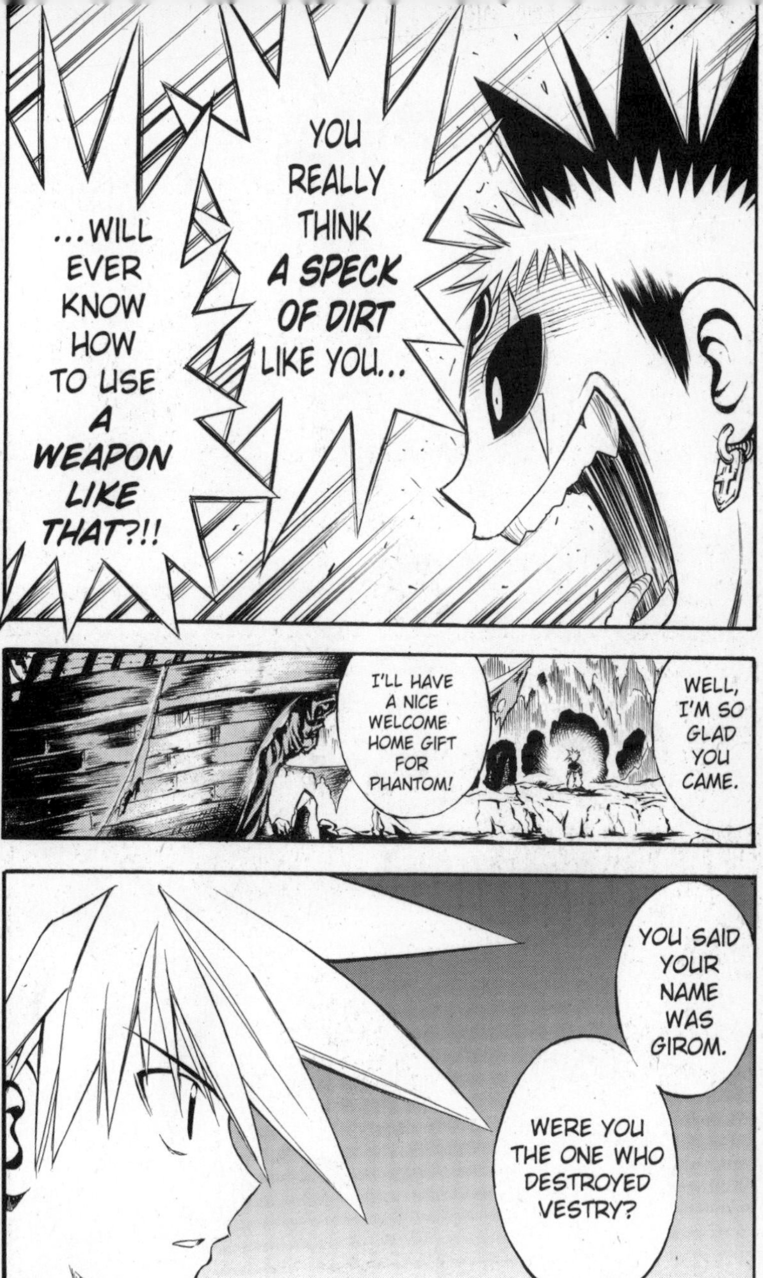
YOU REALLY THINK A SPECK OF DIRT LIKE YOU...
...WILL EVER KNOW HOW TO USE A WEAPON LIKE THAT?!!
WELL, I'M SO GLAD YOU CAME.
I'LL HAVE A NICE WELCOME HOME GIFT FOR PHANTOM!
YOU SAID YOUR NAME WAS GIROM.
WERE YOU THE ONE WHO DESTROYED VESTRY?

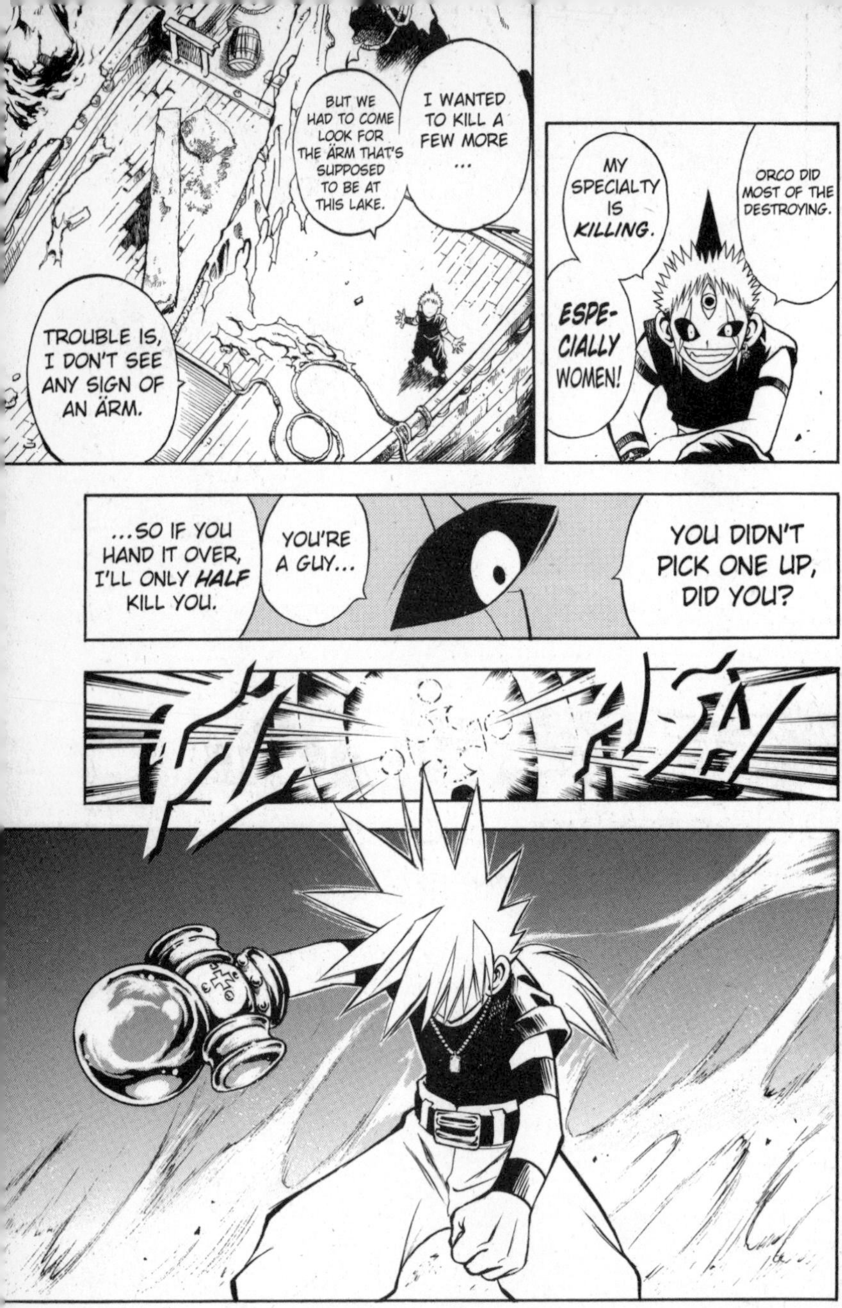
ORCO DID MOST OF THE DESTROYING.
MY SPECIALTY IS KILLING.
ESPECIALLY WOMEN!
I WANTED TO KILL A FEW MORE ...
BUT WE HAD TO COME LOOK FOR THE ÄRM THAT'S SUPPOSED TO BE AT THIS LAKE.
TROUBLE IS, I DON'T SEE ANY SIGN OF AN ÄRM.
YOU DIDN'T PICK ONE UP, DID YOU?
YOU'RE A GUY...
...SO IF YOU HAND IT OVER, I'LL ONLY HALF KILL YOU.

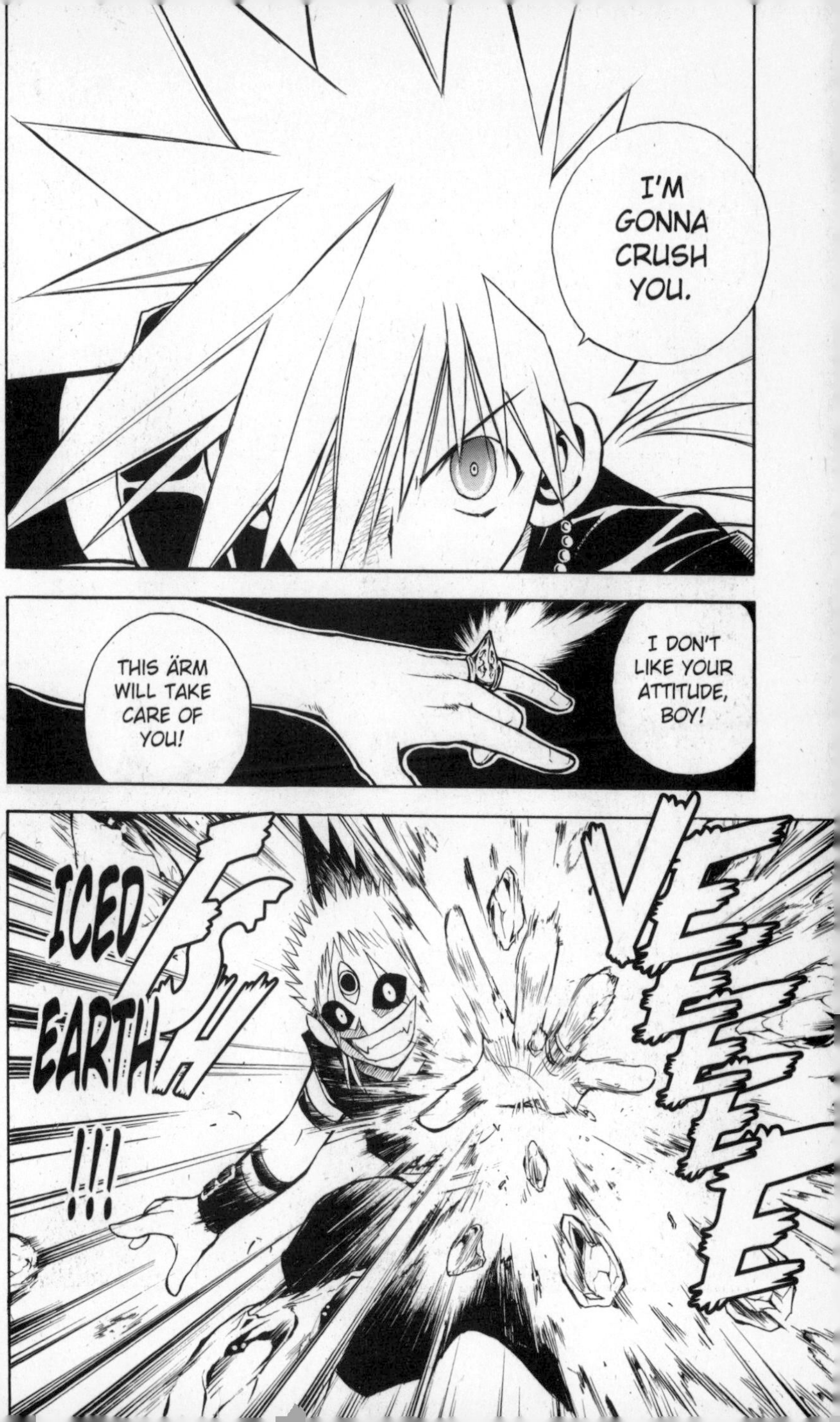
I'M GONNA CRUSH YOU.
I DON'T LIKE YOUR ATTITUDE, BOY!
THIS ÄRM WILL TAKE CARE OF YOU!
ICED EARTH!!!

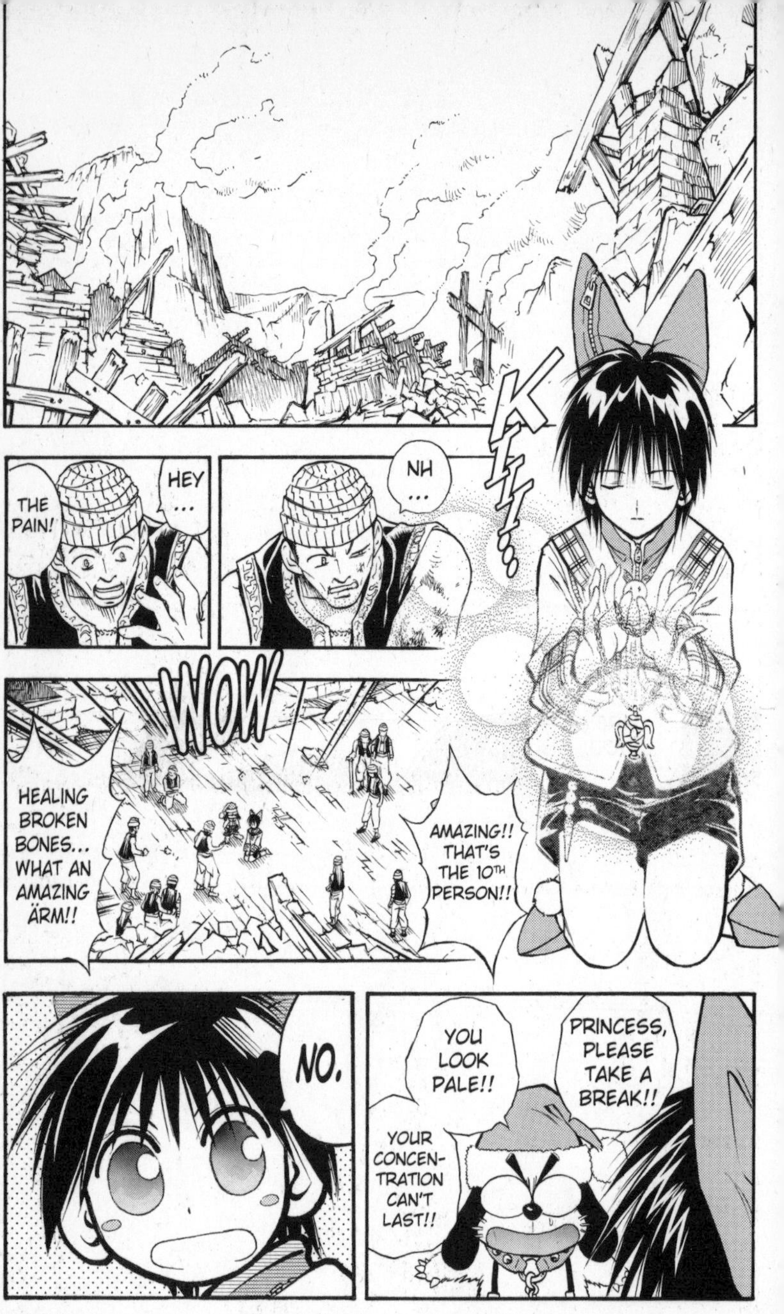
KIII...
NH ...
HEY ...
THE PAIN!
WOW
AMAZING!! THAT'S THE 10TH PERSON!!
HEALING BROKEN BONES... WHAT AN AMAZING ÄRM!!
PRINCESS, PLEASE TAKE A BREAK!!
YOU LOOK PALE!!
YOUR CONCENTRATION CAN'T LAST!!
NO.

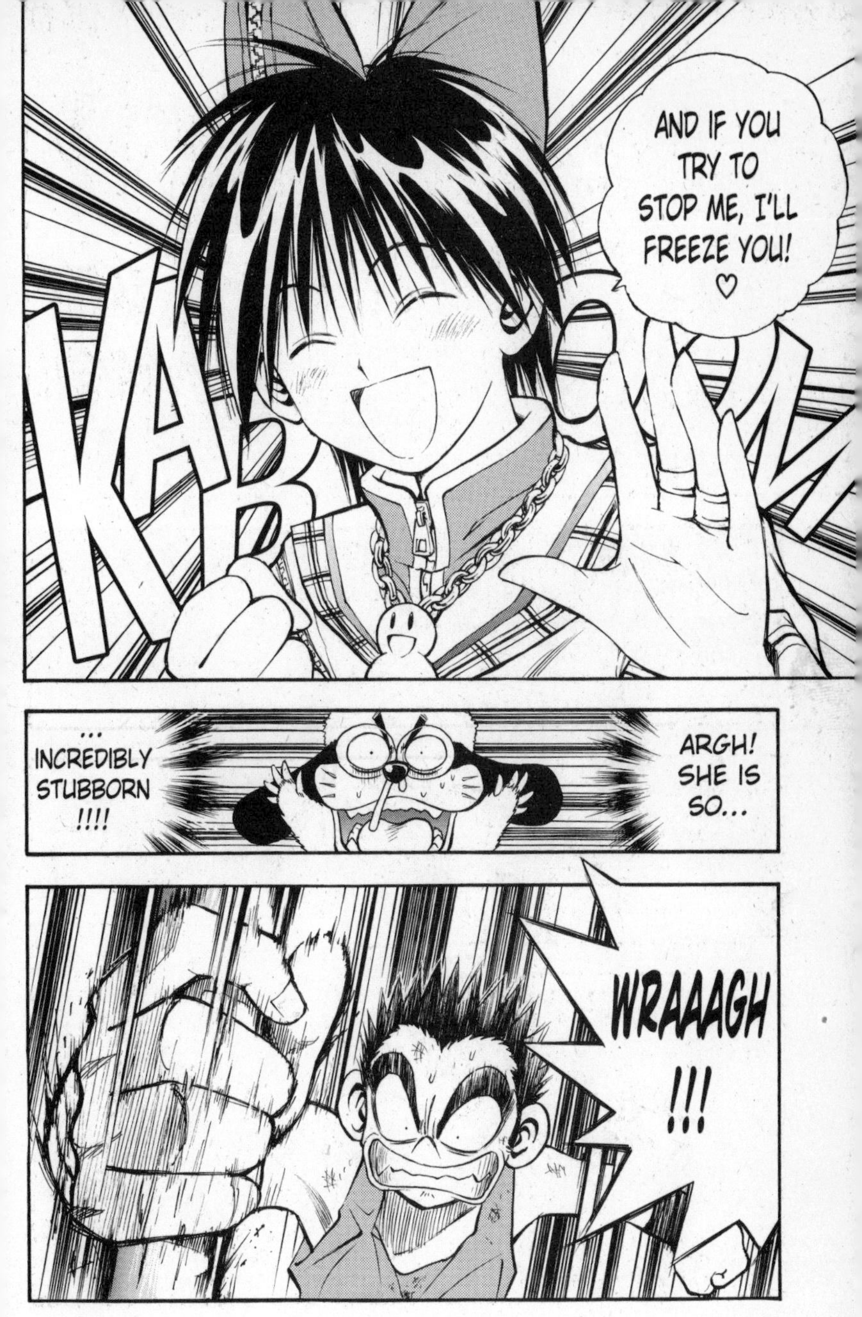
AND IF YOU TRY TO STOP ME, I'LL FREEZE YOU! ♡
ARGH! SHE IS SO...
... INCREDIBLY STUBBORN !!!!
WRAAAGH !!!

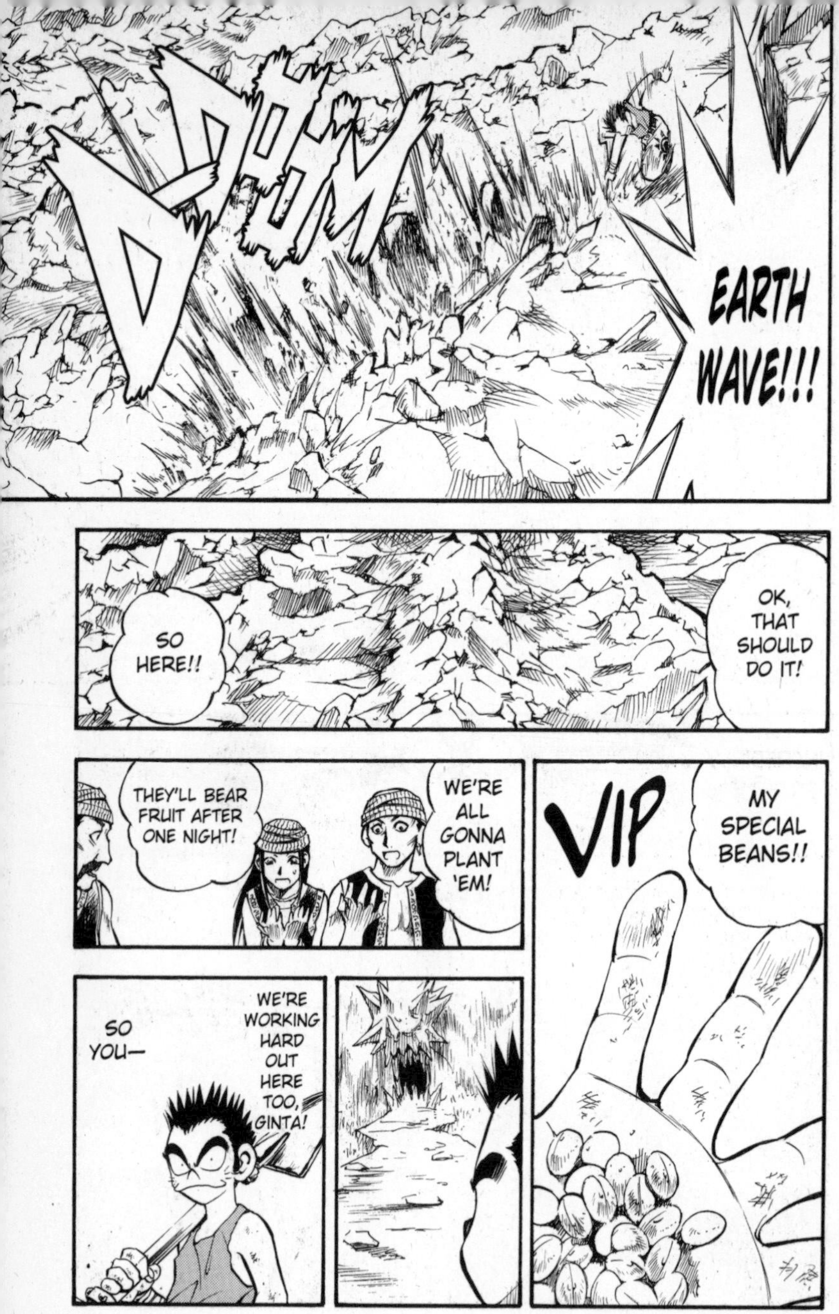
EARTH WAVE!!!
DOHM
OK, THAT SHOULD DO IT!
SO HERE!!
VIP
MY SPECIAL BEANS!!
WE'RE ALL GONNA PLANT 'EM!
THEY'LL BEAR FRUIT AFTER ONE NIGHT!
WE'RE WORKING HARD OUT HERE TOO, GINTA!
SO YOU—

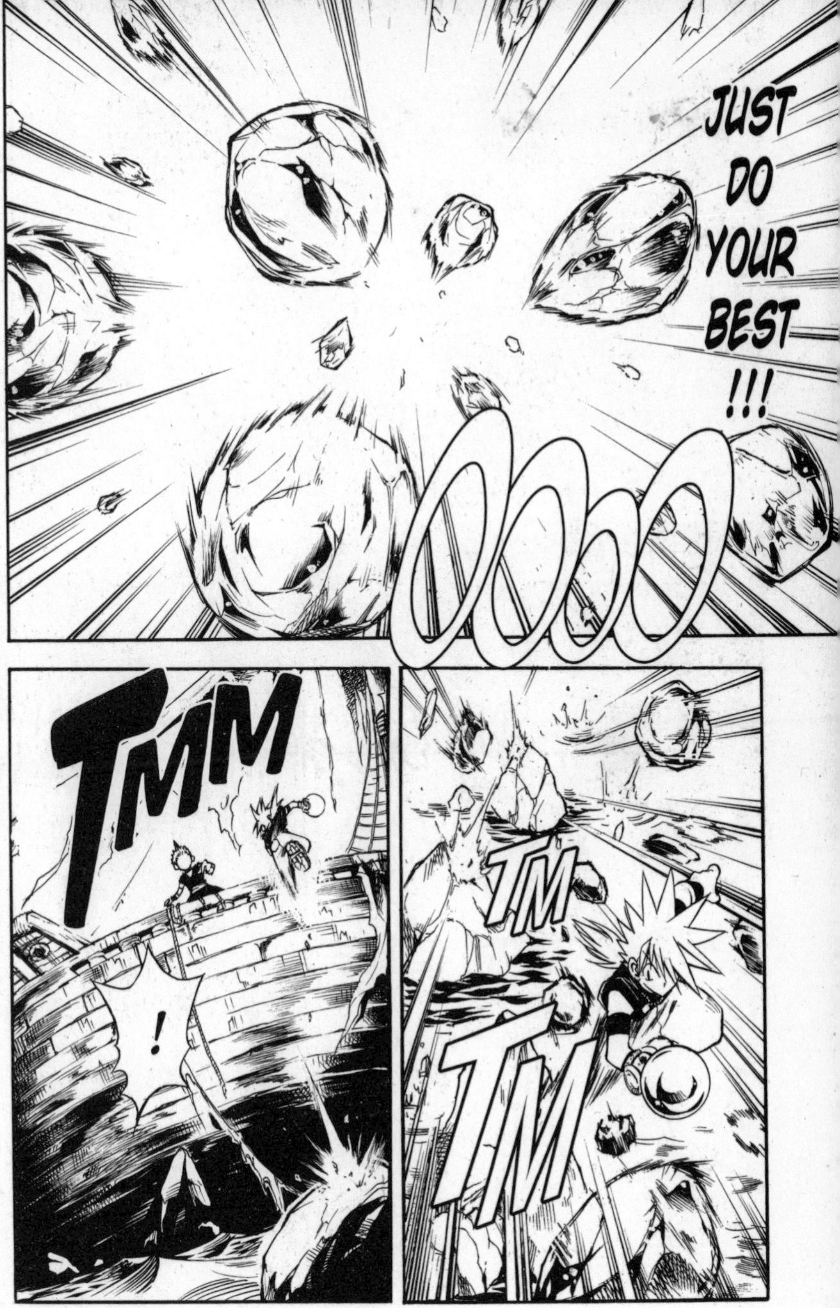
JUST DO YOUR BEST!!!
TM
TM
TMM
!

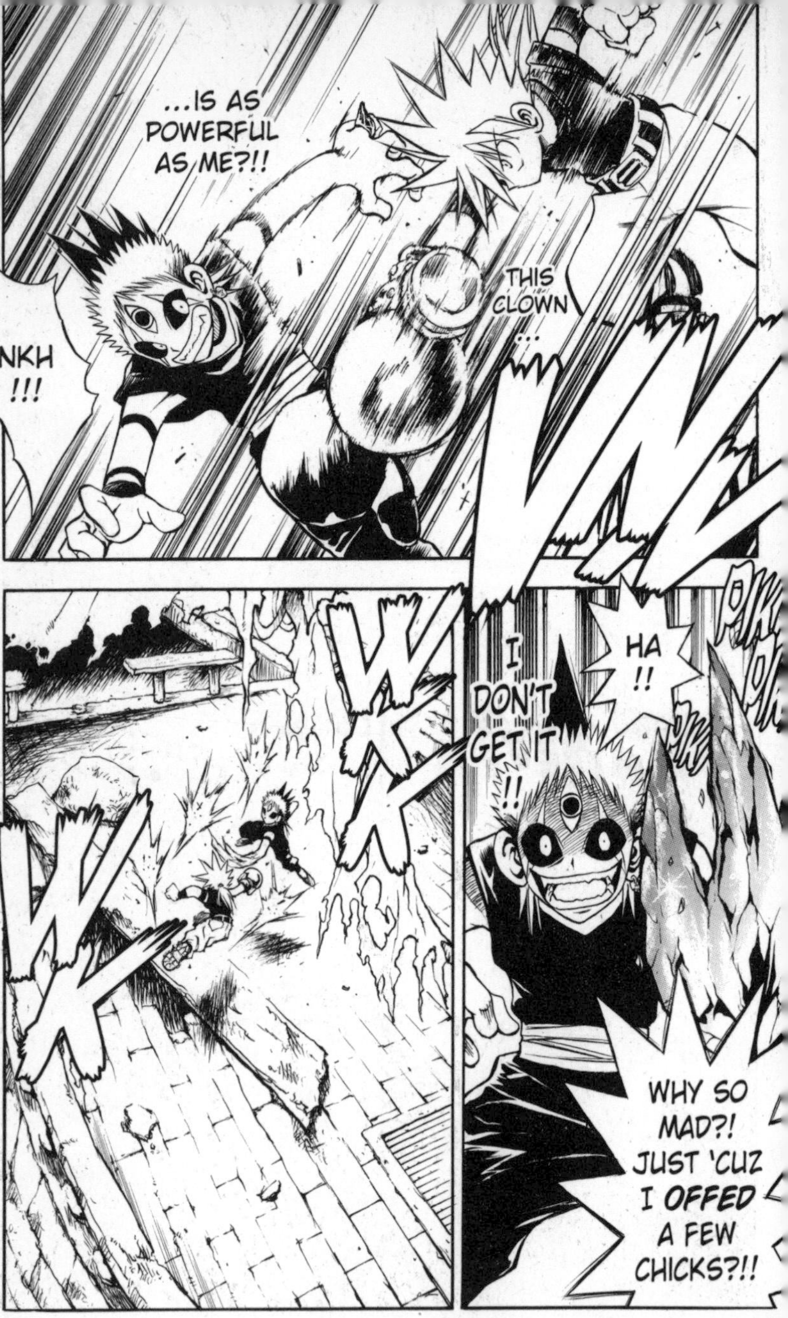
THIS CLOWN...
...IS AS POWERFUL AS ME?!!
NKH!!!
HA!!
I DON'T GET IT!!
WHY SO MAD?! JUST 'CUZ I OFFED A FEW CHICKS?!!

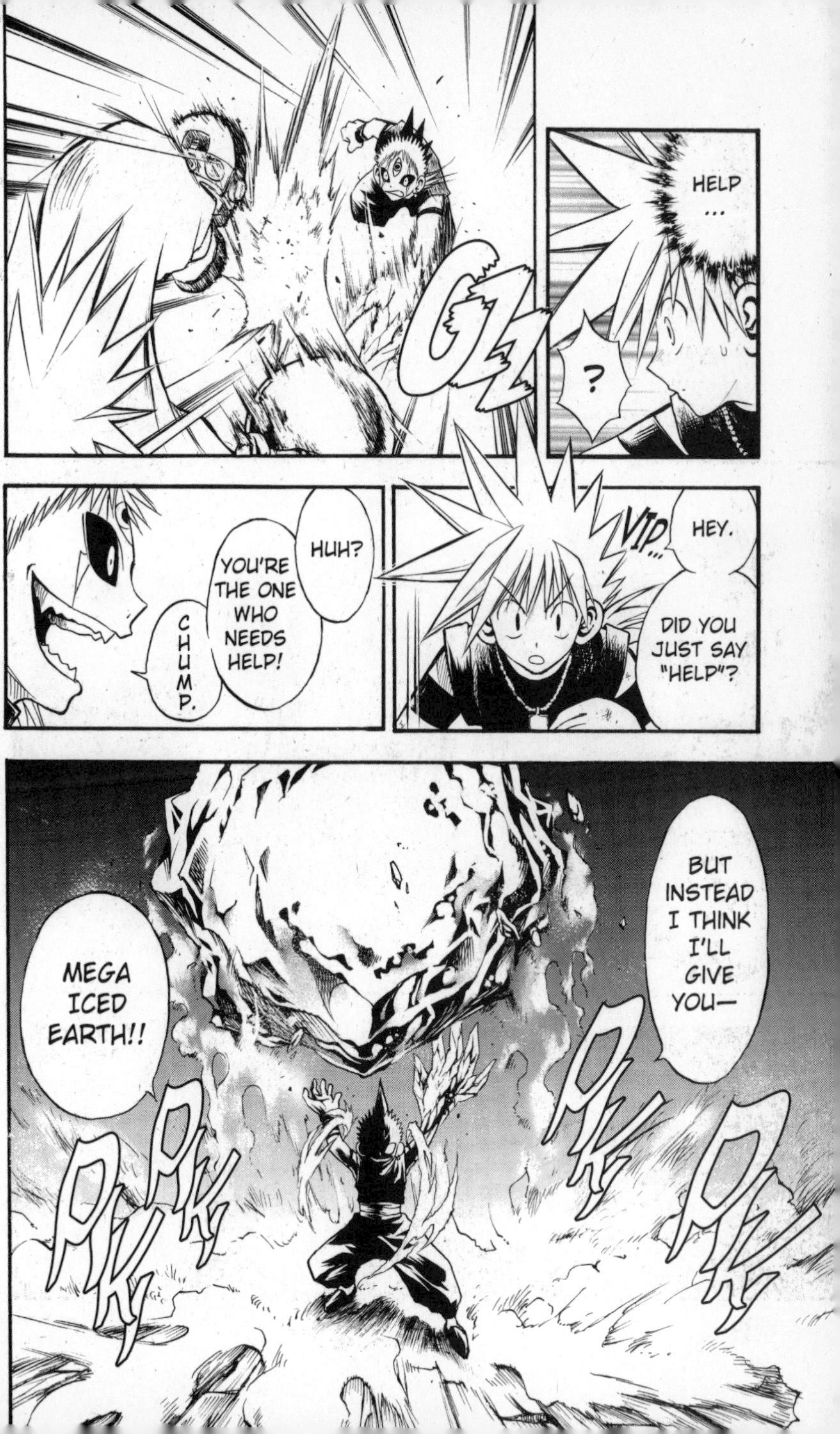
HELP ...
?
GL
VIP...
HEY.
DID YOU JUST SAY "HELP"?
HUH?
YOU'RE THE ONE WHO NEEDS HELP!
CHUMP.
BUT INSTEAD I THINK I'LL GIVE YOU—
MEGA ICED EARTH!!

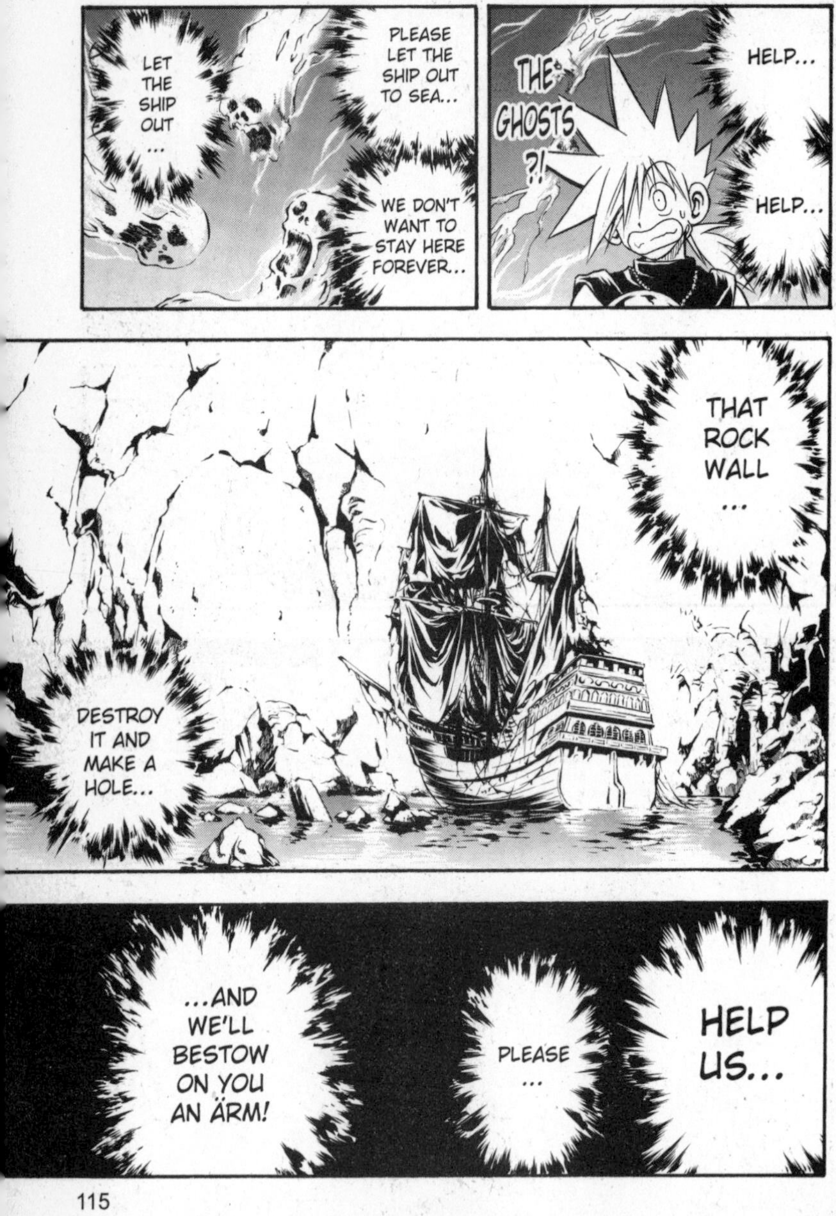
HELP...
THE GHOSTS ?!
HELP...
PLEASE LET THE SHIP OUT TO SEA...
LET THE SHIP OUT ...
WE DON'T WANT TO STAY HERE FOREVER...
THAT ROCK WALL ...
DESTROY IT AND MAKE A HOLE...
HELP US...
PLEASE ...
...AND WE'LL BESTOW ON YOU AN ÄRM!

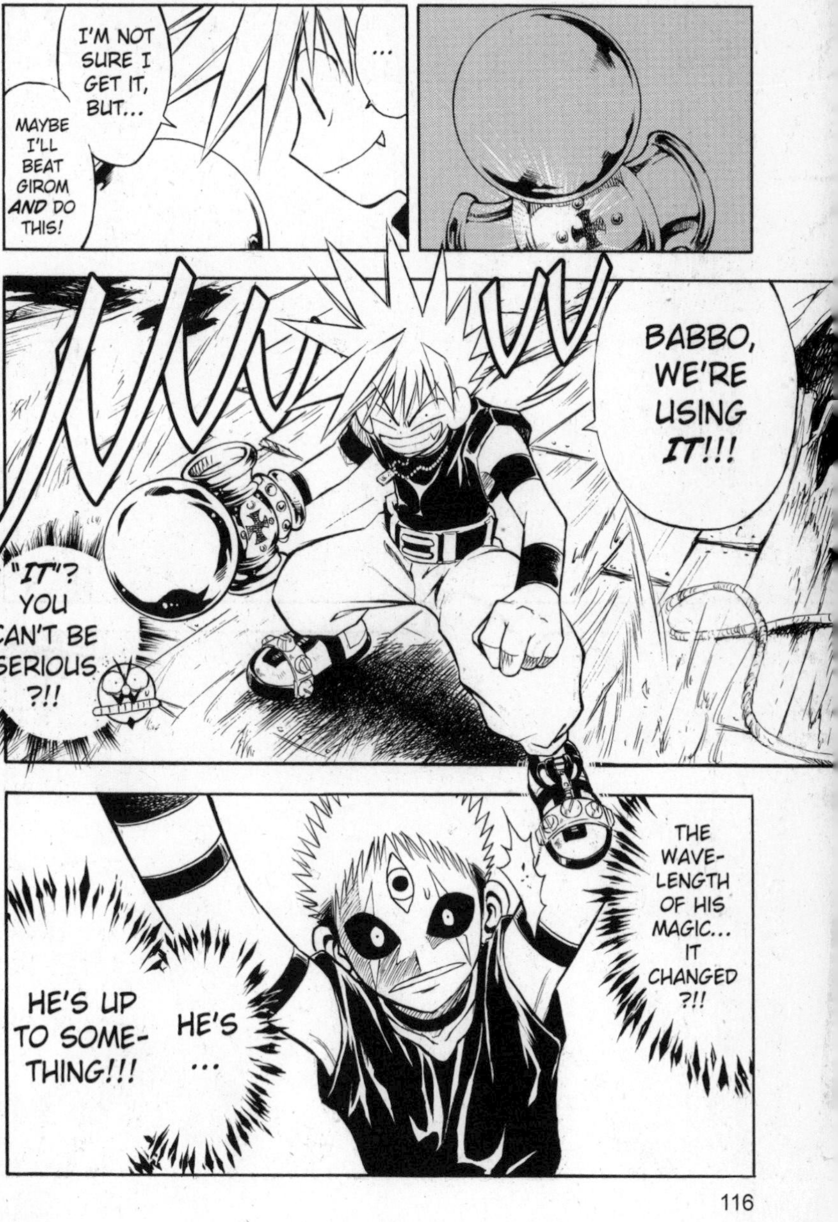
...
I'M NOT SURE I GET IT, BUT...
MAYBE I'LL BEAT GIROM AND DO THIS!
BABBO, WE'RE USING IT!!!
"IT"? YOU CAN'T BE SERIOUS?!!
THE WAVELENGTH OF HIS MAGIC... IT CHANGED?!!
HE'S...
HE'S UP TO SOMETHING!!!

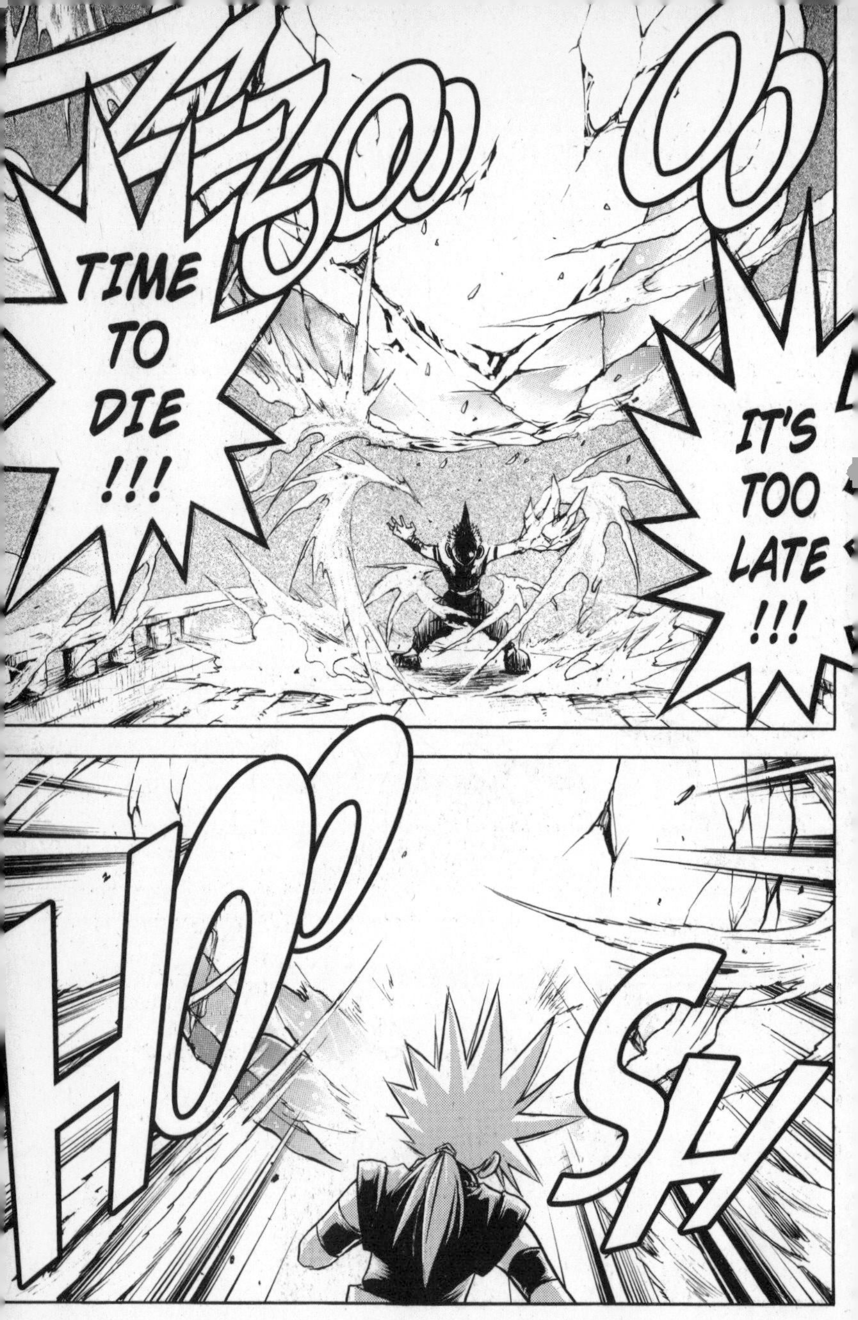
IT'S TOO LATE!!!
TIME TO DIE!!!
HOOSH

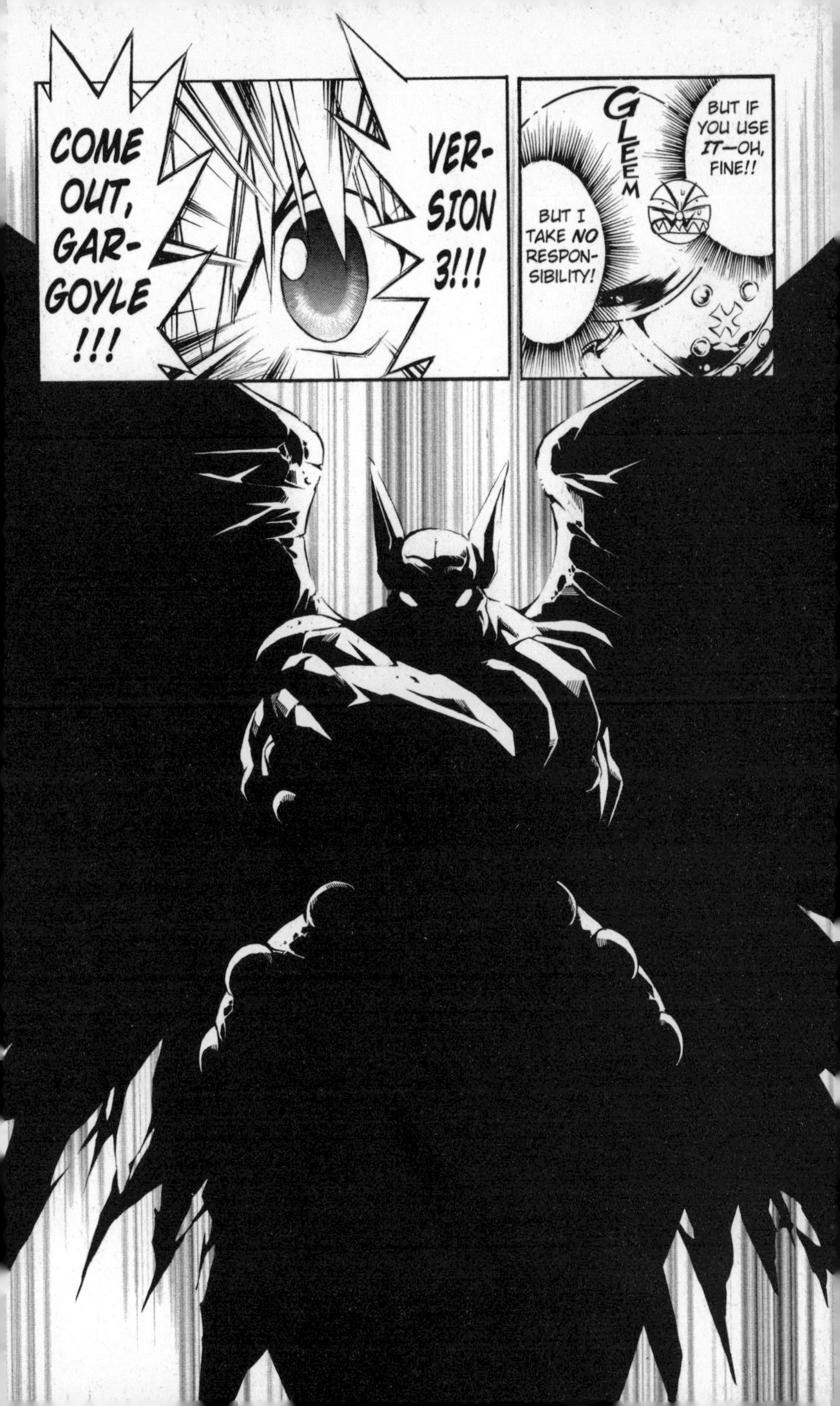
GLEEM
BUT IF YOU USE IT—OH, FINE!!
BUT I TAKE NO RESPONSIBILITY!
VERSION 3!!!
COME OUT, GARGOYLE!!!

AKT.38/ BATTLE OF THE UNDERGROUND LAKE ⑤Gargoyle

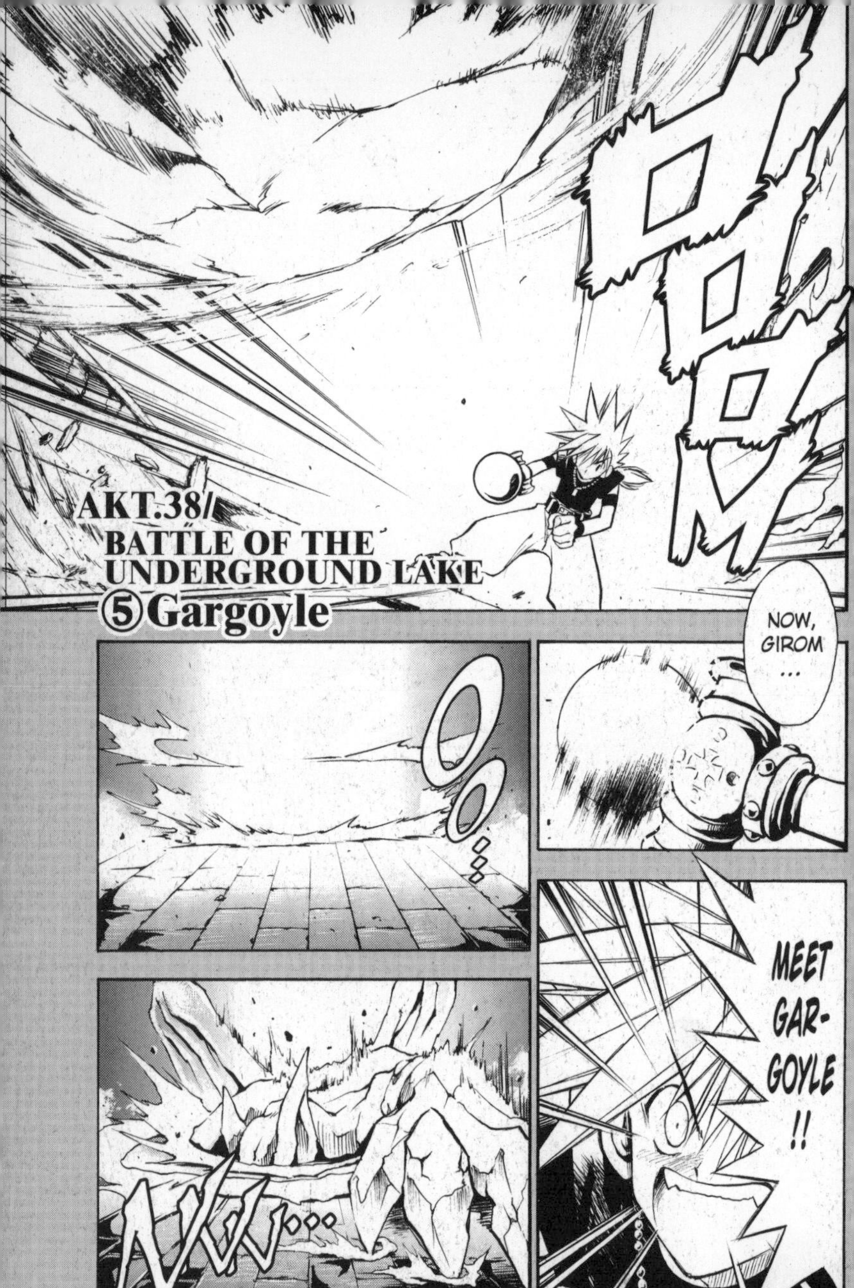
NOW, GIROM ...
MEET GAR-GOYLE !!

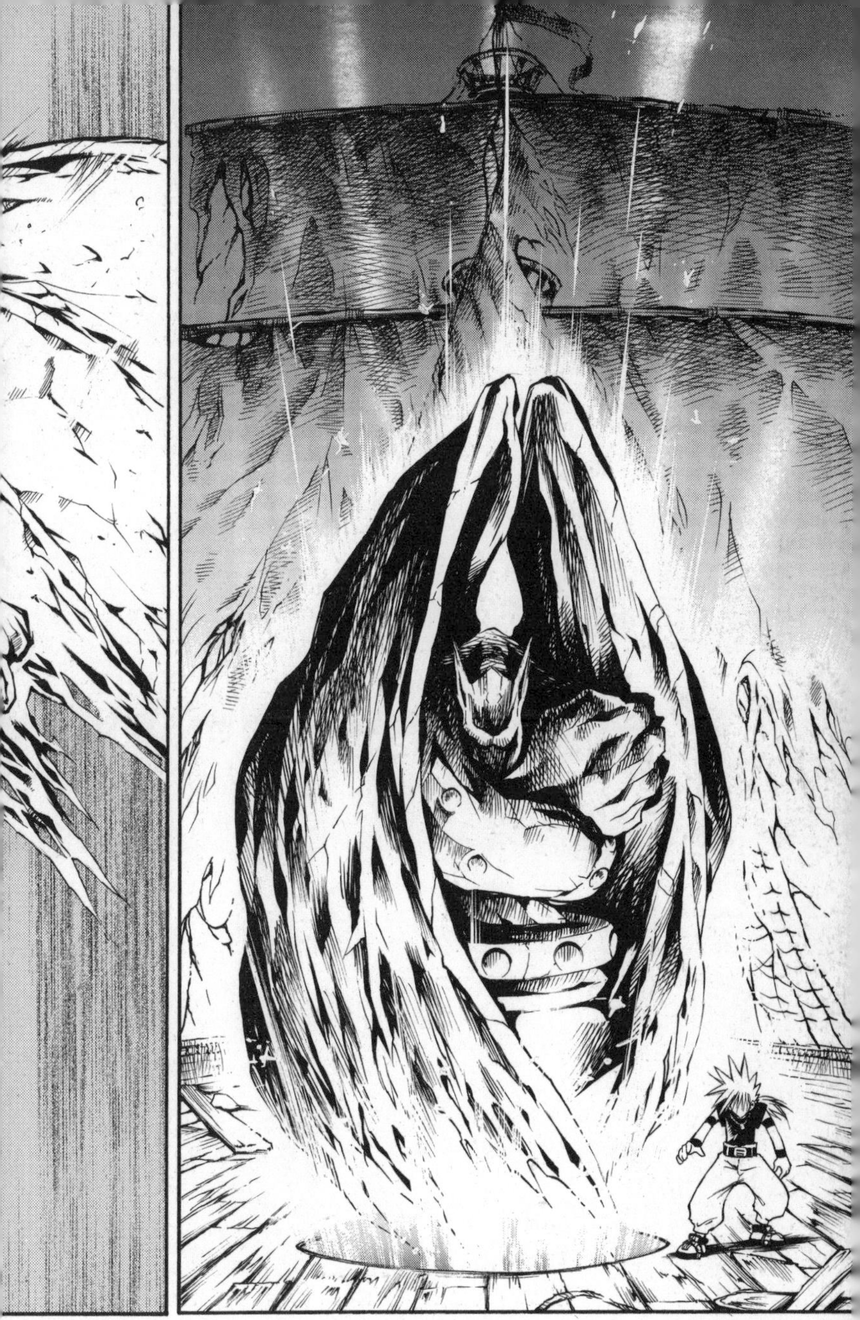

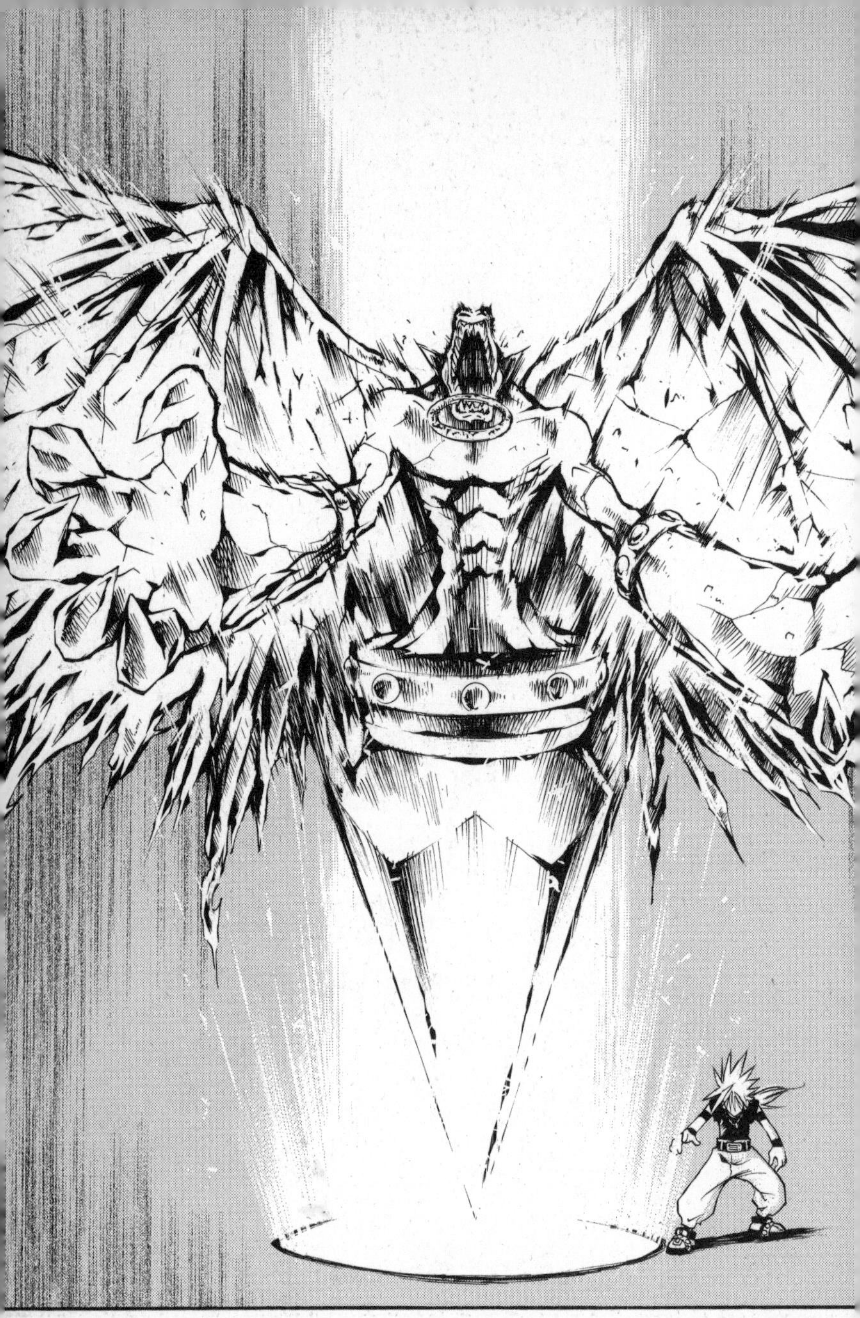

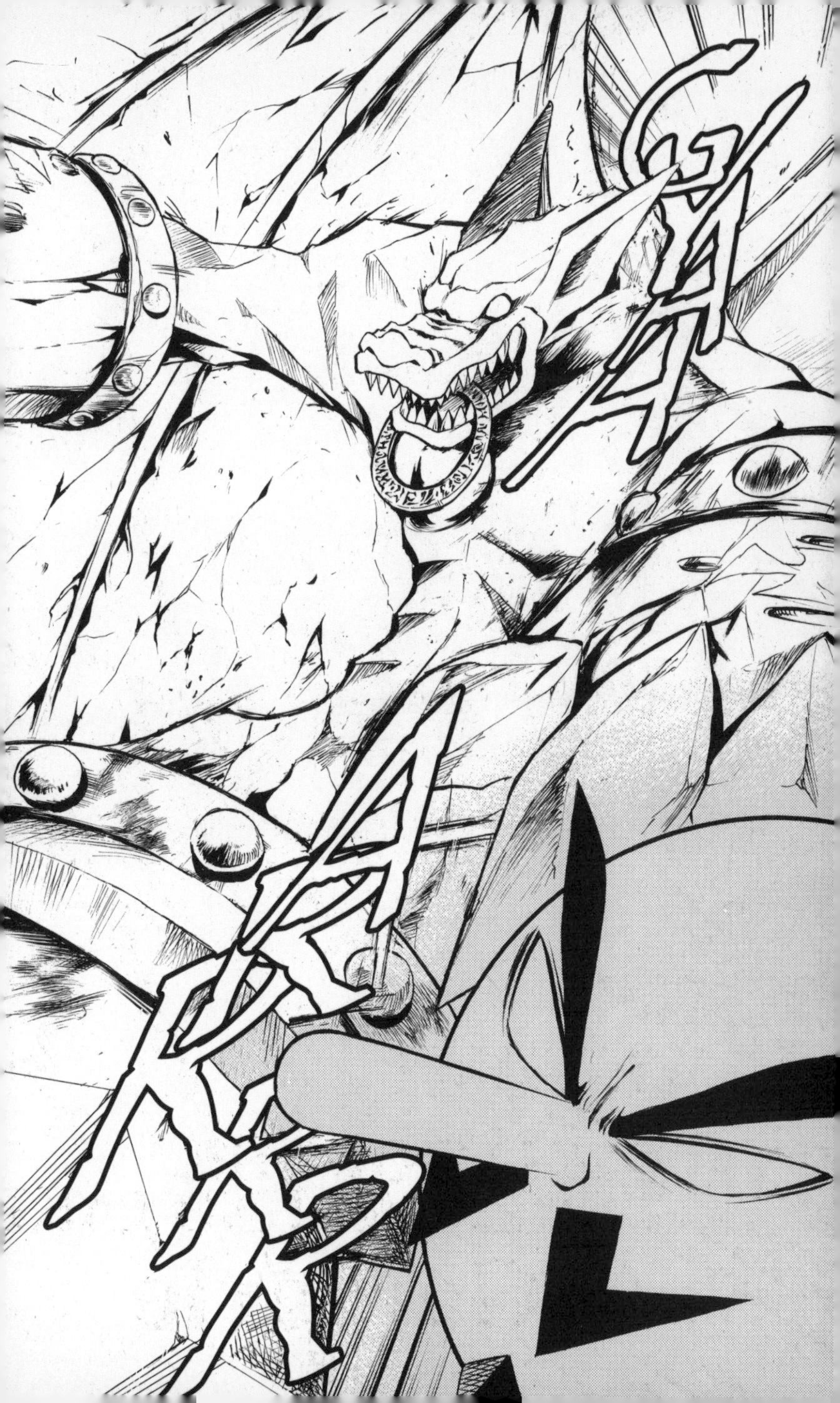

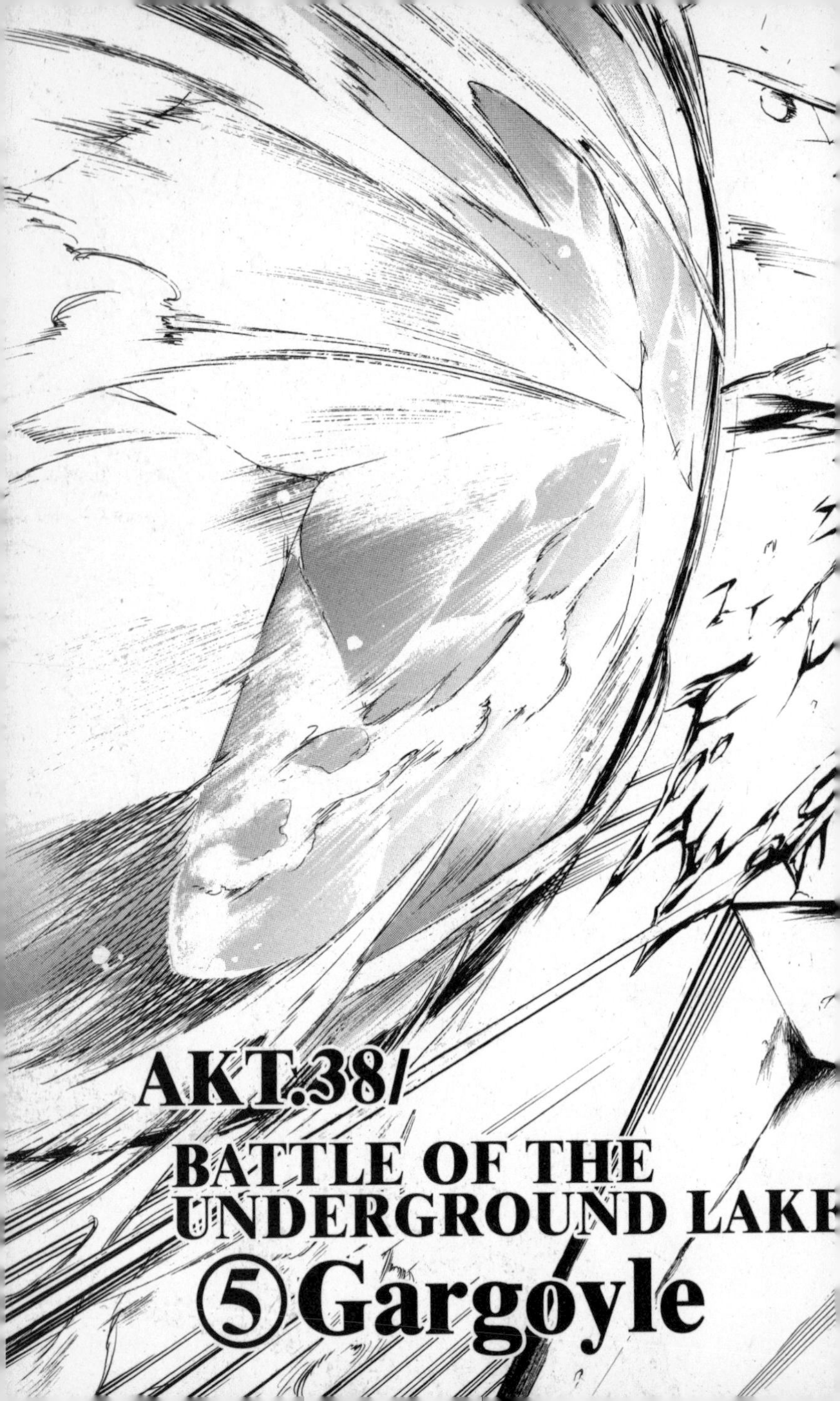
AKT.38/
BATTLE OF THE UNDERGROUND LAKE
⑤Gargoyle

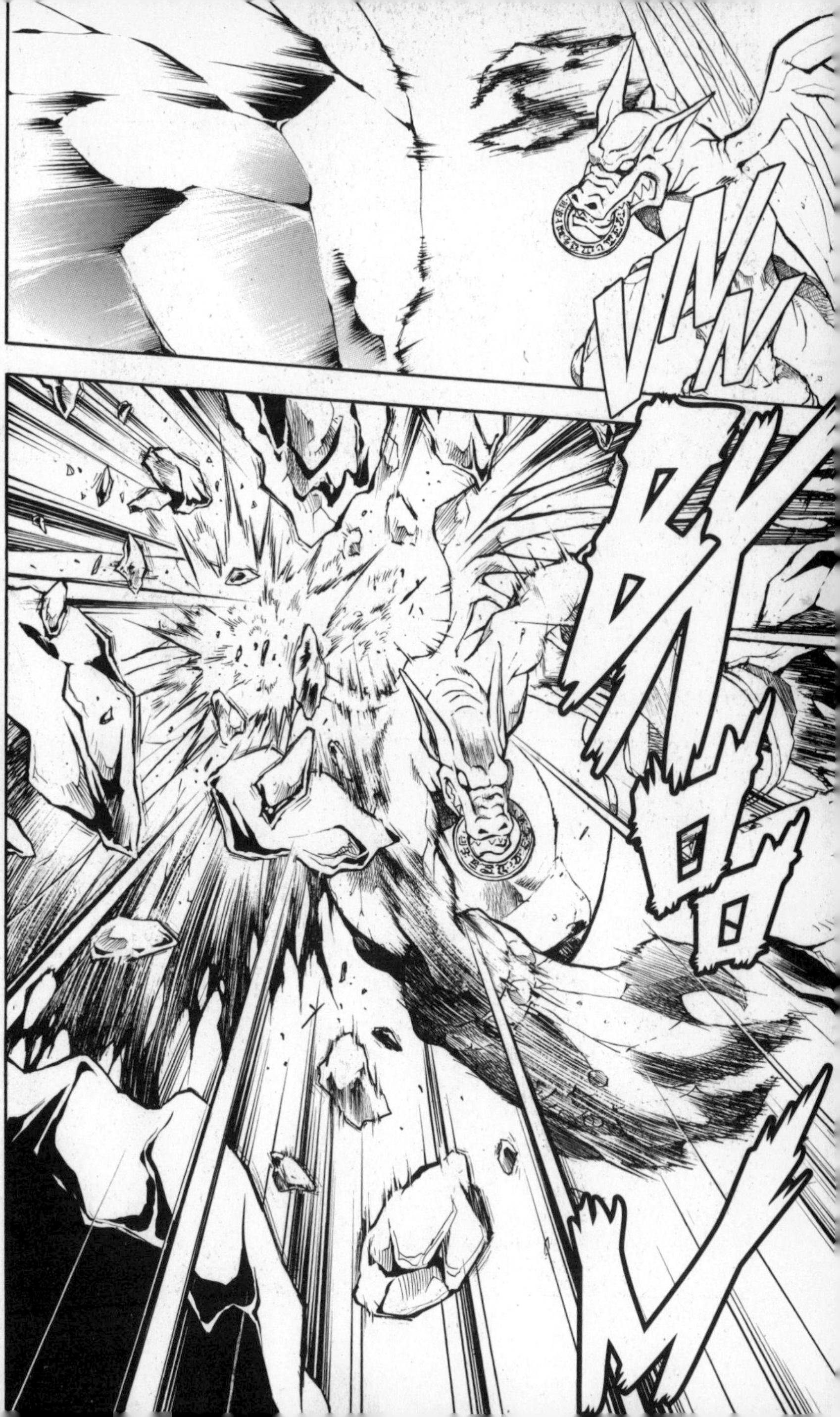

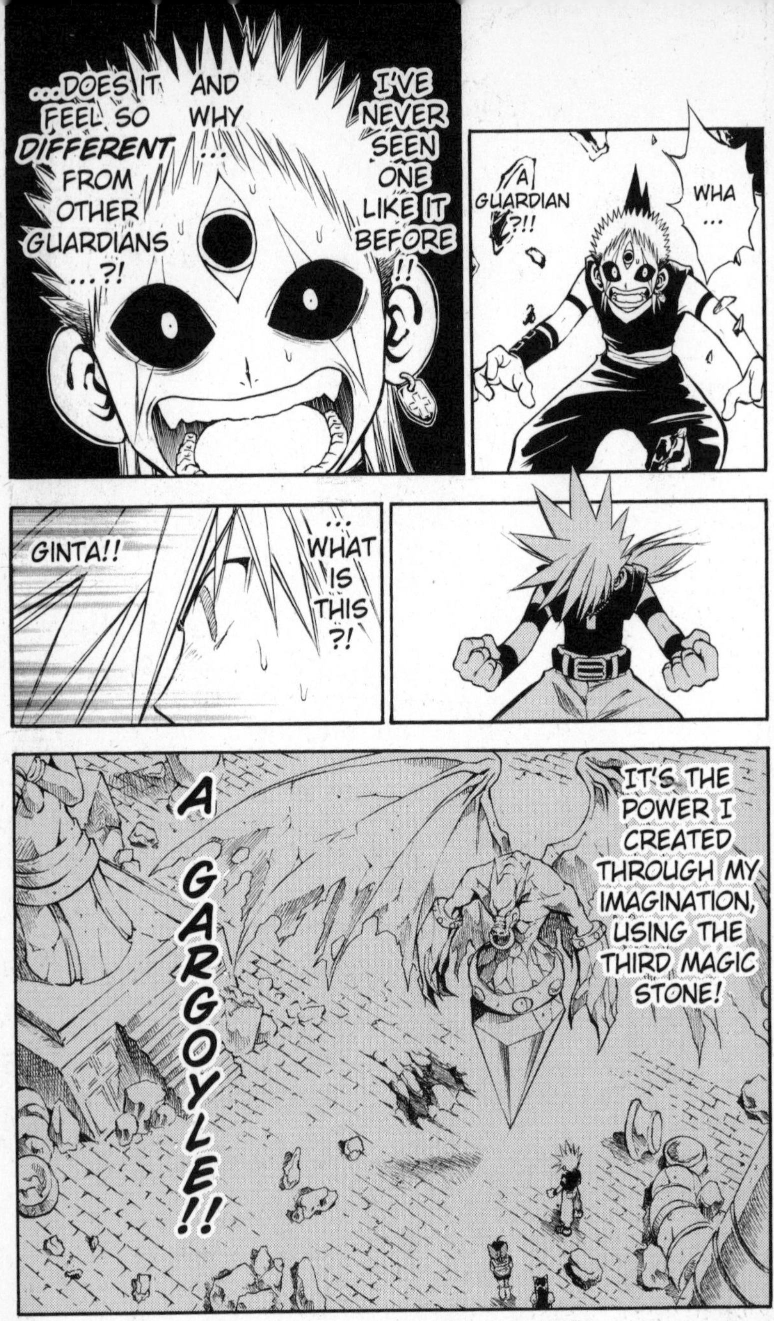
WHA...
A GUARDIAN?!!
I'VE NEVER SEEN ONE LIKE IT BEFORE!!
AND WHY...
...DOES IT FEEL SO DIFFERENT FROM OTHER GUARDIANS...?!
...WHAT IS THIS?!
GINTA!!
IT'S THE POWER I CREATED THROUGH MY IMAGINATION, USING THE THIRD MAGIC STONE!
A GARGOYLE!!

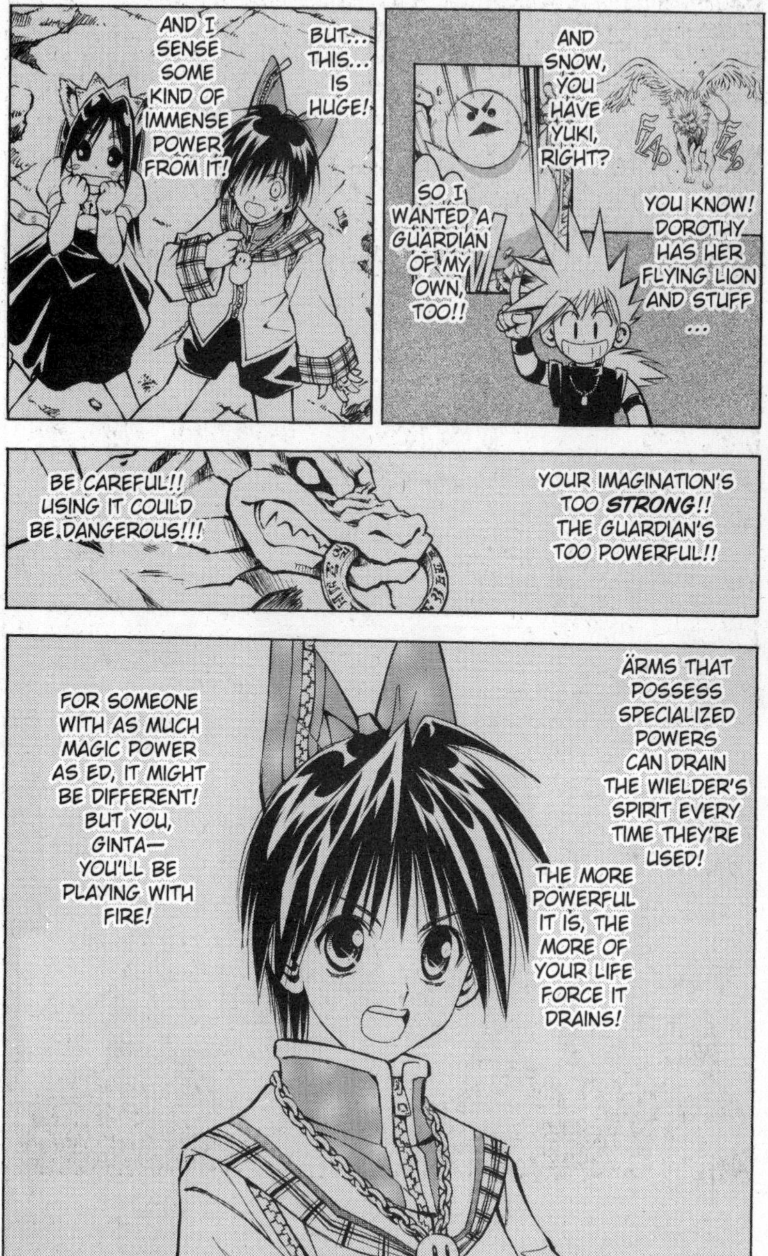
YOU KNOW! DOROTHY HAS HER FLYING LION AND STUFF...
FLAP FLAP
AND SNOW, YOU HAVE YUKI, RIGHT?
SO I WANTED A GUARDIAN OF MY OWN, TOO!!
BUT... THIS... IS HUGE!
AND I SENSE SOME KIND OF IMMENSE POWER FROM IT!
YOUR IMAGINATION'S TOO STRONG!! THE GUARDIAN'S TOO POWERFUL!!
BE CAREFUL!! USING IT COULD BE DANGEROUS!!!
ÄRMS THAT POSSESS SPECIALIZED POWERS CAN DRAIN THE WIELDER'S SPIRIT EVERY TIME THEY'RE USED!
THE MORE POWERFUL IT IS, THE MORE OF YOUR LIFE FORCE IT DRAINS!
FOR SOMEONE WITH AS MUCH MAGIC POWER AS ED, IT MIGHT BE DIFFERENT! BUT YOU, GINTA— YOU'LL BE PLAYING WITH FIRE!

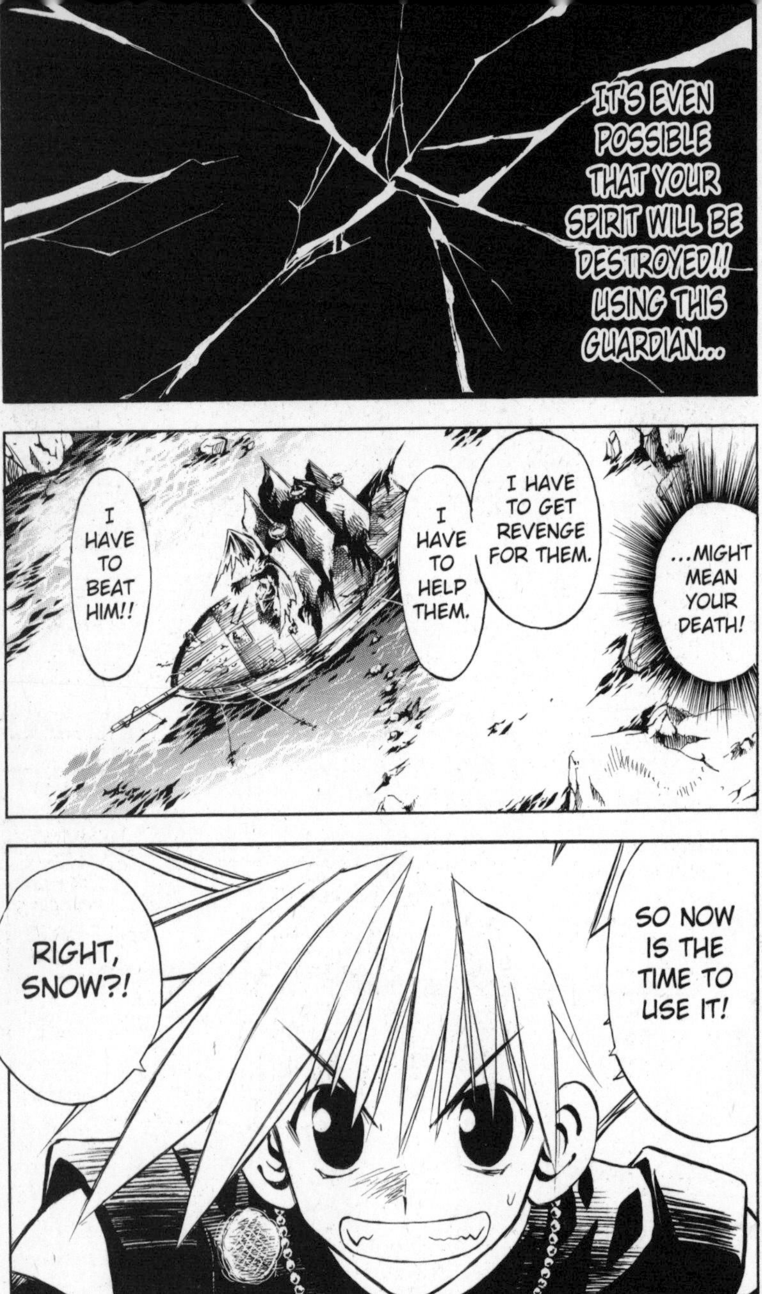
IT'S EVEN POSSIBLE THAT YOUR SPIRIT WILL BE DESTROYED!! USING THIS GUARDIAN...
...MIGHT MEAN YOUR DEATH!
I HAVE TO GET REVENGE FOR THEM.
I HAVE TO HELP THEM.
I HAVE TO BEAT HIM!!
SO NOW IS THE TIME TO USE IT!
RIGHT, SNOW?!

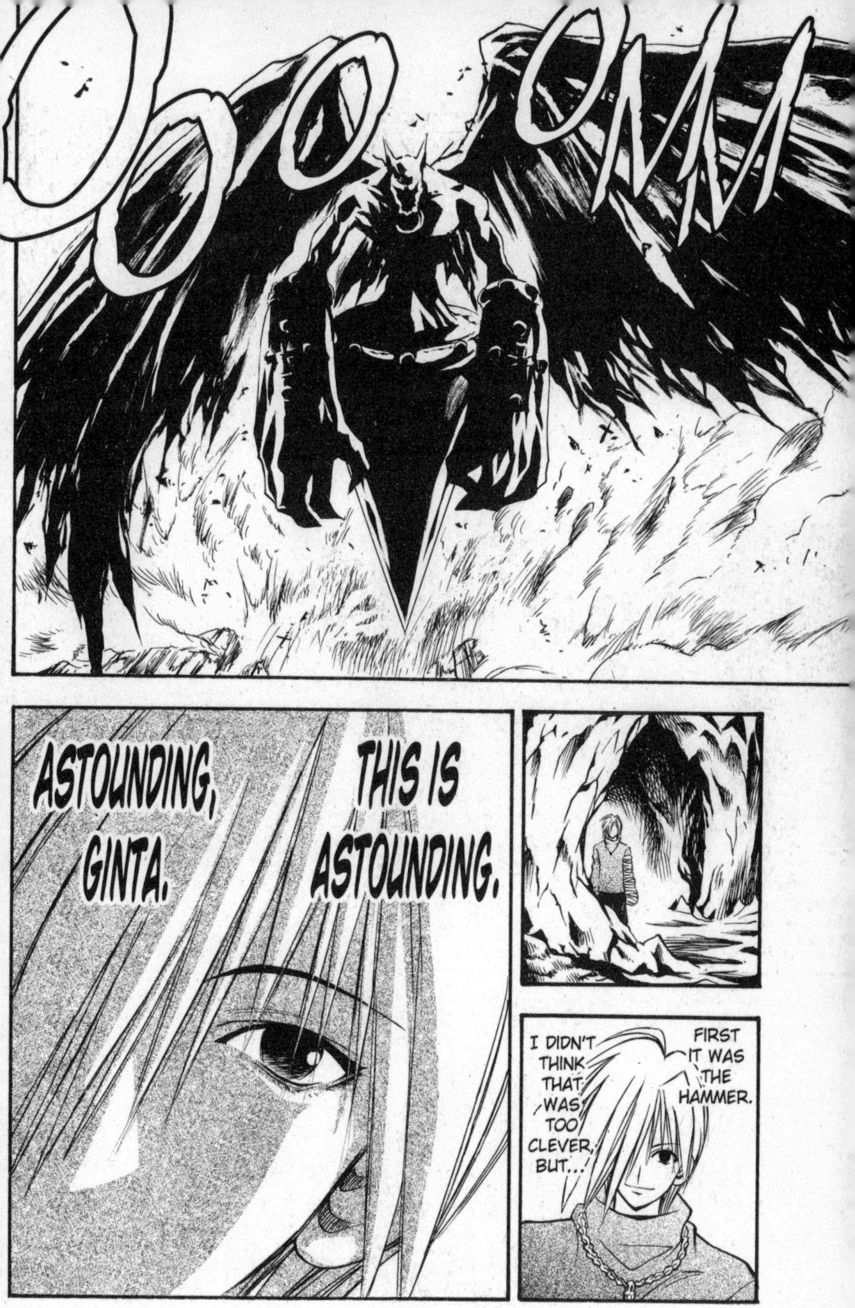
OOOOMM
FIRST IT WAS THE HAMMER.
I DIDN'T THINK THAT WAS TOO CLEVER, BUT...
THIS IS ASTOUNDING.
ASTOUNDING, GINTA.

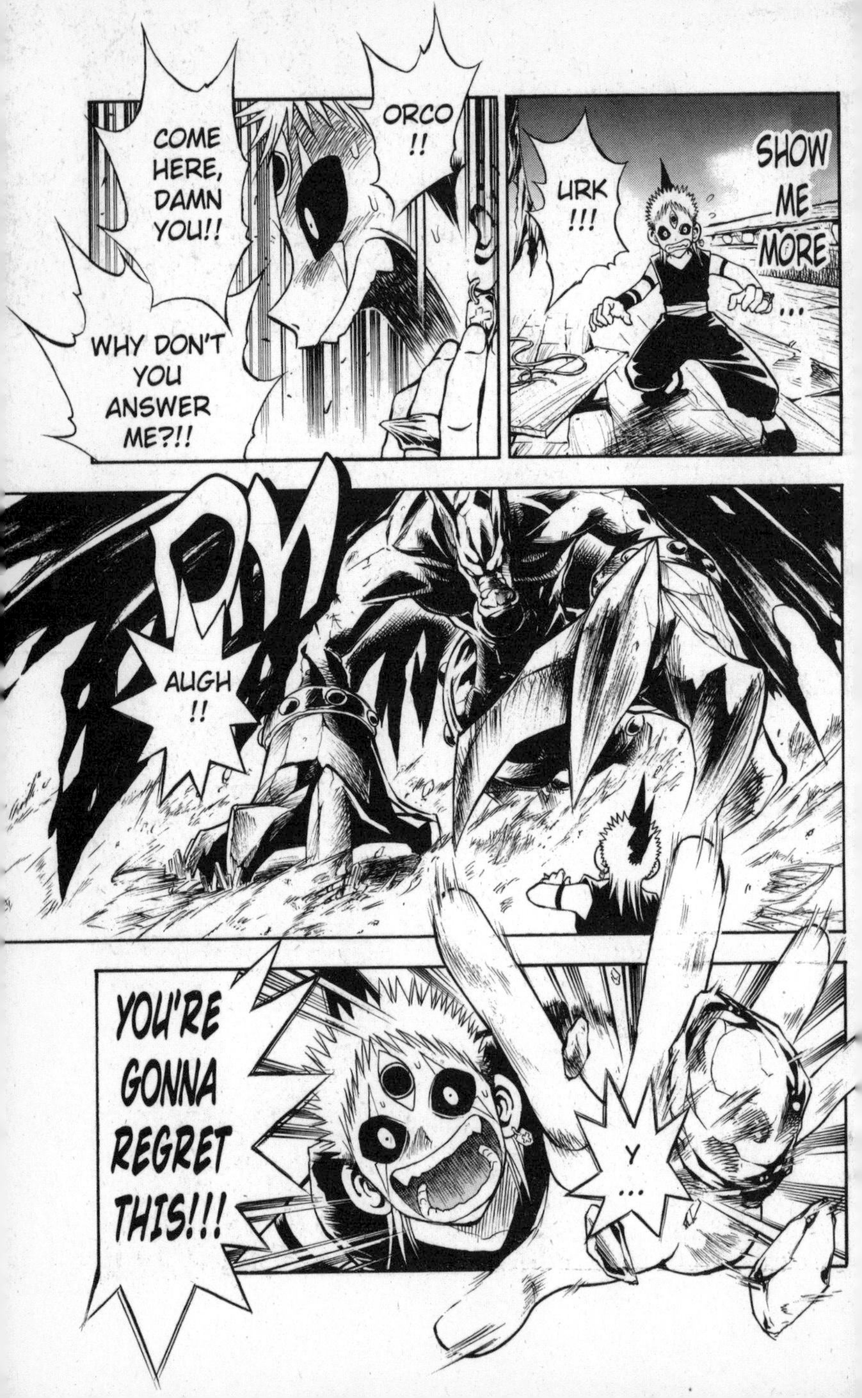
SHOW ME MORE...
URK!!!
ORCO!!
COME HERE, DAMN YOU!!
WHY DON'T YOU ANSWER ME?!!
AUGH!!
Y...
YOU'RE GONNA REGRET THIS!!!

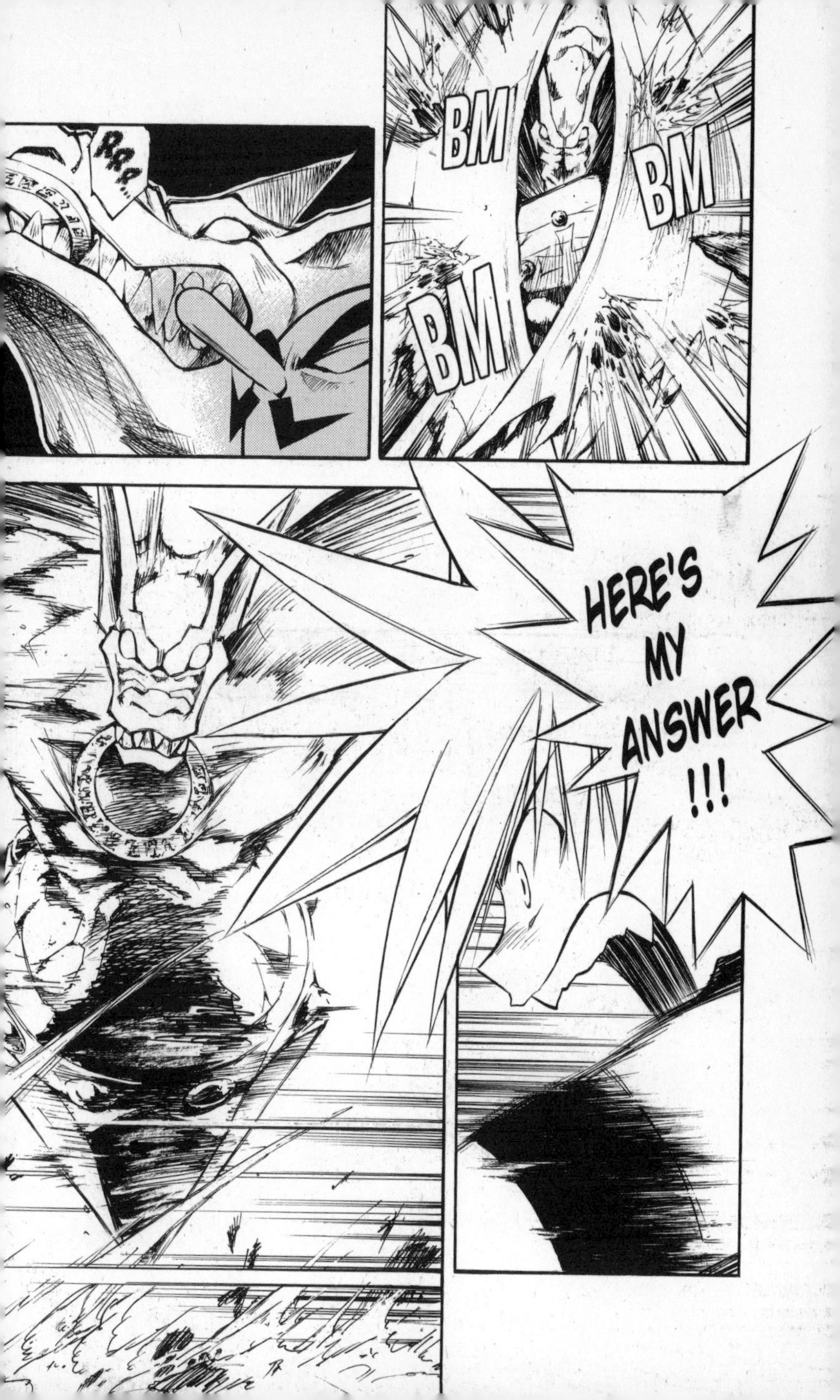
BM
BM
BM
RRR...
HERE'S MY ANSWER!!!

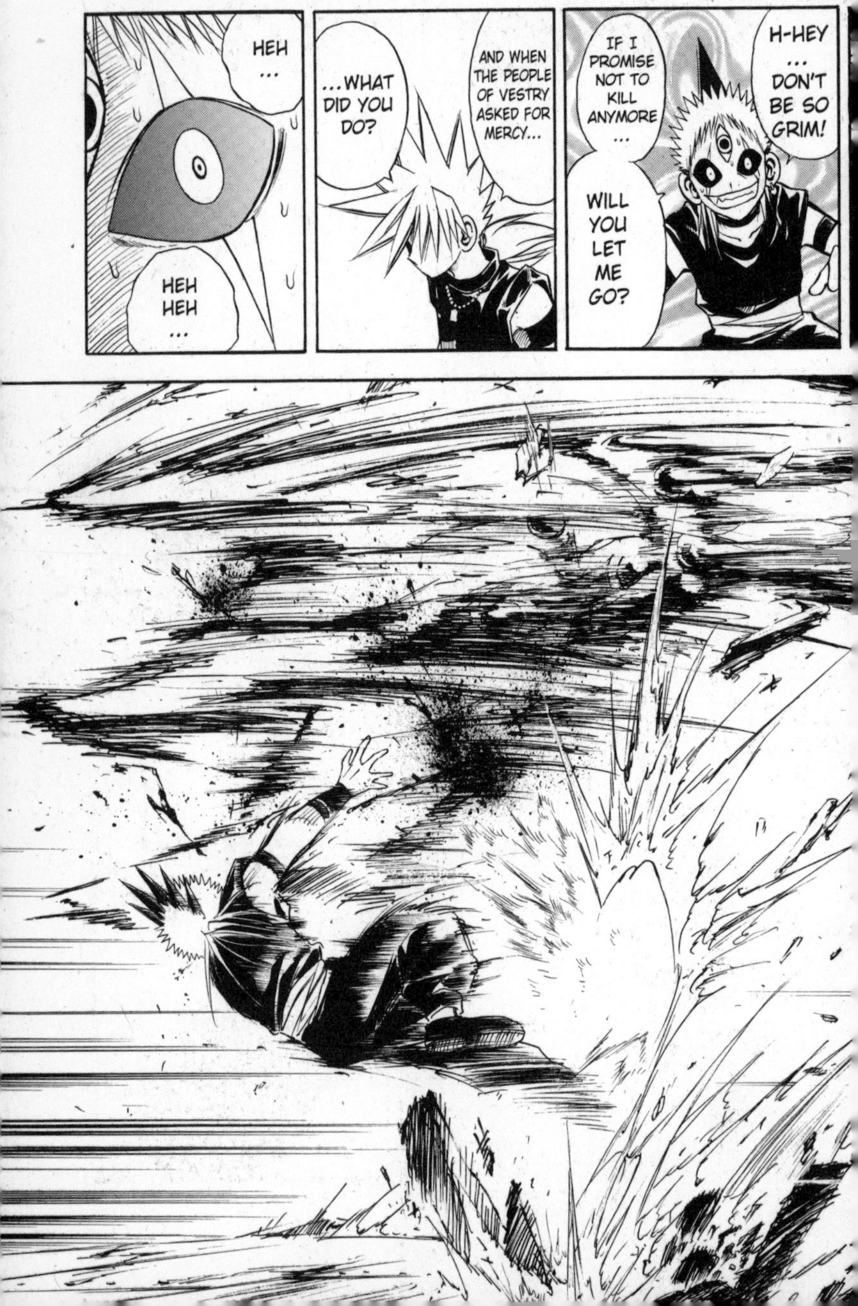
H-HEY ... DON'T BE SO GRIM!
IF I PROMISE NOT TO KILL ANYMORE ...
WILL YOU LET ME GO?
AND WHEN THE PEOPLE OF VESTRY ASKED FOR MERCY...
...WHAT DID YOU DO?
HEH ...
HEH HEH ...

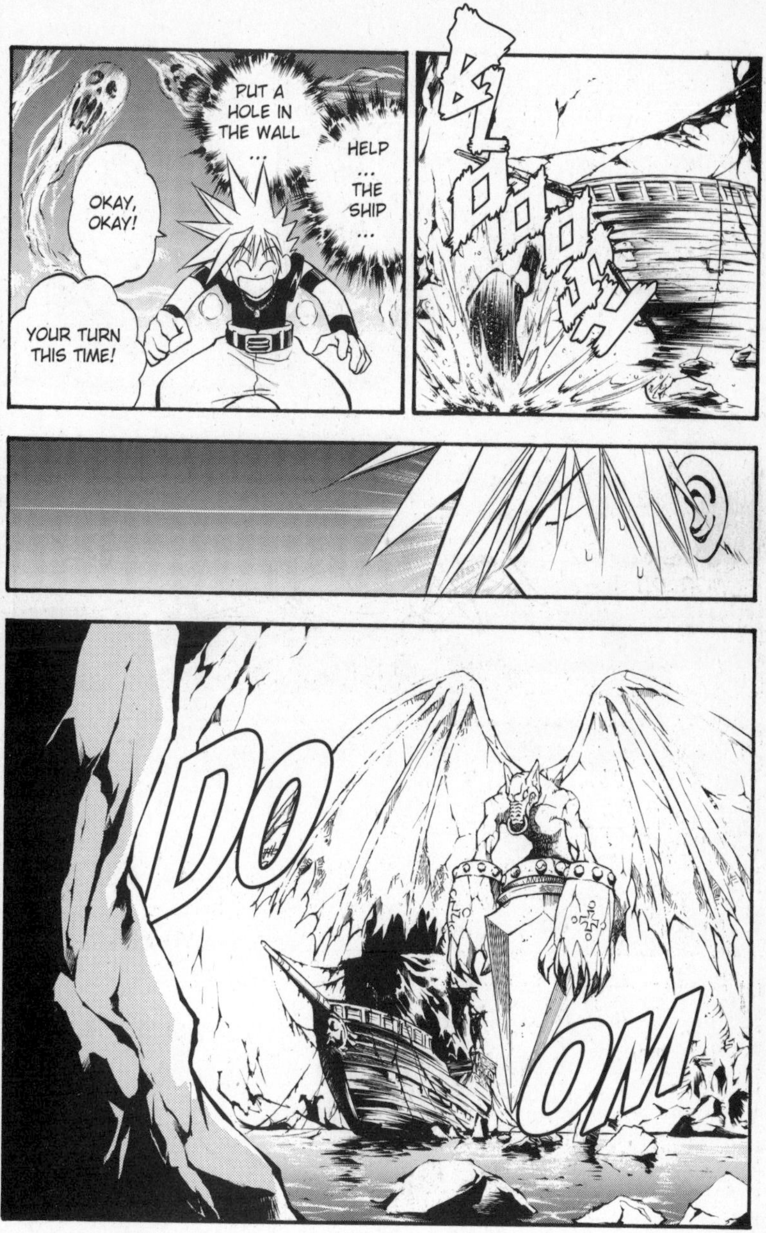
BLOOOSH
HELP ... THE SHIP ...
PUT A HOLE IN THE WALL ...
OKAY, OKAY!
YOUR TURN THIS TIME!
DOOM

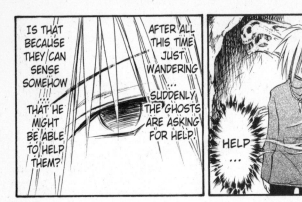

HELP ...
HELP ...
AFTER ALL THIS TIME JUST WANDERING ... SUDDENLY THE GHOSTS ARE ASKING FOR HELP.
IS THAT BECAUSE THEY CAN SENSE SOMEHOW ... THAT HE MIGHT BE ABLE TO HELP THEM?
GUESS IT OUGHTTA BE—
SINCE I'M FROM THE OTHER WORLD!!
SOME JERK NAMED ALVISS BROUGHT ME...
WITH AN ÄRM CALLED THE "GATEKEEPER CLOWN."
YOU KNOW ABOUT BOSS?!
WELL, I'M BETTER!

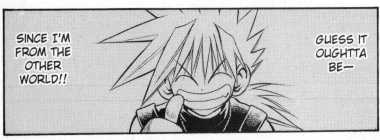

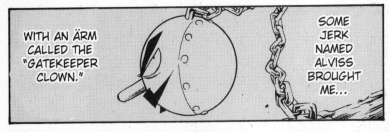

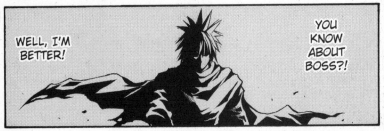

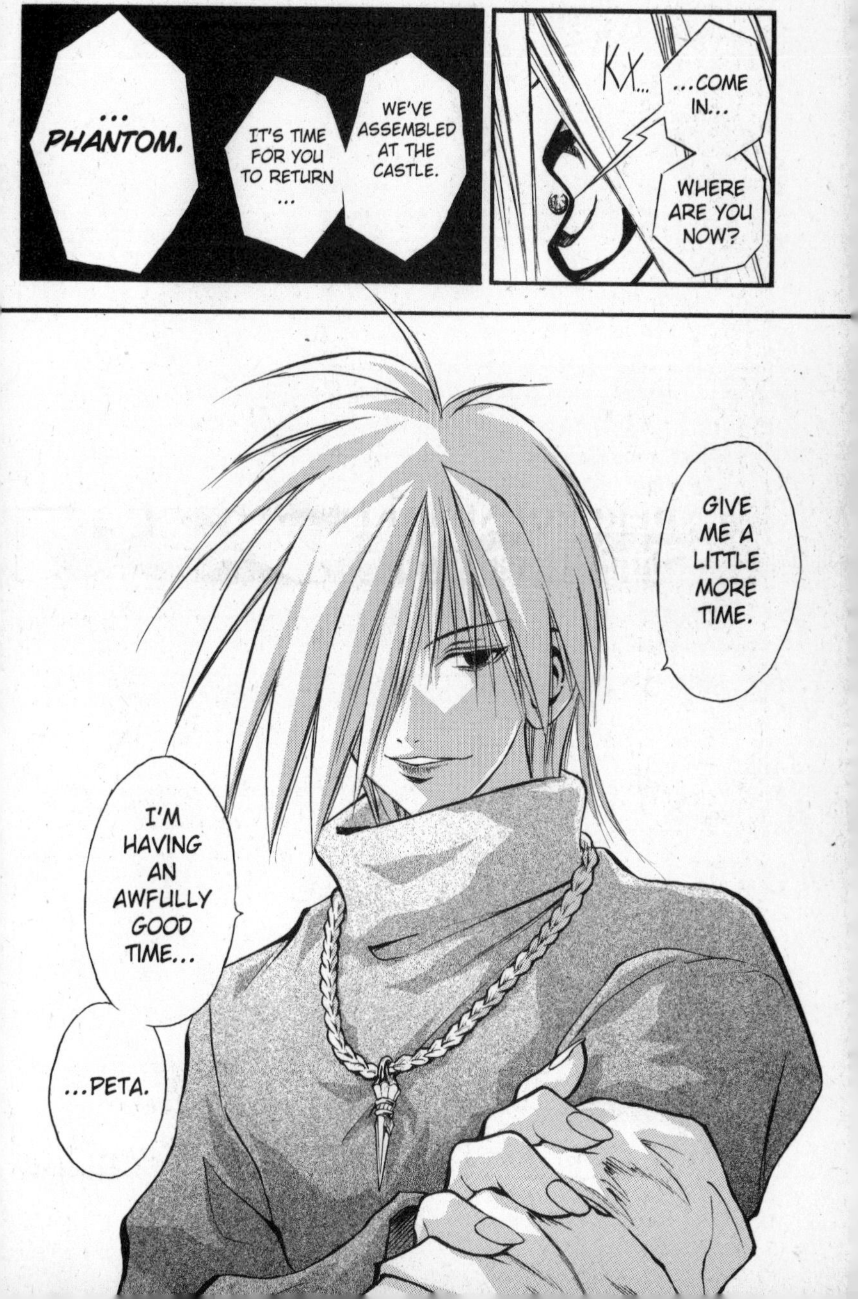
KX...
...COME IN...
WHERE ARE YOU NOW?
WE'VE ASSEMBLED AT THE CASTLE.
IT'S TIME FOR YOU TO RETURN ...
... PHANTOM.
GIVE ME A LITTLE MORE TIME.
I'M HAVING AN AWFULLY GOOD TIME...
...PETA.

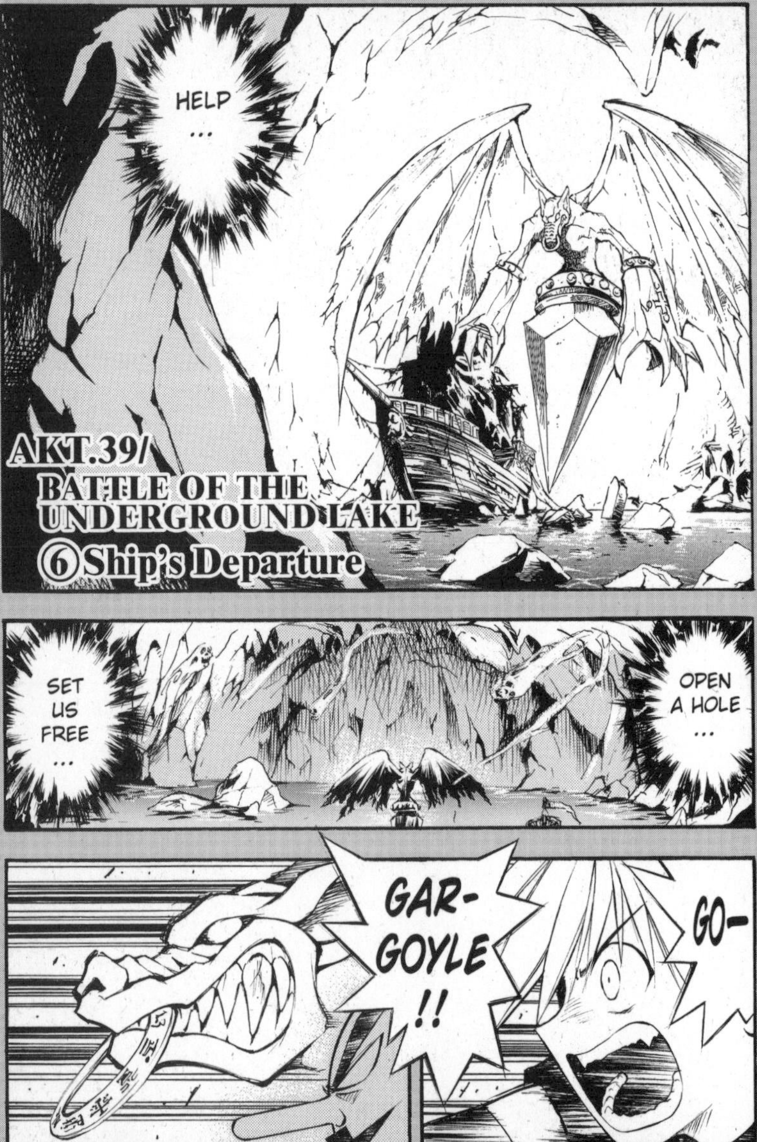
HELP ...
AKT.39/
BATTLE OF THE UNDERGROUND LAKE
⑥ Ship's Departure
OPEN A HOLE ...
SET US FREE ...
GO-
GAR-GOYLE!!

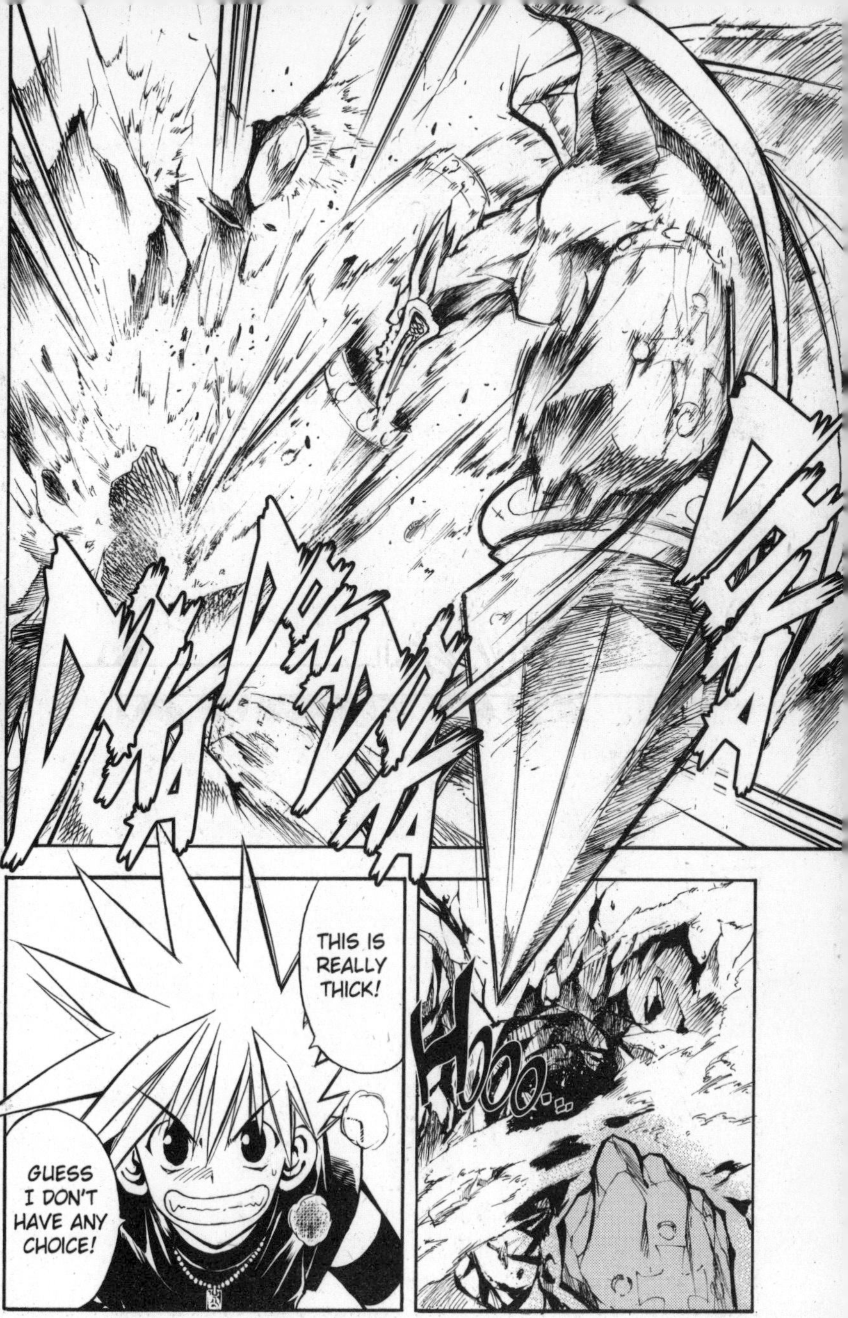
DOKA
DOKA DOKAA
DOKA
FOOO...
THIS IS REALLY THICK!
GUESS I DON'T HAVE ANY CHOICE!

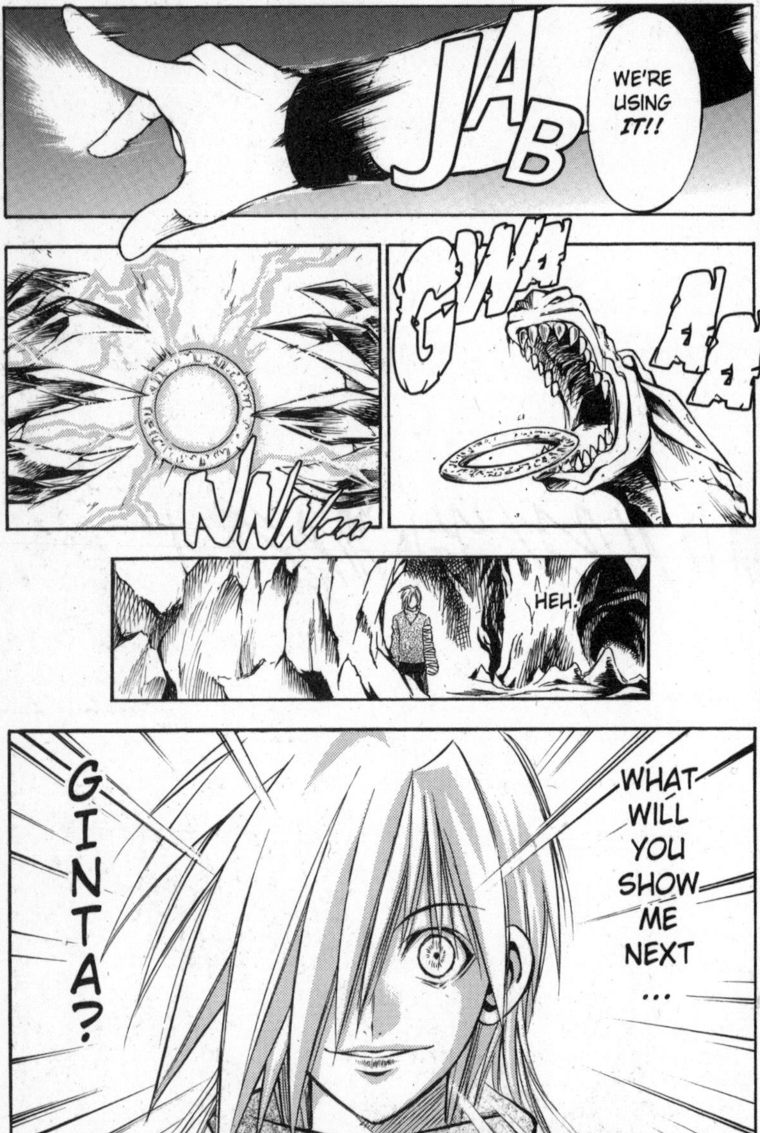
WE'RE USING IT!!
JAB
GWAAAA
NNN...
HEH.
WHAT WILL YOU SHOW ME NEXT...
GINTA?

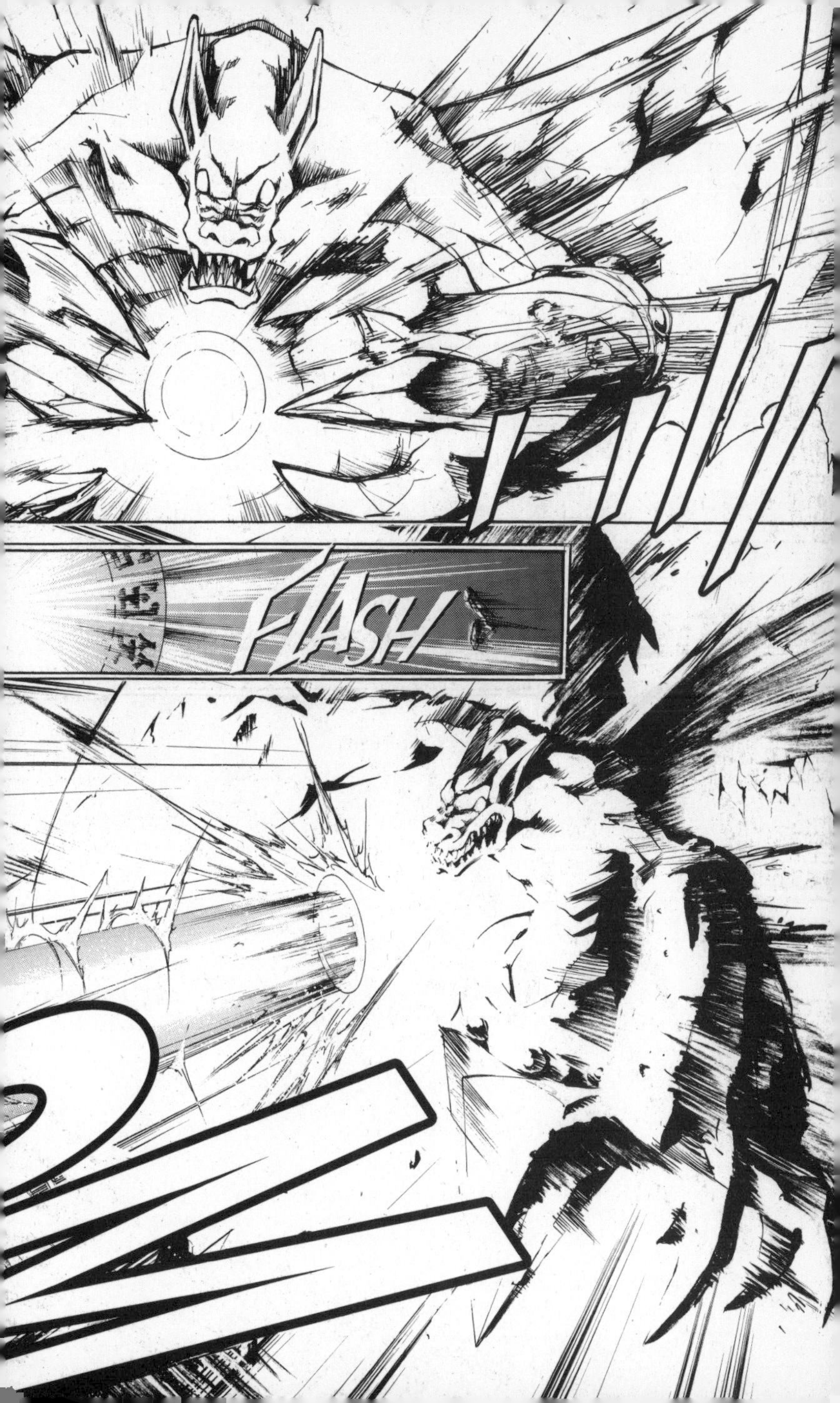
FLASH

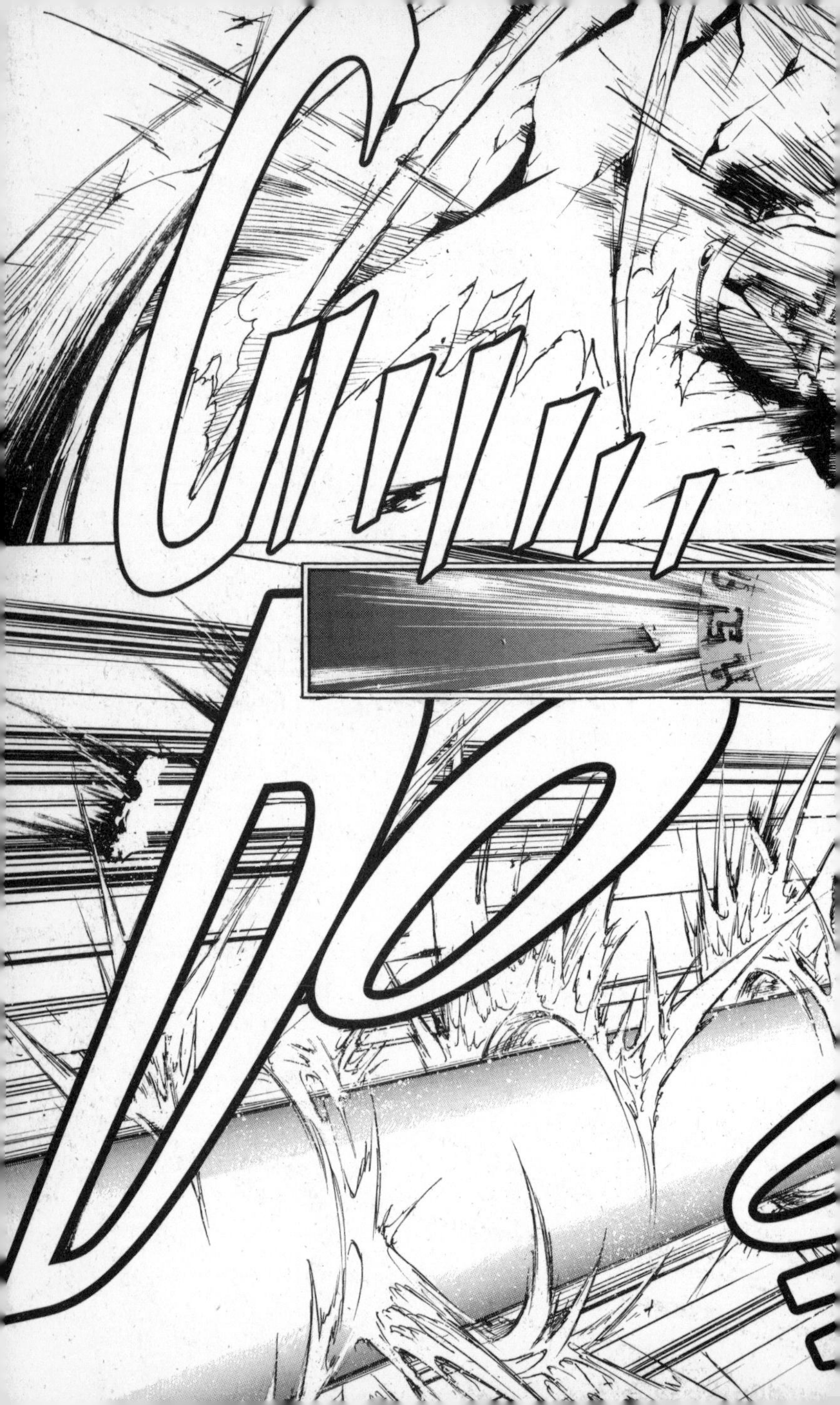

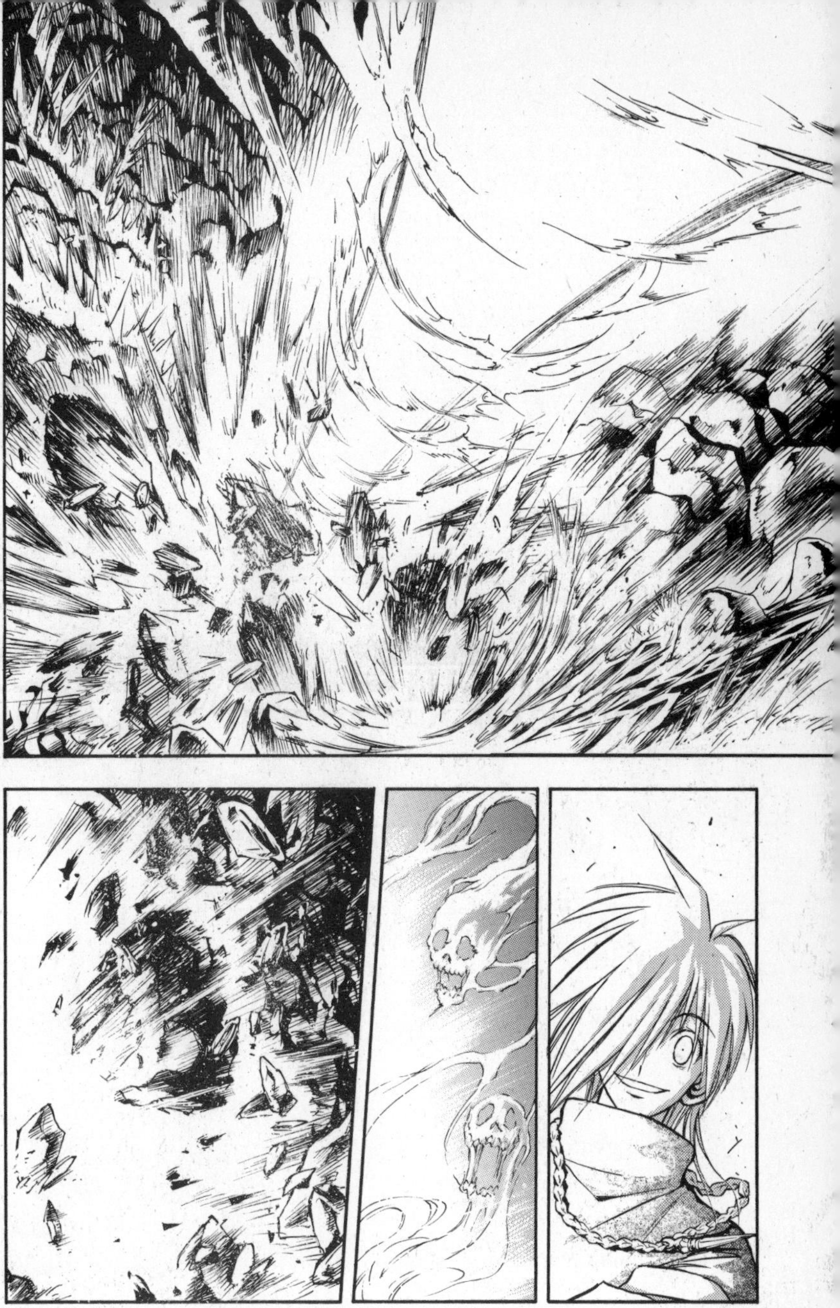

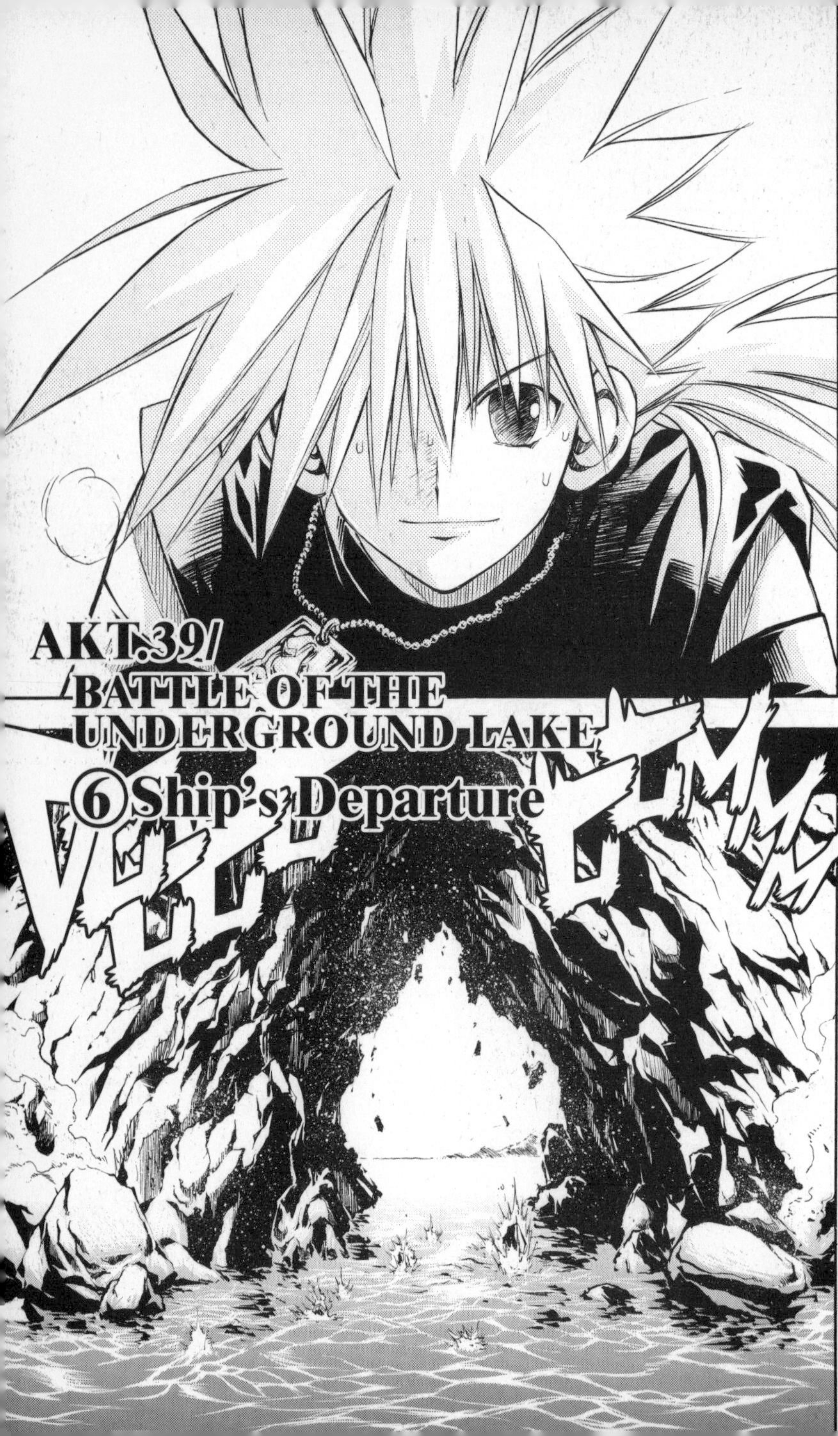
AKT.39/
BATTLE OF THE UNDERGROUND LAKE
⑥Ship's Departure

7

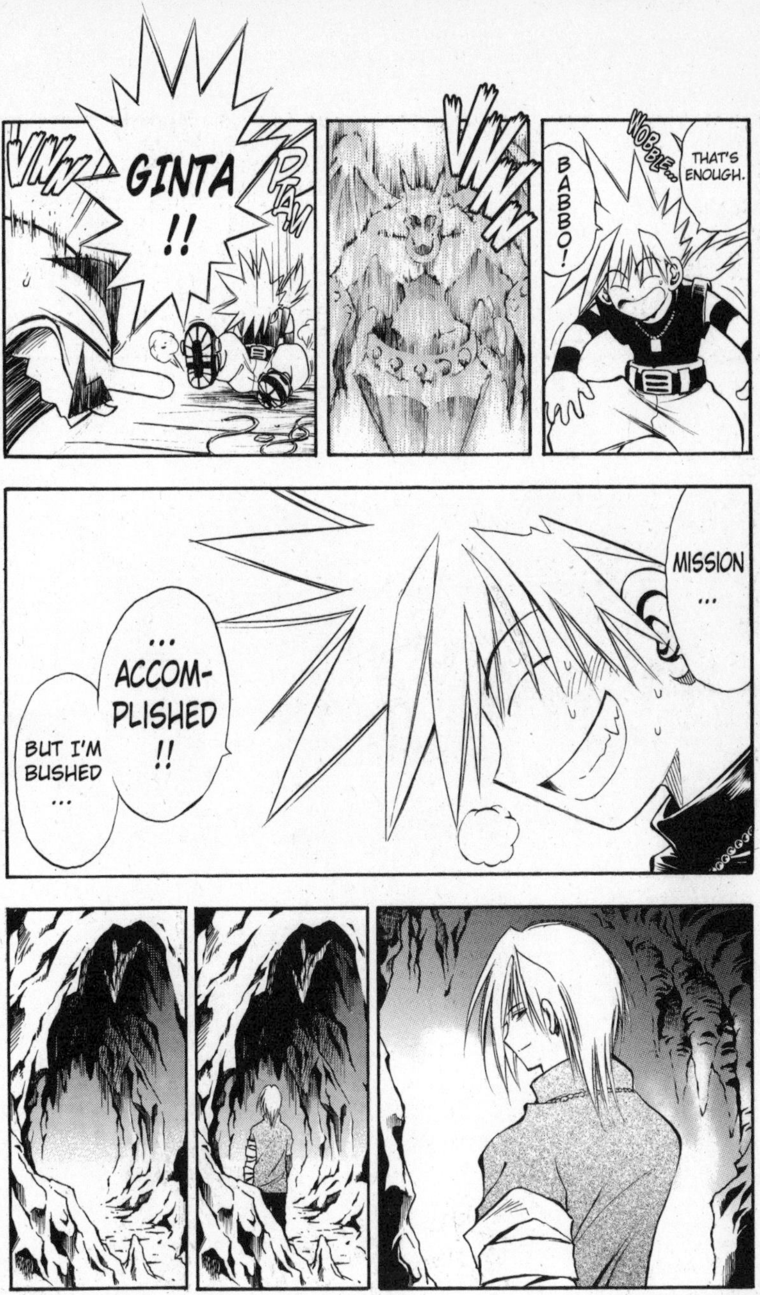
THAT'S ENOUGH.
WOBBLE...
BABBO!
VNNN
PTAW
GINTA !!
VNNN
MISSION ...
... ACCOM-PLISHED !!
BUT I'M BUSHED ...

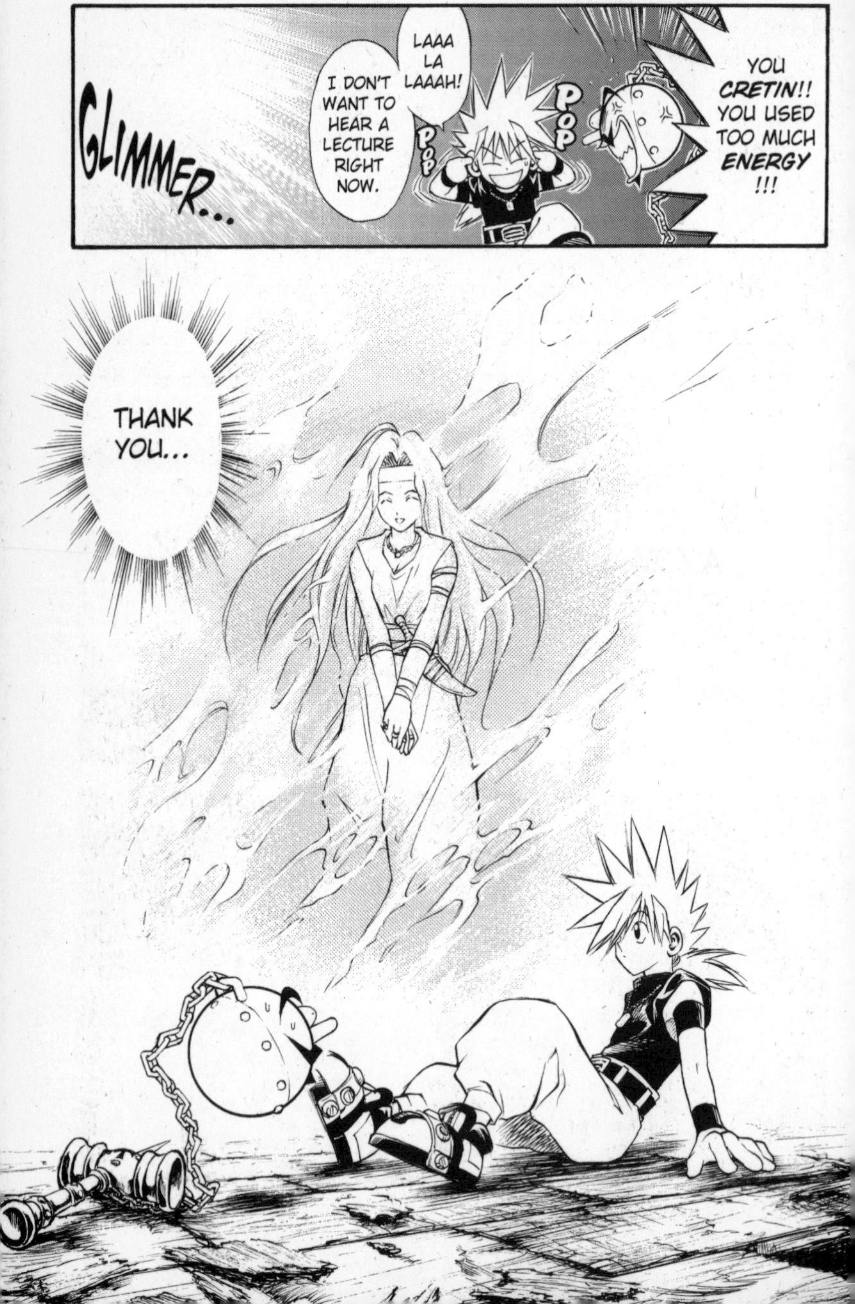
YOU CRETIN!! YOU USED TOO MUCH ENERGY!!!
POP
POP
LAAA LA LAAAH!
I DON'T WANT TO HEAR A LECTURE RIGHT NOW.
GLIMMER...
THANK YOU...

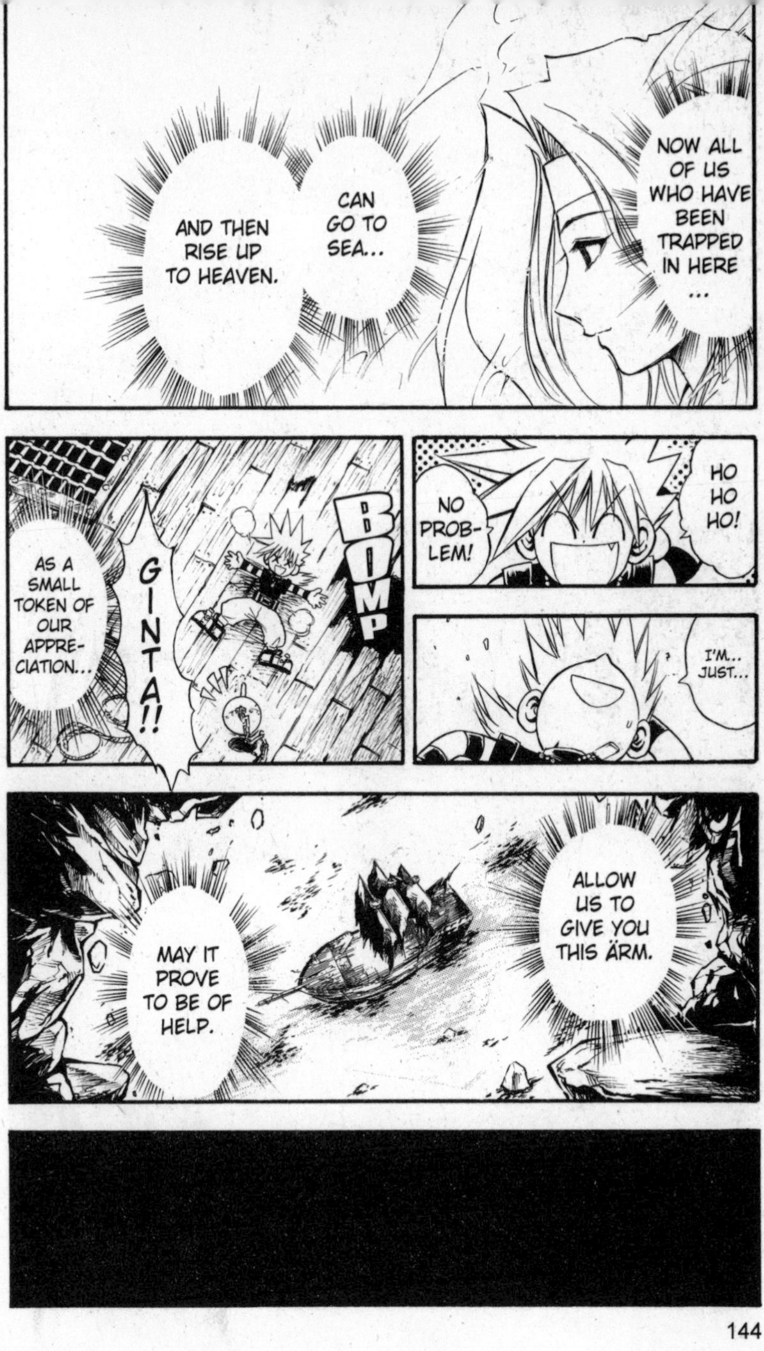
NOW ALL OF US WHO HAVE BEEN TRAPPED IN HERE...
CAN GO TO SEA...
AND THEN RISE UP TO HEAVEN.
HO HO HO!
NO PROBLEM!
I'M... JUST...
BOMP
GINTA!!
AS A SMALL TOKEN OF OUR APPRECIATION...
ALLOW US TO GIVE YOU THIS ÄRM.
MAY IT PROVE TO BE OF HELP.

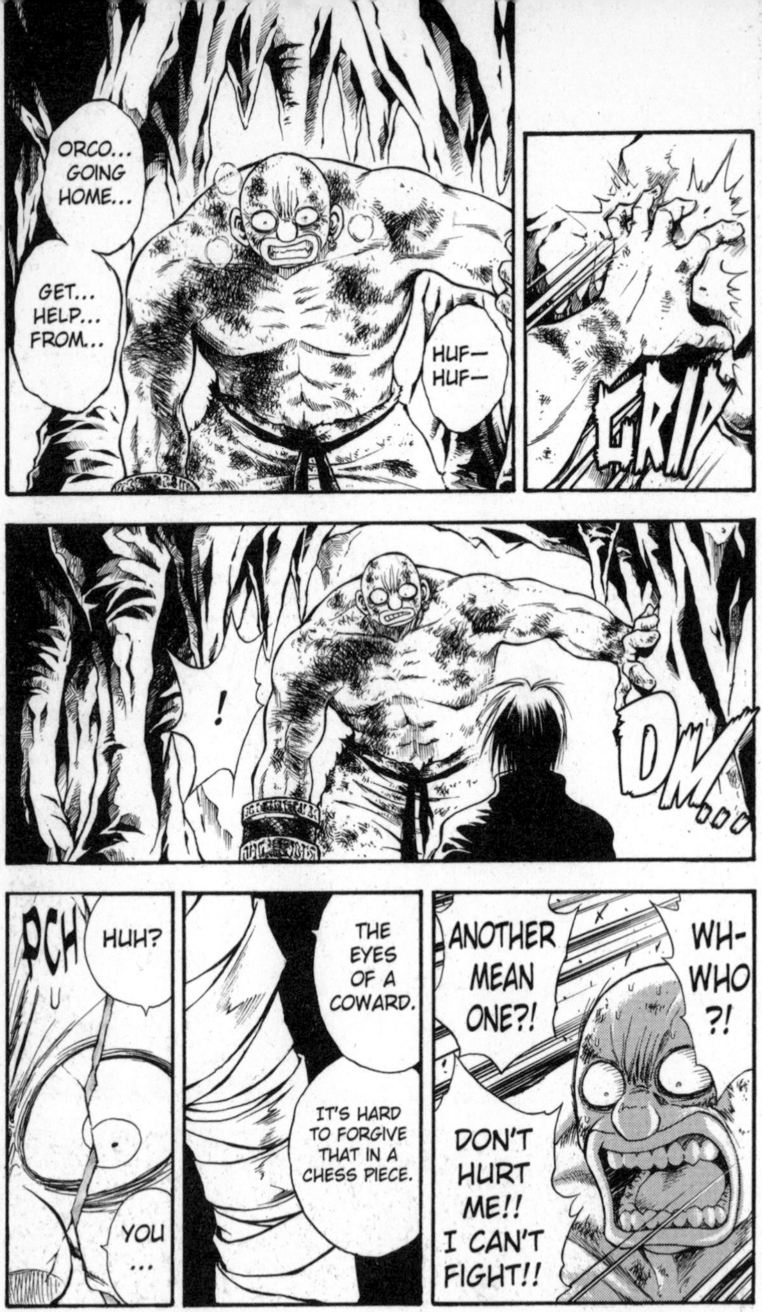
GRIP
ORCO... GOING HOME...
GET... HELP... FROM...
HUF— HUF—
DM
!
WH-WHO?!
ANOTHER MEAN ONE?!
DON'T HURT ME!! I CAN'T FIGHT!!
THE EYES OF A COWARD.
IT'S HARD TO FORGIVE THAT IN A CHESS PIECE.
PCH
HUH?
YOU...

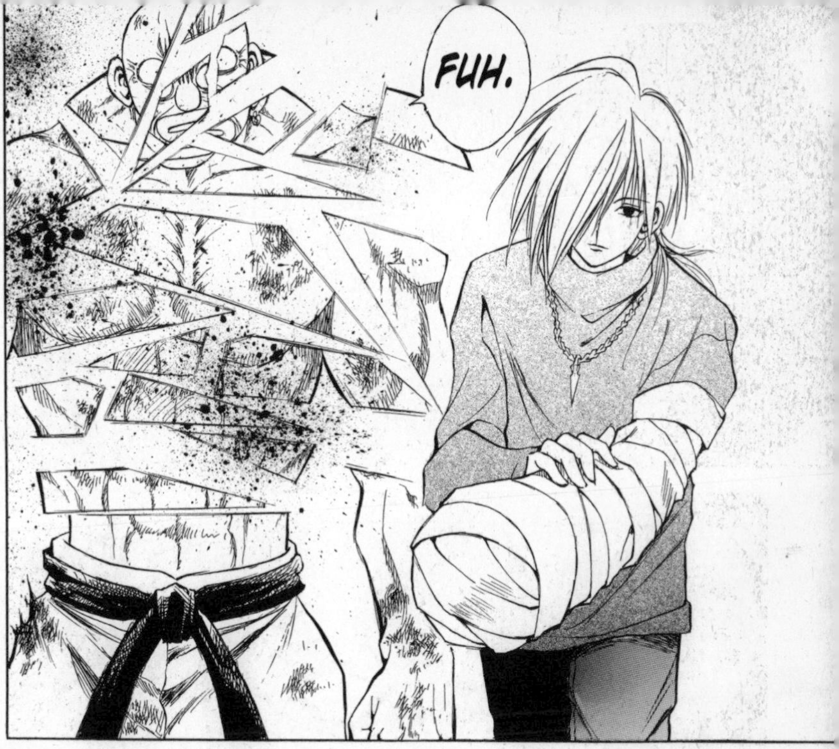
FUH.
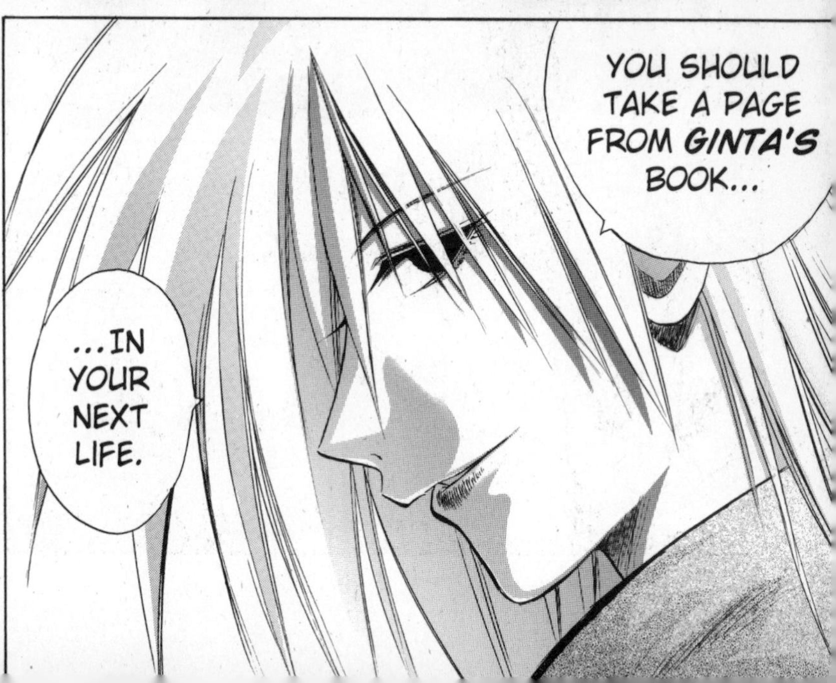
YOU SHOULD TAKE A PAGE FROM GINTA'S BOOK...
...IN YOUR NEXT LIFE.

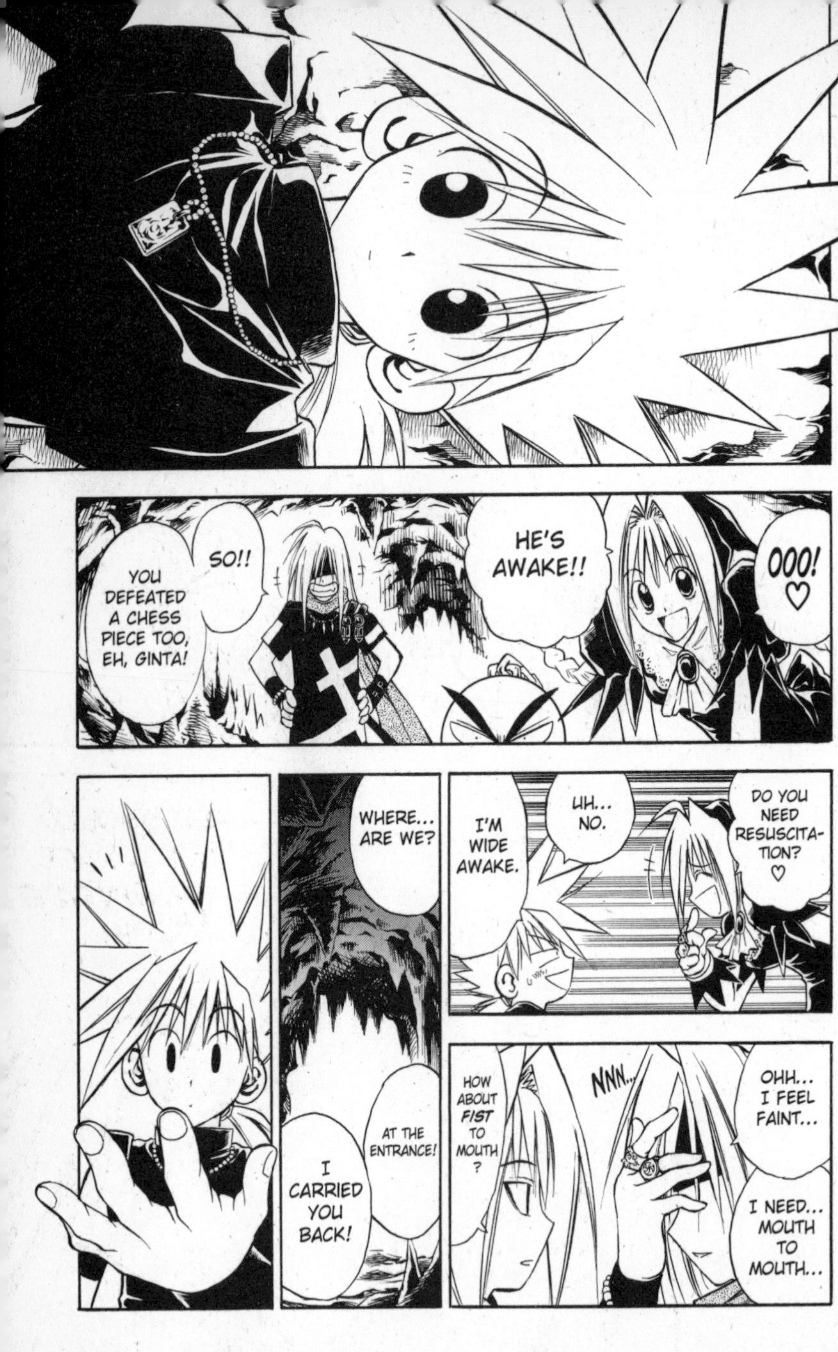
OOO! ♡
HE'S AWAKE!!
SO!!
YOU DEFEATED A CHESS PIECE TOO, EH, GINTA!
DO YOU NEED RESUSCITATION? ♡
UH... NO.
I'M WIDE AWAKE.
OHH... I FEEL FAINT...
I NEED... MOUTH TO MOUTH...
NNN...
HOW ABOUT *FIST* TO MOUTH?
WHERE... ARE WE?
AT THE ENTRANCE!
I CARRIED YOU BACK!

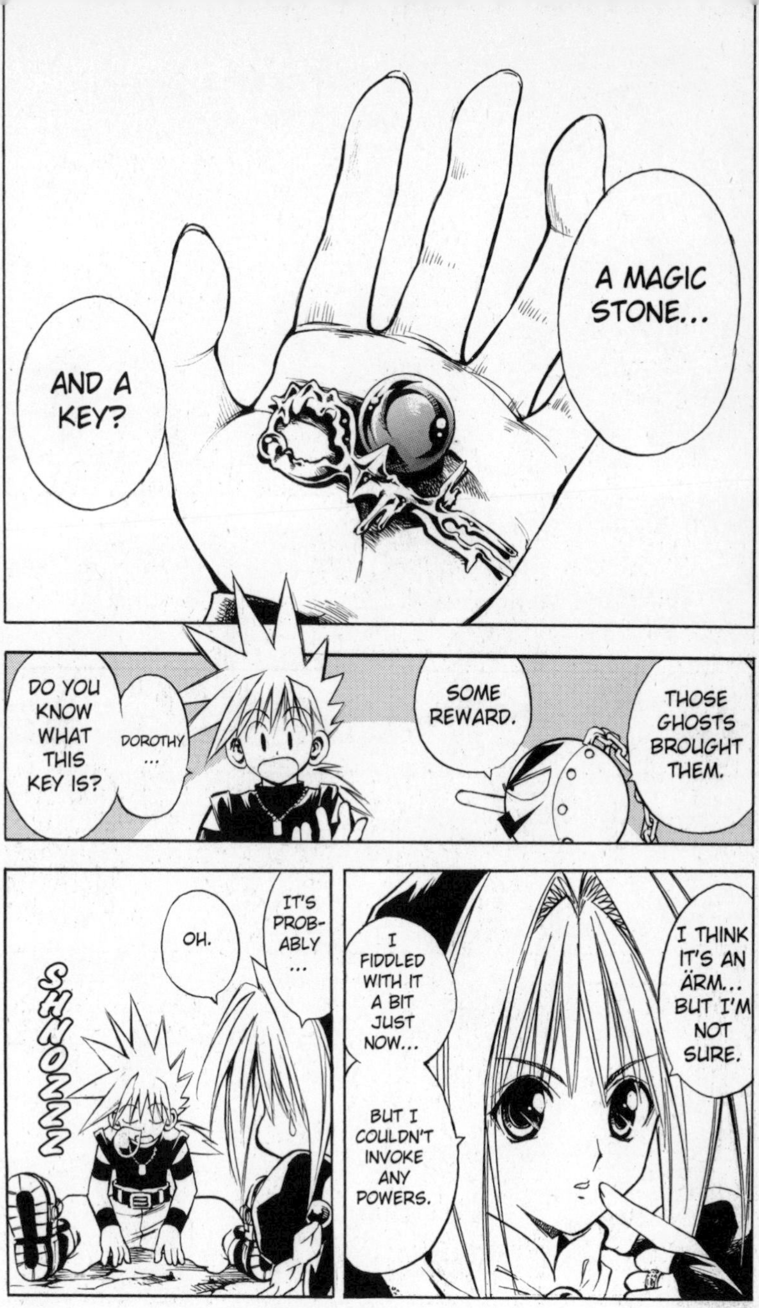
A MAGIC STONE...
AND A KEY?
THOSE GHOSTS BROUGHT THEM.
SOME REWARD.
DOROTHY...
DO YOU KNOW WHAT THIS KEY IS?
I THINK IT'S AN ÄRM... BUT I'M NOT SURE.
I FIDDLED WITH IT A BIT JUST NOW...
BUT I COULDN'T INVOKE ANY POWERS.
IT'S PROBABLY...
OH.
SHNOZZZ

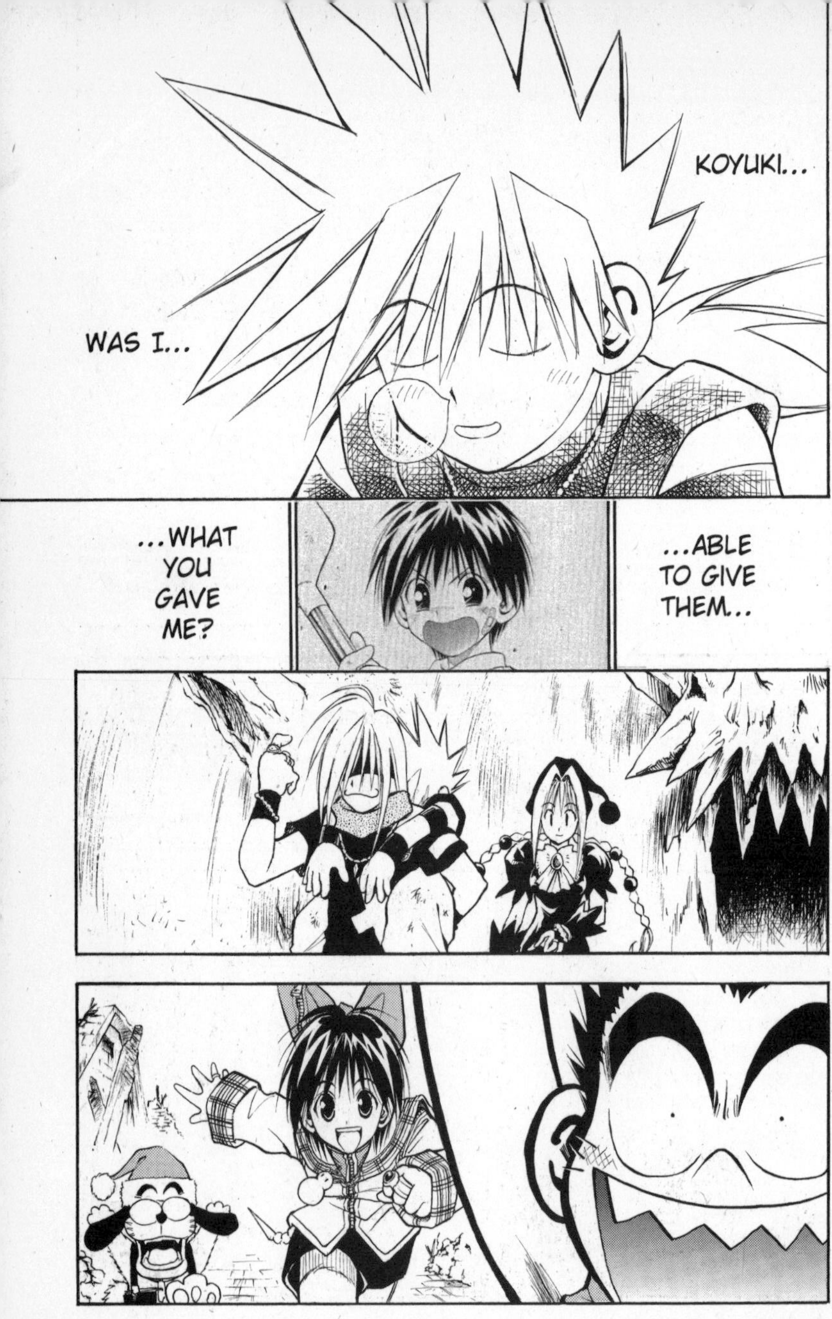
KOYUKI...
WAS I...
...ABLE TO GIVE THEM...
...WHAT YOU GAVE ME?

INCRED-IBLE.
YEAH!
A KID LIKE THAT...
AGAINST THE CHESS PIECES...
AND HE WON!!
YEAH!
!
HEY...
ISN'T THAT ...
A SHIP ...?
THANK YOU...
MY BRAVE YOUNG WARRIOR!

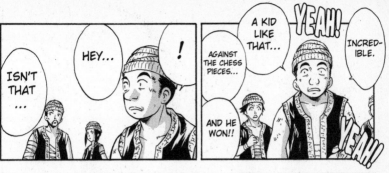

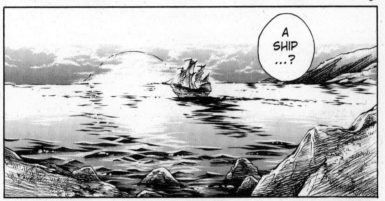

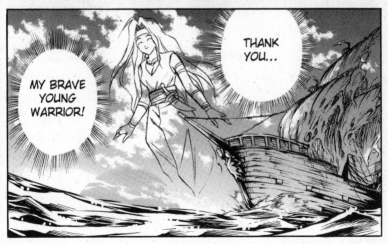

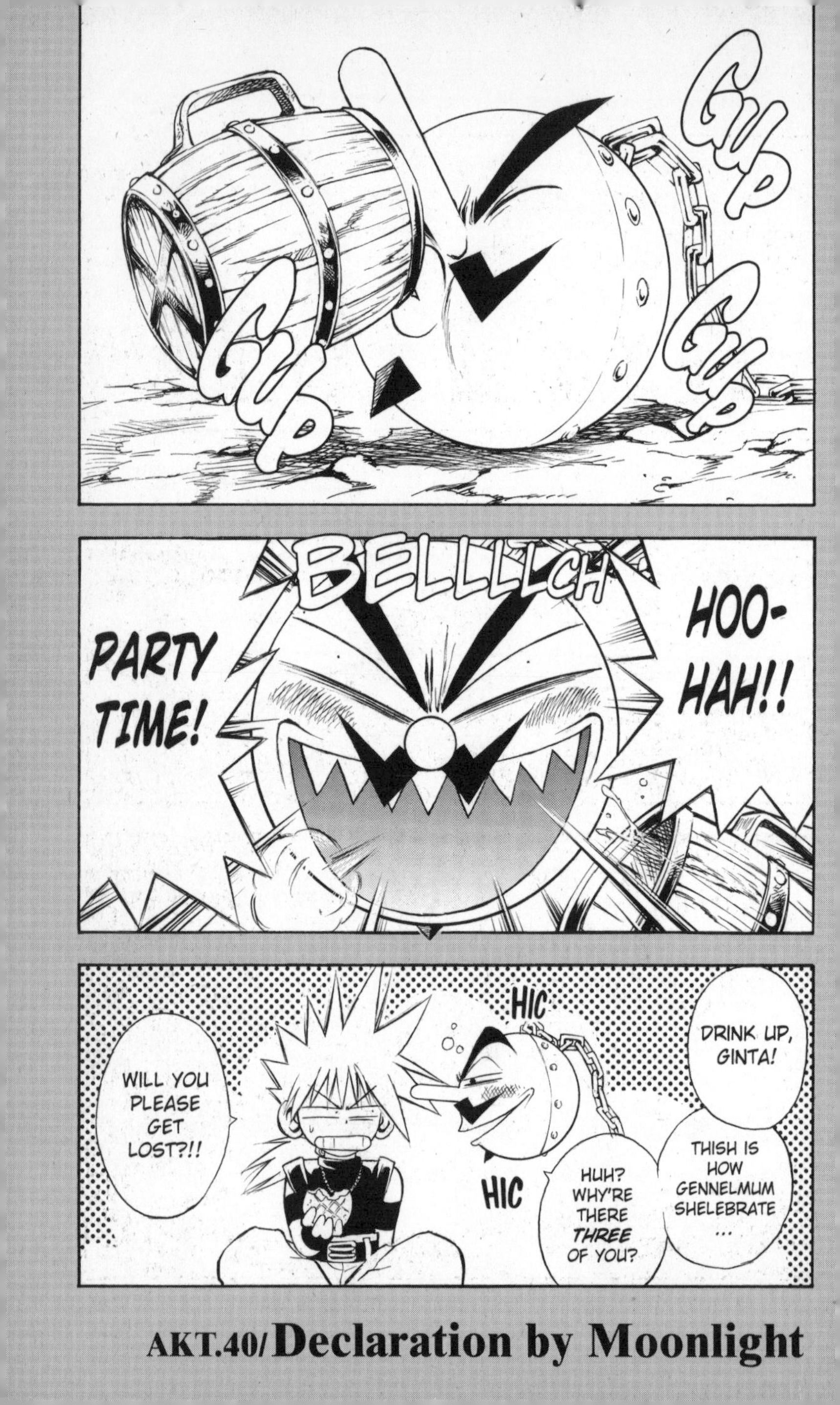
GULP
GULP
GULP
BELLLLCH
HOO-HAH!!
PARTY TIME!
HIC
DRINK UP, GINTA!
THISH IS HOW GENNELMUM SHELEBRATE ...
HUH? WHY'RE THERE *THREE* OF YOU?
HIC
WILL YOU PLEASE GET LOST?!!

AKT.40/ Declaration by Moonlight

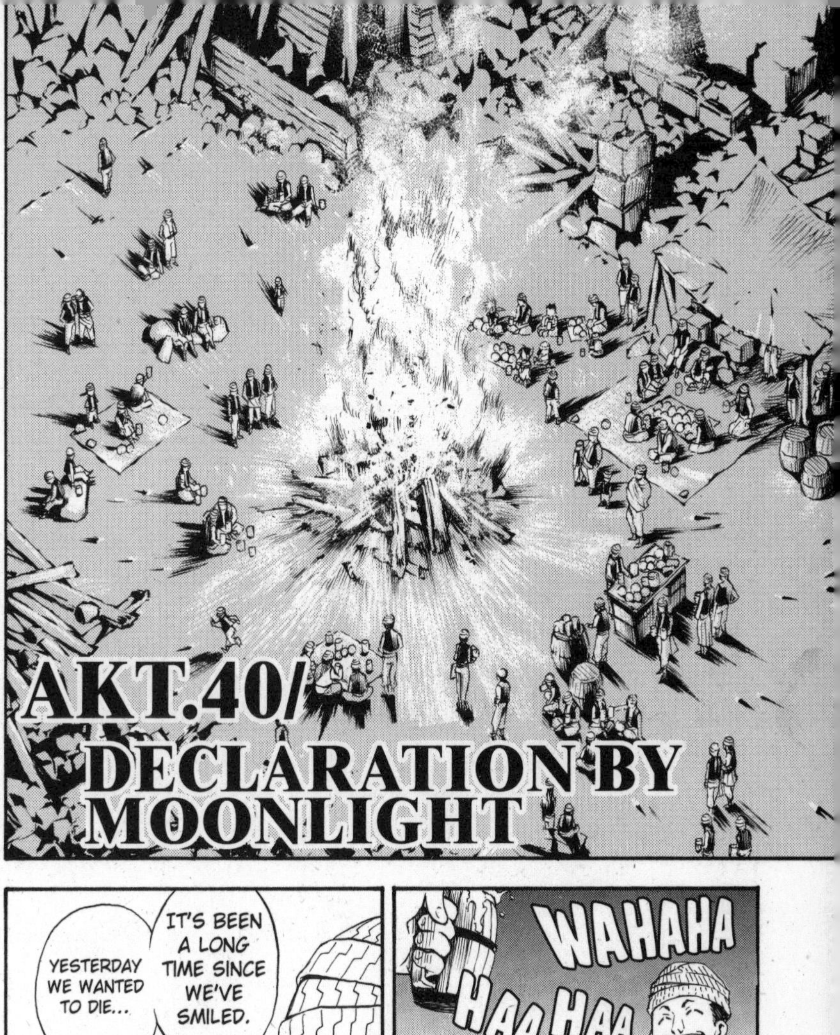
AKT.40/
DECLARATION BY MOONLIGHT

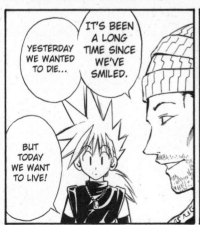

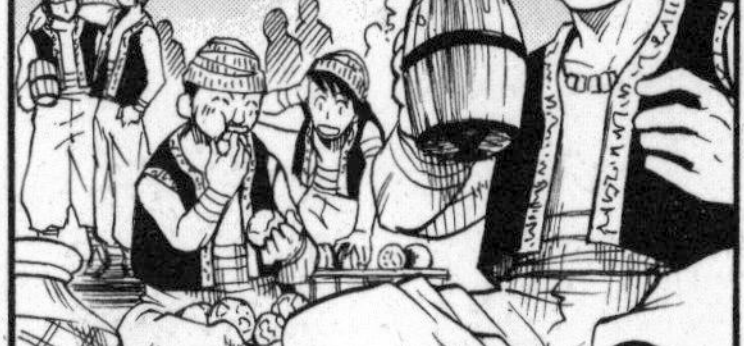
WAHAHA
HAA HAA

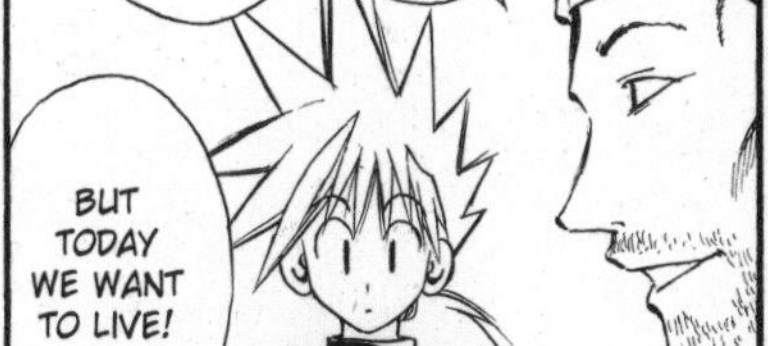
IT'S BEEN A LONG TIME SINCE WE'VE SMILED.
YESTERDAY WE WANTED TO DIE...
BUT TODAY WE WANT TO LIVE!

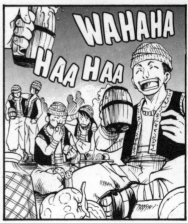

SUCH AN...
...ABUNDANCE OF FOOD!
THANKS TO JACK!!
HO HO!
IT'S NOTHING!!
BLOOOM
I WOULDN'T EXACTLY CALL THAT *NOTHING*.
IN FACT... DON'T YOU THINK IT'S A LITTLE *TOO MUCH*?
P... POSSIBLY...
KINDA CAUGHT ME OFF GUARD TOO...
NOT ONLY HAVE MY *OWN* MAGICAL POWERS INCREASED...
BUT THESE EARTH NATURE STONES I GOT FROM DOROTHY...
...SEEM TO BE PRETTY POTENT!!

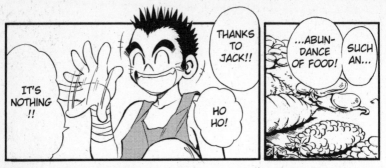

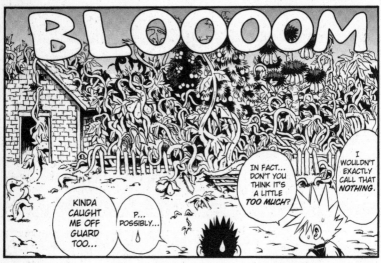

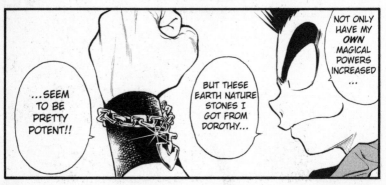

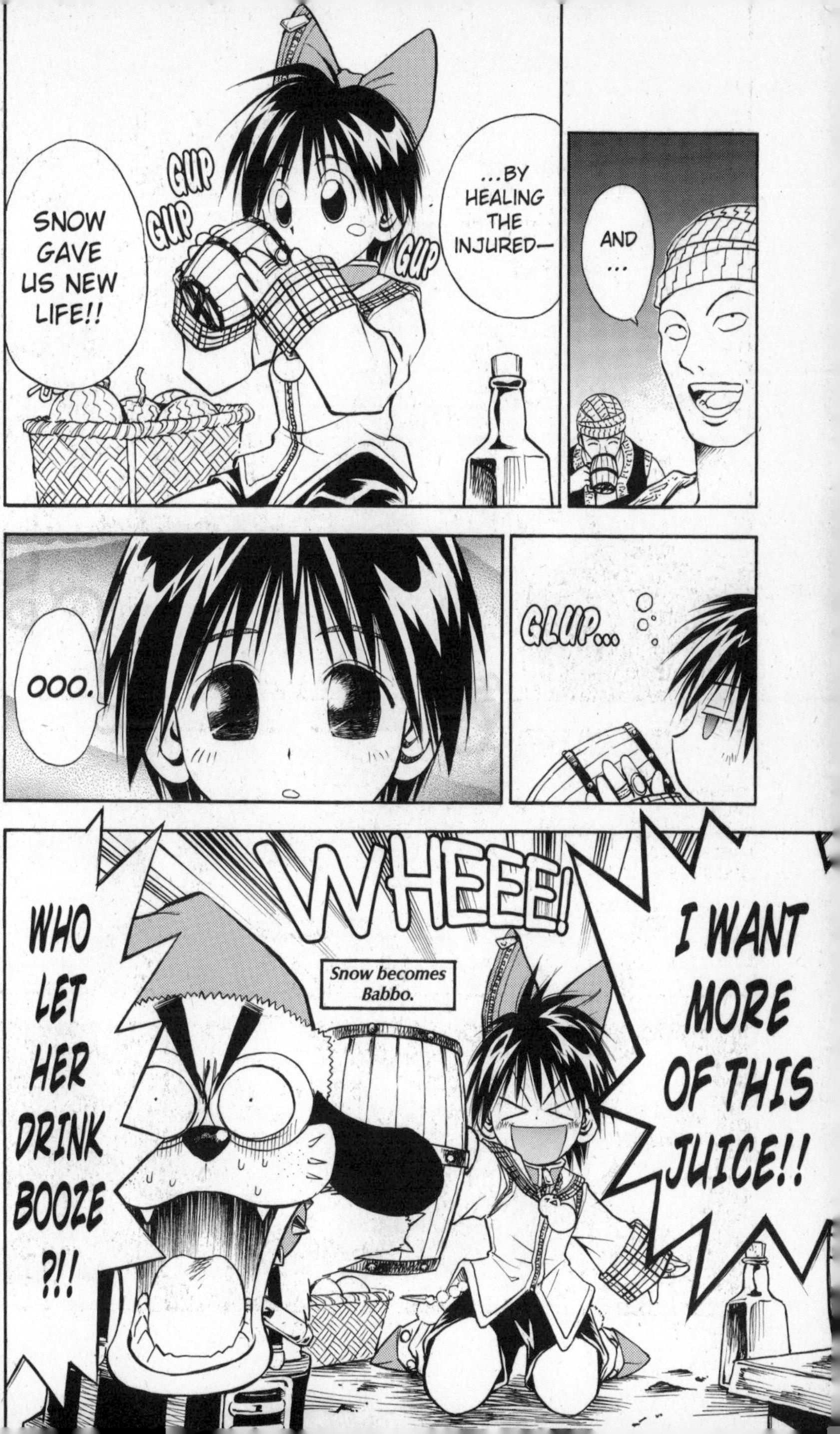
AND ...
...BY HEALING THE INJURED—
GUP
GUP
GUP
SNOW GAVE US NEW LIFE!!
GLUP...
OOO.
WHEEE!
I WANT MORE OF THIS JUICE!!
Snow becomes Babbo.
WHO LET HER DRINK BOOZE ?!!

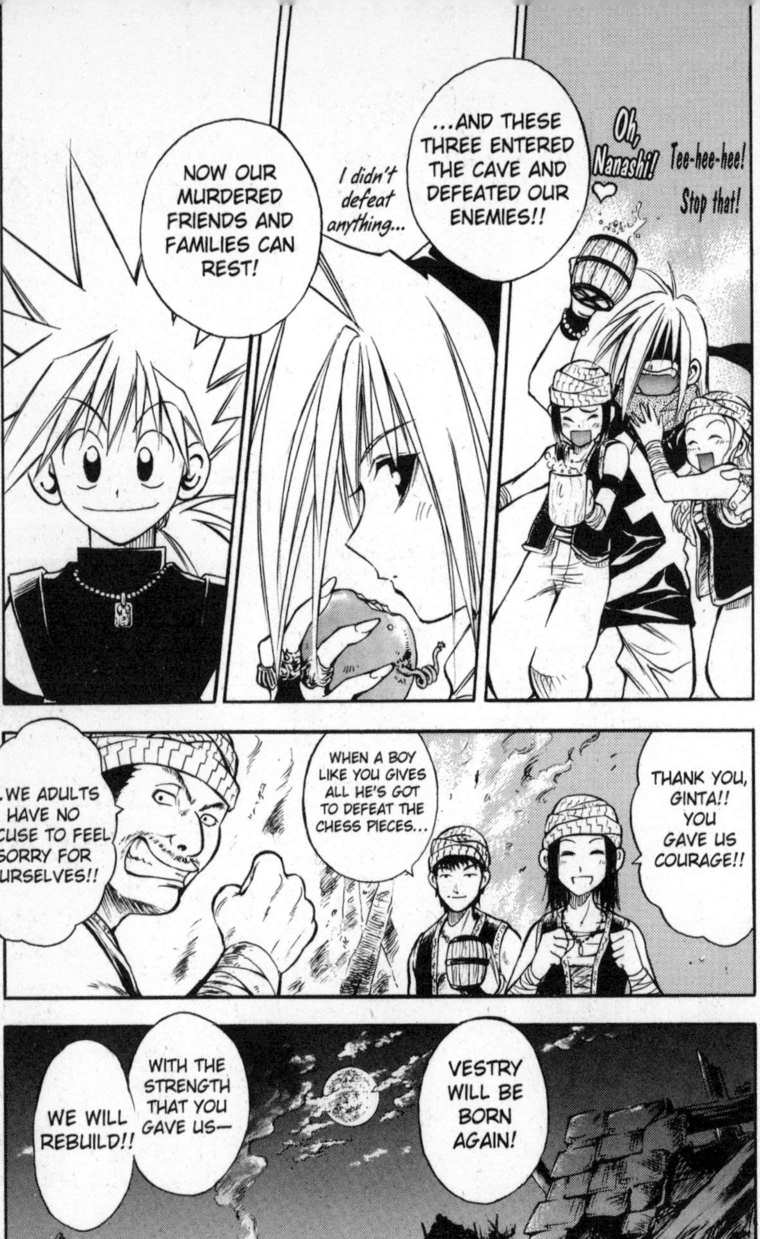
Tee-hee-hee! Stop that!
Oh, Nanashi! ♥
...AND THESE THREE ENTERED THE CAVE AND DEFEATED OUR ENEMIES!!
I didn't defeat anything...
NOW OUR MURDERED FRIENDS AND FAMILIES CAN REST!
THANK YOU, GINTA!! YOU GAVE US COURAGE!!
WHEN A BOY LIKE YOU GIVES ALL HE'S GOT TO DEFEAT THE CHESS PIECES...
...WE ADULTS HAVE NO EXCUSE TO FEEL SORRY FOR OURSELVES!!
VESTRY WILL BE BORN AGAIN!
WITH THE STRENGTH THAT YOU GAVE US—
WE WILL REBUILD!!

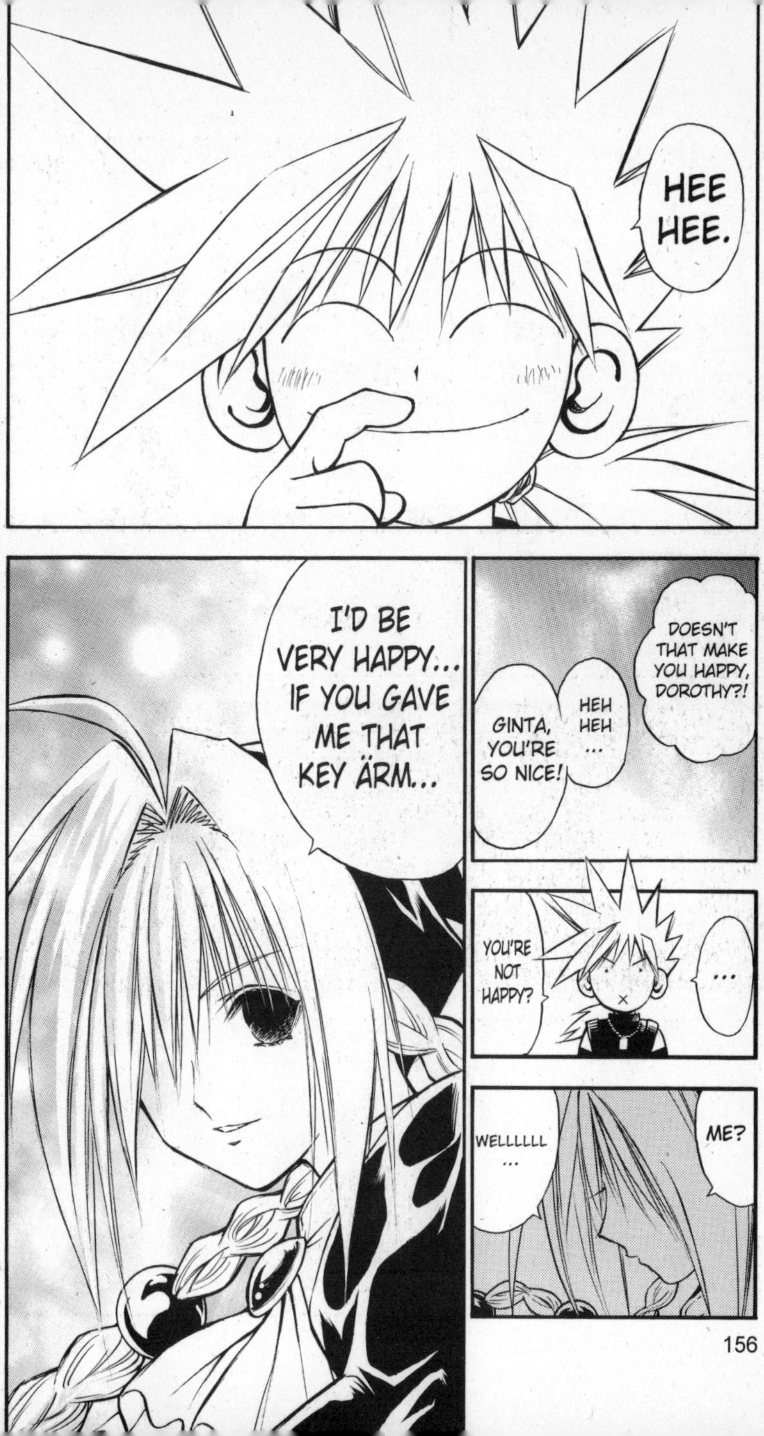
HEE HEE.
DOESN'T THAT MAKE YOU HAPPY, DOROTHY?!
HEH HEH ...
GINTA, YOU'RE SO NICE!
...
YOU'RE NOT HAPPY?
ME?
WELLLLLLL ...
I'D BE VERY HAPPY... IF YOU GAVE ME THAT KEY ÄRM...

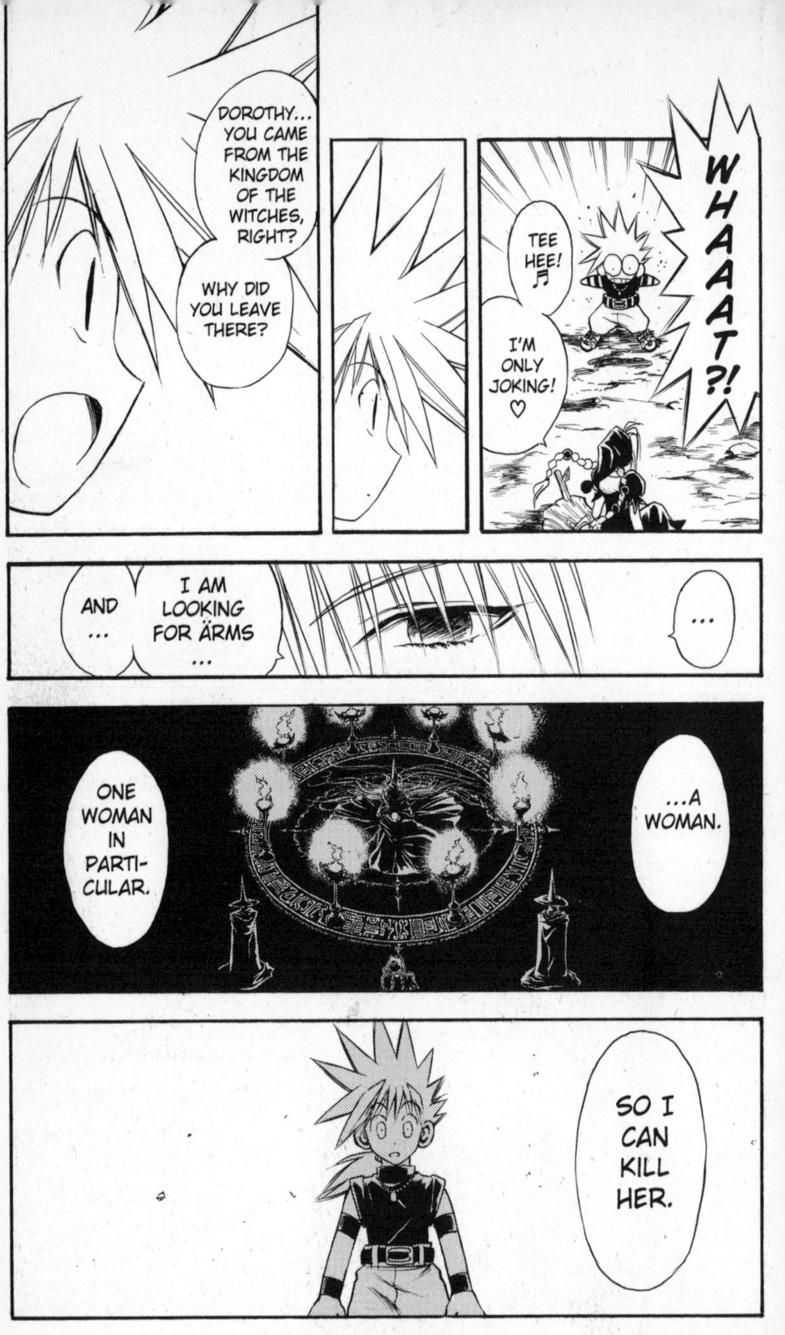
WHAAAT?!
TEE HEE! ♬
I'M ONLY JOKING! ♡
DOROTHY... YOU CAME FROM THE KINGDOM OF THE WITCHES, RIGHT?
WHY DID YOU LEAVE THERE?
...
I AM LOOKING FOR ÄRMS ...
AND ...
...A WOMAN.
ONE WOMAN IN PARTI-CULAR.
SO I CAN KILL HER.

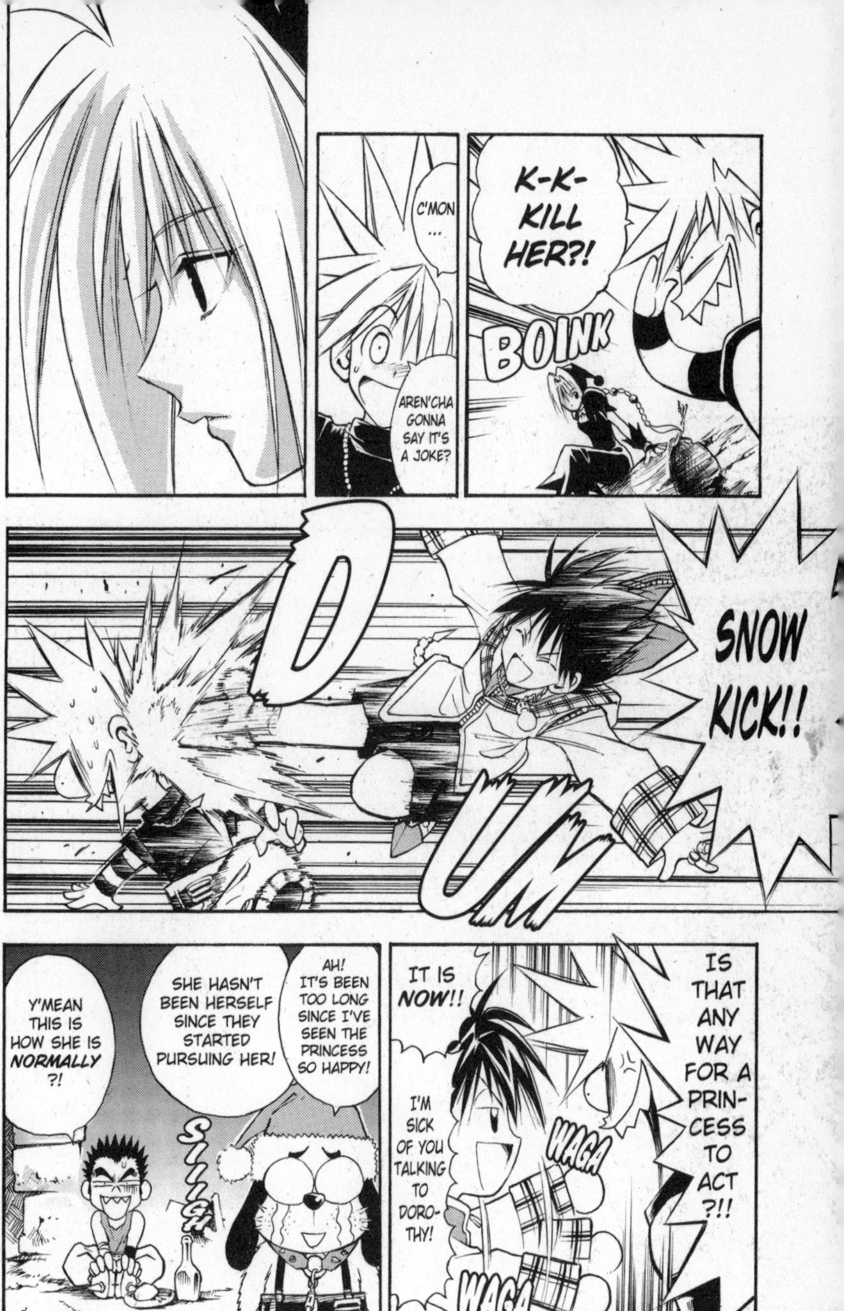

K-K-KILL HER?!
BOINK
C'MON ...
AREN'CHA GONNA SAY IT'S A JOKE?
SNOW KICK!!
DUM
IS THAT ANY WAY FOR A PRINCESS TO ACT?!!
IT IS *NOW*!!
I'M SICK OF YOU TALKING TO DOROTHY!
WAGA
WAGA
AH! IT'S BEEN TOO LONG SINCE I'VE SEEN THE PRINCESS SO HAPPY!
SHE HASN'T BEEN HERSELF SINCE THEY STARTED PURSUING HER!
Y'MEAN THIS IS HOW SHE IS *NORMALLY*?!
SIIGH

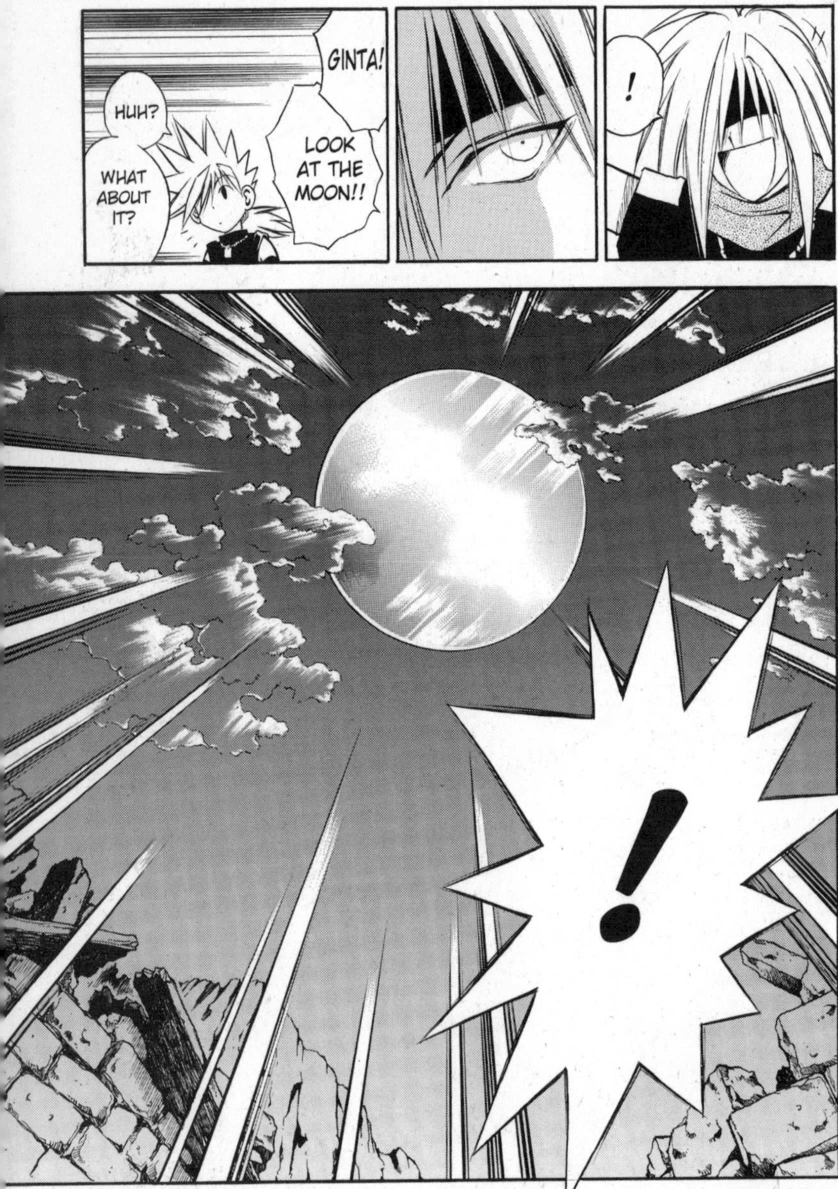
!
GINTA!
LOOK AT THE MOON!!
HUH?
WHAT ABOUT IT?
!

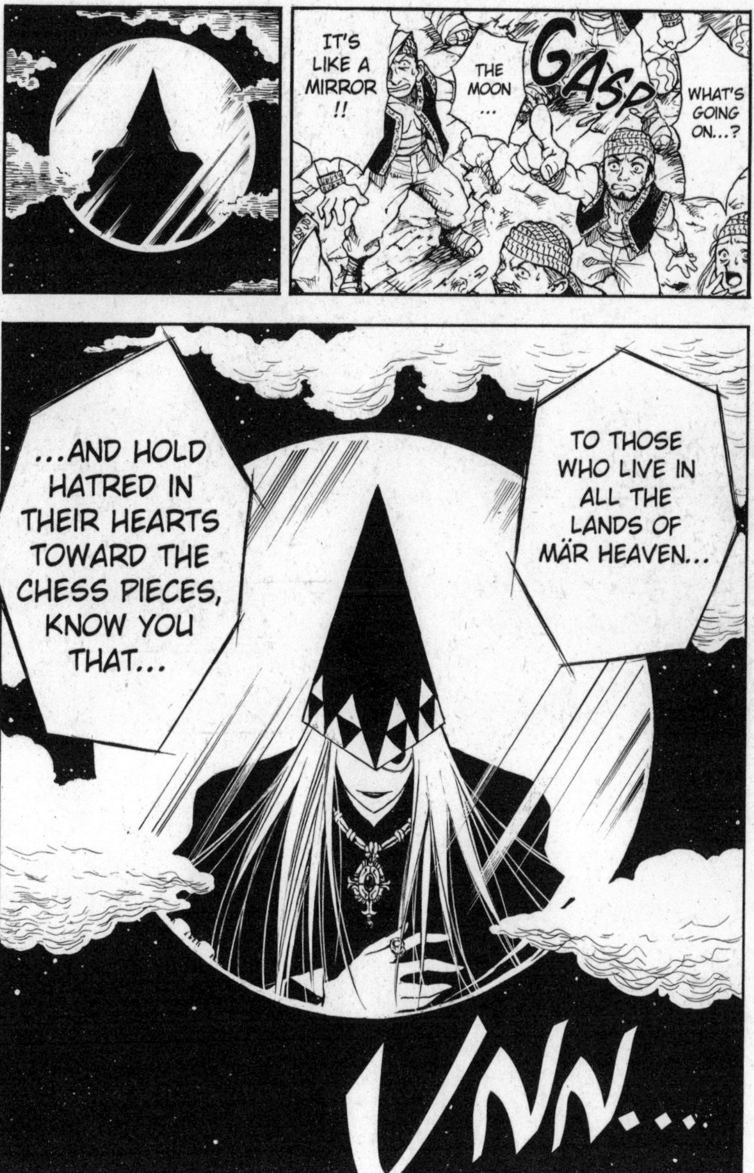
WHAT'S GOING ON...?
GASP
THE MOON ...
IT'S LIKE A MIRROR !!
TO THOSE WHO LIVE IN ALL THE LANDS OF MÄR HEAVEN...
...AND HOLD HATRED IN THEIR HEARTS TOWARD THE CHESS PIECES, KNOW YOU THAT...
VNN...

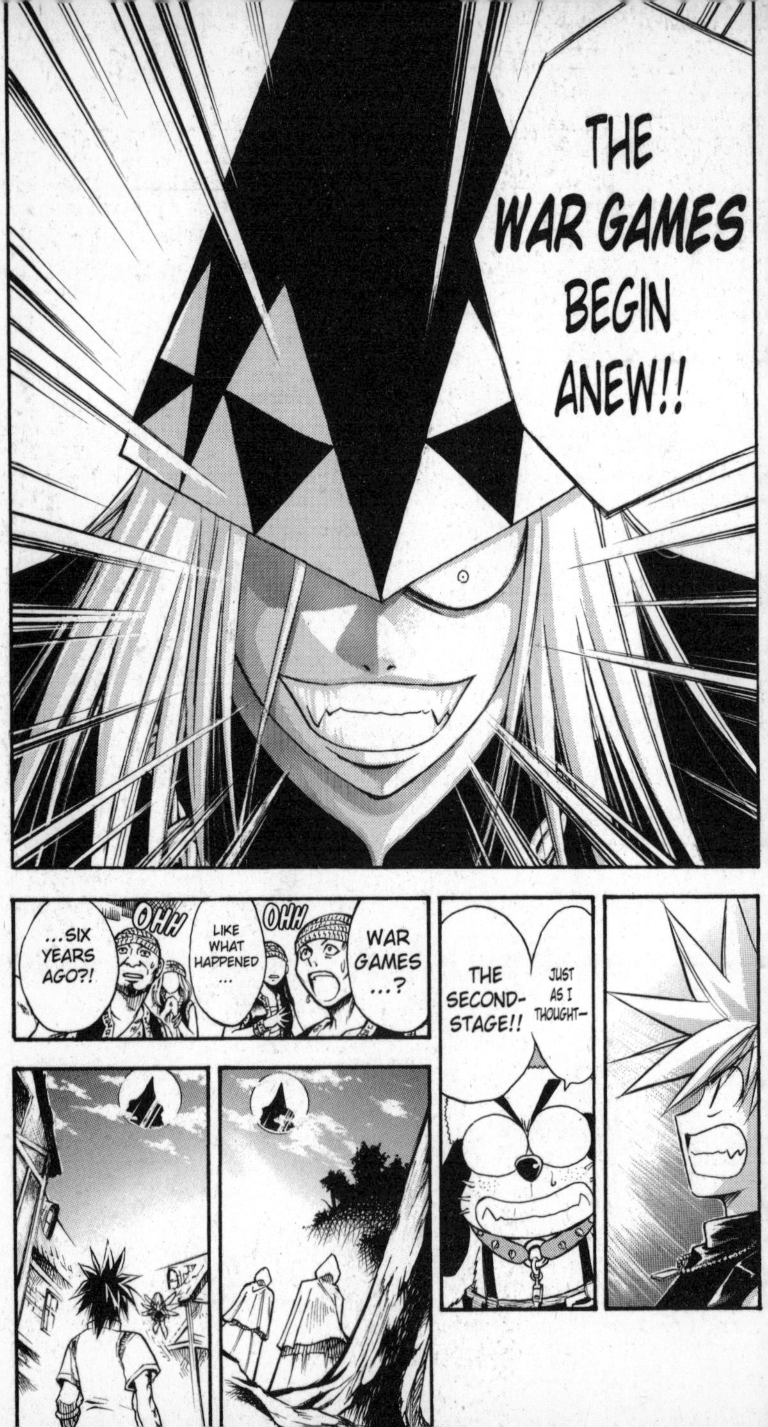
THE WAR GAMES BEGIN ANEW!!
JUST AS I THOUGHT—
THE SECOND-STAGE!!
WAR GAMES ...?
OHH
LIKE WHAT HAPPENED ...
OHH
...SIX YEARS AGO?!

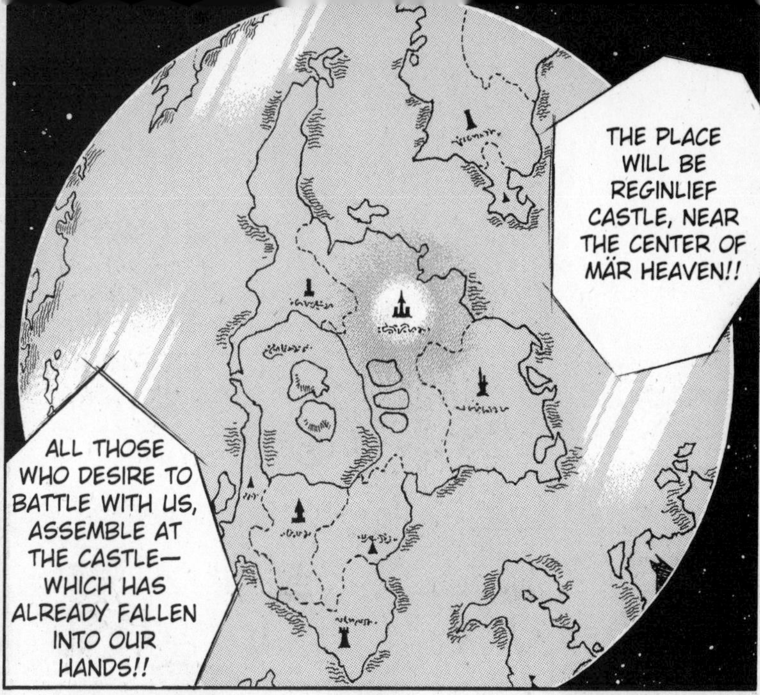
THE PLACE WILL BE REGINLIEF CASTLE, NEAR THE CENTER OF MÄR HEAVEN!!
ALL THOSE WHO DESIRE TO BATTLE WITH US, ASSEMBLE AT THE CASTLE— WHICH HAS ALREADY FALLEN INTO OUR HANDS!!

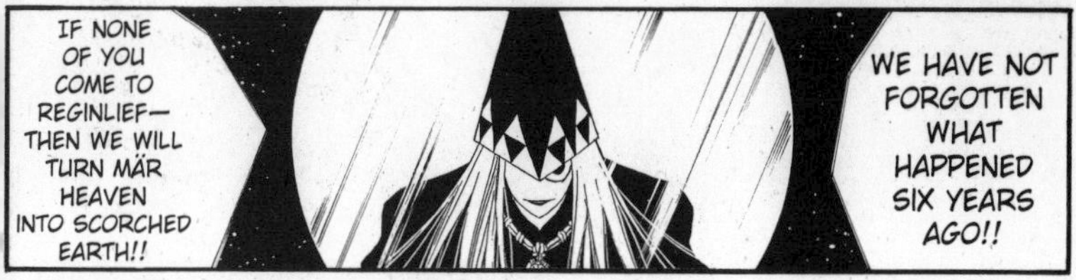
WE HAVE NOT FORGOTTEN WHAT HAPPENED SIX YEARS AGO!!
IF NONE OF YOU COME TO REGINLIEF— THEN WE WILL TURN MÄR HEAVEN INTO SCORCHED EARTH!!

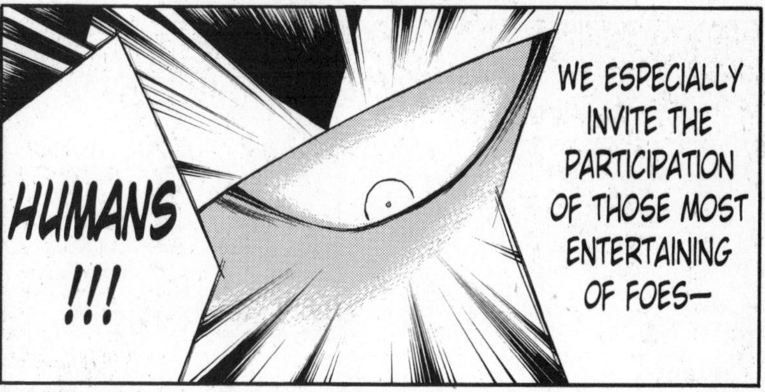
WE ESPECIALLY INVITE THE PARTICIPATION OF THOSE MOST ENTERTAINING OF FOES—
HUMANS !!!

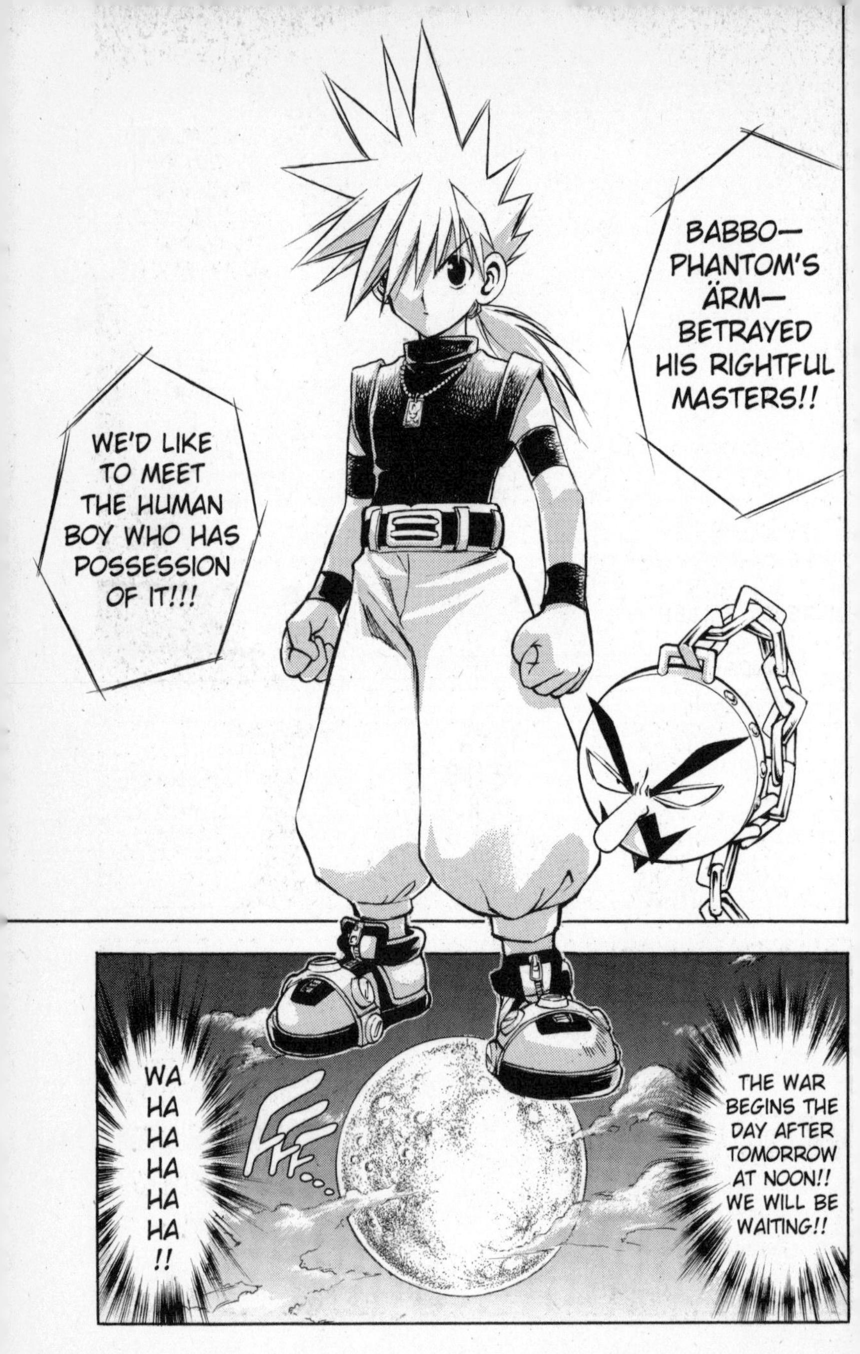
BABBO— PHANTOM'S ÄRM— BETRAYED HIS RIGHTFUL MASTERS!!
WE'D LIKE TO MEET THE HUMAN BOY WHO HAS POSSESSION OF IT!!!
THE WAR BEGINS THE DAY AFTER TOMORROW AT NOON!! WE WILL BE WAITING!!
FFF...
WA HA HA HA HA HA !!

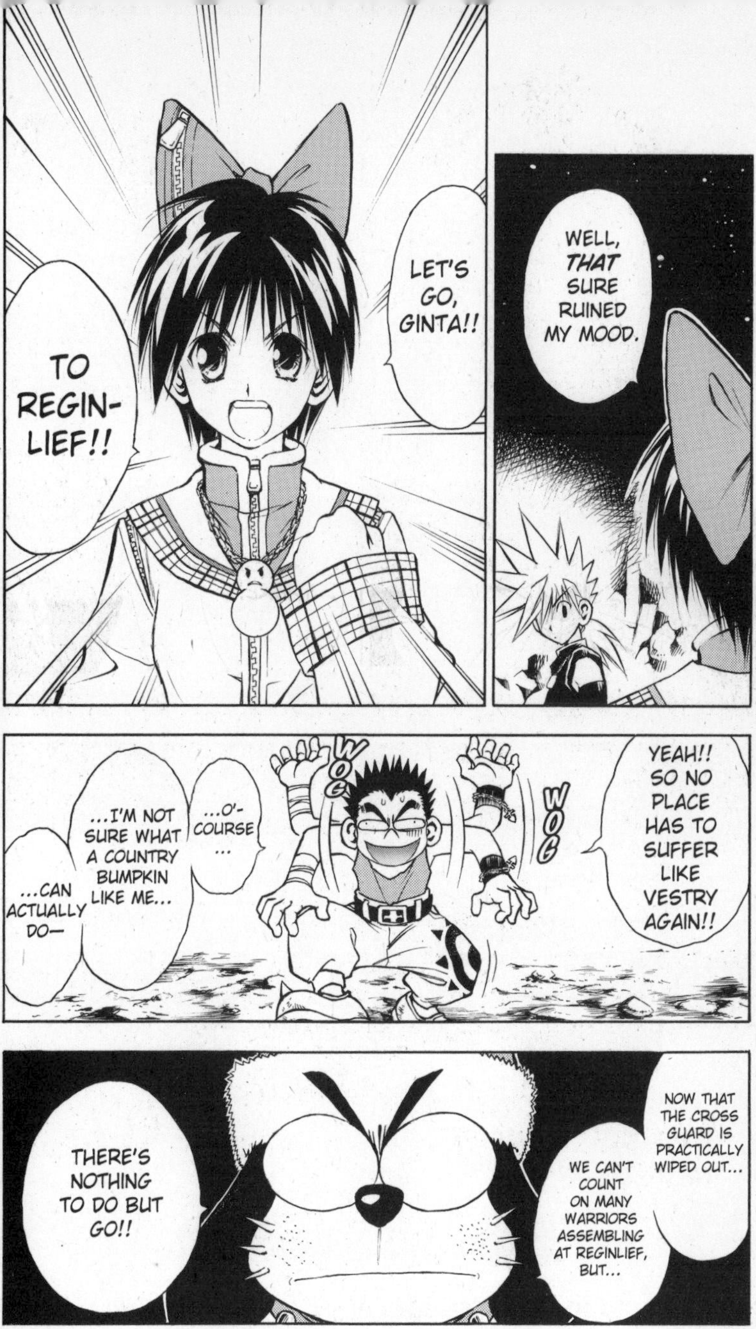

WELL, THAT SURE RUINED MY MOOD.
LET'S GO, GINTA!!
TO REGIN-LIEF!!
YEAH!! SO NO PLACE HAS TO SUFFER LIKE VESTRY AGAIN!!
WOG
WOG
...O'-COURSE...
...I'M NOT SURE WHAT A COUNTRY BUMPKIN LIKE ME...
...CAN ACTUALLY DO—
NOW THAT THE CROSS GUARD IS PRACTICALLY WIPED OUT...
WE CAN'T COUNT ON MANY WARRIORS ASSEMBLING AT REGINLIEF, BUT...
THERE'S NOTHING TO DO BUT GO!!

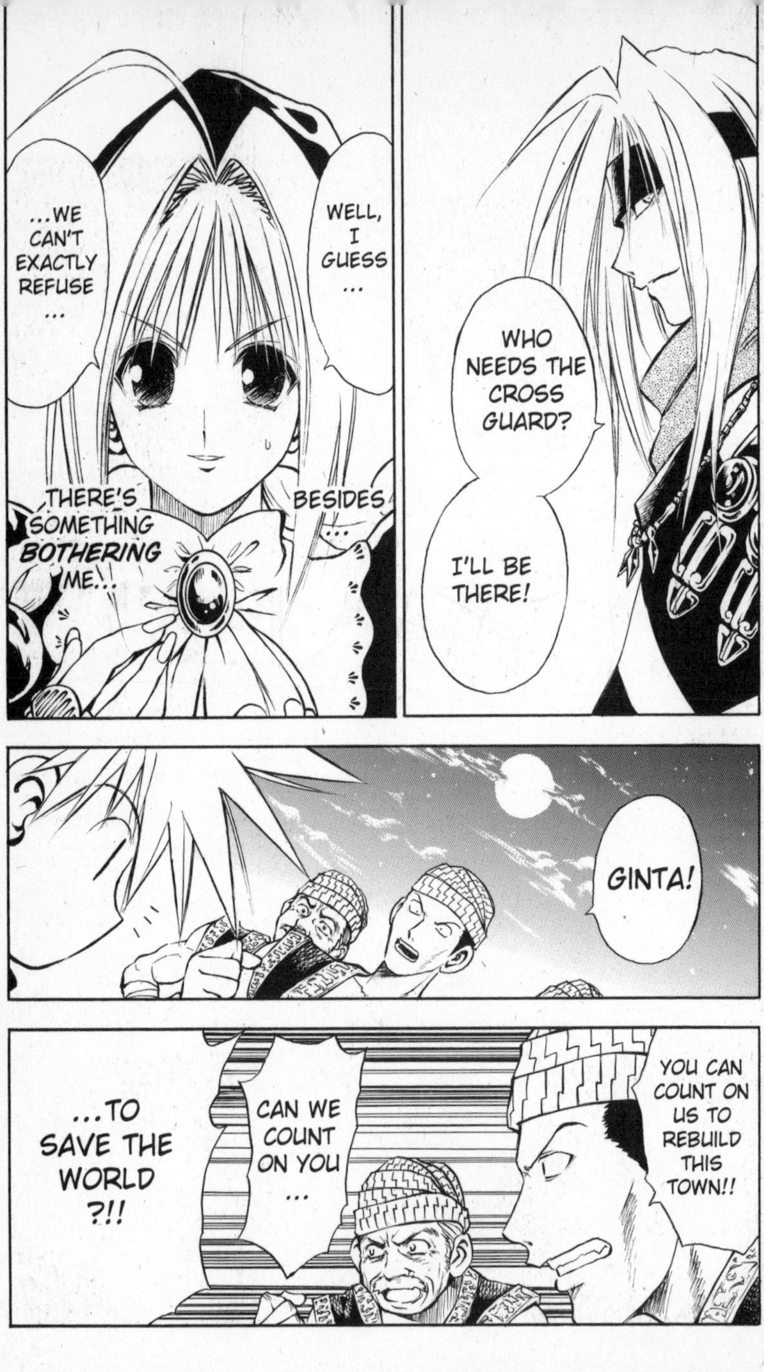
WHO NEEDS THE CROSS GUARD?
I'LL BE THERE!
WELL, I GUESS...
...WE CAN'T EXACTLY REFUSE...
BESIDES...
THERE'S SOMETHING *BOTHERING* ME...
GINTA!
YOU CAN COUNT ON US TO REBUILD THIS TOWN!!
CAN WE COUNT ON YOU...
...TO SAVE THE WORLD?!!

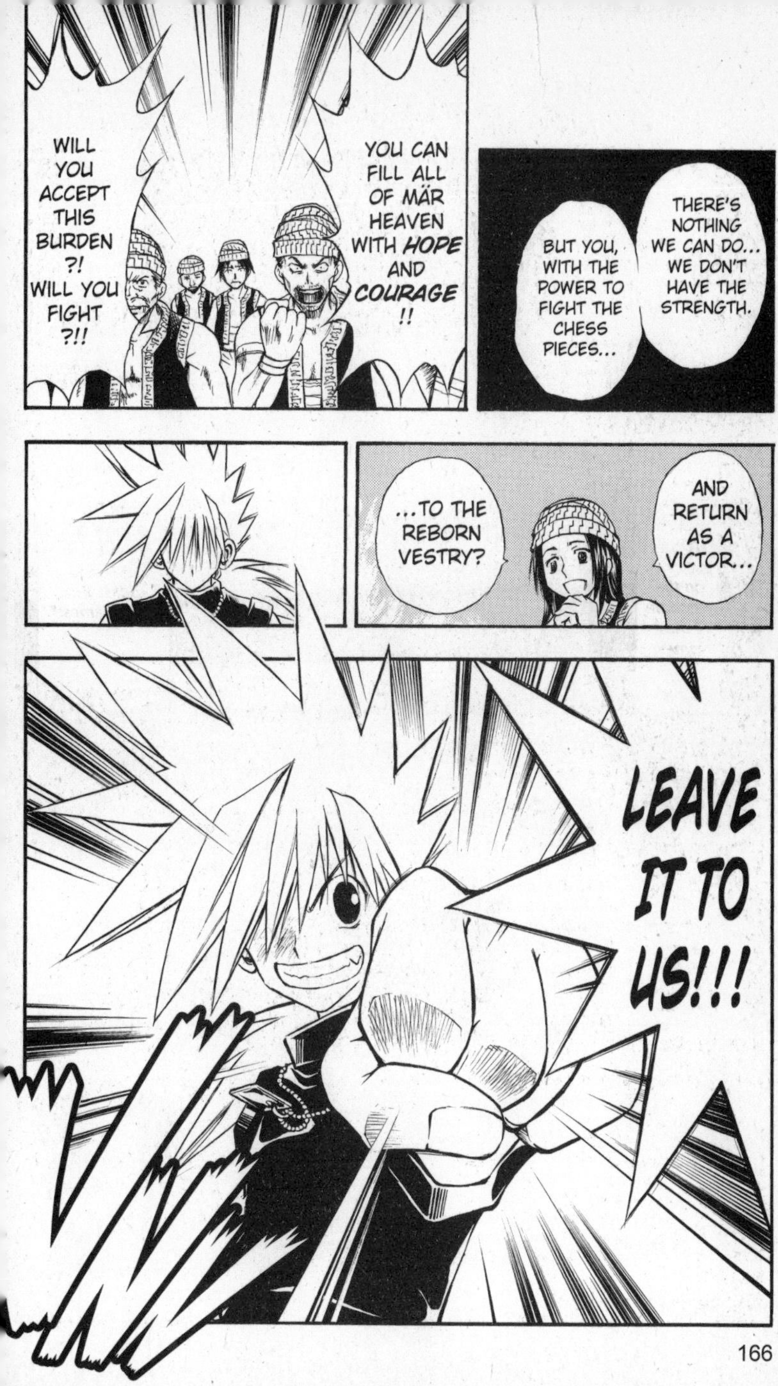
THERE'S NOTHING WE CAN DO... WE DON'T HAVE THE STRENGTH.
BUT YOU, WITH THE POWER TO FIGHT THE CHESS PIECES...
YOU CAN FILL ALL OF MÄR HEAVEN WITH HOPE AND COURAGE!!
WILL YOU ACCEPT THIS BURDEN?! WILL YOU FIGHT?!!
AND RETURN AS A VICTOR...
...TO THE REBORN VESTRY?
LEAVE IT TO US!!!

AKT.41/THE TEST

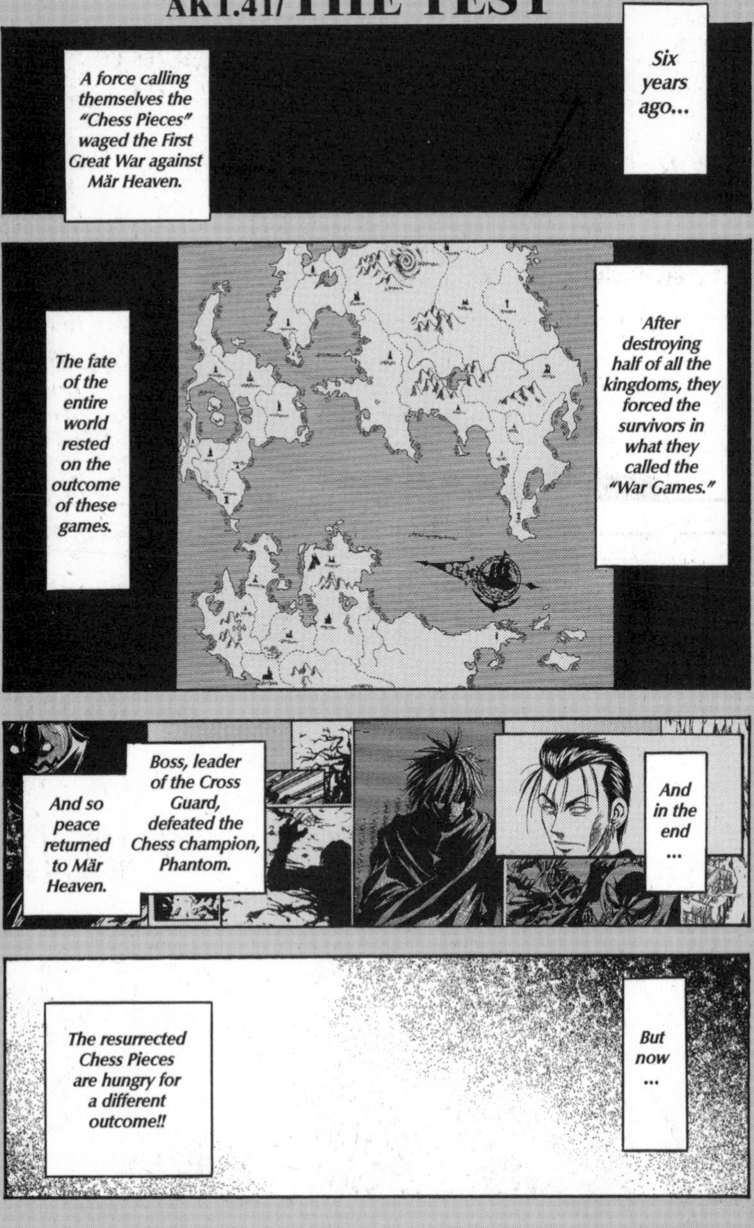

Six years ago...
A force calling themselves the "Chess Pieces" waged the First Great War against Mär Heaven.
After destroying half of all the kingdoms, they forced the survivors in what they called the "War Games."
The fate of the entire world rested on the outcome of these games.
And in the end ...
Boss, leader of the Cross Guard, defeated the Chess champion, Phantom.
And so peace returned to Mär Heaven.
But now ...
The resurrected Chess Pieces are hungry for a different outcome!!

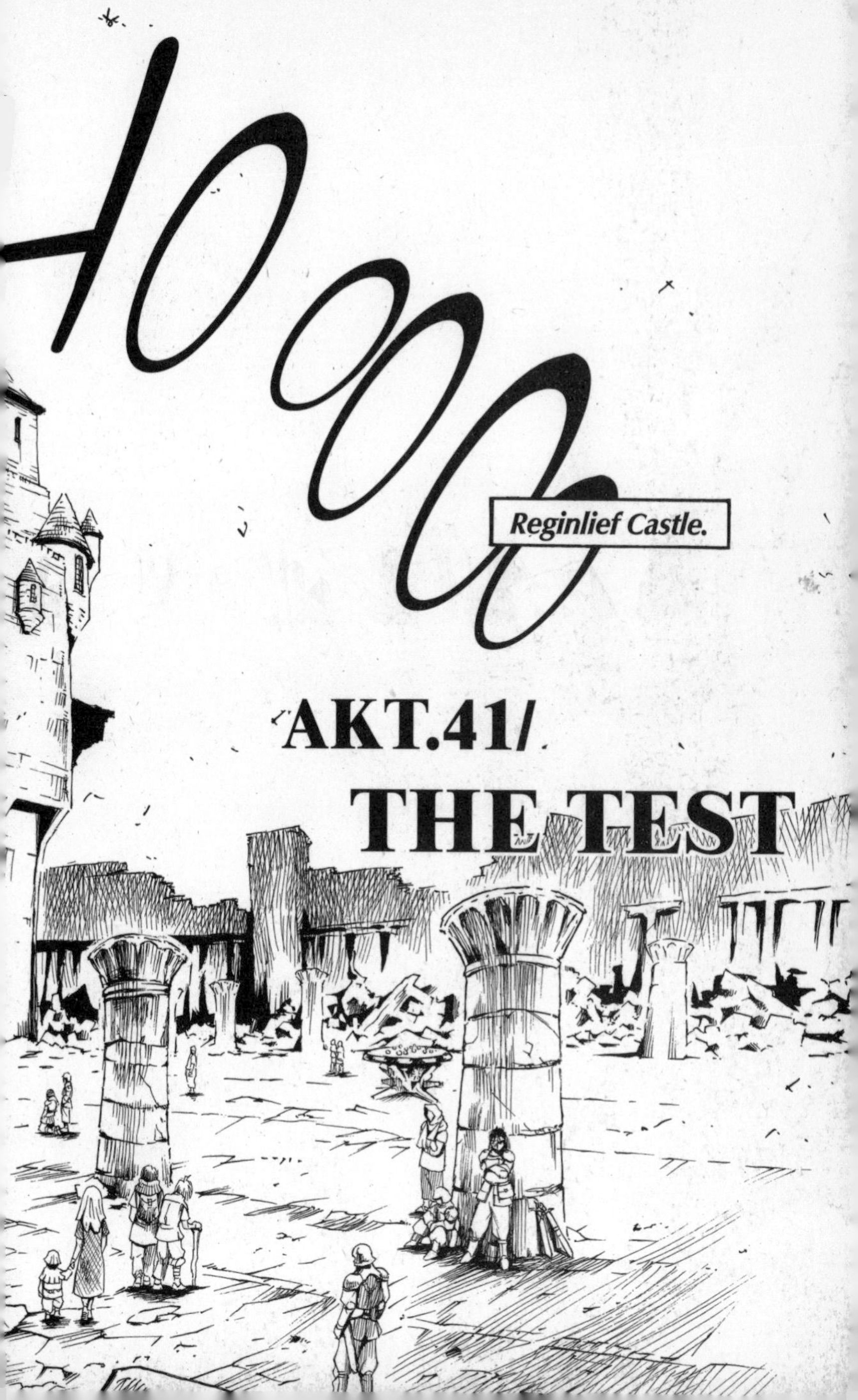

Reginlief Castle.
AKT.41/ THE TEST

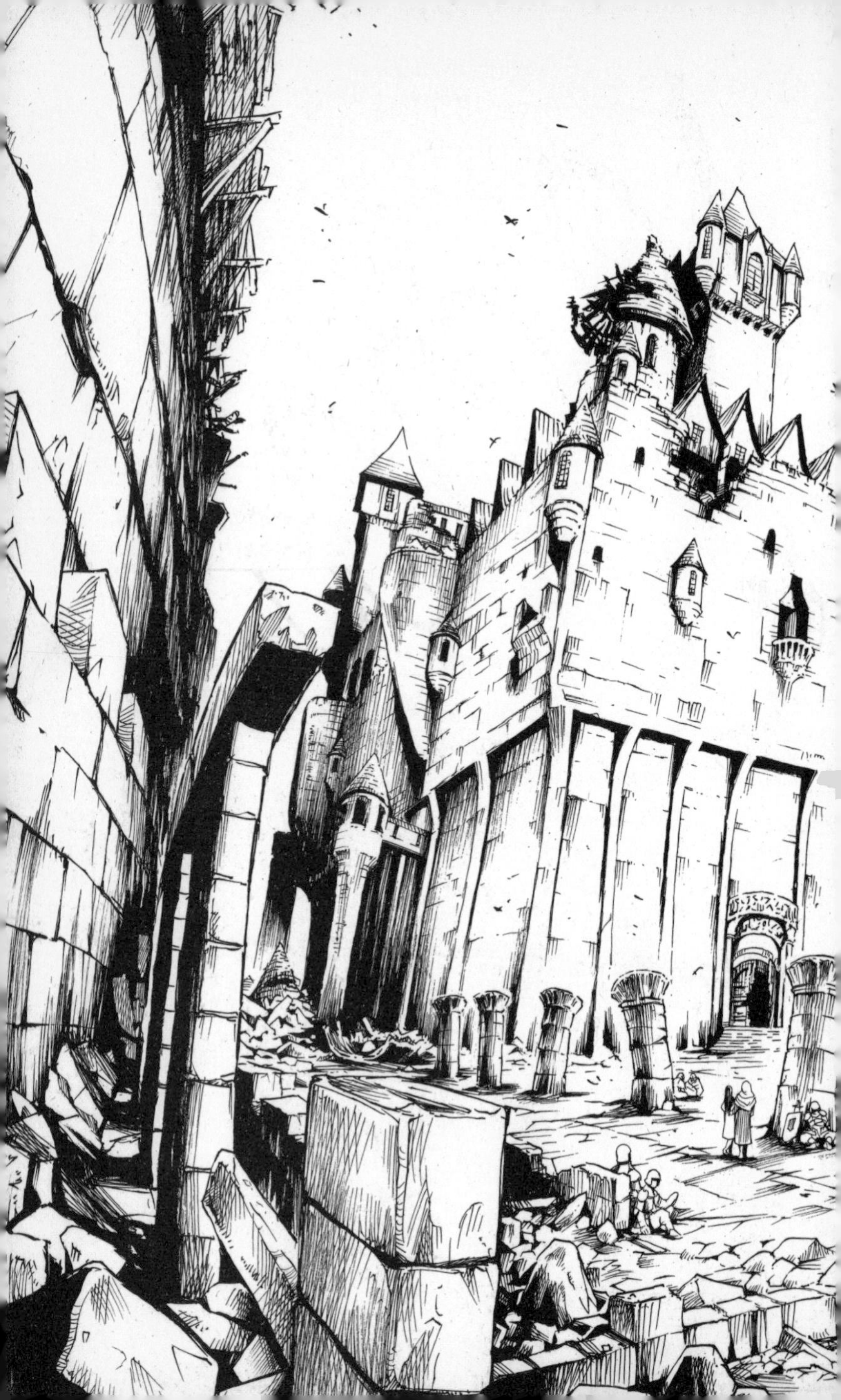

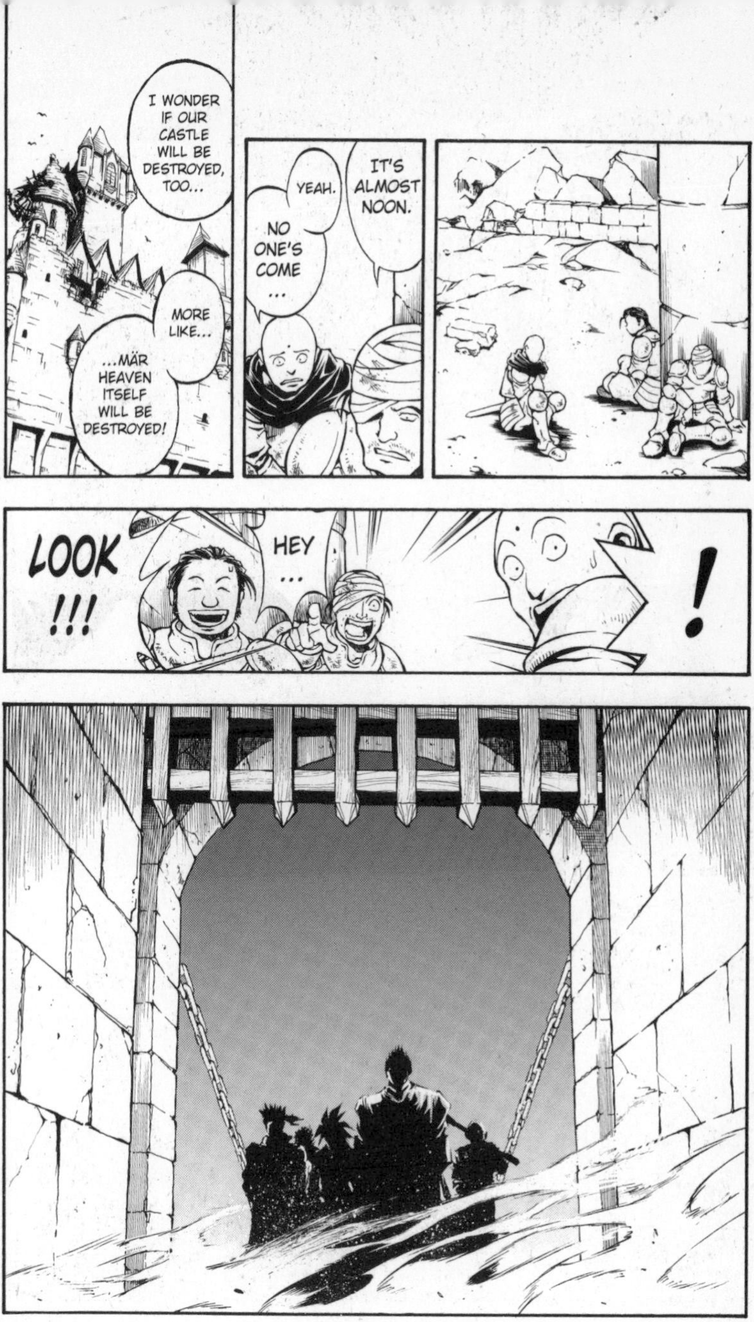
IT'S ALMOST NOON.
YEAH.
NO ONE'S COME ...
I WONDER IF OUR CASTLE WILL BE DESTROYED, TOO...
MORE LIKE...
...MÄR HEAVEN ITSELF WILL BE DESTROYED!
!
HEY ...
LOOK !!!

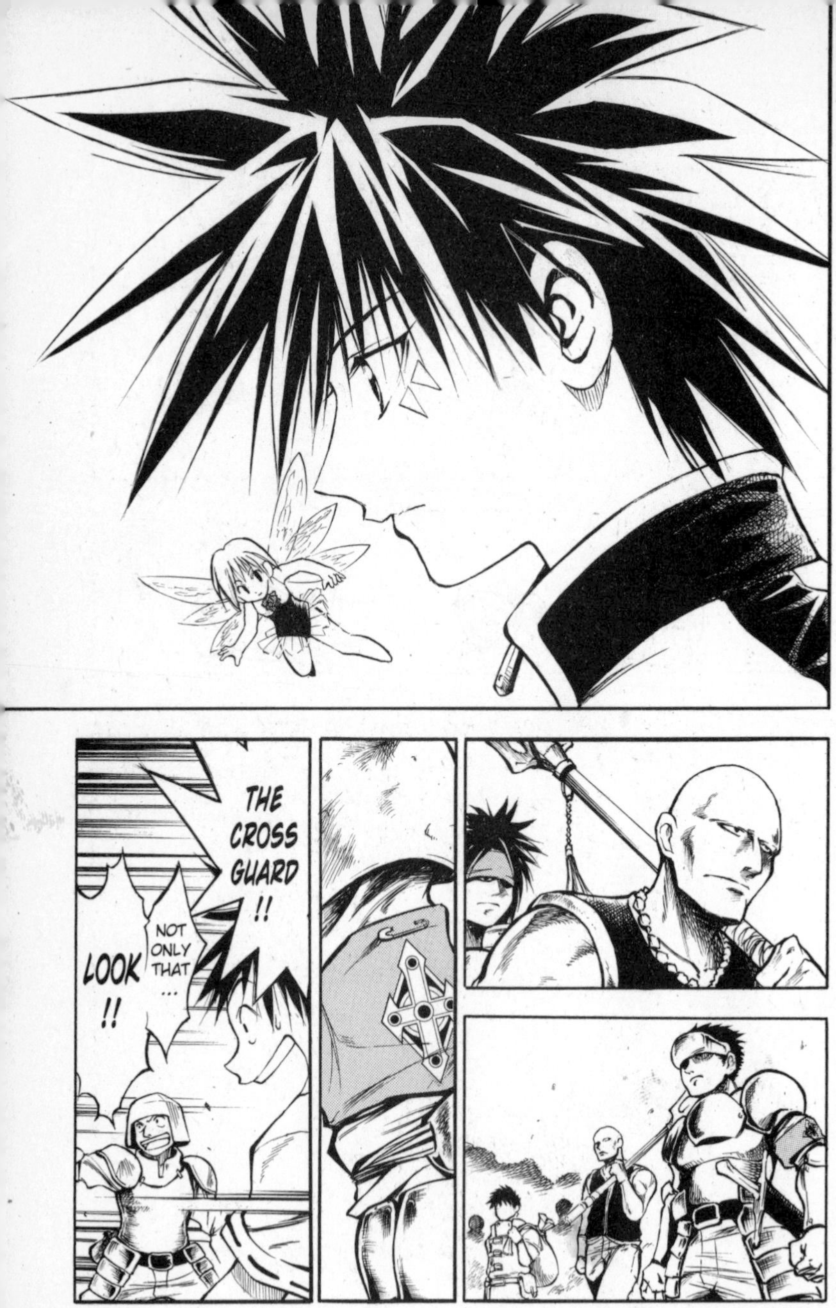
THE CROSS GUARD !!
NOT ONLY THAT ...
LOOK !!

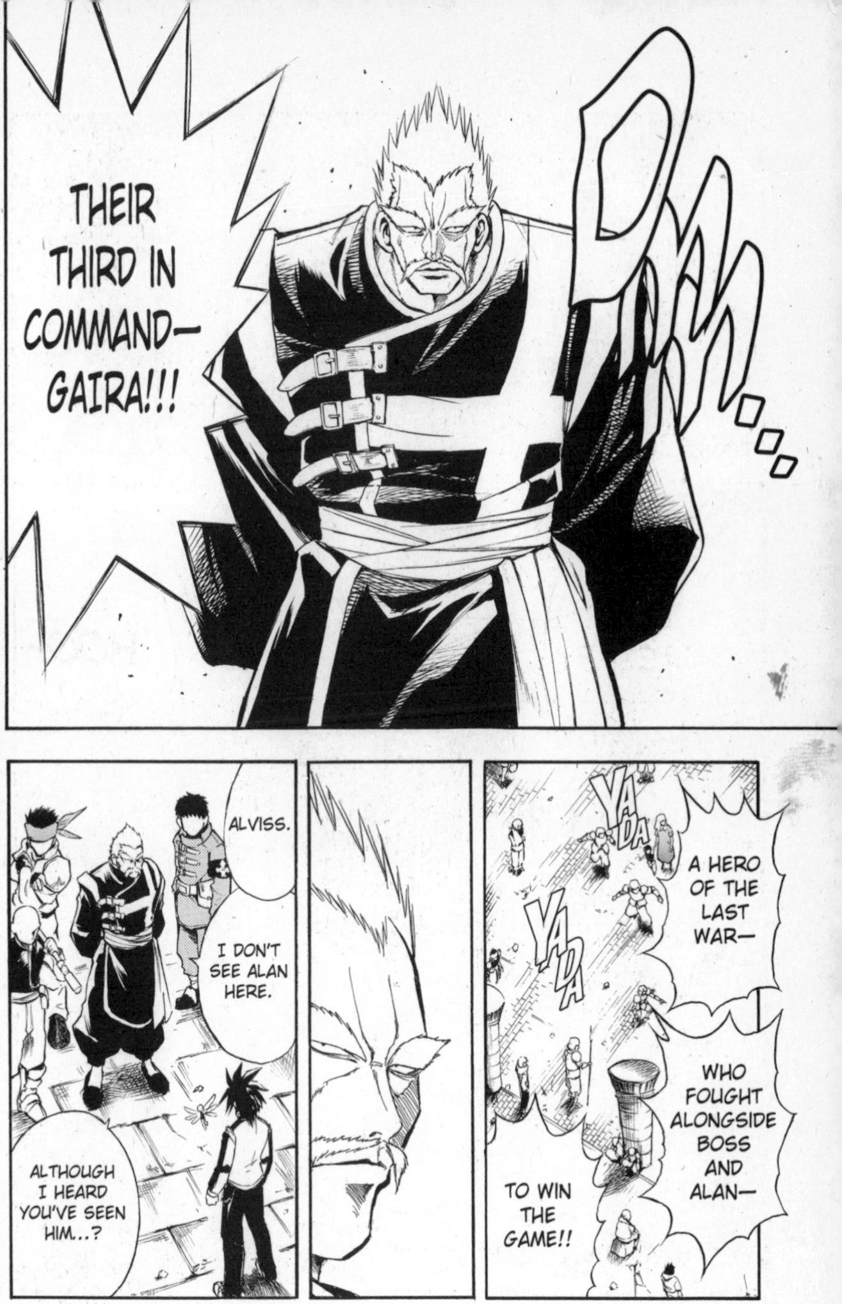
DAN...
THEIR THIRD IN COMMAND—GAIRA!!!
YADA
YADA
A HERO OF THE LAST WAR—
WHO FOUGHT ALONGSIDE BOSS AND ALAN—
TO WIN THE GAME!!
ALVISS.
I DON'T SEE ALAN HERE.
ALTHOUGH I HEARD YOU'VE SEEN HIM...?

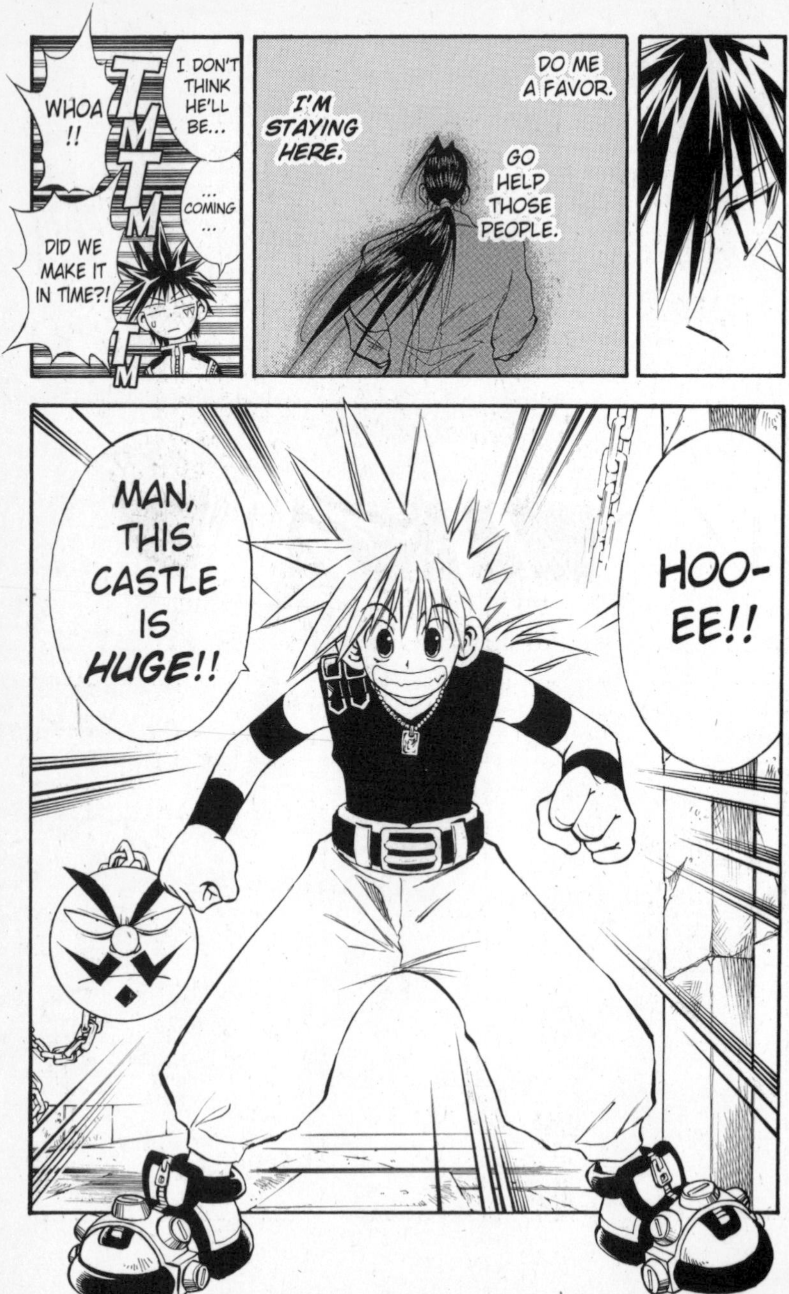
DO ME A FAVOR.
GO HELP THOSE PEOPLE.
I'M STAYING HERE.
I DON'T THINK HE'LL BE...
...COMING...
TMTMTM
WHOA!!
DID WE MAKE IT IN TIME?!
HOO-EE!!
MAN, THIS CASTLE IS HUGE!!

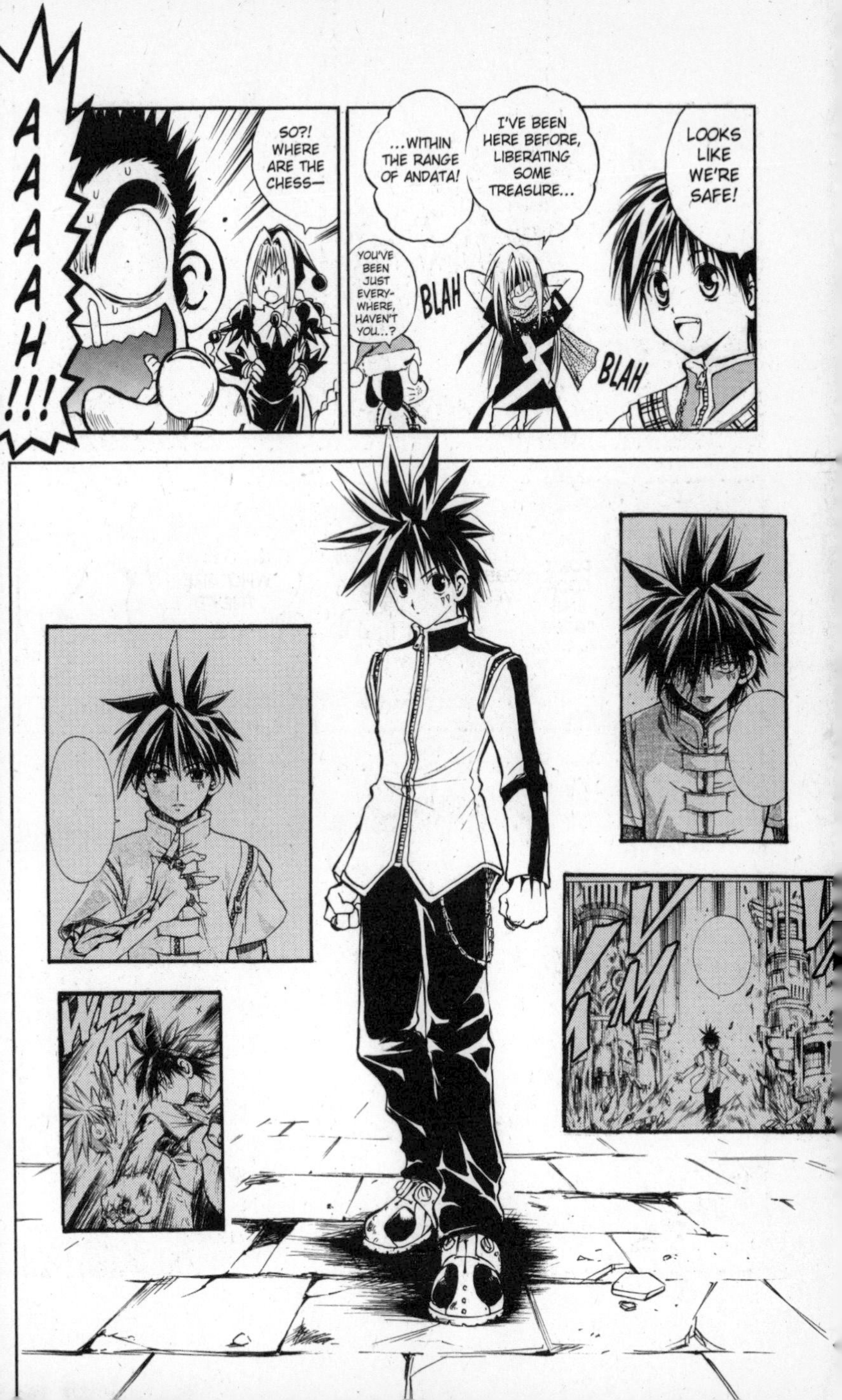
LOOKS LIKE WE'RE SAFE!
I'VE BEEN HERE BEFORE, LIBERATING SOME TREASURE...
...WITHIN THE RANGE OF ANDATA!
BLAH
BLAH
YOU'VE BEEN JUST EVERY-WHERE, HAVEN'T YOU...?
SO?! WHERE ARE THE CHESS—
AAAAAH!!!

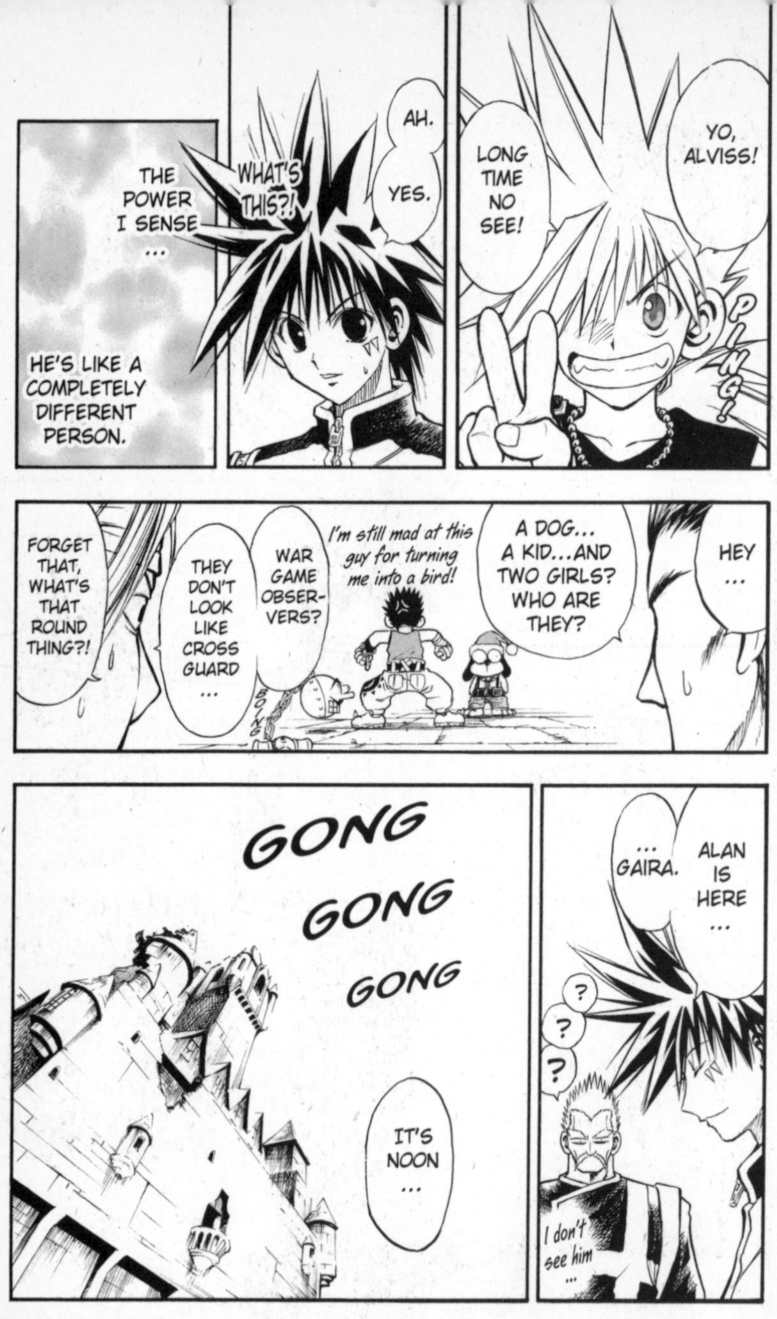
YO, ALVISS!
LONG TIME NO SEE!
PING!
AH.
YES.
WHAT'S THIS?!
THE POWER I SENSE ...
HE'S LIKE A COMPLETELY DIFFERENT PERSON.
HEY ...
A DOG... A KID...AND TWO GIRLS? WHO ARE THEY?
I'm still mad at this guy for turning me into a bird!
WAR GAME OBSERVERS?
THEY DON'T LOOK LIKE CROSS GUARD ...
FORGET THAT, WHAT'S THAT ROUND THING?!
BOING
ALAN IS HERE ...
... GAIRA.
? ? ?
I don't see him ...
GONG
GONG
GONG
IT'S NOON ...

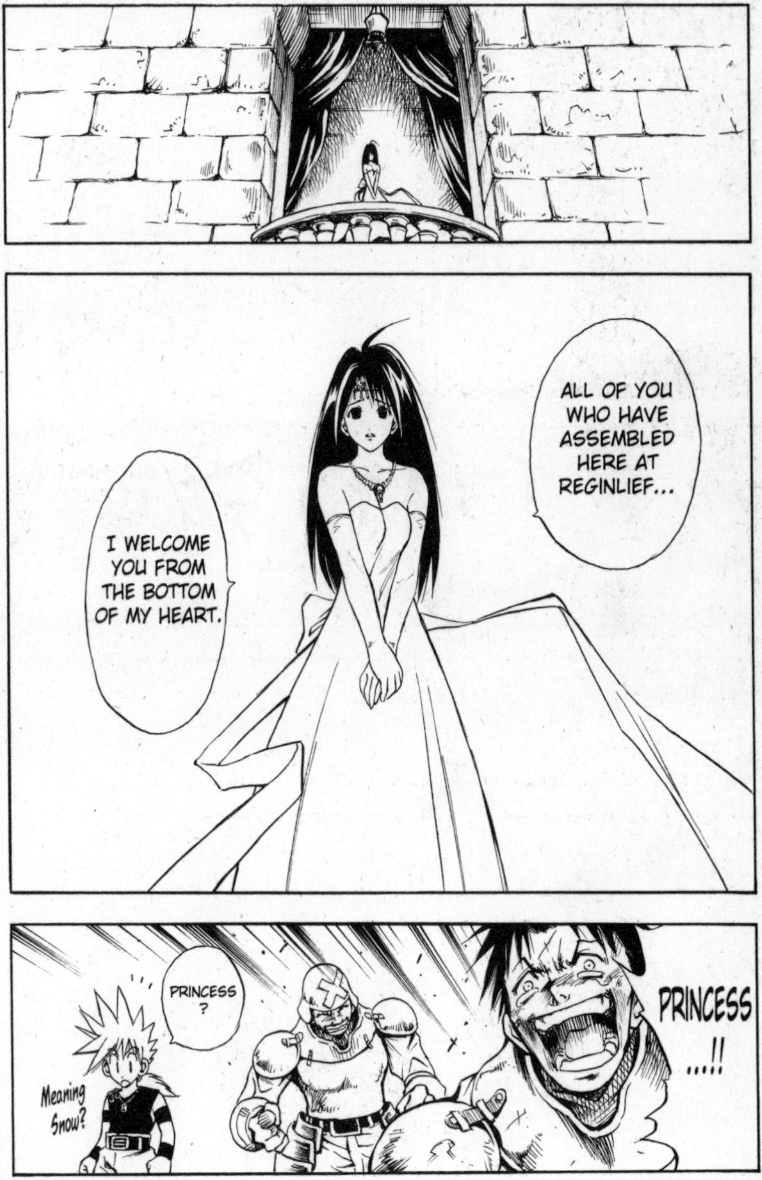
ALL OF YOU WHO HAVE ASSEMBLED HERE AT REGINLIEF...
I WELCOME YOU FROM THE BOTTOM OF MY HEART.
PRINCESS ...!!
PRINCESS ?
Meaning Snow?

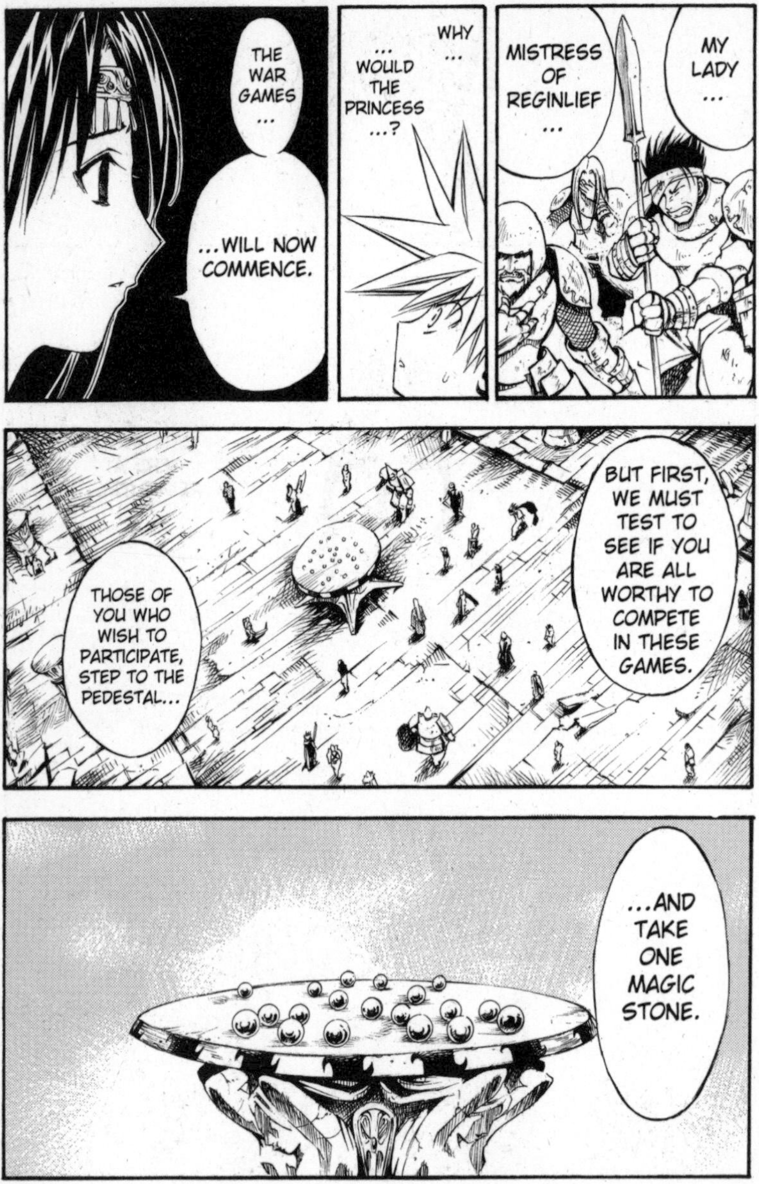
MY LADY ...
MISTRESS OF REGINLIEF ...
WHY ...
... WOULD THE PRINCESS ...?
THE WAR GAMES ...
...WILL NOW COMMENCE.
BUT FIRST, WE MUST TEST TO SEE IF YOU ARE ALL WORTHY TO COMPETE IN THESE GAMES.
THOSE OF YOU WHO WISH TO PARTICIPATE, STEP TO THE PEDESTAL...
...AND TAKE ONE MAGIC STONE.

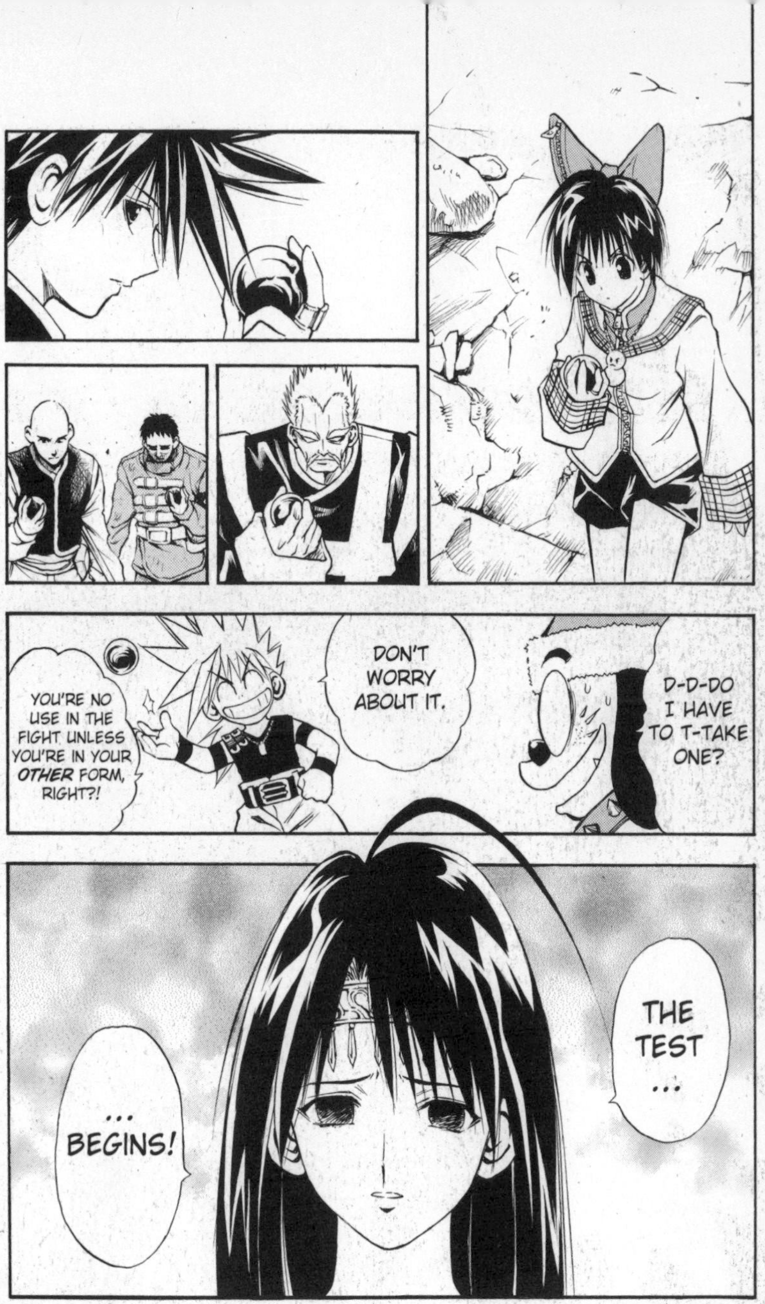
D-D-DO I HAVE TO T-TAKE ONE?
DON'T WORRY ABOUT IT.
YOU'RE NO USE IN THE FIGHT UNLESS YOU'RE IN YOUR *OTHER* FORM, RIGHT?!
THE TEST ...
... BEGINS!

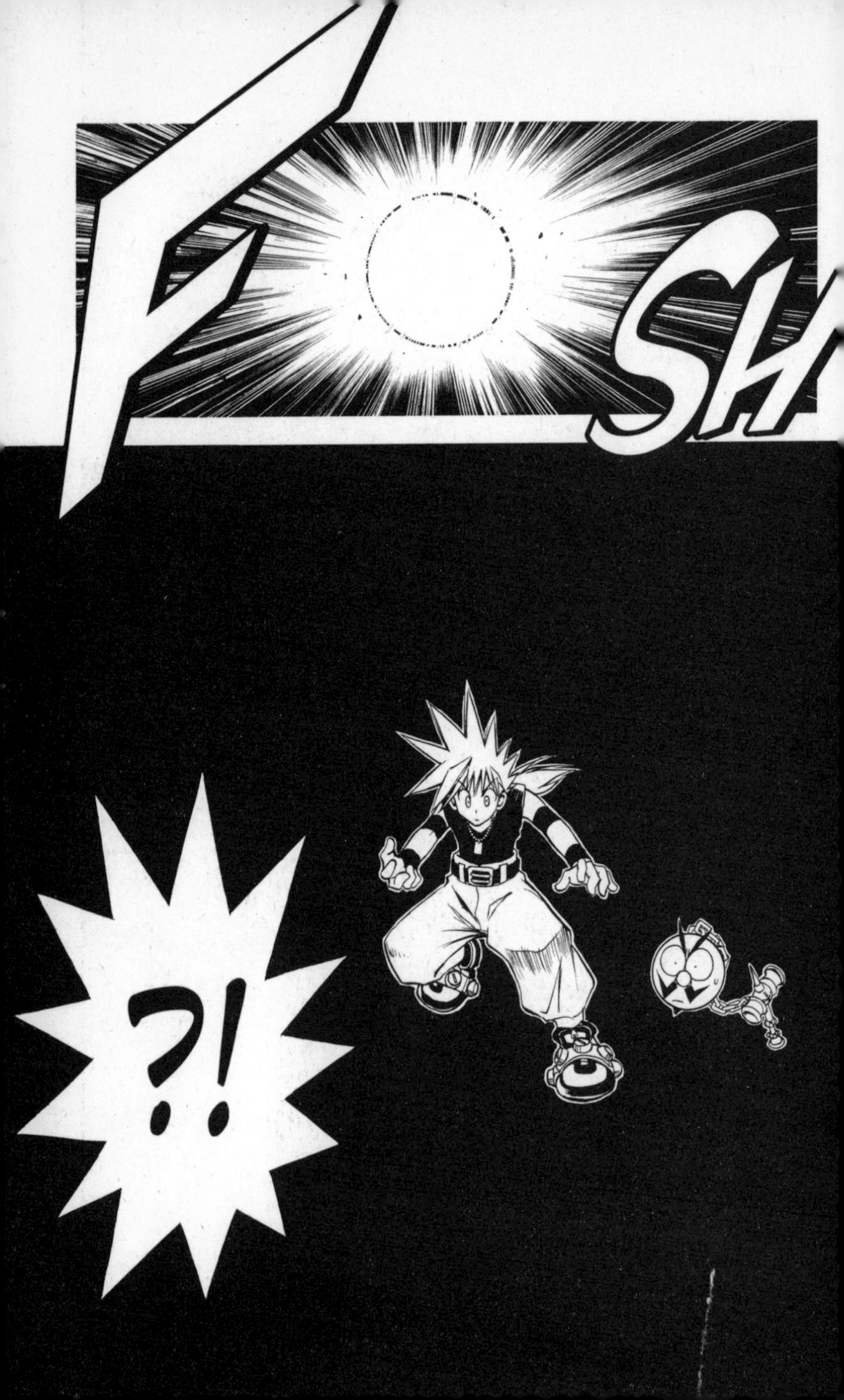
SH
?!

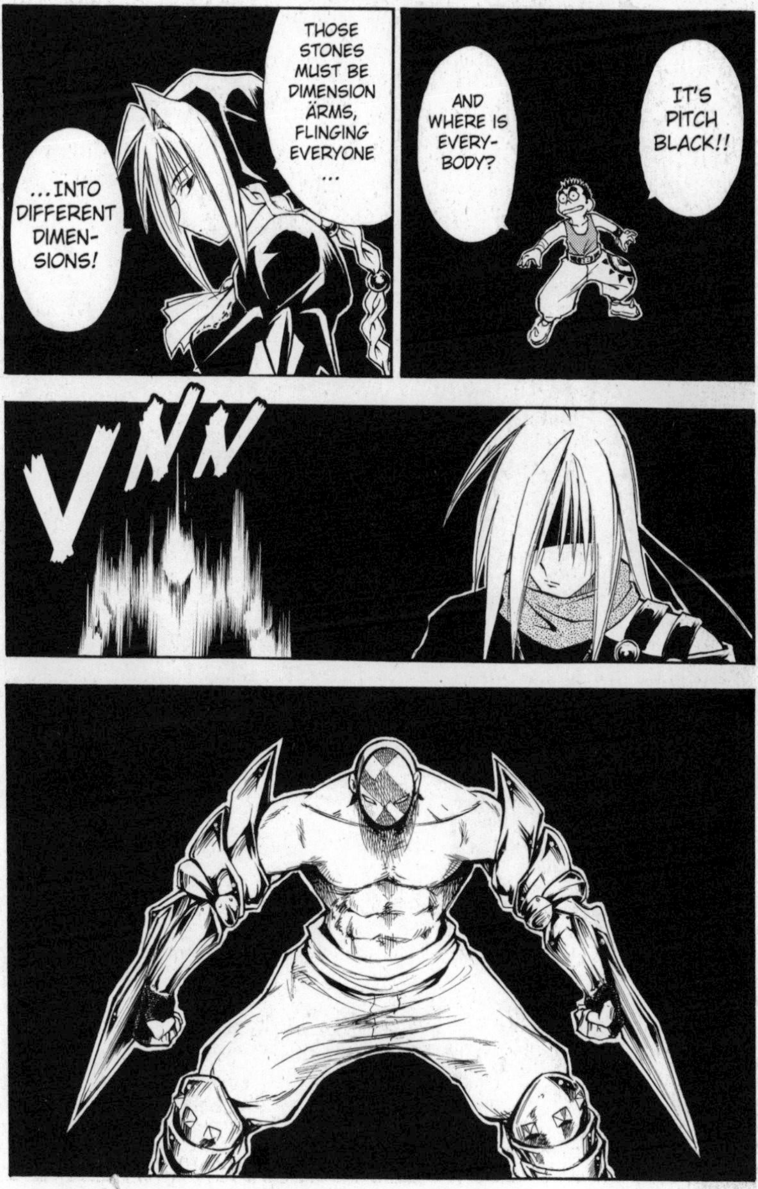
IT'S PITCH BLACK!!
AND WHERE IS EVERY-BODY?
THOSE STONES MUST BE DIMENSION ÄRMS, FLINGING EVERYONE ...
...INTO DIFFERENT DIMEN-SIONS!
VNN

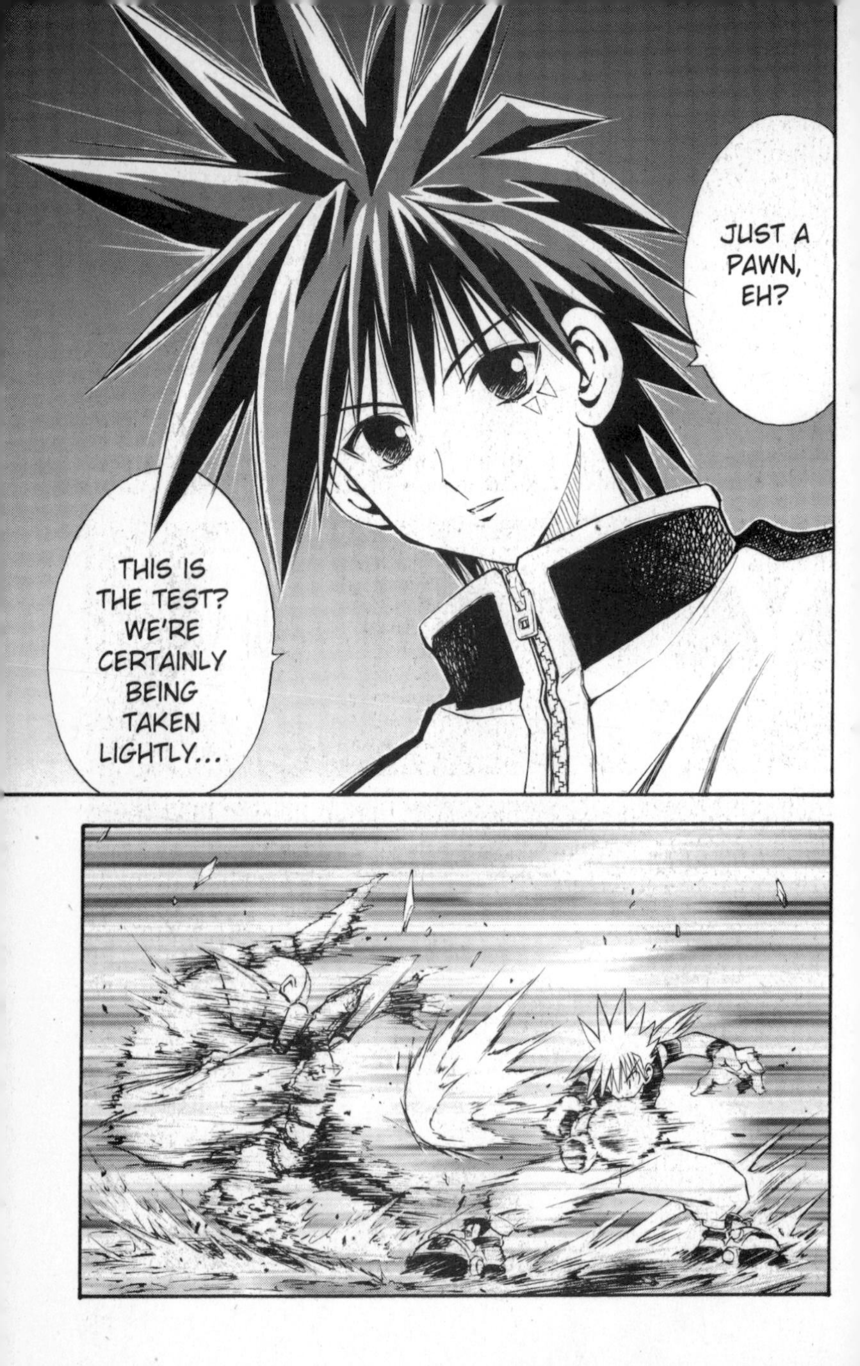
JUST A PAWN, EH?
THIS IS THE TEST? WE'RE CERTAINLY BEING TAKEN LIGHTLY...

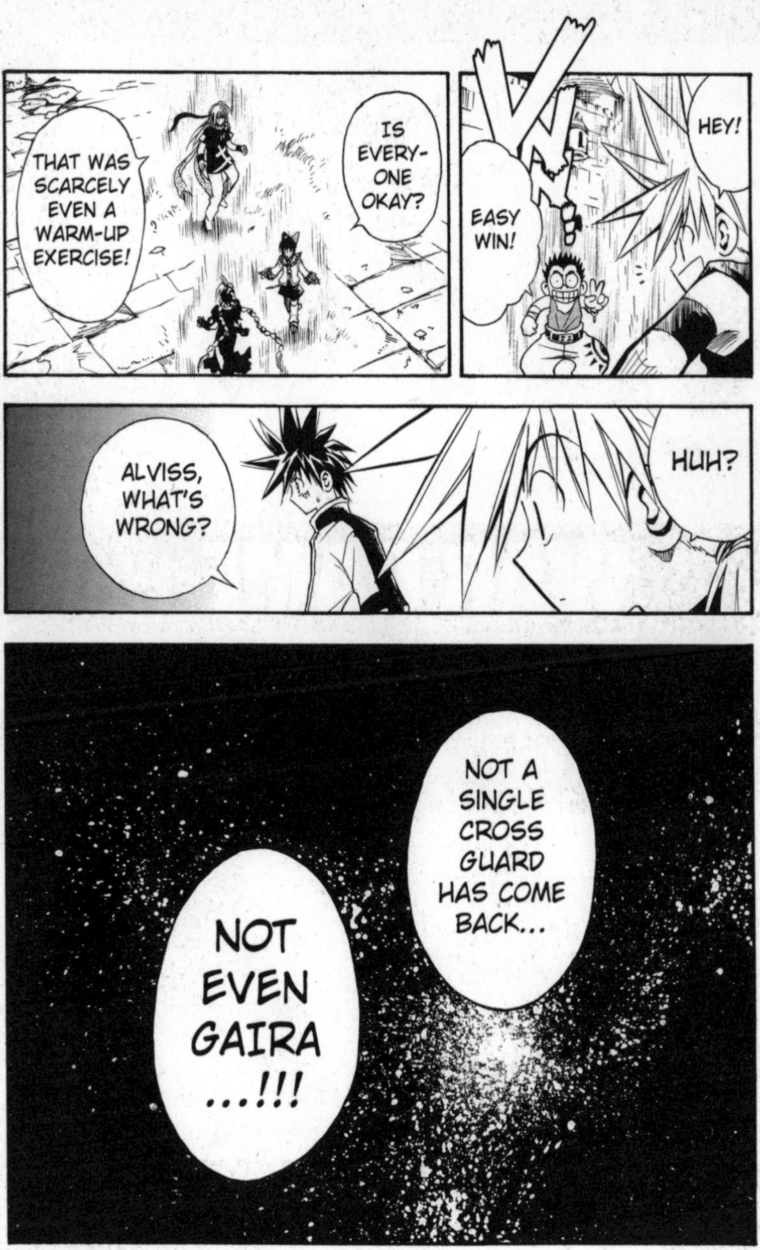
HEY!
EASY WIN!
IS EVERY-ONE OKAY?
THAT WAS SCARCELY EVEN A WARM-UP EXERCISE!
HUH?
ALVISS, WHAT'S WRONG?
NOT A SINGLE CROSS GUARD HAS COME BACK...
NOT EVEN GAIRA ...!!!

THE EXCITEMENT BUILDS...

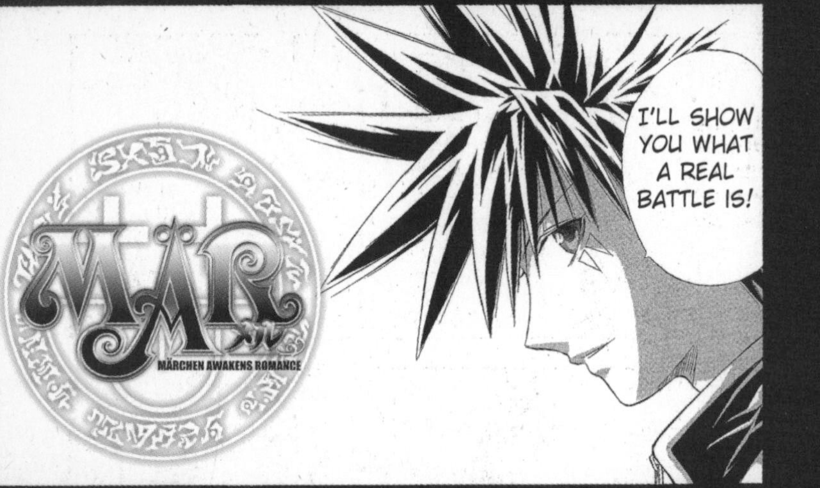
I'LL SHOW YOU WHAT A REAL BATTLE IS!
MÄRCHEN AWAKENS ROMANCE

WAR GAME

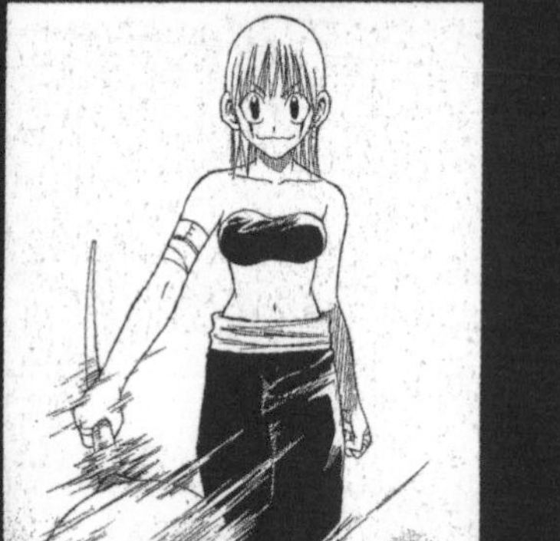

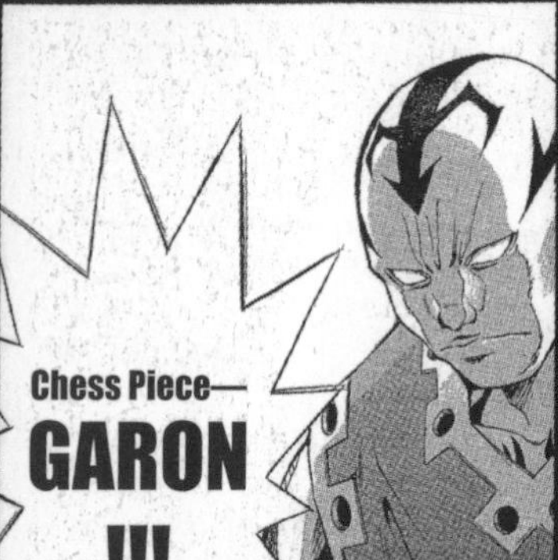
Chess Piece— GARON !!!

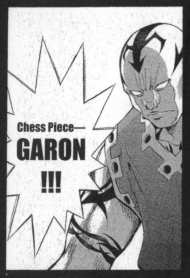

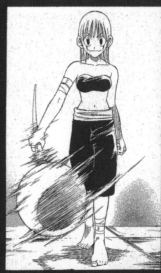

Volume 5

COMING SOON!

ACID VOMIT

Written by: GB
Title lettering: Anzai

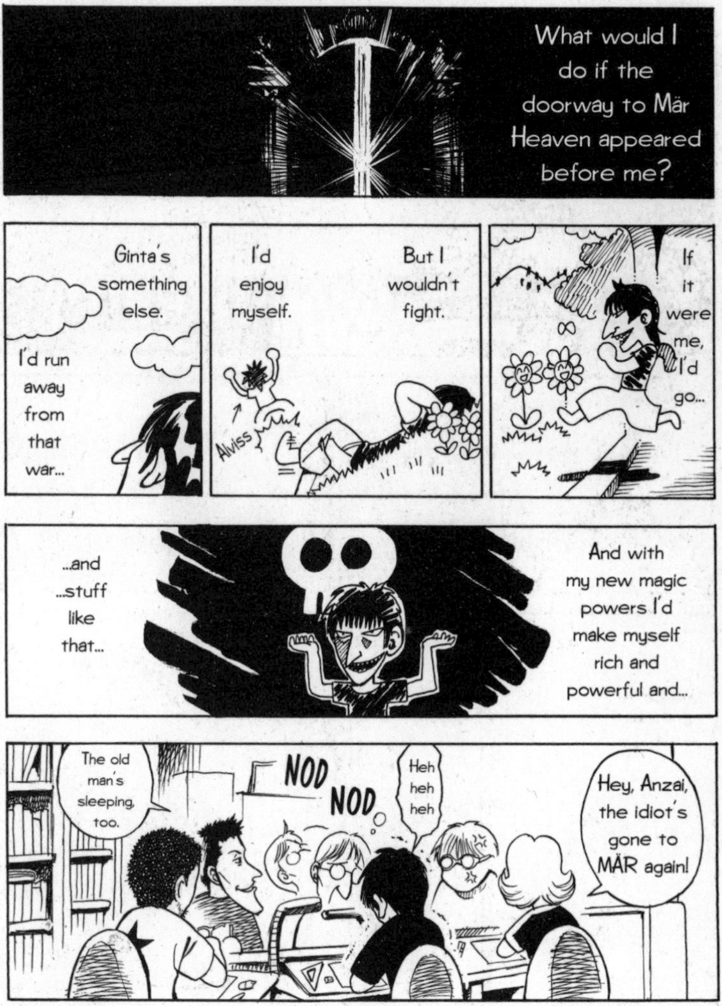
What would I do if the doorway to Mär Heaven appeared before me?
If it were me, I'd go...
But I wouldn't fight.
I'd enjoy myself.
Alviss
Ginta's something else.
I'd run away from that war...
And with my new magic powers I'd make myself rich and powerful and...
...and ...stuff like that...
Hey, Anzai, the idiot's gone to MÄR again!
Heh heh heh
NOD NOD
The old man's sleeping, too.

By Fuse X

The Real Mär Heaven

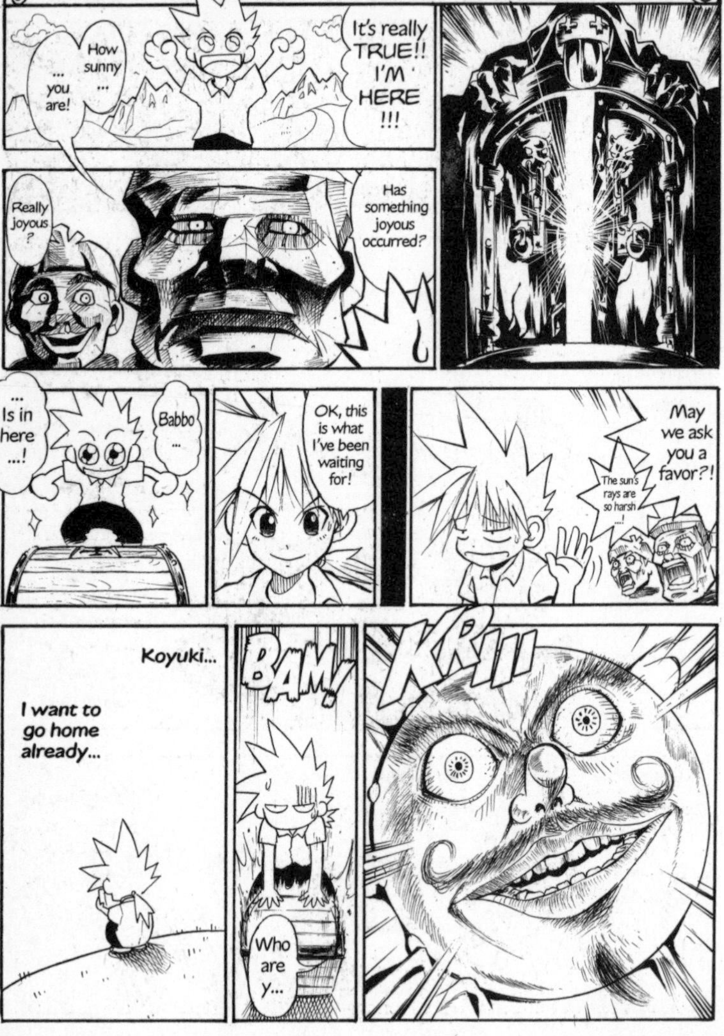
It's really TRUE!! I'M HERE!!!
How sunny...
... you are!
Has something joyous occurred?
Really joyous?
May we ask you a favor?!
The sun's rays are so harsh...!
OK, this is what I've been waiting for!
Babbo...
... Is in here...!
KRIII
BAM!
Who are y...
Koyuki...
I want to go home already...

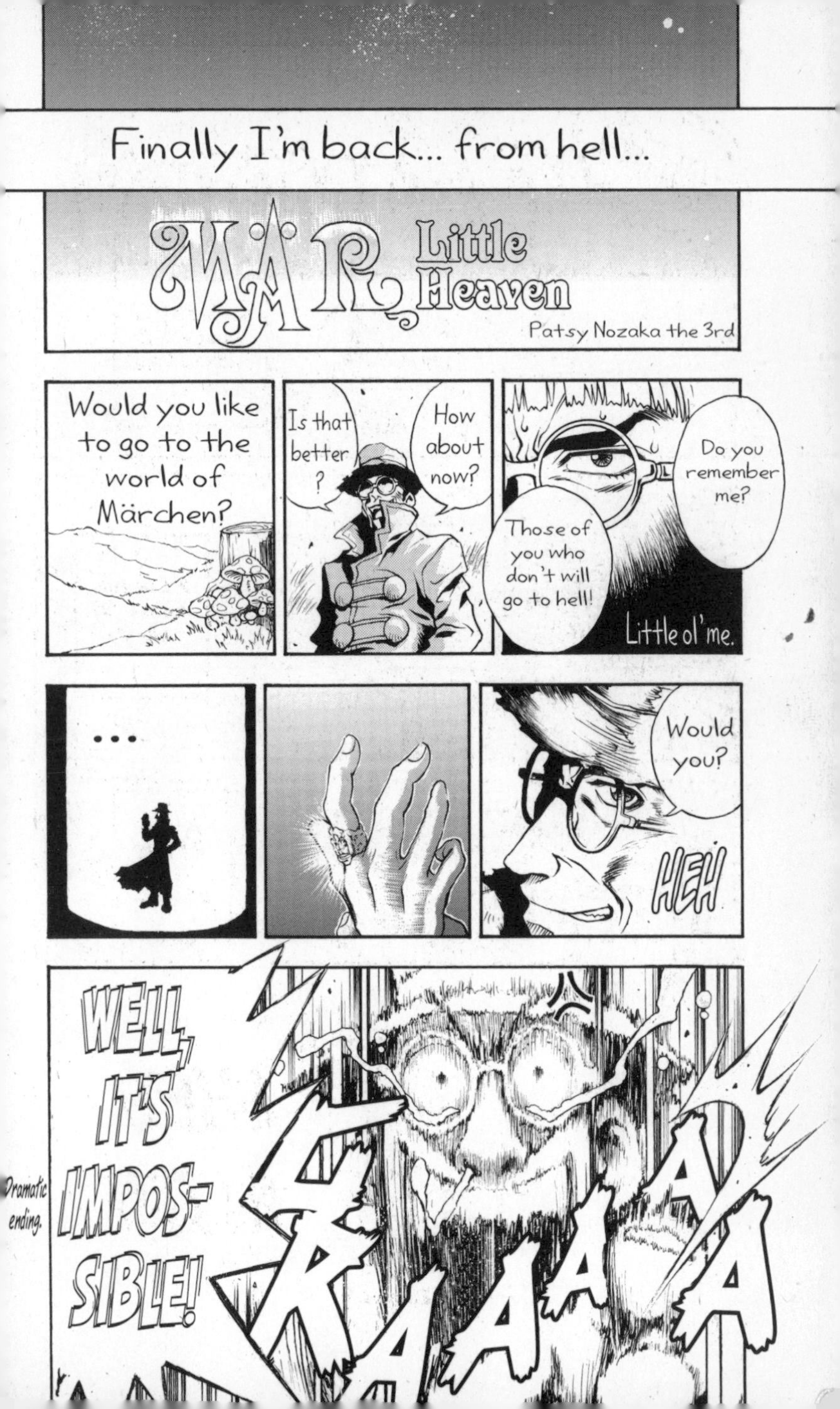

Finally I'm back... from hell...
WAR Little Heaven
Patsy Nozaka the 3rd
Do you remember me?
Those of you who don't will go to hell!
Little ol' me.
How about now?
Is that better?
Would you like to go to the world of Märchen?
Would you?
HEH
...
WELL, IT'S IMPOS-SIBLE!
Dramatic ending.

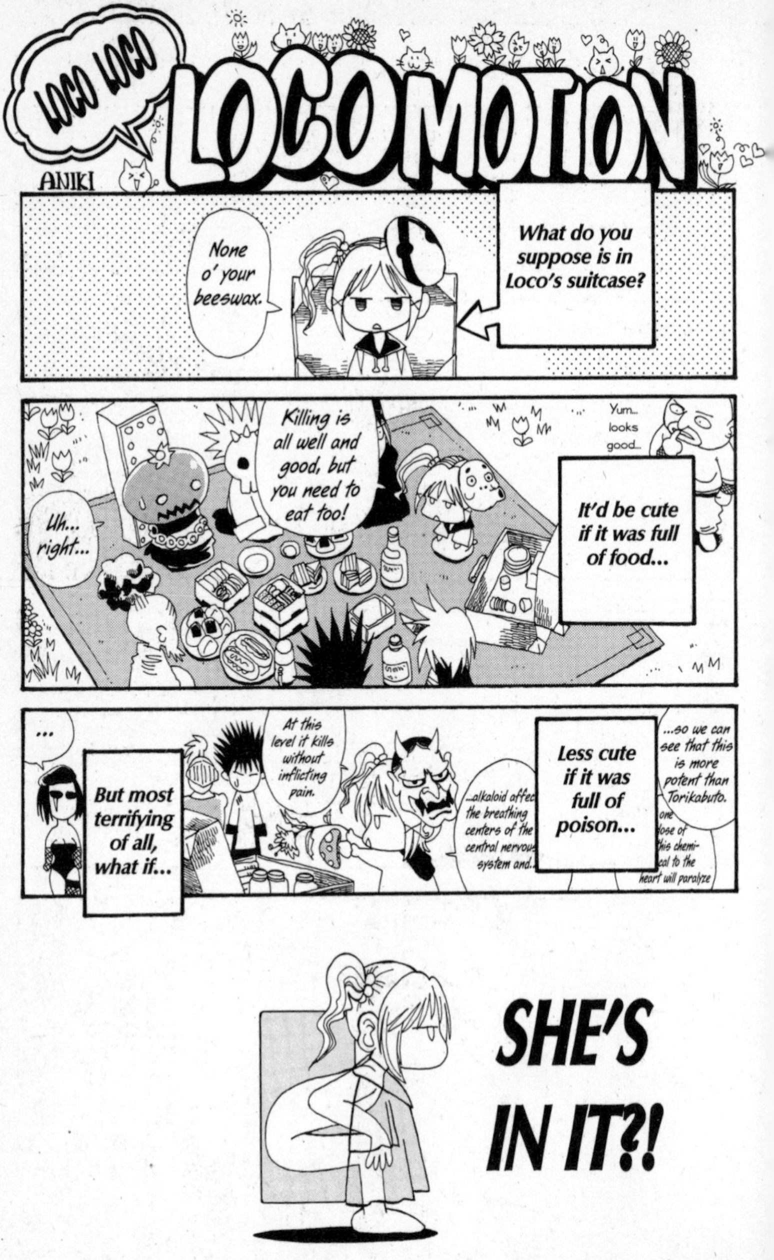
LOCO LOCO
LOCOMOTION
ANIKI
What do you suppose is in Loco's suitcase?
None o' your beeswax.
Yum... looks good...
It'd be cute if it was full of food...
Killing is all well and good, but you need to eat too!
Uh... right...
...so we can see that this is more potent than Torikabuto. one dose of this chemical to the heart will paralyze
Less cute if it was full of poison...
...alkaloid affec the breathing centers of the central nervous system and...
At this level it kills without inflicting pain.
But most terrifying of all, what if...
...
SHE'S IN IT?!

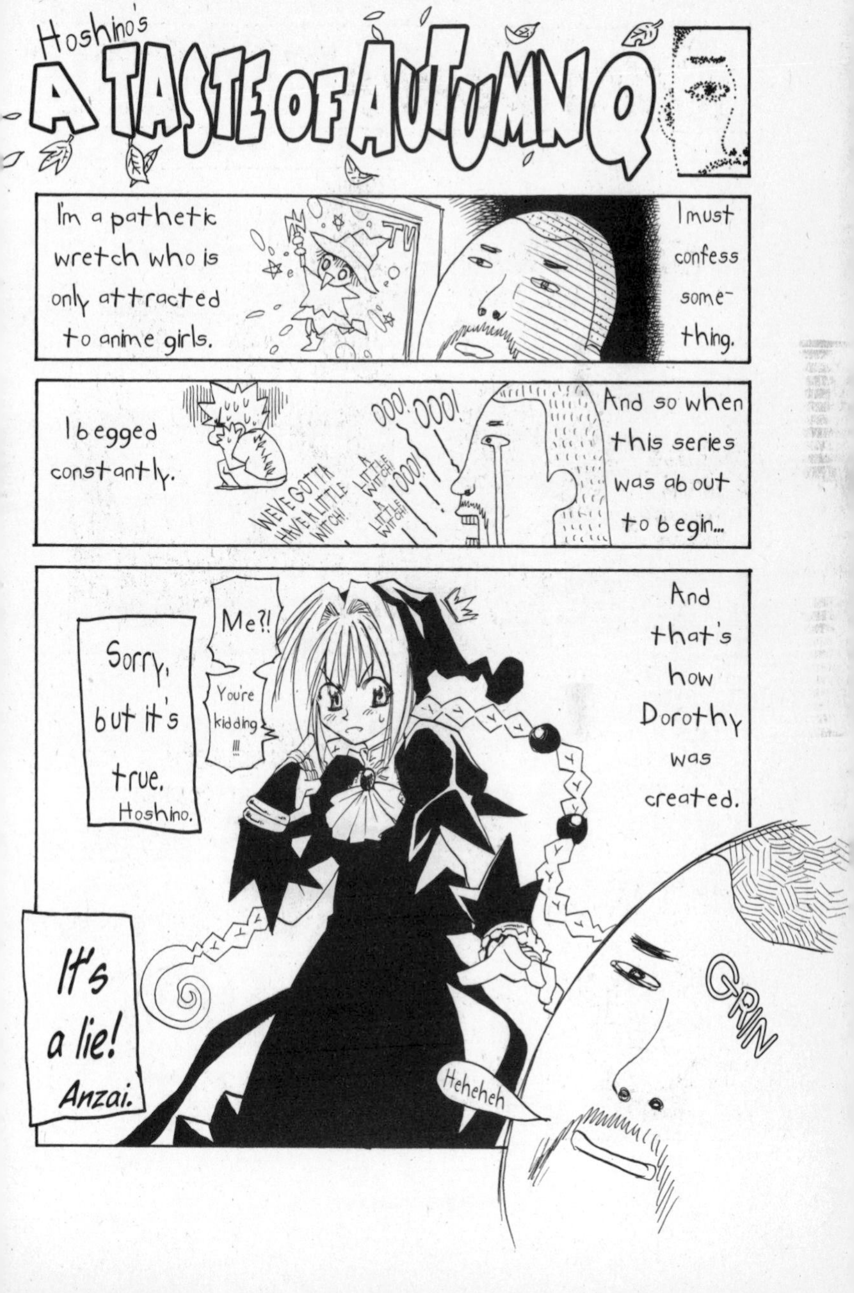
Hoshino's
A TASTE OF AUTUMN
I must confess some-thing.
I'm a pathetic wretch who is only attracted to anime girls.
TV
And so when this series was about to begin...
OOO! OOO!
OOO!
A LITTLE WITCH!
A LITTLE WITCH!
WE'VE GOTTA HAVE A LITTLE WITCH!
I begged constantly.
And that's how Dorothy was created.
Me?!
You're kidding!!!
Sorry, but it's true. Hoshino.
GRIN
Heheheh
It's a lie! Anzai.

Extra Bonus

(Illustration Contest)

Nobuyuki Anzai

Grand Prize

Ms. Jura

Aichi Prefecture ▶

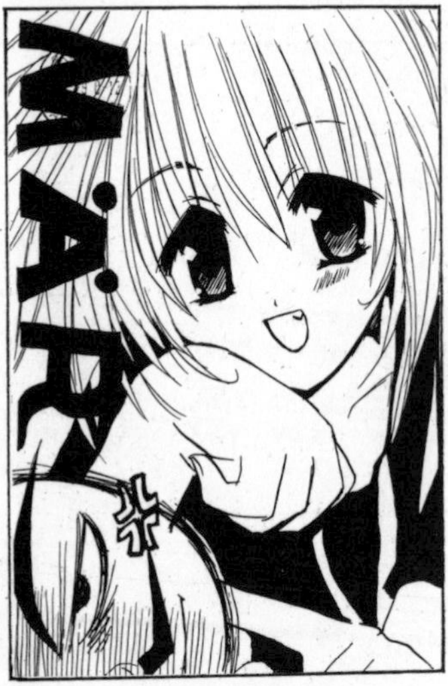
MÄR

Sakura Fubuki

Nagasaki Prefecture ▶

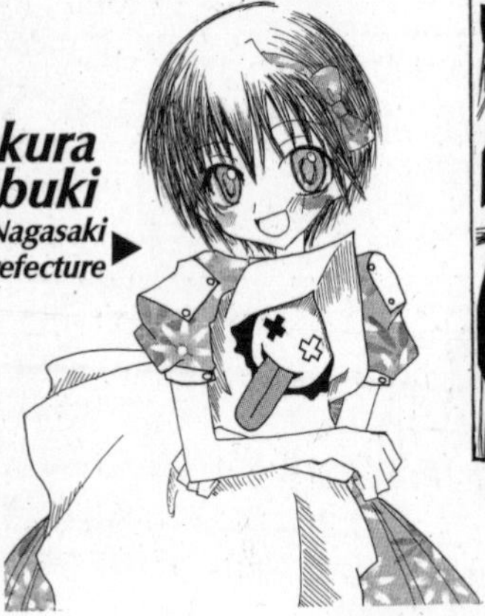

Suguri Yamaguchi ▼

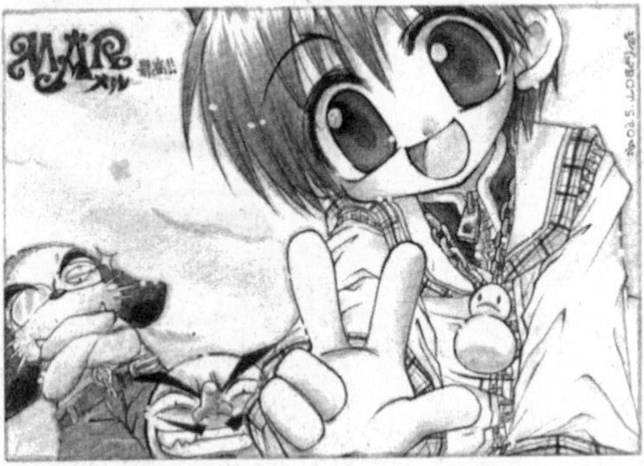

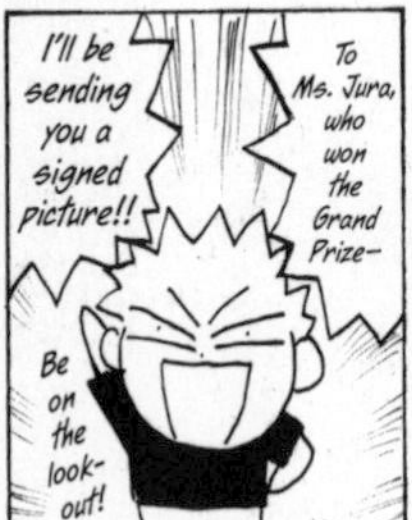
To Ms. Jura, who won the Grand Prize—
I'll be sending you a signed picture!!
Be on the look-out!

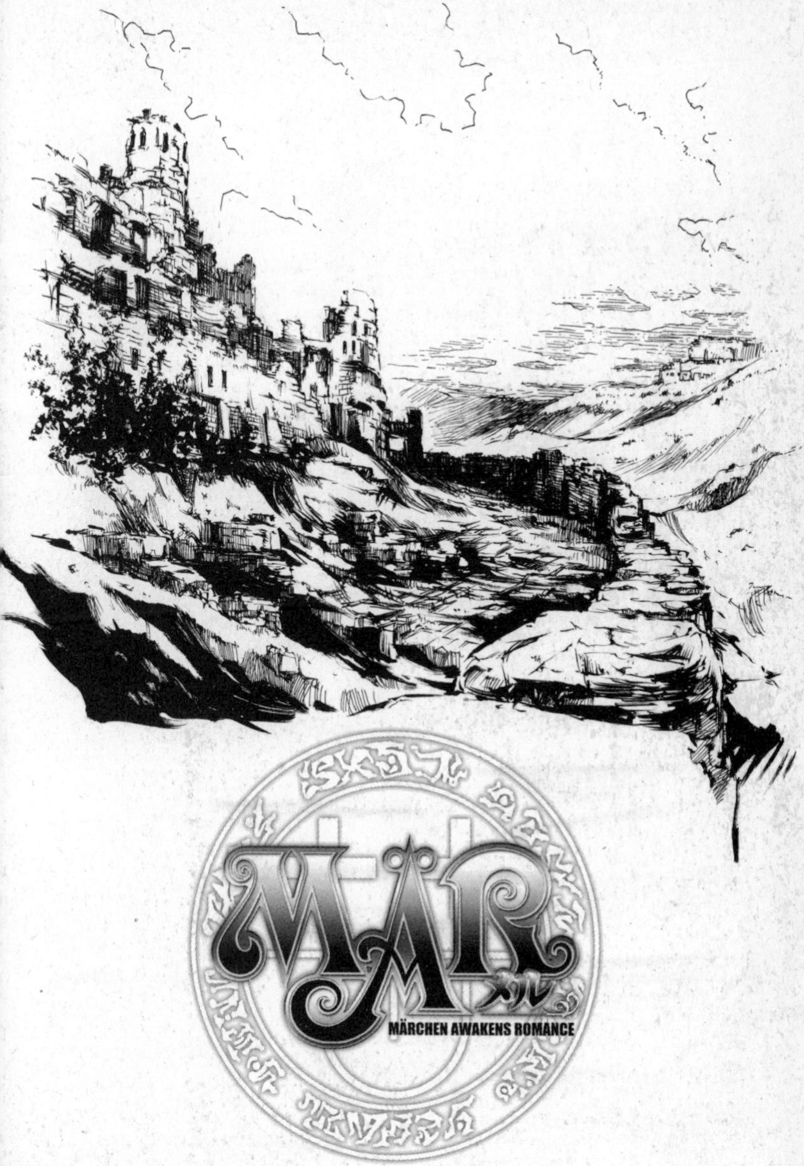

MÄR

MÄRCHEN AWAKENS ROMANCE

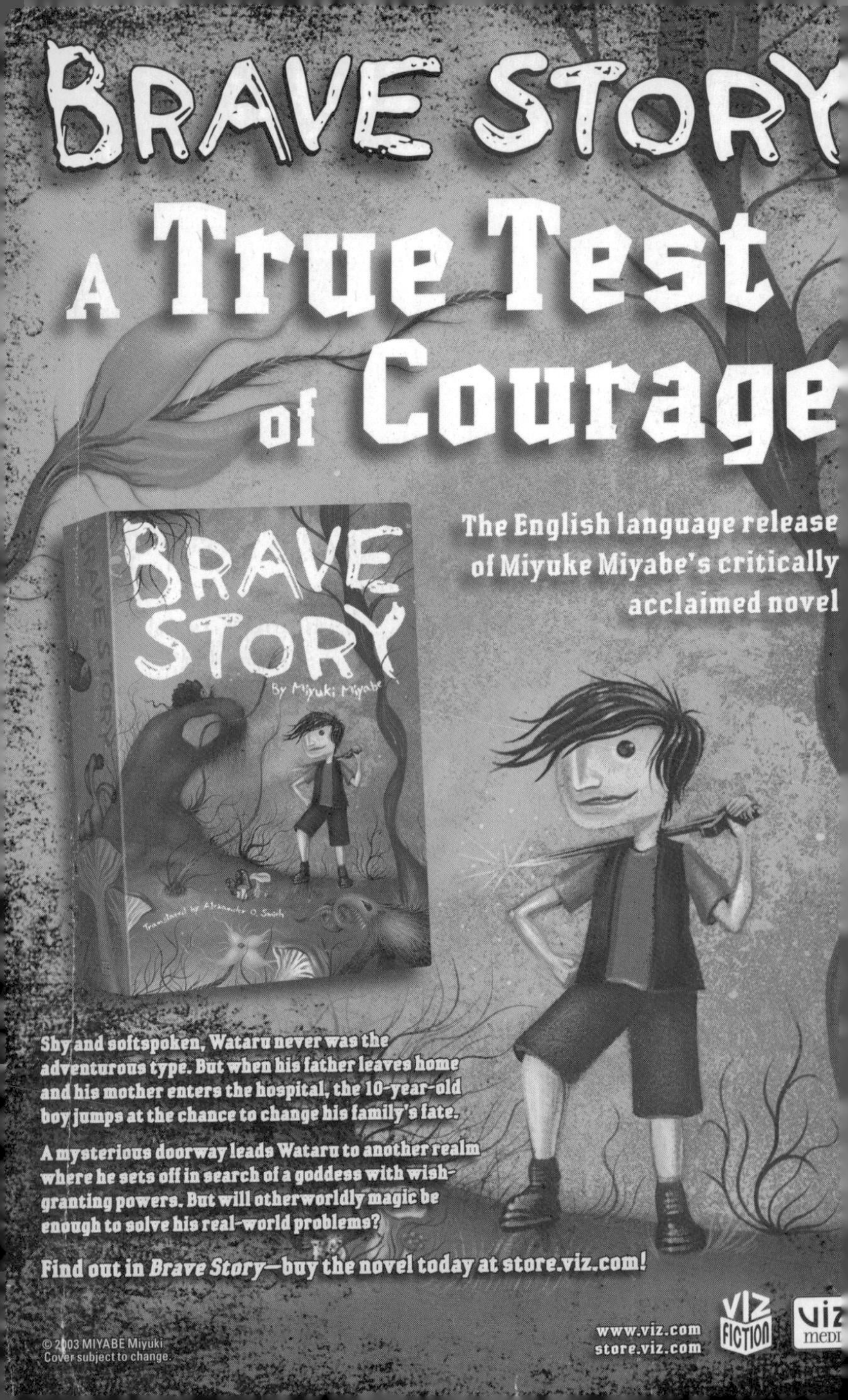
BRAVE STORY
A True Test of Courage
The English language release of Miyuke Miyabe's critically acclaimed novel
BRAVE STORY
By Miyuki Miyabe
Translated by Alexander O. Smith
Shy and softspoken, Wataru never was the adventurous type. But when his father leaves home and his mother enters the hospital, the 10-year-old boy jumps at the chance to change his family's fate.
A mysterious doorway leads Wataru to another realm where he sets off in search of a goddess with wish-granting powers. But will otherworldly magic be enough to solve his real-world problems?
Find out in *Brave Story*—buy the novel today at store.viz.com!
www.viz.com
store.viz.com
VIZ FICTION
© 2003 MIYABE Miyuki
Cover subject to change.

LOVE MAN
LET US KNOW WHAT YOU THINK!

THE URBANA FREE LIBRARY

W9-AYS-525

OUR MANGA SURVEY IS NOW
AVAILABLE ONLINE. PLEASE VISIT:
VIZ.COM/MANGASURVEY

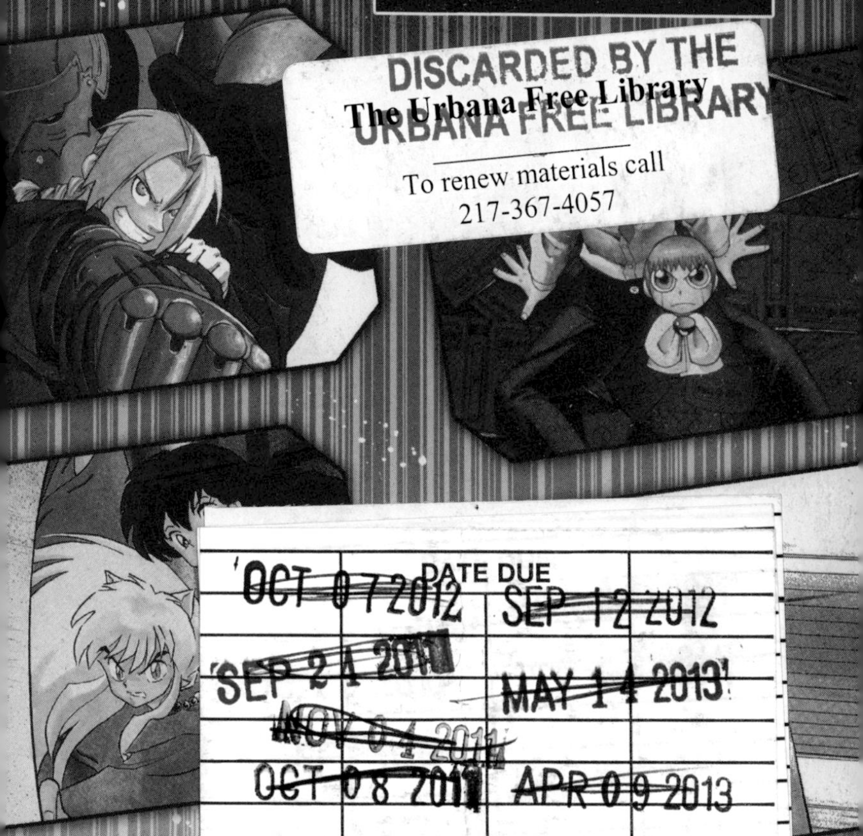

DISCARDED BY THE
URBANA FREE LIBRARY
The Urbana Free Library

To renew materials call
217-367-4057

DATE DUE	
OCT 07 2012	SEP 12 2012
SEP 2 1 2011	MAY 1 4 2013
NOV 0 4 2011	
OCT 08 2011	APR 09 2013
NOV 0 8 2011	
APR 1 2 2012	AUG 0 8 2012
JUL 1 2 2012	

HELP US N
YOU LOVE

FULLMETAL ALCHEMIST © Hiromu Arakawa
AOKI URASAWA'S MONSTER © 1995 Na